MW00759128

Alexander Tcherepnin

RUSSIAN MUSIC STUDIES

Malcolm Hamrick Brown, founding editor

French publicity photo

ALEXANDER TCHEREPNIN

The Saga of a Russian Emigré Composer

Ludmila Korabelnikova

Translated by
Anna Winestein

Edited by
Sue-Ellen Hershman-Tcherepnin

INDIANA UNIVERSITY PRESS
Bloomington and Indianapolis

This book is a publication of

Indiana University Press
601 North Morton Street
Bloomington, IN 47404-3797 USA

http://iupress.indiana.edu

Telephone orders   800-842-6796
Fax orders   812-855-7931
Orders by e-mail   iuporder@indiana.edu

The paper used in this publication meets the minimum requirements of American National Standard for Information Sciences—Permanence of Paper for Printed Library Materials, ANSI Z39.48-1984.

Manufactured in the United States of America

Library of Congress Cataloging-in-Publication Data

Korabel'nikova, L. Z. (Liudmila Zinov'evna)
    [Aleksandr Cherepnin. English]
    Alexander Tcherepnin : the saga of a Russian emigré composer / Ludmila Korabelnikova ; translated by Anna Winestein ; edited by Sue-Ellen Hershman-Tcherepnin.
        p.   cm. — (Russian music studies)
    Includes bibliographical references and index.
    ISBN 978-0-253-34938-5 (cloth : alk. paper) 1. Tcherepnin, Alexander, 1899–1977. 2. Composers—Biography.
I. Winestein, Anna. II. Hershman-Tcherepnin, Sue-Ellen. III. Title.
    ML410.C49K6713 2008
    780.92—dc22
    [B]
                                                                                    2007004425

1 2 3 4 5   13 12 11 10 09 08

This book is dedicated to

the memory of composer Ivan Tcherepnin (1943–1998),

with heartfelt appreciation of his formidable talent,

quiet sparkle, and magnanimous spirit.

We are all here in this world on a round trip from the unknown to the unknown. We have to hold together while we are here and try to do our best in every direction, continuing what our predecessors have done and preparing the way for our successors.

—Alexander Tcherepnin

Contents

Preface

Alexander Nikolaevich Tcherepnin (1899–1977), one of the leading composers of the Russian emigration, left behind a prodigious heritage. His ballets and operas have appeared on numerous stages around the world. Indeed, the composer's first ballet commission came from the legendary Anna Pavlova! His symphonic compositions have been conducted by Gabriel Pierné, Charles Munch, Serge Koussevitzky, and Rafael Kubelik. His cello sonatas were performed by Paul Grümmer, and his violin sonata by Yehudi Menuhin. One hundred and nine instrumental and vocal compositions have opus numbers, and a host of these and others have been issued by twenty different publishing houses worldwide. Hundreds of articles and reviews about Tcherepnin and his compositions have been printed by both newspapers and magazines in French, German, Czech, Serbo-Croat, English, Chinese, and Japanese. Yet for decades his fate as a Russian expatriate prevented his music and even his name from sounding in his motherland. Furthermore, until now no creative biography devoted to him has appeared in English.

My initial title for this book was "Artist on the Threshold of Eras." Tcherepnin witnessed more than three-quarters of the twentieth century. He not only played an active role in the musical avant-garde of the twenties and thirties but survived the "second wave" of the avant-garde in the fifties and sixties and continued to actively compose until the end of his days. Such a creative odyssey was inevitably fraught with drama.

To what epoch did Alexander Tcherepnin belong? Among Russian composers we can say that the first two decades of the century were clearly the "Rachmaninov era," regardless of how much we appreciate Rachmaninov's subsequent compositions. Stravinsky? That era lasted his entire life. Many in the West would say that the Prokofiev era comprised the first third of the century. But in Russia we would probably disagree. And Shostakovich? Tcherepnin's junior by several years, he died two years earlier but basically lived through the same eras. Yet Dmitri Dmitrievich lived in what was already another country, and who knows what he may have written, and what mankind may have lost, if he, too, had left.

The twentieth century, as many have observed, found itself to be the heir and owner of the music of all eras and continents. At the same time its banner proclaimed "new," that which lies ahead. Never before did "novelty" in art mean so much, aspire so purposefully, or imply so much expressiveness. Alexander Tcherepnin was in every way the son of this restless century. In his view, the heritage of the past—of Russian art especially—was something alive, important, and precious. Yet it was also inconceivable for him to write music as it had been written before. A diary entry from 1976 is full of historic drama: "If Tchaikovsky had lived to my age he would have been 77 years old in 1917, i.e., five years after *Pierrot Lunaire* and four after *The Rite of Spring,* and fifteen after *Pélleas,* and even after Prokosha's [Prokofiev's] Second Piano Concerto. . . . How could he then have composed, having heard all this? How could he remain true to himself—or else be resigned to imitation, or futile treading of water?"[1] And yet Tcherepnin loved Tchaikovsky.

Tcherepnin's life can be seen as an epic journey—a journey in both time and space. It was an aesthetic journey, epic in the evolution of his creative attitudes and activities, of his views of his contemporaries, of the surrounding "world of music," and of the broader, relentlessly changing world. Journeying in the geographic sense also marked the composer's life and musical thinking. These wanderings would cover three continents—Europe, Asia, and North America, taking Tcherepnin from St. Petersburg to Tiflis, Constantinople, Paris, New York, Shanghai, Chicago, and innumerable other cities. Indeed, late in his life Tcherepnin recollected a striking episode from his youth when this fate had been foretold.

> At a party, a clairvoyant looked at me and said, "You know what I see for you? Wanderings . . . Wanderings . . . Wanderings." I thought, "She's a foolish old woman." I was sure I would always stay in the hometown that I loved so much. At that time one could not travel more than twenty kilometers. St. Petersburg was surrounded by White armies, German armies—you couldn't even make your way on foot. But my traveling started three months later, and hasn't stopped yet.[2]

Wanderings also accompanied the preparation of this book. Having begun in the late 1980s and early 1990s to research the musical culture of the Russian emigration, I received support from George Soros's Cultural Initiative Fund for a trip to Paris. Thanks to this grant, I worked in the Souvchinsky archive at the Bibliothèque Nationale in 1991 and searched for other, mostly irrevocably lost archives. I also avidly read émigré newspapers and magazines, and met with descendants of the musicians of the "first wave" of emigration. It was among the latter that I found my "Virgil," Professor André Lichké, to whom I am fervently grateful. The scores and sound recordings I acquired during this trip, such as those received from the son of composer Ivan Wyschnegradsky, became the basis of the first Russian research on émigré composers.

In a visit two years later I met Tcherepnin's son, Serge, also a composer. He not only presented me with some of Tcherepnin's scores, which are rare in Russian libraries, but also informed me that the family archive had been transferred to the Sacher Foundation. The largest scholarly center in Europe devoted to musical documentation of the twentieth century, this foundation in Basel also contains the archive of Stravinsky and those of numerous other leading contemporary musicians.[3]

The Tcherepnin materials had not yet been filed and catalogued when, in 1995, the Foundation gave me the opportunity to work with their documents over the course of several months. To be sure, sorting out all the richest materials of the collection was impossible in the limited time available, but my major, fundamental sources stem from there. These are musical manuscripts that include unpublished compositions, diaries, the composer's comments concerning techniques of composition as a whole and techniques specifically of his own work, an enormous quantity of letters in a variety of languages including Chinese and Japanese ideograms, press responses, and numerous other items. Other miscellaneous materials were at that time kept in New York, in the hands of the Tcherepnin Society, and in Paris. An overwhelming portion of the Russian-language materials—such as diaries, correspondence with parents, friends, and colleagues, and so on—had never been read.[4] Neither Tcherepnin's wife, Lee Hsien Ming, a pianist of Chinese origin, nor two of their three sons could read Russian.[5]

Although my assessment of these materials could not be truly comprehensive, it seemed impossible to postpone the preparation of a book about Tcherepnin, especially with the approach of the one hundredth anniversary of his birth. Amid the thawing political climate of his last years, Alexander himself had renewed contacts with the USSR. He even visited Moscow, Leningrad, and Tbilisi in 1967, giving composer's concerts. Tcherepnin also repeatedly expressed an ardent interest in the appearance of a book about him. Concerning his approaching seventieth birthday he wrote the Moscow musicologist Grigori Shneerson from Paris in 1968: "It would be good if, by this time, there were interest in and an opportunity to create and publish even a brief monograph about my life and creative work. I could provide exhaustive materials, photos, and examples for this purpose."[6] In another letter soon after, Tcherepnin explained further:

> I am very excited that you consider a monograph about the Tcherepnin family of interest to our homeland. . . . Materials printed abroad are numerous, and Willy Reich is now preparing an expanded and up-to-date edition of my biography. . . . I shall try to act on my long-standing plan to write a lengthy autobiography, beginning with the life of my dear father and culminating with the lives of my sons. . . .
>
> It would be interesting to compare more than twenty of the opuses I composed during childhood and youth in my motherland with the evolution of life and creativity abroad, and to end with examples of [Russian] a cappella choruses, both liturgical and folk, composed after my departure, and nurtured by contact with the native world! You see the "arc" of my life is complete: Petrograd–Tiflis–Paris–New York–the entire world–New York–Paris–Moscow–Tbilisi–Leningrad! And this "conclusion" has given me a new sense of my life. It brings into focus everything that has always stimulated me and my art. It has given me hope that my entire life—which has been similar to a novel one could not invent—and my creative work will enter the sphere of Russian music, to which I have never ceased feeling I belong.[7]

The aforementioned monograph by Willy Reich was issued in German and followed by a French translation.[8] Its 119 pages include, besides the author's text, an index of compositions, a bibliography, fifty-four illustrations, and about sixty musical examples of varying size and schema. The uniqueness of this book lies in the fact that the author, a friend of Tcherepnin, had the opportunity to consult with him constantly. This lends the text a kind of authenticity, although in a later diary entry Tcherepnin remarked on several mistakes. Many years later, the composer's widow and several other admirers of his music, mostly pupils and members of the Tcherepnin Society, employed a corrected version of the Reich text as the foundation of an English book, *Alexander Tcherepnin: A Compendium,* which incorporates some 600 pages of additional materials. These include emendations specified by Tcherepnin for a future English edition, his reminiscences, excerpts from interviews, texts of different versions of curriculum vitae, and detailed analytical essays devoted to major compositions. The latter were written by Benjamin Folkman, as was the chapter about the composer's last years. The book contains valuable documentary appendixes. Completed in 1995, the book has for various reasons remained unpublished.

I learned of the existence of this work from Ivan Tcherepnin and his wife, Sue-Ellen, during their 1997 stay in Moscow. Their friendship was invaluable and poignant as were my conversations with Ivan, who together with his brother Serge formed the third generation of the Tcherepnin compositional dynasty. The untimely death of Ivan Tcherepnin on April 11, 1998, was a great sorrow for me. I dedicate this book to the memory of this gifted composer and delightful individual, whom his father called "Ivushka" in diaries. With the generous approval of Benjamin Folkman, the author/editor of the English book, Sue-Ellen Hershman-Tcherepnin gave me her own computer printout of the compendium, which has served as the source for a number of the memoir fragments and appendixes in this book. There is also an invaluable reference book titled *Alexander Tcherepnin: A Bio-Bibliography,* prepared in Chicago by Dr. Enrique Arias and published in 1989.[9] Arias, as had Reich, focused primarily on the composer's music.

For quite evident and primarily language-related reasons, the subject of Russian musical emigration is almost completely unaddressed in these foreign texts. Two chapters in the present book, "The Air and Bread of Emigration" and "A Russian Composer," examine broad questions of the lifestyle of Russian musicians in the countries of the Diaspora, and include little-known and forgotten names. This specialized information is necessitated by the absence of works devoted to the musical culture of the Russian Diaspora, and the importance of achieving a broad and comprehensive understanding of twentieth-century Russian music. One of the first books to tackle this question is a recent monograph, *Russian Music and the Twentieth Century* (*Russkaia muzyka i dvatsatyi vek*).[10] Finally, there is an ethical aspect, a feeling of historical duty, owed to musicians, who found themselves outside a Russia they had not willingly abandoned.

This biography is of a historico-documentary nature and involves a twofold task. The first is to acquaint the reader with the facts of Tcherepnin's life and music, important articles, reviews, and other responses to his work that were published during his career. The second task is to add to the literature about Tcherepnin and indeed the musical culture of the Russian emigration. This includes exposing the public to the invaluable documents of the Basel archive as well as to the Russian émigré press of Paris and Shanghai. Moreover, numerous previously unread Tcherepnin letters were discovered in Moscow archives. In Tbilisi, with the heartfelt help of Maria Kirakosova, copies were obtained of nearly eighty critical articles written by the young Tcherepnin that had been completely forgotten. A list of these was found in the Moscow archive of the musicologist and lexicographer Grigori Bernandt. Any portrait of Tcherepnin is also inseparable from a portrait of his family—his parents Nicolas and Marie Tcherepnin, and the closely related Benois family. Further strokes are added by other characters encountered along his life path, who also figure in these pages.

In this first biography, the task of analyzing all or even the central opuses of the composer could not be simultaneously accomplished. Nevertheless I hope that Tcherepnin's likeness and the spirit of his music arise from the documentary narration. In addition to its historical perspective, this book considers the perception of Tcherepnin's activity as a composer and pianist via the publication and performance of his compositions. Reviews and responses, many penned by outstanding music critics, help portray the works in their historical context.

Several appendixes provide additional perspectives. Two include pieces by Tcherepnin: "A Short Autobiography" and his theoretical tract, "Basic Elements of My Musical Language." These will serve as a basis for further in-depth studies of the creative life of Alexander Tcherepnin. With the exception of the "Short Autobiography," printed in *Tempo* magazine in 1979, these are published here for the first time in any language. A discography is also included (Appendix 3).

For this English-language version I have had the opportunity to correct several errors that appeared in the original Russian edition. I must also acknowledge my deep gratitude to numerous people, establishments, and organizations; without their help I could not have carried out this work. I thank Alexander Tcherepnin's sons, Ivan, Serge, and Peter, and Sue-Ellen Hershman-Tcherepnin for their enthusiasm and gifts of editions, recordings and illustrations; Benjamin Folkman, author of the yet unpublished English book, along with his colleagues Mosco Carner, Marjorie Glock, Lily Chou, and Phillip Ramey, for their generous permission to use the materials they collected; Gennady Rozhdestvensky, who provided notes and photos of the composer, whose music he has performed; employees of the Paul Sacher Foundation, whose interest and assistance made it a pleasure to work in this archive; and Tatyana Gladkova, director of the Turgenev Library in Paris, and Tatyana Duga-Jablonsky, my Parisian student, for help in searching through and copying the periodical press.

A significant part of the Russian émigré periodical press is present even in Russia. For a long time the employees of the Émigré Department of the Russian State Library, "The Russian Emigration" Library Foundation, aided the use of these materials. Important documents were discovered and copied with the permission of the directors and help from archivists of the Russian State Archive of Literature and Art, and the Glinka Central State Museum of Musical Culture.

Since many of the Tcherepnin materials I owned (including editions and recordings of his music) were otherwise unavailable to Russians, I asked colleagues of the Department of Music of the State Institute of Art Studies, as well as other musicians, to become acquainted with them. Their impressions are especially noteworthy and appreciated.

This book received understanding and support from the Russian Humanitarian Scholarship Fund (Project # 99-04-16207). Financial support also came from the Tcherepnin Society, for which I wish to again thank its president, Benjamin Folkman, and its chairman, Peter Tcherepnine.

Musical examples are borrowed from copies of editions stored in the libraries of the Moscow Conservatory, the Union of Composers of Moscow and the State Central Museum of Musical Culture, as well as from autograph manuscripts at the Paul Sacher Foundation.

Ludmila Korabelnikova

Acknowledgments

I wish to thank the many individuals who made this publication possible: Ludmila Korabelnikova, whose scholarly devotion has so beautifully illuminated the Tcherepnin musical legacy; translator Anna Winestein for her steadfast dedication to this project; Benjamin Folkman for his thorough review and astute suggestions, along with additional help from Phillip Ramey; Vera Klepikov and Alexey Shabalin for their invaluable clarification of Russian musical terms; Mao-chun Liang and Lei Liang for identification of key figures from Alexander Tcherepnin's years in China; Leonid Winestein for help with myriad logistical and technical aspects; my brothers-in-law Peter Tcherepnine and Serge Tcherepnin for their insight and moral support; and last but not least, very special thanks to the staff of Indiana University Press, for patience and counsel during preparation of the manuscript.

Sue-Ellen Hershman-Tcherepnin

Abbreviations

SCMMC	(ГЦММК) The State Central Museum of Musical Culture, Moscow
RSALA	(РГАЛИ) The Russian State Archive of Literature and Art, Moscow
PSF	The Nicolas and Alexander Tcherepnin Archive, Paul Sacher Foundation, Basel
BFM	Benjamin Folkman et al., Manuscript, "Alexander Tcherepnin: A Compendium," 1995
A. T.	Alexander Tcherepnin
M. T.	Marie Tcherepnin
N. T.	Nicolas Tcherepnin

Alexander Tcherepnin

1 Introduction

From his earliest years Alexander Tcherepnin was destined to be a composer of the twentieth century, of East and West—that is, a Russian composer. He began to "remember himself" at a very early age, and his stories of his family and childhood are captured in numerous letters, interviews, autobiographical notes, and recollections of people close to him. One of the closest among these, a pianist, composer, musicologist, lexicographer, and theorist who had attended the Petersburg Conservatory—Nicholas Slonimsky—prepared an article for Tcherepnin's seventieth birthday. As editor of two noted musical encyclopedias—*Baker's Biographical Dictionary of Musicians* and *Thompson's International Cyclopedia of Music and Musicians*—and as the author of the chronicle *Music after 1900,* where he devoted twenty paragraphs to Tcherepnin, Slonimsky had obtained extensive and vital information firsthand from the composer.

> Sasha Tcherepnin, a tall boy for his age, was a familiar figure at the St. Petersburg Conservatory fifty-odd years ago, as he was seen walking down the corridors accompanied by his father Nicolas Tcherepnin, professor of composition and conducting, teacher of a generation of Russian composers, and himself a composer of stature. Paradoxically, it was Sasha's mother, not his father, who gave him his first music lessons. As soon as he learned to manipulate the piano keys, he began making up tunes of his own. There was so much music lying around the house that he picked up the rudiments of notation intuitively. He learned notes and the Russian alphabet at the same time. Now, at seventy, he cannot even remember when he could not read Russian words or musical notes.

> The Tcherepnin household in St. Petersburg was the crossroads for musicians, writers and artists. Sasha's maternal grandfather was the French painter Albert Benois, whose brother was Alexandre Benois, stage designer for Diaghilev's Ballets Russes and the author of the scenario for Stravinsky's *Petrushka,* as well as that of the ballet *Le Pavillon d'Armide* by Tcherepnin-*père.* Among Tcherepnin's maternal ancestors was the Italian composer Catterino Cavos who settled in Russia early in the nineteenth century and identified himself with the cause of Russian music. His position is of historical importance, for he anticipated Glinka by twenty years in writing an opera on the story of Ivan Susanin, and it was Cavos who conducted the first performance of Glinka's opera *A Life for the Tsar* on the same subject. Another maternal ancestor was Johann Friedrich Kind, the author of the libretto of Weber's *Der Freischütz.* Through the Benois branch of the family Tcherepnin is related to the actor Peter Ustinov, whose maternal grandmother was a Benois. Ustinov often comes to see Tcherepnin in Paris, in London or in New York, to discuss and play music.

Alexander Tcherepnin's life is exceptionally well documented. Since the age of six, he has kept a diary, punctiliously recording events of his life, personal and professional. Miraculously, all of its bulk has been preserved, packed away in trunks in Paris, in New York and in other places. At some future time this diary will provide an inexhaustible fount of intimate information on artistic life during the first two-thirds of the twentieth century. There are delightful vignettes in this monumental manuscript. At the age of fourteen Sasha was busily engaged on the composition of a grand national opera *The Death of Ivan the Terrible,* improvising on the family piano. To imitate the sound of a huge bell, which he needed for the last act, he got hold of a sheet of iron, throwing it on the floor with a tremendous clatter.

It so happened that the apartment below was occupied by Hippolytus Tchaikovsky, brother of the composer, an elderly man unaccustomed to such un-Tchaikovskian noises. One day Tcherepnin found a *carte de visite* slipped under the door of his apartment, with an imploring message, "Dear Sasha, please have pity on a sick old man. I can endure your piano exercises with equanimity, but not your improvisations." Tcherepnin complied, and a few days later there came another message from Tchaikovsky's brother: "I have now recovered from my illness, and you are free to resume your practicing, and even your improvisations."

Tcherepnin-*père* became aware of his son's musical experiments rather late in the game. As he looked over Sasha's scribblings, he observed with a sigh, "Alas, you are bound to be a composer!" He used to call his son's pieces *bloshki,* little fleas, because their melodic leaps were so wide and so unpredictable. One of these "fleas," composed in 1913, and eventually published as No. 4 in a piano album, *Pièces sans titre,* Op.7, is a specimen of bitonal harmonies rather bold for the period. . . .

Composing and keeping a diary became an almost physiological necessity for young Tcherepnin, like food and drink. In fact, he continued to write music even when food gave out in icebound Petrograd (Russianized from St. Petersburg during the German war) in the year of the Revolution. The Petrograd winter of 1917–18 was the most severe since Napoleon's armies invaded Russia in 1812. People used furniture for fuel and went to bed wrapped up in furs. Daily bread rations were reduced to a quarter of a pound, and even for that the emaciated Petrograders had to stand in line. A Russian music critic bartered his grand piano for twelve pounds of black bread. Malnutrition began at birth, and babies, few of whom survived, were fed frozen potatoes. Obesity became an unknown condition. Glazunov, the beloved director of the Petrograd Conservatory, whose corpulent figure was a sightseeing landmark in Russian musical circles, lost half of his imposing avoirdupois in a single year. Sasha Tcherepnin, who was tall but not broad and had little excess fat to expend, was stricken with scurvy.

It was in this state of bodily distress that he wrote his funereal 13th piano sonata, which opens in the nethermost regions of the keyboard with a theme from the Russian Mass for the Dead. Eighty-seven opus numbers and 41 years later Tcherepnin used the same subject as the cantus firmus of his Fourth Symphony. This "Hunger Sonata," as it might well be called, was eventually published under the redeeming title *Sonatine romantique.*

Amazingly, concert life was still going on in Petrograd under the siege of cold and hunger. Some lucky artists were paid in kind, receiving a few pounds of bread, horsemeat and sometimes such luxuries as butter, flour and sugar. When cats and dogs began to disappear from the streets of Petrograd, and dogmeat sandwiches were sold openly near the closed food markets, the Tcherepnins made plans to leave. Like most people fleeing the doomed city, they headed south.[1]

The episode connected with Hippolyte Tchaikovsky had clearly imprinted itself in Sasha's memory—it appears in Reich's monograph, the obituary by A. Skidan,[2] as well as other sources such as Guy Freedman's interview. Facts from Tcherepnin's lost childhood diaries are imperfectly preserved. Thus Slonimsky incorrectly describes the composer's grandfather as a "French watercolorist." Although he was of French extraction and continued to paint in France after emigration, Albert Benois was a Russian artist and the founder of the Russian Imperial Watercolor Society. Albert and his younger brother, Alexandre, had married two sisters, Marie and Anne Kind, respectively. Marie Karlovna Benois-Kind was a remarkable pianist whom Sergei Taneyev had long and seriously courted. In a July 16, 1927 letter sending birthday greetings, Alexander added: "I wish to remember grandmother (as I see her now walking with you down the path in Ollila [a village near St. Petersburg]), and to reflect together on how she lives on in us . . . how her blood flows and lives in our veins. And as in [Maeterlinck's] *The Blue Bird,* in my mind I wish to go into her garden and tell her that we are thinking of her, and carry on in our lives what she so energetically began."[3]

In the aforementioned interview with Guy Freedman, Tcherepnin said:

> My father was Greek Orthodox, my mother the daughter of a French émigré—she was Catholic but her mother was Protestant—and as a child I went to three churches: to the Russian church with papa, to the Catholic church with mama, and to the Protestant church to please my grandmama. Similarly, I was exposed to the three Russian composers. I heard Rimsky, Glazunov and Prokofiev and, as you can guess, my choice was Prokofiev.[4]

The development of Alexander's creativity in Petersburg and later in Tiflis testifies to his remarkable acoustical sensitivity, musical impressionability and memory, formed vitally in his early youth. The first opera he saw onstage was Glinka's *A Life for the Tsar,* and at home at night he often fell asleep to the sounds of compositions by Rimsky-Korsakov, Borodin, or his father. Since Nicolas Tcherepnin conducted at the Mariinsky Theater as well as in Diaghilev's "Russian Seasons," ballet would later play an important role in Tcherepnin's work.

The artistic life of Petersburg in the decade preceding the revolution was extraordinary, brimming as never before with varied and brilliant events—theatrical productions; exhibitions; concerts; and new literary, musical, and painterly groups and associations. Nicolas Tcherepnin was in one way or another involved with many of them. Alexander, his beloved and only son, was a part of all this. Nicolas Tcherepnin took Sasha and Marie Albertovna with him to Paris for the Diaghilev Seasons. There, in 1909, he inaugurated the enterprise by conducting a performance of his own ballet *Le Pavillon d'Armide* with a libretto and staging by Alexandre Benois, and with Anna Pavlova in the leading role. The same evening he also conducted a production of an excerpt from the Borodin opera *Prince Igor,* the *Polovetsian Dances,* which would later prove to be of great importance. The following season saw the premiere of the famous ballet *Scheherezade.* Six decades later Tcherepnin recognized the strength of these childhood impressions in a letter, "I remember how in 1909 [actually 1910] everyone in Paris was singing the praises of Bakst's scenery and costumes for *Scheherezade,* and how everything—choreography, scenery, illumination, costumes—remained etched in my memory as something extremely intense, remarkable."[5]

Alongside the symphonic and chamber concerts of the Imperial Russian Musical Society, the Russian symphonic concerts, and the quartet evenings of Mitrofan Belaieff, Petersburg offered the Ziloti concerts, which had been presented since 1903 as a subscription series, and the Koussevitzky concerts, inaugurated in 1910. Young Tcherepnin attended many of these performances, whose programs responded to the burning need for the "new." In addition to European and Russian classics, the Ziloti concerts showcased and sometimes premiered many orchestral compositions by Debussy, Ravel, Duc, Roger-Ducasse, Reger, Enesco, Elgar, Albeniz, Stravinsky, Prokofiev, Vasilenko, and Steinberg, as well as Scriabin, Rachmaninov, Glazunov, and Liadov. The 1912 arrival of Arnold Schoenberg in St. Petersburg coincided with a Ziloti performance of his *Pelleas and Melisande.*[6] The Koussevitzky concerts, particularly admired for the conductor's brilliant interpretations, also presented novel programs, premiering Myaskovsky's *Alsator,* Scriabin's *Prometheus,* many Prokofiev compositions, and, in February 1914, the *Rite of Spring* in its first Russian performance since its Moscow premiere.

Another outstanding development amid the Petersburg musical avant-garde was the "Evenings of Modern Music" (1901–12) centered around Vyacheslav Karatygin, a formidable music critic, scholar, and new music advocate, and a close associate of the magazine *Apollon.* These evenings would serve as the stage for the debut of works by Stravinsky, Prokofiev, Myaskovsky, and Kuzmin, as well as performances of compositions by Reger, Debussy, Ravel, and Roussel. Very pleased with Karatygin's review of Schoenberg's *Pelleas,* Stravinsky hastened to recommend that the "Evenings" present Schoenberg's "latest composition—*Pierrot Lunaire*—where the extraordinary warehouse of his creative genius shows itself most powerfully."[7] Karatygin's musical activities were financed by Belaieff, who included Nicolas Tcherepnin on his advisory board and took him into his circle. Indeed, Tcherepnin senior repeatedly figures in Karatygin's articles and reviews. Even before accepting a full-time teaching position at the conservatory in 1919, Karatygin lectured there and elsewhere on the history of music and aesthetics. Enrique Arias noted that at the conservatory Tcherepnin-*fils* "took special interest in the lectures on history and aesthetics by Professor Karatygin. This interest in a broad general education prepared Alexander for his later research into the philosophic and historical roots of the Russian musical tradition."[8]

Musical-theatrical explorations were an important part of the artistic atmosphere of prerevolutionary Petersburg. Between 1909 and 1913 Nicolas Tcherepnin conducted Vsevolod Meyerhold's productions of Wagner's *Tristan and Isolde,* Gluck's *Orpheus and Eurydice,* and Strauss's *Elektra* at the Mariinsky Theater. He also conducted and oversaw other performances, especially the operas of Rimsky-Korsakov. Indeed, Sasha's earliest piece of musical criticism, published in the October 19, 1917 issue of the newly founded Petrograd newspaper *The Common Cause,* concerns the musical theater. It is a review of a Mariinsky Theater revival of Mussorgsky's *Boris Godunov.* The young author insightfully and quite frankly evaluates the work of the conductor Nikolai Malko, as well as the performers of individual arias.

The extent to which musical experiences were impressed upon our protagonist during his Petersburg years cannot be precisely determined. However, he was undoubtedly aware of the effect that many of these events had on him. Indeed, the articles he wrote about Prokofiev, Myaskovsky, and other "new" composers that were published in Tiflis (now Tbilisi) from 1918 to 1920 testify to this—as do his early compositional experiments. Although he was never literally his father's pupil, Alexander considered Nicolas his most important teacher and was thoroughly familiar with his music. Writing to his father in connection with the planned Paris performance of Nicolas's cantata *Joyzelle dans le jardin,* Alexander observes, "Dad, you know how I've always been a fan of *Joyzelle*— let me remind you that in St. Petersburg there is orchestral material for it *copied by me.*"[9]

Alexander's actual teachers have never received proper attention, and even in his *Short Autobiography* they are mentioned only in passing. Yet young Tcherepnin's instructors were among his formative influences, and one name that arises in later documents is that of Viktor Beliaev.

> Viktor was the teacher who prepared me for entrance into the Petrograd Conservatory more than half a century ago. We became especially close during his brief stay abroad during the NEP [New Economic Policy] era. We saw each other in Paris. Later he made a special trip to Donaueschingen, where Scherchen was conducting the first performance of my *Concerto da Camera,* which had won a prize at the competition sponsored by the Schott Publishing House. After returning home he wrote a huge article about my music in the former magazine *Music* [actually *Modern Music*] and also arranged many performances of my chamber pieces in Moscow and Leningrad.[10]

Indeed Tcherepnin's Second Sonata for Cello and Piano was heard at the December 2, 1926 concert of the Leningrad branch of the Association of Contemporary Music, alongside Shostakovich's Piano Sonata Op. 12, performed by the composer.[11] At the time he taught Tcherepnin, Beliaev (who had been a pupil of Liadov and Glazunov) was a young professor of theory at the conservatory, and had published a textbook on counterpoint and musical form, as well as essays on and reviews of Taneyev, Rimsky-Korsakov, and Mussorgsky. An adherent of "new" music, in 1912 he had described Schoenberg as "among the most interesting people of our musical era." In the 1920s Beliaev would write about Paul Hindemith, Nikolai Myaskovsky, Samuel Feinberg and Alexander Mosolov.

Leocadia Kashperova, a devoted protégée of Anton Rubinstein, was another of Alexander's early teachers. She was renowned as a pianist and teacher, and even Stravinsky had studied piano with her. The press praised her world premiere performance of Glazunov's Second Sonata (Op. 75) at one of the "Evenings of Modern Music." She became close to Balakirev in his late years and was the first to perform some of his works. Kashperova also graduated from the Petersburg Conservatory, conducting her own composition—a cantata set to text from Dimitri Merezhkovsky's *Orvasi*—for her graduation performance. A number of her compositions were published by Peter Jurgenson, and even more by Vasily Bessel. Although her Symphony is uninviting, her *Children's Stories in Song*, which allude to Mussorgsky and are set to her own text, have some appeal. In later recollections Tcherepnin called her "an interesting figure."

Tcherepnin also briefly joined the class of the now forgotten Nikolai Aleksandrovich Sokolov, a student of Rimsky-Korsakov and member of the Belaieff circle. Tcherepnin's classmate in that course, Vyacheslav Karatygin, remarked on the breadth of Sokolov's views on Debussy, Reger, and Scriabin: "Irrespective of personal sympathies or antipathies, N. A. established curious, often quite unexpected, but insightful, sharp connections and comparisons in relation to certain sound combinations.... N. A.'s general views on the work of different composers, on the relationships of unmediated imagination and technique, on the essence of the creative process, were remarkable for their deep thoughtfulness."[12] Karatygin valued highly Sokolov's extraordinary work *The Foundations of Polyphony: Melodic Figurations*, which remained unpublished because of the liquidation of Koussevitzky's Russian music publishing house. Sokolov transcribed several large-scale compositions by Borodin for piano four-hands and composed numerous works himself, among them an orchestral *Divertissement* that was transcribed by his pupil Ivan Wyschnegradsky, a bright representative of the Russian musical avant-garde. Even Shostakovich studied with Sokolov, although much later.

Other individuals also made a deep impression on young Sasha Tcherepnin.

> Ossovsky was a friend of my father's ... we frequently visited his family. Ossovsky was interested in my early compositions, and insisted that I perform them for him and leave the manuscripts for review. I was [also] on familiar terms with Akimenko—he encouraged my writing, and invited friends to his place so they could hear my works; this friendship was preserved abroad. I was even closer to Spendiarov, with whose family my parents and I often stayed in Yalta around 1907, and whom we saw constantly at their summer residence in the Soudak. We spent those summers either nearby in the manor of an aunt, a Benois by birth, who had married General von Horvath (they had one thousand acres of barren, hilly terrain along the sea), or in Soudak itself....

Playing four-hands with Spendiarov, I performed his Crimean sketches, and performed his concertos in the original or my transcription. He took an interest in my works, and I gave a concert every summer in a recital hall at the Soudak hotel "Gul Tepe." Spendiarov's daughters, Marina and Tanya, were my first loves. Although at such an age these loves were Platonic, they were inspirational, judging by the quantity of the compositions I then dedicated to them.[13]

Ossovsky and Spendiarov were both students of Rimsky-Korsakov. Later a prominent musicologist, Ossovsky began teaching at the Petrograd Conservatory in 1915, and worked closely with the Belaieff circle. He was a consultant for the Ziloti concerts and prepared all the program notes for performances between 1906 and 1917. His enthusiasm for contemporary music was undeniable. Spendiarov, one of the classicists of Armenian music, was probably a vital link for Tcherepnin between the Eastern and European musical traditions.

Certainly other Petersburg acquaintances, friendships, and ties that were broken or interrupted by emigration remained long vivid in Tcherepnin's memory. "A lot of time has passed since we trained in the Leningrad Conservatory," he wrote to Yuri Shaporin in 1960, "but the memory of it cannot be erased: I see it as if it were yesterday—our classes, the assemblies, your figure (resembling mine in build). I remember our teachers, our colleagues and the broad current that produced us and remains the solid foundation of my entire life and activity."[14]

Dialogue with emigrants such as Prokofiev, the world-class conductor Nicolai Malko, the future head of the Leningrad symphonic school Vladimir Scherbachev, and the prominent Soviet conductor Alexander Gauk also frequently brought Tcherepnin back to his roots. "Malko, whom I remembered from St. Petersburg, I met in Copenhagen after the Second World War," recalled Tcherepnin, "[and] later I saw him often in Chicago, where we were neighbors after 1949. . . . He performed my compositions in Chicago and England—my *Symphonic March* is dedicated to him."[15] In Petersburg Nicolas Tcherepnin's pupils also shaped Alexander's environment, causing him to gravitate toward "modern" music, pushing him to shun academicism. Gauk testifies that Tcherepnin senior was the first to "accustom us not to be led by common truths and canonized traditions. In Tcherepnin's class the newest French composers, Debussy, Ravel, and Dukas, could be heard and discussed. It was possible to discuss Richard Strauss's orchestration, although the composer was not much indulged in the conservatory. . . . Tcherepnin always trod an independent path and aimed at the unexplored."[16] In class an "elevated atmosphere" reigned, Gauk continues, "the presence of Prokofiev gave a certain incisiveness to judgments and reinforced the sensation of modernity." Indeed, for Prokofiev, Tcherepnin senior felt "an extraordinary tenderness, concern, and indubitable faith in his great talent as a composer."[17]

Prokofiev himself recalled, "Among my teachers, Tcherepnin was the most lively and interesting musician . . . from Tcherepnin I received a lot."[18] From Prokofiev's autobiography we learn how his teacher encouraged his compositional imagination, anticipated his future, and, among many other things, directed him toward conducting. A significant memory was Tcherepnin "sitting beside me with a score during the endless rehearsals of the student orchestra. He would say, 'listen to how wonderful the bassoon sounds here!'—and I would gradually enter the world of Haydn and Mozart scores. . . . Here my Classical Symphony was conceived, although born five or six years later."[19] Most importantly, Tcherepnin encouraged from the young composer precisely those pieces that shocked nearly all the conservatory's other musicians. It was no accident that Karatygin then called neoclassicism "one of the main currents of French modernism."[20]

In an album of serious and lighthearted written notes that Prokofiev entitled "What Do You Think of the Sun?" an entry by Nicolas Tcherepnin immediately follows entries by Mayakovsky and Chaliapin. Tcherepnin made the entry after an open dress rehearsal of the *Classical Symphony* and it reads, "When you left today to conduct your sparkling symphony, a sunbeam was playing on your gentle face. Whether it was a sympathetic smile for the elements natural to you, I do not know, but I am convinced that may have been the case."[21]

The memoirs of Tcherepnin junior testify to his attitude toward Prokofiev.

> There was several years' difference between Prokofiev and myself—that is, I was twelve and he was twenty. When I looked at him, a tall young man, I myself was still a boy. I admired him and his music immensely.
>
> . . . Both Nicolas Benois and I were ardent followers of Prokofiev; we called him "The Great" and counted years from Prokofiev's birthday—April 11 (old style), which we took as the beginning of our year and called January 1. Once we sent him a birthday card saying, "Happy New Year!" to which he answered: "Congratulations on your commitment to the lunatic asylum."
>
> . . . I remember once, in 1918, just prior to the revolution, on a bitterly cold night, when we were all hungry, he played his last recital of his own works in St. Petersburg. There was only a handful or so of people present in the hall—some fifteen or twenty. Nikolai Benois, my cousin, and I clapped our hands as loudly as possible until they were red at the end of each work and elicited many encores—trying to give the impression of success despite the poor attendance. My father was the only professor at St. Petersburg Conservatory who encouraged Prokofiev. At the conservatory's graduation concert, Prokofiev played his First Piano Concerto. Although it was not customary for a student to play his own composition at a graduation concert, my father proposed this nevertheless, and persuaded the other faculty members to permit Prokofiev to do so. Glazunov, at that time the conservatory director, got up and stormed out of his first-row seat in a motion of protest as Prokofiev proceeded to play the first [Allegro]. Prokofiev had my father's permission to come to the music library at our home, consult scores there, and study them whenever he liked. During that period he brought all his compositions to my father for comment and advice, listening very attentively to all of my father's counsel. Naturally I was full of interest and did not miss any of these sessions. I can still recall him telling me with an emphatic tap on my head, "Remember, what you've just heard should not be known outside this house!" I remember the first work

that he brought to father was "Kudesnec," for voice and piano. When he had left, my father told me, "This man has great talent." Prokofiev dedicated three works to my father. The first, Sinfonietta Op. 5, he told us he had been able to compose without a piano. The second was his Piano Concerto No. 1, and the third, Scherzo for Four Bassoons, was later published as a piano piece. When I was sixteen I composed a piece for orchestra called *Laugh, Laugh, Laugh.* Prokofiev was in my room and looked at this work. Then he said to my father, "It's fascinating how Sashinka has learned craftsmanship. You should try this piece with your orchestra at the conservatory." My father asked me to copy out the material and said he would play it. But he never did, alas, and I was too timid to broach the subject with him myself.[22]

The young musician steeped himself in Prokofiev, whose influence he would always acknowledge. Only eight years separated them, but at the dawn of the twentieth century in Russian music this effectively represented a full generation. Prokofiev's name arises in comparison with the prodigious Scriabin in a later observation which is both characteristic and unfair.

Nearly all my fellow students belonged to the Scriabin cult; they saw him as a musical and philosophic prophet, and followed him. In spite of the fact that I had romantic feelings toward Scriabin's daughter, Elena, who was in piano class then, I was not attracted to Scriabin's music. His early works seemed to me conventional, [and] the later ones seemed far-fetched, pretentious. Many of his sonatas (except the 9th and 10th) seemed to mill the wind, caught in the mousetrap set by the composer himself. His orchestral works—especially the *Divine Poem* and the *Poem of Ecstasy*—shocked me with their colorless and heavy instrumentation, and *Prometheus* with its fixations and affectation. And although in the course of fifty years I have changed many of my estimations, my opinion of Scriabin has remained the same, only perhaps I am now able to see in his music—relieved of its home-made, high-flown philosophy—some [motivic] and rhythmic aspirations in harmony with the present day.
... Mozart, Tchaikovsky, Reger, Prokofiev were in those days in harmony with my thinking. To counter the cult of Scriabin, I created the undisputable and enthusiastic cult of Prokofiev.[23]

This attitude toward Prokofiev remained constant and is especially evident in Tcherepnin's recollections of his youth.

Tcherepnin grew up amid the dominant aura of the Rimsky-Korsakov school and the surviving members of the "Mighty Five" St. Petersburg nationalists.[24] He also had a powerful icon of the new Russian musical creativity in the form of Igor Stravinsky. But the younger musician never admitted to following "Prince Igor," and his attitude toward Stravinsky was complex. Perhaps this was not due to music but to musical life: Tcherepnin to Diaghilev to Stravinsky. In the exact same year as Sasha's birth, Stravinsky had intended to begin music theory lessons with Tcherepnin senior, but this plan failed, and Stravinsky instead enrolled with Feodor Akimenko.

In a wonderfully illuminating letter to the musicologist Grigori Shneerson, Tcherepnin describes at length his sense of Stravinsky:

I have a particular opinion about Stravinsky that I have never found in books about him, and that he personally far from agrees with (is even annoyed when I speak with him about it). I see him as a folklore musician—a typical successor of Rimsky-Korsakov—and I find unity and progression in all his creations from the earliest to the most recent, serial works.

He is not a creator of material but a skillful sculptor who remains himself no matter what material he uses. Russian folklore up to *Les noces* [Small weddings] was his material. American ragtime was added as is, and also combined with Russian material in *Story of a Soldier*. Pergolesi served as the source for *Pulcinella;* Bach for the Octet and *Apollo;* Meyerbeer for *Oedipus;* Rossini for *Card Game;* Alexander Scarlatti for the opera *Oedipus Rex;* Serialism for *Threni* and Movements for Piano and Orchestra. I forgot also to mention Tchaikovsky as well, for *Le Baiser de la fée*. Using the imperishable sources of folklore or the great masters, he remains outside the influence of folklore or the great masters, as he fabricates from this material creations that are entirely dissimilar to the original creations. Always remaining Stravinsky, that is to say himself, he finds a novel approach to every source. A well-known parallel can be made between Stravinsky and Picasso. As any great artist, Picasso studied human anatomy, i.e., the anatomy of "life." Only instead of reproducing what he sees, or the impressions he receives, he uses the immortal lines of the living organism for an abstract construction. And people marvel: why is an eye lodged in the middle of a backbone? Picasso's strength is in his knowledge of anatomy and his use of its eternal lines for a free design. And, like Stravinsky, Picasso uses different sources but always remains himself. If we now compare Prokofiev and Stravinsky, it seems to me that Prokofiev is as consonant with his own epoch as Tchaikovsky was. And Stravinsky in his approach, in my opinion, is similar to Rimsky-Korsakov, only perhaps he is more universal thanks to a greater variety of material. He is as consonant with our world as Rimsky was with his epoch and native land.[25]

Savenko was the first to use the literary term "Acmeism," which refers to a style of early-twentieth-century Russian poetry, to describe Stravinsky's creativity.[26] Clarity as opposed to foggy symbolism; simplicity as a rejection of metaphorical complexity; a love for the "thing," the subject, the phenomenon; the novelty of expressive language—all this the sensitive young Tcherepnin absorbed from the Petersburg atmosphere. Prominent Acmeists such as Nikolai Gumilev, Anna Akhmatova, and Sergei Gorodetsky published manifestos in the pages of *Apollon* magazine.[27] Both Stravinsky and the elder Tcherepnin (and the younger after 1916) composed music to Gorodetsky's words. Note that Prokofiev's *Scythian Suite* was produced for Gorodetsky's ballet-scenario *Ala and Lolli*. "A new century has poured new blood into Russian poetry," asserted Gumilev in the aforementioned article. "The beginning of the second decade is precisely that phase of a century when the features of its future face can be discerned for the first time."

Later judgments about the music of other composers whose works were often heard in St. Petersburg throw light on Alexander Tcherepnin's creative stance, which was formed, or at least incubated, in those years. "When I was young," Tcherepnin observed, "I felt that Debussy is one to be fought. I felt that Rachmaninoff and Fauré would . . . not even need to be fought as they were already finished."[28] He also remembered, "Contrary to most of my colleagues in the conservatory, I saw the music of the future in simplification and not in complication, in clearness. . . . I fought the impressionists in those days and, not having understood the genius of Debussy, called his music 'sketchy and formless.' "[29] The anti-romantic, anti-impressionistic predispositions of his younger years are reflected in these statements. More significant still, they are reflected in his creative work.

Perhaps the most important factor in young Tcherepnin's Petersburg experiences, one that would forever shape his artistic destiny, was his place as a member of the Benois clan. The painter, book illustrator, theatrical artist and theatrical figure, and preeminent art historian Alexander Nikolaevich Benois was "leader, soul, and inspiration of 'The World of Art.' "[30] Many artists, writers, directors, and musicians who were close to Benois surrounded Tcherepnin. Nearly all of them would later reunite in emigration. Mstislav Dobuzhinsky cites the less well-known name of the artist and critic Stepan Jaremich, who "was inseparable from Benois . . . a great friend of Benois' children, who called him Stip. He always took part in their often very talented contrivances. Later [in the 1910s] he once helped Koka Benois and his friend Sasha Tcherepnin with all seriousness to write some terribly long nonsensical history in an ultra-Hoffmannesque spirit."[31] Sasha's cousin, Nikolai (Koka) Benois, subsequently became the principal scenic artist of Milan's La Scala; in 1925, incidentally, he designed *Petrushka*.

Years later, while explaining the origin of the literary pseudonyms of the Tiflis period (discussed in the following chapter), Tcherepnin paints in passing the picture of childhood related by Dobuzhinsky:

> Some of these pseudonyms are connected to my childhood, which is in turn tied up with the Benois family—Alexandre Benois' son and my bosom friend Koka, Alexandre Benois' daughter Lelya, and the daughter of Leonty Benois, Nadia. In childhood we were all engrossed in reading E. T. A. Hoffmann, Tieck, Novalis, and Edgar Poe, were afraid of ghosts, and lived in some singular world of imagination. We had our own country—Laetsia—where I was initially "prince," under the name of Olaf-khar, and then was replaced by Koka, under the name Pilikikius. Lelya had the nickname Brambilla Kofetois, Nadia was Khilaida Kofetois. The geographic location of our country was indeterminate . . . but mostly Laetsia existed in our imagination. Baedeker guidebooks, railway indexes, maps, etc., were even put together. And then began productions in my puppet theater (an exact copy of the stage of the Mariinsky Theater bought by my father from a needy stage worker and presented to me before I was ten). Pilikik (Koka) and I (Olaf-khar) wrote plays together. Pilikik, or Pik for short, produced scenery and cardboard puppets, I composed music, and performances took place in my parents' apartment at 25 Torgovaya Street (now, apparently Profsoiuz Street). The theater was set up in the doorway between my room and my parents' bedroom. Pik and I operated "offstage" in my room, and in my parents' bedroom were chairs

Example 1.1

for invited guests, among them my parents, relatives, [my] grandfather Albert Benois, and frequently Uncle Shoura and Aunt Atya [Alexandre and Anne Benois]. Then a journal, "Tik-Tak" began to be "published" in a run of one copy, whose employees were the very same Koka and I. But for the sake of variety, articles were signed under different pseudonyms; among mine were Platon Valanchal and Karl Agafia Fiuldan. The magazine was "illustrated," and included poems, articles, and music.[32]

What music did young Tcherepnin compose? He began to improvise early and composed extensively. He told Guy Freedman, "I began composing at a very early age. My first memory relates to when I was five: I looked through the window of our home in St. Petersburg and I thought, 'For goodness' sake, how old I am growing. Now, what would I like to do?' And I concluded that I would like to be a composer."[33]

Years later he applied for entrance to the Petrograd Conservatory with a "portfolio" of operas, ballets, orchestral works, choral works, five piano concertos, twelve piano sonatas, and additional chamber and vocal compositions. Such a quantity and selection of compositions testifies to his unquenchable thirst for self-expression through musical sound. Having not yet received regular music instruction, he could not compose from a base of studied techniques. The composer recalled that it was only after having joined Sokolov's class that he started to analyze what he had up to then created intuitively. The spontaneity of a primal impulse—whether a theme (or, more often, a motif), a brief sound cluster, a rhythmic figure, etc.—became a basic feature that would not disappear over time. Rather this impulse increasingly began to interact with rational (and rationalistic) methods of composition. As we shall see, this "system" first developed its basic features during practice sessions, and was then reflected upon, advanced, augmented, and structured. In this way it became the basis of further creativity.

Among the childhood creations,[34] dedicated mostly to "Uncle Kolya and Aunt Tanya" Benois, many carry a purely domestic, "amateur" character, to which Sasha's sweet, playful hand-drawn covers testify. "Alexander Tcherepnin. Sonatina. For piano 2-hands. Price 40 Kopeks. Property of the Publisher. 1913. For dear Uncle Kolya! From Sasha. April, 14 1913." The Sonatina consists of two parts: a fourteen-measure Allegro and a nine-measure Largo. Already what brevity! The composer would struggle against such brevity as well as against abruptness until the end of his days. There is no key signature, and accidentals are written next to individual notes. "New Year. Op. 33 [a joke?]. Edition of the Laetsk Ministry of Arts. 1913" is a very dissonant little piece. "Piano Suite. Museum of Laetsk Duke Olaf. Op. 89 [a joke!]. January 11, 1915. For dear Aunt Tanya from Sasha"—stated in three lines—demands a certain pianistic skill. The beginning of "Musical Moment. For dear Uncle Kolya from Sasha. December 6, 1915" is characteristic in many respects—for its combination of chromatic and diatonic scales, the Russian flavor of its theme, and its melodic variety. This passage also subsequently reappears twice: in the second movement of the youthful fourth piano concerto, and in No. 4 of the eight *Pièces sans titres,* for piano, Op. 7 (musical example 1.1).[35]

Among the very earliest efforts is an overture to an opera, "*Dispute of Two Ancient Greek Philosophers about What Is Graceful*—For dear Uncle Kolya and Aunt Tanya! From Sasha. December 24, 1912." Its four pages are marked by a love of ostinato that would remain ever constant. Another special piece was the seventeen-page "Lunch of the Phantoms—a 'Dramatic Pantomime.' December 6, 1912." Sasha's plot description naïvely recalls his father's ballet *Pavillon d'Armide,* "a moonlit night, Catherine's room, on the wall a portrait of the groom, the knight d'Aumont Clery, dead for forty-five years." Significant musical features include rapidly changing meters, a sophisticated texture which often grows out of single-voiced motives, dissonant harmonies, and varied rhythmic patterns. The piece gains momentum with undulating fourths and fifths in the "Scene with bells." A series of seconds is introduced at "The Appearance of the Phantom," a technique which would later prove to be one of the composer's favorites.[36]

Another pre-conservatory composition similarly preserved only in the archive shows Tcherepnin already writing in the style of a Prokofiev piano concerto, aping his model's characteristic unromantic, percussive jabs of the solo piano. The piece is of special interest for a program note by its author illuminating his personality and outlook on the problem of creativity. The clean manuscript is entitled, "On the Threshold: Diptych for Piano and Orchestra. Score. Composed September 1916. Orchestrated from October 1916 until December 1917." The following inscription is found on the back of the title page:

> This diptych opens a new era in the history of my creativity. During the summer of 1916 I reflected a lot on questions of religion and the universe, and the music of this diptych recalls and reproduces these thoughts and feeling in music. It seems to me that all human life is the struggle of the spirit against the flesh. When the flesh wins, the person "lives" for corporeal life; when the spirit wins, the person "dies" for it. On the other hand, the spirit released from the burden of flesh can rise and penetrate worlds which it could not have before, when weighted down by the body. And sooner or later we shall see these worlds, both I who am writing these lines and you who are reading them. But until then we shall struggle long and hard; and the picture of this struggle, the struggle which takes place in me and in you, is recorded in this diptych. Here the only winner is the flesh. And how could it be otherwise, since I am seven-

Example 1.2

teen years old! But beginning with this composition the struggle of the spirit and the flesh will hold my creativity entirely in thrall. And my last composition, should I have the strength to write it down, will be a victory of the spirit. Now the struggle continues, and its flow is embodied in my compositions.[37]

The two contrasting dimensions are reflected in measures 1–2 and 5–6 (musical example 1.2).

The music, however, is not at all philosophical. The piano part is virtuoso, especially in its etude-like cadenzas. Incessantly knocking solo ostinatos are pierced by brass instrument calls.

It is amazing that many pieces written prior to Tcherepnin's entrance in the conservatory achieved such high quality that they were not only performed by the composer in Petrograd, Tiflis, and abroad but were also published in the 1920s, both by Belaieff's "Russian" publishing house and by the French publisher Durand. Some of the works were edited by Isidore Philipp. Examples of this precocity include the 1915 piece that would become No. 4 in Op. 7; No. 7 of the popular *Bagatelles,* Op. 5, composed in 1912; and the ninth and tenth of the *Ten Etudes* Op. 18, composed, respectively, in 1914 and 1917. The Scherzo eventually published as Op. 3 was also performed in Soudak. The short pieces of this period, numbering some two hundred, went by the household name *bloshki* ("little fleas"). That not all of them have survived is apparent from a touching 1965 reminiscence:

When he returned from his first trip to the USSR, [Charles] Munch brought me a handmade case filled with a clump of Russian earth taken from the porch of the Church of St. Nicholas in Leningrad. The Benois house at 15 Glinka Street, where I lived during the year of our departure, was a corner building, and from my window the Church of St. Nicholas of the Sea was visible. After

I received the Russian soil, I wrote about it to my uncle, Alexandre Benois, in Paris. He then sent me a watercolor of the church of St. Nicholas of the Sea so that I would have what I had seen from our windows together with the soil. I have kept both in New York. Munch also photographed the Benois house on Glinka Street for me. . . . And who knows—perhaps in the attic of this house still remains the large enameled chest with my diaries and manuscripts.[38]

The circumstances surrounding the creation of the future *Sonatine romantique* Op. 4, in the spring of 1918, are recounted by the composer:

During Holy Week I was laid up in bed with a temperature, ill with scurvy from lack of food. My house was directly opposite the St. Nicholas Cathedral where I usually went each year with my father for the Easter service. That year I was unable to go but heard the bells peal and from the window watched the procession, and thus somehow participated in the service. During the Saturday service some seamen from the Kronstadt left with weapons in hand and began to shoot, and from the window I heard rifle shots on a background of choral song. The romantic sonatina was written within four days: the first part on Thursday, the second on Friday, the third on Saturday, and the fourth on Easter Sunday. In Russia there was a custom that on Easter any interested person could enter the church and ring the bells for his own pleasure. In youth I did it many times but now could call these bells only on the piano.

In the *Sonatine romantique* the bells of St. Nicholas Cathedral can be heard in the third movement, which is pentatonic but without Oriental coloring. The shots can be heard in the fourth movement; and the church chanting, here a doleful prayer, in the first and last movements. The Canzonette movement drew on an earlier romance written to the words of a poem by Konstantin Balmont. According to Tcherepnin, his early music was marked by "freedom and intuition." Nevertheless the *Sonatine romantique* demonstrates an early formal clarity and an economic use of the means of expression.

Although little biographical documentation survives about most of the Petersburg pieces, we find a wealth of information concerning the *Bagatelles* Op. 5. In the Freedman interview Tcherepnin characterized *Bagatelles* as "absolutely anti-impressionistic and anti-eclectic, rather like Prokofiev, but perhaps with chromatism, which Prokofiev did not always use."[39] Dating from the years 1912–1918, these *bloshki* reached print in no fewer than four editions in Paris. In 1958 and 1960 they appeared in concerto-like arrangements—one for piano and full orchestra, one for piano and strings—made by Tcherepnin at the request of the well-known pianist Margrit Weber. It was in 1967 that the author of this book heard *Bagatelles* in Moscow, performed by Tcherepnin himself.

2   In the Hills of Georgia

In midsummer 1918 Nicolas, Marie, and Sasha Tcherepnin fled Petrograd for Tiflis. There the Mensheviks had seized power in November 1917, creating an independent Georgian Republic that would exist for almost four years, no longer part of the Russian Empire nor yet a Soviet Socialist Republic. Although for political reasons this period is scantily covered in Soviet historiography, the cultural life of the capital—Tiflis—was brilliant and intense during this time. There was a simultaneous influx of prominent writers, artists, actors, and musicians escaping hunger in Petersburg and Moscow, and Georgian professional music began to blossom.

The Caucasus, especially Georgia, had already been inextricably tied to Russian artistic classics for a century. Providence brought Sasha Tcherepnin to the place where Griboedov wrote *Woe from Wit* and Leo Tolstoy wrote *The Cossacks.* Here Pushkin created *The Captive of the Caucasus* and other poems inspired by Georgia, and Lermontov produced *Mtziri, The Demon,* and *A Hero of Our Time.* Borodin, Glinka, and Balakirev all drew Eastern influences from Georgia, although only the latter two had actually traveled there. In fact, the Russian Musical East, mainly of the Caucasus-Transcaucasus region, was one of the hallmarks of the "Mighty Five" Petersburg school.[1] Igor Stravinsky is also known to have taken an interest in Georgian folklore, although much later and from a modernist perspective. Despite this heritage of Eastern exploration, Tcherepnin's three years of stable life in Tiflis marked a decidedly novel "immersion" for him: not only in ethnicity but also in the substance of life and the life of art.

During these years the Tiflis Opera Theater saw premieres of works by Zakharia Paliashvili, Dimitri Arakishvili, and Viktor Dolidze. Concurrently the Georgian Musical Society was formed and operated actively alongside a branch of the Russian Musical Society and the Russian Conservatory. The conservatory, which had been created shortly before through the reorganization of a music college, underwent significant development. Indeed, it was Nicolas Tcherepnin who was invited to direct the conservatory and conduct the Opera Theater Orchestra.

Upon arrival, Tcherepnin Jr. immediately began to show his bright and versatile talent. Yet despite the importance of these next three years for his musical formation, this period is mentioned only briefly in existing literature. Neither Willy Reich's book nor Enrique Arias's *Bio-Bibliography* elucidates the extensive scope of Tcherepnin's literary activity in Tiflis, nor does any previous commentator from Georgia, Russia, or the West deal with this important subject.

Tcherpnin's numerous articles (usually signed "A. T.") not only form a significant chapter in Russian musical criticism but also mark an original layer of his artistic heritage. They also are a "thermometer" of his Tiflis life—a piggybank of impressions that in one way or another were later reflected in his work. In a 1969 letter responding to an inquiry by musicologist-lexicologist Grigori Bernandt, Tcherepnin provided the names of selected publications and newspapers that had printed his Tiflis writings and, more important, identified his literary pseudonyms. This letter serves as the starting point for the search to characterize his musico-critical works.

> Dear Grigori Borisovich, I have found here my articles in the Transcaucasian (Tiflis) press (during 1918–21) pasted in by my mother, and I cannot bring myself to make you a list. Besides, almost nowhere are printed the dates and names of newspapers or magazines in which the article appeared. . . . But here are some titles: . . .
>
> The *Caucasian Word* was the first newspaper where I worked (its art editor was Vladimir Ananov). The newspaper was frequently closed by the Georgian government of that time. . . . The majority of the articles and reviews appeared in 1918 and 1919. I seem to remember that I was invited to become the musical editor of the newspaper *Struggle* in 1920, but by this time I was very much occupied with writing concertos, composing, working at the Tiflis Chamber Theater, etc., and so wrote less frequently and did not cut out articles. Consequently, except for an article on *Don Giovanni,* I have preserved nothing else from my involvement with *Struggle.*[2]

Tcherepnin's writings appear in the newspapers *Caucasian Word, Future Day, Unity, New Day, Word, Struggle,* and the *Tiflis Gazette,* in the magazine *Art,* and in other publications. A large-format leather album with clippings of the articles is held at the Paul Sacher Foundation. From these we learn about the music heard daily at the theater as well as in evening programs of different societies and circles. The author used various signatures: large, more important items were signed "Alexandre Tcherepnin" or "A. Tcherepnin"; others "A. T.," "A. T-n," "Fuldan," "Platon Valanchal," and "Es."[3] These texts vividly describe the musical and theatrical life of Tiflis in the years 1918 to 1921. They clearly reveal an experienced visitor to Petersburg theaters, concerts, and exhibitions (which the author sometimes mentioned directly).

The repertoire revealed in Tcherepnin's reviews is extensive. At the State Opera Theater this included Rimsky-Korsakov's *The Tsar's Bride* (conducted by Nicolas Tcherepnin), Tchaikovsky's *Eugene Onegin* and *Queen of Spades,* Mozart's *Don Giovanni,* Napravnik's *Dubrovsky,* Verdi's *Rigoletto* and *Aida,* Massenet's *Manon,* Offenbach's *Tales of Hoffmann,* Bizet's *Carmen,* Puccini's *Madame Butterfly,* Paliashvili's *Absalom and Eteri* (a review spread over two issues), and, on the stage of the Artistic Society, Tigranyan's *Anush.* As in the earlier Petersburg impressions, here we see the formation and discovery of an attitude toward different aspects of opera, especially libretto, which would later appear in Tcherepnin's own operas. Regarding *Madame Butterfly* he writes,

There are operas in which the composer takes on ambitious goals, where the center of gravity lies in music that is superb by itself, and the libretto fades into the background. There are operas in which magnificent music is combined with beautiful scenic action. And there are operas in which a scenically alive libretto dominates the music. This last type of opera has the greatest success [and in this category] belongs Puccini's *Madame Butterfly.* A deeply touching and scenic libretto accompanied by sincere music, not lacking a certain spice and exoticism, has made it popular around the world.[4]

A heroine in a kimono, the Far East in European music, all this went into the "piggybank." Tcherepnin writes sympathetically about *Tales of Hoffmann:* "full of lively content, beautiful in musical essence . . . the plot filled with fantasy, abounding in various entertaining episodes." The critic's judgments are especially convincing when he speaks about Russian opera, such as the recitatives in Dargomizhsky's *Mermaid.* During 1919 Tcherepnin's reviews of performances of the State Opera were published weekly in the Menshevik *Struggle,* and sometimes a single week would see the staging of one new production and the revival of three older ones! In connection with successive performances of *The Tsar's Bride* and *Queen of Spades* we find reflections on Tchaikovsky as "lyricist" and on Rimsky-Korsakov as "epicist, storyteller." Tcherepnin's "The Week in Opera" reviews indicate that he attended the theater no less than twice a week for the whole season, and witnessed a set of productions typical for theater at that time. These included Thomas's *Mignon,* Humperdinck's *Hansel and Gretel,* Massenet's *Werther,* and Gounod's *Faust.* His opinions of stage direction and individual singers are subtle and exact. Although she had amazed him on the concert stage, Nina Kotshetz was reproached for excessive "dramatization" of some lyrical opera roles and for overly precise declamatory diction that sometimes sacrificed the main value—"pure vocal melodiousness of sound."

The symphonic and chamber music programs, and the solo evenings of pianists, violinists, and singers which Tcherepnin mentions, include dozens of works from Bach and Handel to Rebikov and Prokofiev. The Russian classics, perfectly familiar to the young critic, are richly represented. He finds fault with a performance of Borodin's Second Quartet: "this masterpiece of Russian chamber music . . . the ending, close in spirit to his 'Bogatyrskaya' Symphony [Symphony No. 2], sounded boring and tense." Quite often these articles far exceed critical response to the music performed and contain reflections of a historical character. In the article, "About Rubinstein and from Rubinstein," we find a mature view, remarkably acute for its time, of the linear development in German music from Phillip Emmanuel Bach through the Viennese Classicists, Romanticists, and Wagner, which "cleanly and naturally . . . led to Reger, Strauss, Schoenberg." Tcherepnin compares the work of Anton Rubinstein with "the business of Peter the Great." He also connects "Neoclassicism, headed by Medtner and Prokofiev . . . forging a path through the milieu of Russian music" with the "fundamental principles" established by Rubinstein.

The twenty-fifth anniversary of Tchaikovsky's death, widely celebrated in Tiflis, spurred a whole series of articles. Although many of the opinions expressed then seem obvious and even banal now, at that time the development of the theme of death—from the Adagio of the Third Quartet to the ending of the Sixth Symphony—had not been addressed by scholarly literature.[5] In general, Tcherepnin writes about Tchaikovsky with remarkable sincerity: "While I admire Beethoven's magnificence, while I am amazed by the brilliant technique of Liszt, Tchaikovsky I love. . . . Great is the artist who in his works has found a way to the human heart, and great is the composer who makes us love his creations. For him, Death does not exist."[6] These confessions of a musician who had already demonstrated a stylistic and linguistic affinity for the "Mighty Five," a school philosophically opposed to Tchaikovsky, are nevertheless quite organic for a subsequent epoch. They are connected with his attitude toward Russia's spiritual and cultural heritage, and were absorbed in childhood and destined to accompany him throughout his life. Tcherepnin's final discussion of this theme seems dramatically apt in light of the historical shocks his country was then experiencing, and perhaps prophetic as well, for the Tcherepnin family would soon leave Russia forever, a departure as yet unsuspected by the man who authored "A Week of Tchaikovsky."

> Territories that definitively belong to Russia can be violently torn away from her; but no one can take away Pushkin, Dostoevsky, Turgenev, Vrubel, or Tchaikovsky. And now, in a moment of terrible doubt and tests, the awareness that behind the Russian people there is such an integral spiritual treasure allows us to look forward more bravely and have faith in a brighter future.

Articles about contemporary Russian music form a special segment of Tcherepnin's critical works at age twenty. They reveal his early maturity, as well as the "baggage" he carried from Petersburg. In the article "On Sergei Prokofiev" that appeared in *Art and Literature,* edited by Sergei Gorodetsky, the author reminds us of the two Russian schools of composition that had developed from Rimsky-Korsakov and Tchaikovsky:

> The entire current of Russian music of the beginning of this century lay in the vein of these two schools. But new forces were already fermenting. New talents were preparing to set Russian music on a new path. And the bright embodiment of this living force was Sergei Prokofiev, who openly broke with both the clichéd routine of *Kuchkism* and the extremes of Impressionism. . . . Prokofiev's talent—imperious, merry, and always free—has something in common with Mozart's.

Sarcasms, Visions, Fugitives, the *Scythian Suite,* two concertos, and the not yet staged *Gambler* all fall within Tcherepnin's analytical scope! Another article, "On Myaskovsky," discusses its subject as a symphonist and heir to Tchaikovsky, a role that "required not only a talent full of tension, but also a deep thinker." Tcherepnin compares the evolution of Myaskovsky's creativity to his world-view, predicting the composer's future to be one of "large symphonic forms." A certain one-sidedness marks an article devoted to Michael Gnesin. Surveying his songs, his Symphonic Fragment *After Shelley, The Victorious Worm,* and other compositions, Tcherepnin compares Gnesin's compositions to "Vrubel's nightmarish pictures," the "terrible visions of Dante's hell," and "Heine's last sufferings." Only "the most recently published work, *Rosarium,*" proves an exception. These opinions are notable not for objectivity or validity but for the personality of the author—his tastes, his awareness, his talents as musician and writer—all of which shines through them.

The oft-performed music of Nicolas Tcherepnin is naturally discussed in the reviews. Alexander writes the following about the second gathering of the Georgian Musical Society.

> The soloist, Boris Zalipsky, performed three romances of Tcherepnin. The first two of these, "Tsarskoselskoe Lake" and "The Candle Has Burnt Down," belong to the composer's early period, but they already reveal the tenderness and refinement of feeling that was fated to be poured out in both series of "Fairy Tales." But the third, "Birch," which was written rather recently and has at its heart a nostalgia for the tenderly beloved homeland, ranks with Tcherepnin's best, most experienced romances. . . . The composer accompanied and was warmly greeted by the public.

About "An Evening of Nicolas Tcherepnin's Compositions" at the National Conservatory, Alexander writes:

> In his broad opening address I. S. Aisberg characterized Tcherepnin as predominantly a lyricist and simultaneously heir to the Russian Mighty Five, a school Tcherepnin had left. Yes, in Tcherepnin's creativity, saturated with intimate and graceful subjectivity, deep experience and a certain contemplation of that experience are simultaneously present. The combination of these two apparently incompatible sources indeed forms the basic secret of Tcherepnin's creativity. . . . The performance by the author himself of "Fairytale of the Fisherman and the Fish" caused great excitement. In six sketches Tcherepnin embodied in music the brightest motifs of Pushkin's marvelous tale. This work, though deeply Russian, shows at the same time an absolutely new approach to the subject, and is a big step forward against the clichéd *Kuchkism.*

Noteworthy here is both the mention of "clichéd *Kuchkism*" and how well Alexander understood the "mystery" of his father's creativity. From other articles we learn about Nicolas Tcherepnin's performances in ensembles—at Nina Kotshetz's concerts, as conductor and director of the Conservatory Orchestra and Chorus, as the performer of Tchaikovsky symphonies, and so on. It is in Tiflis that father and son start performing together in concerts.

Alexander Tcherepnin's work as a music critic served him well and helps us understand his acoustical experiences, opinions, and preferences, but it represents only one facet of his activities. Another was his active concert life in Tiflis and other cities of the Transcaucasus, where his repertoire was quite extensive. Surviving programs document violin and piano concerts (with Iolanta Mirimanova) offering sonatas by Beethoven, Grieg, Saint-Saëns, and piano soirées predominantly featuring Russian music from Rubinstein to Medtner and Prokofiev. In each concert Tcherepnin also played his own music, and many evenings were devoted entirely to his works. Thus he began to establish himself in the role of composer-pianist, which the following decades would affirm.

Another Tiflis motif for Tcherepnin was his meeting and collaboration with the remarkable actress Elizabeth Zhihareva, a bright star of Russian Silver Age theater who is almost forgotten today. Zhihareva studied with Vladimir Nemirovich-Danchenko, making her debut in 1903 at the Moscow Art Theater. Subsequently playing the provinces, she returned again to Moscow, performing at the theaters of Korsh and Nezlobin, and the Small Theater. A notable dramatic actress and an extraordinary personality, she played Katherine in Ostrovsky's *The Storm*, Nastasia Fillipovna in a dramatization of Dostoevsky's *The Idiot*, Jeanne d'Arc, and Hedda Gabler. In Tiflis Zhihareva created and directed the Chamber Theater, where she took many leading parts.

Concerning her performance of the title role in Hermann Sudermann's drama *Magda*, Leo Gal wrote in *Obnovlenie*, "in the person of Mrs. Zhihareva the theater has, undoubtedly, a star of the first order, an actress of Divine favor, a true artist who draws culture and beauty onstage from the light of her soul."[7]

Destiny again led Sasha Tcherepnin to the theater as if by the hand. Composing music for plays, it seems he began to assume the duties of musical director of a theater. A notice in *Struggle* mentions "the forthcoming production at the Chamber Theater (dir. by Zhihareva) of R. Rolland's play, *The Triumph of Reason*, music and choruses to be written by A. Tcherepnin,"[8] although music is not mentioned in the review of the premiere. Some of his Tiflis theater music is preserved, however, notably a violin solo from his music for Oscar Wilde's *Salome*.[9] The *Salome* score receives considerable attention in another review in the same newspaper:

> In *Salome* the entire first scene takes place to the music of the talented young composer Alexander Tcherepnin, who shows in it much feeling and taste. This music (executed on a harmonium) creates an intense mood and serves as an interesting background for the play, responding to the quite prophetical words of Herodias that there must be tragedy. The Dance of Salome (a violin solo) is a bit sketch-like.[10]

It is important to remember that Tcherepnin was familiar with the autumn 1917 performances of *Salome* and Gerhart Hauptmann's *Hannele* in Petrograd at Mardzhanov's theater.

Alexander Tcherepnin's use of "voices without words" as accompaniment to vocal parts in a different production of *Hannele* is an interesting musical-scenic discovery, which predates the use of this technique by many others (musical example 2.1).[11] To be sure, the wordless chorus and the arpeggios in fourths and fifths in the orchestra are found several years earlier in Nicolas Tcherepnin's *Narcissus and Echo*.

The harmonium is often used instead of a pit orchestra. According to the December 8, 1920, issue of *Struggle*, "A. N. Tcherepnin" appeared "at the harmonium" in a program at Zhihareva's theater commemorating the tenth anniversary of Tolstoy's death (the only such observance at a Tiflis theater). "In

Example 2.1

the musical portion of the celebration," Tcherepnin accompanied a cantata by Anton Arensky, "sung with uplifting sentiment and harmony by the young chorus of the opera studio."

The actress Tamara Tsulukidze draws a powerful portrait of Zhihareva in the Tiflis setting:

> I recall unforgettable impressions from my youth—"Evenings of poetry and music" given by the then well-known actress Elizabeth Timofeevna Zhiha-reva. She staged them in the building of the conservatory. Accompanied by piano, she read the poems of Vasily Kamensky, Shelley, fragments of Hamsun . . . alone. All evening long . . . poems by Balmont, Anna Akhmatova, Blok. . . . How they sounded in her performance! Never would I encounter such a huge range of vocal effects. From deepest organ-like sounds to thin violin-like notes, from the booming beat of the drum to a choking shrill whisper. It was a truly peerless music of speech.[12]

According to T. Tsulukidze, Tcherepnin accompanied Zhihareva on those poetry evenings.

A chance mention in a 1928 letter to his parents elucidates the character of his musical accompaniments in Tiflis: they were at least partly improvisations.

> Yesterday received a very kind letter from Frau Gutheil-Schoder. She is an ex-singer, heroine of all Strauss's operas, with a reputation [that enables her to fill] any German hall. And I have developed a project to try to do an evening of "Poetry and Music" with her, and in fact I will write music for this in a totally different manner than I did with Zhihareva, i.e., completely excluding improvisation. And based predominantly on rhythm, with possible percussion.[13]

Tcherepnin did not forget Elizabeth Zhihareva. She wrote him in 1925 from Riga, where she was working at the Chamber Theater under Ekaterina Roschina-Insarova's direction, and reproached Sasha for not staying in touch.

> Here things are not bad, but no better! Ah, Sasha, how death is everywhere! Where is life? Where is the real thing? My soul is so torn by such duality! I feel that amid the gloom and horror of Russia, light nevertheless breaks through; and for me there is no thought more terrible than the awareness that if I return there, I shall not understand that life, and shall be dead for them [Soviet Russians]. . . . Why did I leave? This is the shame, this is the mistake! . . . Send me the music for Blok's *Stranger*.[14]

Tcherepnin quickly answered Zhihareva.

> I throw aside all other affairs in order to answer you immediately.... With what
> tenderness I remember the Chamber Theater and all our collaborations....
> The more I see and hear actors of opera and drama, the more I understand
> how uniquely gifted and extremely remarkable you are! ... Whoever heard
> your voice, whoever saw you in *Elektra,* in *Salome,* will never forget.[15]

Returning to Tiflis on the cusp of the 1920s we see one more aspect of young
Tcherepnin's life and activity: new Russian poetry. Because Georgia, between
1918 and 1921, falls into the gap between "Russian" and "Soviet" history, the
Literary Encyclopedia entries devoted to the "Poets' Guild," Vasily Kamensky,
and Sergei Gorodetsky do not contain a single word about Tiflis. Yet the "Poets'
Guild" operated there quite actively. Gorodetsky was one of the organizers. Literary critics remarked that the Guild's creative principles were reflected in the
works of Gumilev, Mandelstam, and other members of the association.

> Formed on April, 11, 1918 ... the Poets' Guild was originally an association
> of all sorts of poets, with diverse leanings. Soon after, however, a split devel-
> oped between the basic nucleus ("Acmeists") and the left currents ("Futur-
> ists").... At this moment the Poets' Guild (Acmeists) numbers about twenty-
> five members. Fifteen meetings have taken place since the fall .... A constant
> participant at the gatherings was Alexander Tcherepnin, who performed after
> the recitation of works.[16]

Another mention of Gorodetsky's Poets' Guild describes the reading of "the
newest verses" of members of the group, after which "the young composer
A. Tcherepnin was warmly welcomed."[17]

Among those who "broke away" from the Poets' Guild was the Futurist Kamensky. On May 12, 1919, the following announcement appeared in *The Caucasian Word:* "Theater of the Artistic Association. Wednesday May, 14. Vasily
Kamensky. Solemn lecture to music: Encounterings ... Soundings ... Wreath-
ings (the spring holiday of Futurism and new verses). At the piano, A. Tcherepnin. Scenery by Sergey Sudeikin." Here is the report of the lecture, which
had been preceded by expectations of scandal:

> The first entrance of the poet satisfied the crowd—he was dressed in an open-
> collared, motley shirt of an Eastern fabric. A. Tcherepnin very much matched
> the style of the evening, looking like a musician from Murger's *Scènes de la vie
> Bohème.* Against a background of posters by Sudeikin, the figures of Kamen-
> sky and Tcherepnin made for an entertaining show.... He [Kamensky] is a
> Russian talent. In him ferments strong young wine; from him flows the scent
> of the Volga and Kama. Understandably his favorite hero is Stenka Razin....
> A. N. Tcherepnin selected perfect music, and performed finely, delicately, and
> expressively.[18]

By this time Kamensky's "freedom-loving novel," *Stenka Razin,* had already
been issued in two editions. The work demonstrated the author's colorful palette, and abounded in epic power and liberating force. Tcherepnin surely had

Kamensky's poetics in mind when he later composed a ballet with the same name.

Sudeikin was another important presence. An artist who gravitated toward the World of Art group, he had executed scenery from the designs of Bakst and Roerich for Diaghilev's Paris seasons in 1912. He spent 1919 in Tiflis, where his projects included a poster and twelve decorative panel screens for Kamensky's May 14 lecture. The young Tcherepnin was clearly part of Sudeikin's circle. The artist's wife, Vera (who later married Stravinsky), kept a "Golden Book"—an album for entries by friends—in which Alexander inscribed a few bars from his First Concerto while visiting the couple in Kodjori.

Most important for Tcherepnin in the Tiflis years was his direct acquaintance—not possible from Petersburg—with the music of the peoples of Transcaucasia and the work of Georgian and Armenian composers. He wrote about many of them, including Zakharia Paliashvili, who was considered senior among this group. After studying with Taneyev in Moscow at the beginning of the century, Paliashvili arranged and published national songs, which he described as "in national harmonization" and made phonograph recordings of them. Scholars remark that the composer keenly captured the various dialects of Georgian musical folklore in his compositions. Tcherepnin wrote a detailed review of the premiere of his opera *Absalom and Eteri,* whose choral episodes are based on Kartalino-Kakhetinsky and Svansky songs. At the end of 1919, when Paliashvili's opera had been presented twenty-five times, the critic again praised it, citing the "outstanding beauty of separate episodes, the high technical development of the opera's musical contents, its purely national foundation, its loving attitude toward Georgian national song, its drive to sustain national color."

In the beginning of 1920 Tcherepnin returned to another classic opera—Dimitri Arakishvili's *Legend of Chota Rostaveli.* This composer and ethnomusicologist had, like Paliashvili, trained in Moscow in the early 1900s. A member of the Musico-Ethnographic Commission of Moscow University and the Georgian Literature and Art Society, Arakishvili published more than five hundred examples of vocal and instrumental national melodies. He returned to Georgia in 1918, and his opera was staged almost concurrently with *Absalom and Eteri.* "Its musical contents are exquisite," wrote Tcherepnin, "the beautiful orientalist foundation is skillfully clothed in the best European attire. Its melodies are full of strange Eastern Romanticism, and breathe the hot temperament of the south."

Finally, in a January 1920 article, Tcherepnin responds to the first Georgian operetta based on city folklore, while again commenting on the historical value of the two previous operas: "In the last two years Georgian music has taken a significant turn. The well-known operas *Absalom and Eteri* and *Legend of Chota Rostaveli* have created a whole epoch in the musical creativity of Georgia. The composers of these operas both managed to combine the East and Europe seamlessly, the national and the international. These operas also revive wonderful historical images of the Georgian nation for the audience. Depicting days

Example 2.2

of old, both are full of epic greatness and scope."[19] By contrast, the opera *Keto and Kote,* though demonstrating "the indisputable, vibrant, and mobile talent" of its young creator [Viktor Dolidze], possesses an "eclectic character." But, in the works of Paliashvili and Arakishvili, "an entire national root is shaped according to the rules of European technique. Here Europe lives near the East in the music itself."

We do not yet find the concept of "Asia" anywhere in Tcherepnin's writings. Georgia, though an independent republic, could only be perceived in its cultural tradition as belonging to Russia. However, the idea of Russia as a Eurasian country was undoubtedly stronger "beyond the Caucasus ridge." Caucasian impressions, above all musical ones, would be reflected in both the themes and plots of Alexander Tcherepnin's later compositions, and in the formation of his musical language.

This brings us to Tcherepnin's *Georgian Rhapsody* for cello and orchestra (1922). According to its composer, the score uses national song. Indeed, it belongs directly to the tradition of Russian musical Orientalism, both in general tone color and in detail. One remembers Balakirev's *Islamey:* an appeal to the East in order to create an effective concert piece, reproducing the sounds of native instruments. In *Rhapsody* we find Georgia's emblematic folk dance, the *lezginka,* along with Eastern rhythms and Eastern ornamentation, the harmonic color strengthened by the augmented seconds of Tcherepnin's nine-step scale (musical example 2.2).

The innovations of Balakirev relate to the world of modal harmony. The reader may recall the piano postlude to *Georgian Song*—in minor mode with a lowered fourth degree of the scale. Is this not the path to Shostakovich? It certainly leads to the twentieth century.

Georgia provided living succulence for Tcherepnin's composition. An authentic Georgian song is quoted in Tcherepnin's second movement (musical example 2.3)

Georgian Rhapsody is emotional, and the solo-monologues of the cello are

Example 2.3

satisfying as well as rhythmically fascinating. The transitions between lyrical and rhythmically dancing episodes are expressive. The instrumentation is especially luminous—duets, dialogues of strings and winds, cello as background to a drum.

As suggested earlier, the idea of "Eurasianism" had not yet arisen in Tcherepnin's thoughts and writings, although this concept, replete with its many dimensions and contradictions, would later become vital to the spiritual, cultural, and political life of Russian emigration. But can it be associated, retrospectively, with the phenomenon of the "New Russian School?" That is certainly not possible in the geopolitical sense but one can link "Eurasianism" with the "New Russian" school's global perspective and consciousness—the sense of belonging to the planet's largest continent and to Russia, its largest part; the sense of belonging to Europe and Asia simultaneously. The theme of Eurasianism would be highlighted years later by the composer in connection with *Sobeide.*

Tiflis was not only important as a center of Georgian influence at that time but also remained the center of Armenian culture. It was precisely in these years that the Komitas Society was formed. A Komitas concert on May 21, 1919, elicited the following newspaper response from Tcherepnin:

> Komitas is an extremely interesting figure on the scene of the modern music world! This zealous collector of national songs appreciates the value and necessity of technique and education for the musician. Komitas, although already an archimandrite, leaves for Germany, where for four years he studies with Professor Richard Schmidt. Technique is acquired—and now, at the height of technical knowledge and training, Komitas, free and imperious, denies it, and approaches national song only impressionistically [meaning not the precise style but the spontaneity of impressions.—L.K.]. Also it should be said that the approach of Komitas to national song is so convincing, so truthful, that it is difficult to imagine a more favorable framework or more favorable conditions for its reception. Komitas's arrangement merges with the song, so that you see no laws, no hardened formulas of harmonization: the song and harmonization are created, merged, and cannot be imagined separately.

Becoming acquainted first with Komitas's arrangements and then his compositions, Tcherepnin grasped the most important elements of the Armenian folk-song heritage, beginning with the most ancient. The Komitas Society was headed by Thomas de Hartmann (Foma Hartmann), who had arrived in Tiflis in 1919. Here Alexander became his pupil in counterpoint. The two would meet again in Constantinople and still later in France, where Hartmann became closely tied to the Tcherepnin family, working as a professor at the Russian Conservatory under the directorship of Nicolas Tcherepnin.

In 1962, responding to Shneerson's comment in a 1958 book on Khachaturian, Tcherepnin wrote the author:

> I love [Khachaturian's] music. . . . So it saddens me that we never met: as you perhaps know, in the fall [actually summer] of 1918 my father was invited to be director of the Tiflis Conservatory. I was the only son—and spent three years in Tiflis together with my parents—from August 1918 till August 1921. My father combined the directorship of the conservatory with conducting at the Opera. Paliashvili, Potzhverashvili, Balanchivadze (Meliton), and Arakishvili were his friends. On page 18 you speak of the premiere of *Absalom and Eteri* and quote the words of Khachaturian about the impression this opera made on him. . . . I was also present and experienced the same strong impression. This means that we were with Khachaturian in the same theater—listened to the same music—experienced the same impression! . . . Reading your description of Tiflis it was as though I again visited the city so dear to my heart, especially as your description speaks of Tiflis in an epoch that I knew. Everything that impressed Khachaturian also impressed me, then in my formative period. You will find in my work elements of the folk music of Georgia, Armenia, and Azerbajian (I gave concerts widely across Transcaucasia and listened to folk music everywhere). You will find these traces not only in works of a national character, such as my *Georgian Rhapsody* for cello and orchestra, the *Georgian Suite* for piano and string ensemble, the ballet *Chota Rostaveli*, etc., but also in many completely non-folklore pieces. The nine-step scale on which many of my works are constructed flows out of the sounds of Transcaucasian folk music.[20]

Notable in this letter is the mention of concert performances in countries of Transcaucasia other than Georgia. It is also possible that in the *Basic Elements* section devoted to the folkloric sources of his compositions, the composer missed at least one example—entered undated on a sheet of German-made music paper with the heading: "Record from memory of an Armenian song, heard in the train on the road from Tiflis to Yerevan when on tour: Yerevan, Alexandropol with [two words indecipherable] and the singer Chesnokova in 1920."[21]

Until recently this city song was commonly heard. A minor triad is atypical of Armenian songs, but the Aeolian harmony, and especially the sustained sound of "Dam" [I shall give], are captured precisely (musical example 2.4).

Regarding the composer's account of the derivation of the nine-step "Tcherepnin scale" from "Sounds of Caucasian Folk Music," an analysis shows other

Example 2.4

28   *Alexander Tcherepnin*

inescapable convergences. These are Olivier Messiaen's later "modes of limited transposition," which were admired by Tcherepnin, and the augmented harmonies of B. Yavorsky, then likewise unfamiliar to him. The use of the "simultaneous" major-minor as a foundation is novel and apparently does not arise from the East.

Tcherepnin connected Eastern motifs and their reflection in literary texts to arts other than music. "The product of an artistic family" is how Alexandre Benois describes himself and his son Nikolai, Sasha's friend and childhood comrade. Understanding "artistic" both broadly and in the narrower sense of the visual arts, the same can be said of Benois' great nephew Alexander Tcherepnin.

The young critic writes about the "Exhibition of Georgian Artists" and the "Exhibition of the Union of Armenian Artists," where he meets such estimable figures of twentieth-century painting as Lado Gudiashvili and Martiros Sarian. The exhibition of Armenian painting became an occasion to reflect on the essence of artistic creativity, to express the composer's own credo.

> In painting, as in other arts, true fire is recognized by the presence in the artist of internal emotion. Without internal feeling, without its "lenses," artistic creation is impossible. The artist who has not experienced his image, the artist who depicts only *what* he sees instead of *how* he sees, cannot be called an artist. The whole point of any artistic work, whether visual or not—is in the opening of the inner spiritual world, the images of the soul—for in fact the soul thinks in images, and almost always in images not taken from reality but born from internal experiences. Freeing the soul from the pressure of external impressions, from external influence, is the most important task facing the artist. Not without reason, having surmounted a technical challenge, painting, which always moves forward, has come to Ciurlionis, to Vrubel, the Futurists . . . through self-knowledge and deepening, to merge with the Cosmos.

These verbose and not always comprehensible thoughts of a musician before whom the "technical challenge" still lay provide in effect a spiritual portrait of Alexander Tcherepnin that would be recognizable even decades later.

At the Georgian exhibition the paintings of Mose Toidze, Lado Gudiashvili, and Niko Pirosmanashvili attracted the greatest attention. While Tcherepnin described Toidze and Gudiashvili as "full of principles and saturated with the national spirit of *Tsarina Tamara* and *Chota Rostaveli*," Pirosmanashvili rather confused the critic and, not surprisingly, was misunderstood. The review itself is sincere, as are all Tcherepnin's writings, and deserves to be quoted as a characteristic document of the era.

> At this time painting, music, and literature are all in a phase where anything, once placed in an aesthetic framework, can be examined as a work of art. One of the signboards on Olginskaya Street depicts a rather ineptly drawn polar bear in a naïve and disingenuous pose. . . . You will either pass by, having paid him no attention, or smile. . . . It will not even enter your mind that this signboard could be considered art, especially as a creative achievement. But place the same bear in an aesthetic context, present him at an exhibition, and

Example 2.5

Example 2.6

> the judgment becomes seriously complicated. So it goes with Pirosmanash-
> vili. First his paintings, his charming naïve primitives, seem somehow very
> original and artistic. Is it not so? Did Pirosmanashvili come to primitivism or
> is his work the primitivism of the half-trained student? I am inclined to think
> the latter.

Of course, contact with the East was constant. The biographers of Khachaturian and Pirosmani depict Tiflis at the beginning of the 1920s as a bubbling
multinational city, with street singers, organ-grinders, and multi-voiced songs
flowing from the taverns. All this was absorbed by the eyes and ears of the composer. Stored in his memory, it began to enter his artistic subconscious. It also
started to shape his musical thinking and language, but only later was this realized and implemented in compositions. In the "Indian" ballet *Ajanta's Frescoes* (1923) we encounter traditional Georgian melodic fragments, including
an entire number in "Duduki" (No. 8 in scene 2). In the *Georgian Suite* (1937),
after the Overture and the expressive Dialogue, the two final movements are
named "Allaverdi" and "Prayer of Shamil." Last, according to Tcherepnin's own
note, *Childhood of St. Nino* (Op. 69, 1943) revives the history of the saint who
turned Georgia to Christianity by preaching the Gospel. Indeed, the piece re-
produces the character of Gospel readings in Georgian churches, using a tonic
triad which substitutes a fourth for the third as its basis. In a letter to his father
from London, the composer recalled "our beloved Georgian tonic,"[22] and explained with a few notes (musical example 2.5).

The sheet with the title "Oriental Dance" is undated, but whenever this piano
piece was written, it had its roots in the Caucasus. In fact, its source was more
likely Armenia than Georgia, as evidenced by both the ostinato sustained all
the way through and the chromatic variation of melodic folk motives (over accompaniment in fifths) which divide into smaller units (musical example 2.6).

Thanks to the extensive Georgian diaspora in Paris, friends from Georgia
long remained close to the Tcherepnins. A notice in the émigré newspaper *Po-*

slednie novosti about a concert ball held by the Association of Georgians in France on the occasion of a national Georgian holiday indicates, "A. Tcherepnin's *Georgian Rhapsody* (accompanied by the composer) will be heard, national songs performed by a chorus, etc., at the Salle Victor Hugo."[23] Indeed, Georgians quite often supported Nicolas Tcherepnin financially, especially at the end of his life. One of his last compositions was *Georgian Funeral Dirge.*

During the early years of the Tcherepnins' stay in France, friends from Tbilisi and Russia actively sought contact with the European emigrants, although this became increasingly complicated as time went on. Arakishvili's and Paliashvili's letters to Nicolas Tcherepnin, in unadressed, unstamped envelopes, were obviously transmitted by hand as the opportunity arose. Paliashvili wrote:

> After a break of almost four years, during which I have completely lost track of you, I only recently learned that you are now based in Paris. . . . In 1923 I received your card from Brussels. . . . Wanted to answer you but could not find your address there. Now that I have the chance, I want to share news and talk with you to my heart's content. How are you living, and what are you doing? I receive word here about Sasha's great successes as a pianist and a composer. . . . I heard that in Paris a Russian conservatory has opened and that you are its director. This is wonderful! I am confident that, with your help, such an educational institution will serve as a nursery for Russian musical culture in Paris. But dear Nicolas Nicolaievich, as a Georgian public figure and composer I must ask you to not overlook the culture of small and beautiful Georgia, where you lived three years and headed a similar establishment. . . . This is already the fifth season in which my opera *Absalom and Eteri* is being staged, and it engages the public more and more. . . . During this time I have also written another three-act opera, *Daisi* [*Twilight*]. In two seasons it has played about fifty times. It is written in quite another spirit—in Georgian, but in its form it is closer to European operas. In it are many national scenes, dances, and round dances, and there is also humor. . . . And now, dear Nicolas Nicolaievich, it seems to me that it is time to acquaint Europe with our culture! And it seems to me that musicians and leading people like you could help us with it. . . . You know my *Absalom and Eteri* very well. You even conducted it, and apparently it pleased you so much that when you left here you asked me to supply you with at least some excerpts, if not the whole score.[24]

Unaware of the realities of Parisian life, which had long since separated Nicolas Tcherepnin from Diaghilev, Paliashvili also tried to interest the latter in the staging of his opera. A year later, having received some money from the Manganese Industrial Society "Chemo," Paliashvili was determined to go to Europe:

> From your letter I learned something similar to what I had also considered, that is, to coordinate concerts of Georgian music in Paris, and perhaps in Berlin, where the works of Georgian composers would be staged, including young pupils of our conservatory if you remember them: Taktakishvili, Kiladze, Tuskia, and others. . . . Just like you, I see great value in devising concerts of both a grand and ethnographic character. . . . For this, the encouragement of an expert and art lover such as you is necessary. In your letter you

emphasized this several times, and I never doubted that, for Georgian Music, and in particular for me, you would do everything required, and a lot does depend on you!

At first Alexander's Georgian ties continued uninterrupted. Willy Reich's monograph includes a photograph of the entire Tcherepnin family with Sasha's young musician friends—Nikolai Vygodsky, Iolanta Mirimanova, Maria Kalamkarian, and Tatyana Halatova. This Mirimanova was the very musician who had performed the violin solo in *Salome* at the Chamber Theater and at one of Alexander's sonata evenings. After difficult wanderings with her family, she appeared in Berlin and wrote Sasha in Paris. The tone of the letters suggests that the Tiflis relationship had had a romantic character.[25]

Nikolai Vygodsky graduated from the Tiflis Conservatory in 1920 and from the Moscow Conservatory four years later. He studied organ with A. Gedike, composition with Myaskovsky, taught history of music in this conservatory, led an organ class, conducted concert activity, composed, and at one point was a member of the Russian Association of Proletarian Musicians (RAPM). Repressed by the Soviets, he died before turning forty. Among his twenty or so published articles the very first was about Alexander Tcherepnin's *Bagatelles* and two pieces of his Op. 1, copies of which the composer had sent him from Paris during their active correspondence. Some letters are twelve to fourteen pages long; others, which analyze new works received from the composer, are accompanied by musical examples. Vygodsky's letters brightly describe both his creative life and the lives of other musicians. Although extensive citations of this most interesting and completely overlooked figure are outside the scope of this book, his writings surely deserve comprehensive publication elsewhere. Vividly engrossed both in the compositions of his recent schoolmate, and new music in general, he asks that certain publications be sent from Paris:

> New foreign releases, unfortunately, do not reach us here, and thus the music world of Moscow and the rest of Russia is deprived of opportunities to become acquainted with the newest products of the musical art, and hence to actively keep up with the development of music. It is sad. Russian composers (the most outstanding) are not present in Russia, and thus undoubtedly we lag somewhat behind.[26]

Another time he writes: "Things are interesting here. A very important musical event on the horizon is the birth of a real music journal, *To New Shores*. Organizers and participants: Viktor Beliaev, Myaskovsky, Igor Glebov, Sabaneyev, Meichik, and others."[27]

In the third issue of the magazine to which he refers, a note appears by Vygodsky about piano pieces by Tcherepnin, which Vygodsky showed to Beliaev and Myaskovsky, who "became interested." In response to Tcherepnin's questions, Vygodsky sent Alexander a sonata by Myaskovsky, and wrote: "Roslavetz is here and composes. He has introduced an innovation—a septet of human voices—into the symphonic orchestra. . . . And about Kastalsky: he now writes things with revolutionary content but in the spirit of the Church. Dead stuff!" Contacts would soon dwindle to nothing, but for the moment Tcherepnin found these reports from home significant. Having received a published concerto score, undoubtedly the Second Concerto for piano and orchestra and the First Piano Sonata, Vygodsky sketched his impressions of the latter.

> Rather pleasant. Its strengths: absence of routine in tonal sequences (a, G, g♯, a), musicality (not in the banal sense but in the idea that all the movements are alive—the music is not perfunctory but saturated with great sincerity), the continuity of themes from the first and third parts, simplicity of harmonies, and deep pithiness.

The sonata had been composed back in Tiflis, and Vygodsky asks why others, "in fact a lot more interesting," have not been issued. *Bagatelles* he estimates more critically: where is the "Tiflis force . . . the ambition to overturn the old"?[28]

This brief and exact musicological article is the very first response in the Russian musical press to Tcherepnin's music. Nearby pages contain articles by Leonid Sabaneyev, Alois Hába, Darius Milhaud, Viktor Beliaev, and Nicolai Roslavetz. And among the musicological articles, five are devoted to editions of different compositions by Prokofiev, and others deal with Strauss's *Alpine Symphony*.

The following text is a fine descriptive analysis of the *Bagatelles* and an even more precise portrait of Tcherepnin:

> Alexander Tcherepnin—son of the well-known composer Nicolas Tcherepnin —is an uncommon phenomenon. Only twenty-four years old, he is young. He is fertile. To his pen belong fifteen piano sonatas, two concertos . . . a series of small pieces for piano, romances, etc. He writes constantly, with enthusiasm. He is original, combines depth and childlike naïveté. Modern, he reflects our headlong speed, boiling activity, eccentricity. Few among us know him: his recent years (until 1921) were spent in Tiflis, then isolated from Russia. Now he is in Paris. His creativity evolves. Not satisfied with the present, he searches for new ways. The submitted items belong to the period of his early activity.
> *Bagatelles*, originally named *Primitives*, is a small cycle of plays, each evoking a mood. The form of the *Bagatelles*, despite its historical precedent, is ever lively. It should be to the taste of the present, which has a propensity for novelty. When examining *Bagatelles*, you involuntarily recall by association Prokofiev's *Visions Fugitives*, but the former are more naïve. In A. Tcherepnin's style there is much from Prokofiev: a love of harmonic spice and a certain harmonious "impudence," a propensity for precise rhythms, and a gravitation to expressions of the playfully violent, the direct, the sarcastic. Some words about each bagatelle separately. The first, deliberately solemn, is like a march. It sounds youthful. The second is full of mystery, the picture, the fairy tale, is comically rude. The central meno mosso is the Renaissance of Rimsky-Korsakov, with a dash of a good-natured and ironic smile in comparison with the last. The third: a light gust of wind. The fourth seems to pretend to depth, but the author will not lead us on: this is only a fleeting darkening, a moment of thoughtfulness. The fifth, continuing the fourth, is an obedient, restrained

request. There are two unusually beautiful repeating notes, g♯ and f♯. The sixth is a volley, a rise of spirit, the thirst of creativity. The seventh is wildly playful, a humoristic back page. The eighth: extraordinarily good-natured. The ninth—extremely beautiful harmonically, though simple—carries a slight influence from Grieg. The tenth, the last in the cycle, serves as a coda and has a somewhat rigid, less original construction. All ten, executed successively, create a complete impression. The basic feature that distinguishes the entire cycle is an overlay of the youthful, cheerful, and healthy.

The composer succeeds less with the *Nocturne,* owing to some dryness and formality. But here also, as generally in A. Tcherepnin's work, notes sound warmly and inadvertently entice. In the central part there is an explosion, a furious storm that does not completely harmonize with the overall tone of the piece. The dance begins classically enough, with a sort of cadence. Immediately it breaks into a mad, cheerful jig. In a dizzy whirlwind everything flies, sweeps away the surroundings, rushes madly—and suddenly collapses, a precipice. And again, as if from the beginning, all is quiet and clean—then again the mad gallop, more headlong the further it goes. And the dance breaks off. . . .

The *Toccata* is rather original. Elements of modernism and classicism in the spirit of Bach intertwine—a phenomenon that is not new but always entertaining. Some especially like to take a theme of Bach as a basis (Schumann, M. Reger, etc.). Tcherepnin chooses a theme that comes very close in construction to these. And this is still fresh. Augured by gloomy octaves in the low register, this theme is developed in a "fugue" very originally conceived. Toward the end (in the last two pages) the theme's motif sounds a tremendous, almost ancient *Dies Irae.* The works of A. Tcherepnin considered above do not allow us as yet an opportunity to fully judge his creative persona. A more complete assessment can be made only when we receive his further opuses.[29]

During these years the views of contemporaries, despite their living in different worlds, were in many respects similar, including their understanding of "progress" in music. In a letter to a friend, Vygodsky includes a review of modern music. Not always convincing, but interesting, he isolates certain "lines." Among those "aspiring to the quest for new opportunities" he includes Alois Hába with his quarter-tone technique, as well as Schoenberg, Roslavetz, and, of course, Stravinsky and Prokofiev. Myaskovsky, Gnesin, and Crane are "armed with modern technique, but not revolutionaries." Named among those "late by thirty to fifty years, some quite bright and talented," are Glazunov, Vasilenko, Glière, and Liapunov. "In what is the essence of progress in music?" Vygodsky asks, and concludes: "in the gradual enrichment of the musical arsenal. And on this path there are no borders . . . on to new harmonic, tonal, key, and tonal-system opportunities!"[30]

News of friends and family from the 1919–21 Tiflis years systematically enters the letters. Kamensky sends "a greeting, warm, like Borjomi mineral water"; Grisha Hamburg "shines in the Stradivarius quartet," and so on. These are lively memories and testimonies of the Tcherepnin "Sturm und Drang" era.

As in Petersburg, Alexander composed extensively in Tiflis. He would later name this period "instinctive," when the creation of music came easily to him, especially when connected with the piano, and somewhat with vocal music. Pieces could be immediately executed by him in numerous concerts and by Marie Albertovna at home. Two reviews, essentially two portraits by Vladimir Ananov, inform us of the style of Tcherepnin's music. The first was about a concert on May 22, 1919, which included the youthful Sonata No. 12 in E♭ minor, Suite for piano (Procession, Nocturne, Intermezzo, Blue Fly, Lullaby, Scherzo, University Ballad), *Primitives* (twenty-one items from which the *Bagatelles* would be quarried), and Sonata No. 9 in E Major.[31]

> Alexander Tcherepnin is a monumental young man of twenty, with wavy golden curls, a clear blue gaze, a purely Wagnerian visage of a "simple and pure soul."... Always smiling, cheerful, because life smiled on him with one of the best joys—talent—and has opened this talent to him early and magnificently.... Art for him is not an aspect of life, it is an outlook. He has grown up amid the blossoming of Russian modernism, among its potent boiling and already emerging crystallization. Modernism for him is not a fashionable suit, not an abstruse language, but a native, heart-felt tongue for which it is not necessary to search blindly, painfully. And consequently the search for the new is not combined in him with a groundless destruction of the old.... The new enters into the system with the old, finds itself in living, harmonious development of the very same eternal beginnings.... No surprise then that a feeling for form is so typical of him. Most of his miniature *Primitives* are combined in a tripartite song form. It is also natural that, having played twenty *Primitives*, Tcherepnin formally ends the cycle by repeating the first Primitive in C minor. He is drawn to sonatas, of which he has written more than ten, confronting the genre's structural requirements, though strongly modifying them.... Pure impressionism as a self-absorbed game of pitch colors is foreign to him, and outside of a strict line he cannot imagine these paints.... Here one feels his sympathy toward young innovators; Prokofiev has influenced him in many respects.... The *Primitive* in C minor, written in the form of a rigaudon, is absolutely a Prokofievian "Gavotte." But even stronger than that influence is Tcherepnin's originality, though certainly not yet fully realized.... He has a boisterous youthful temperament, springtime passion. He does not wallow in pensive lyrics but violently aspires to pathos—a certain boiling excess of feeling, a powerful dramatic effect—with which his Sonata No. 9 is rich. His piano playing contains these same qualities.[32]

A second article by the same author appeared almost a year and a half later, and this time Ananov marks a great creative growth.

> When asked how many works he has written, Alexander Tcherepnin answers: "Oh, lots! In Petersburg an entire chest of manuscripts remains, and here—a whole box in the armoire." This giant excess of creativity characterizes Alexander Tcherepnin's figure. His piano playing style is the same—huge, titanic in essence: a mighty virgin soil, a vast, untamed forest.... Behind this powerful growth, behind this spontaneous creativity in his rapid development one can barely keep pace. One phase quickly replaces another, and this is only the gentle youth of a huge talent.... Still equally devoted to form, Tcherepnin

now shows a new gravitation toward impressionism, which he avoided earlier, toward phonic chaos—"noises" as he calls it—for example in the *Apocalyptical Poem,* which ends with an unusual tension of sonority and nervousness. But form still triumphs in the new *Sonata-ballad* where an usual sonata structure does not conclude with the usual coda but rather marries a completely new thematic episode. Psychologically this is extremely effective and significant: the final theme comes after painful experiences and struggle, with a transition of an organ-like character—solemn enlightenment. . . . Both the poem in C minor and the poem in G♯ minor are very graceful in their deep, gentle lyricism and sonority. If Tcherepnin leaned earlier toward Medtner, in these last works he already marks an independent position.[33]

The quantitative side of Alexander's compositional activity shows that writing came easily to him. A completely new creative process would be evident in 1927 during the painful or at least difficult and slow birth of the First Symphony, as he faced constant hurdles to surmount. But for the time being his much noted improvisational ability allowed him to produce plentifully and express himself in his own natural language. In this language we clearly see his relationship to the Petersburg school of the twentieth century, as well as his individual refraction of it. For a definition of the stylistic visage of Alexander Tcherepnin in these and subsequent years, we can hazard the term "neo-*Kuchkism.*" Let us repeat that this refers first of all to the language, for by their "ideology" the composers who belong to this movement are far removed from the deep essence of the "Mighty Five."

In harmonic innovations, and later the nine-step scale, we can clearly observe the Russian, specifically Rimsky-Korsakovian tradition, which does not allow one to ignore key relationships nor to spurn tonal foundations. Such innovations can be heard in the work of both Tcherepnin Sr. and Gretchaninov, even in that of Kastalsky—but certainly not as radically as in Alexander's music, and without such "globalization." Discussing the major-minor coloring of Tcherepnin's music, let us not forget the folkloric sources, from whence came the major-minor thirds of Stravinsky's *Les Noces.* But in the youthful pieces, as well as in his much later work, it is a matter of assimilation of folklore elements rather than their direct reproduction.

The "Russo-Eastern" genesis began later but developed creatively in early compositions. The *Toccata* Op. 1, the first of his works published in Paris, is in fact built entirely on major and minor thirds, which appear immediately in measures 1–6 (musical example 2.7). Like Prokofiev's Toccata, it is written in D minor. A technique (probably picked up from Stravinsky) of metric shift, movement relative to the time signature, appears in measures 31–34 (musical example 2.8).

Feuilles libres (*Loose Pages*) was begun in Tiflis in 1920 (Nos. 1–3) and completed in Monte Carlo in 1924. The first piece of the set embodies the tonal features of the Russian East. It is linked by different kinds of major chords. The lower tetrachord in the following example is in "double *harmonic* major," while at the same time the upper line is in "*melodic* major." This leads to "mi-

Example 2.7

Example 2.8

Example 2.9

norization" of the major, creating a sound that seems to the European ear to be typically Eastern and sensual—as if Balakirev were writing a half-century later (musical example 2.9).[34]

Pages, like many other sets of miniatures, is a collection rather than a cycle.

The Tiflis works are marked by mastery of different instruments. Tcherepnin "knows the ropes" about violin and cello, and according to the testimony of the performers, everything sits well for their instruments. We find that the Sonata for cello and piano (Op. 30, No. 2, F♯ major/minor), and especially its first, toccata-like movement as well as the ending, allude to Prokofiev. Indeed, the entire composition is marked by density, compression, and dynamism. Among relatively large-scale instrumental forms, the First Piano Concerto, which was written in the early Tiflis years and later published as Op. 12, has a development section characteristic of Tcherepnin: not motif work, not *Durchführung,* but a series of episodes: fugato, two slow lyrical fragments preceded and followed by cadenzas, and so on.

Following the tradition of his father, who had created *Wreath for Gorodetsky,* Alexander connected his voice-and-piano works with this same poet. During

1920–22 he wrote approximately twenty songs, which make up Opp. 15, 16, and 17. They were written for and dedicated to his mother, Marie Albertovna, who had been a singer in her youth. The preserved manuscripts of all the songs are dated and supplied with additional notes and commentaries: "To dear Mommy, as a token of sincere sentiment and admiration. Fitlif [Tiflis]."[35] The green musical notebook, penned in elegant calligraphy, holds the following dedication on the reverse side: "To lovely Mommy, so that this small gift may serve as a small reminder of her great musical calling. And may these songs be executed with accompaniment by her loving son Alexander."[36]

Much later, in a letter to Grigori Bernandt dated August 20, 1964, the composer remembered the fine vocal gifts of his mother, and explained:

> She was very shy, did not perform publicly (only in front of me was she free of embarrassment, and I accompanied her performances of songs of Glinka, Tchaikovsky, my father, Schubert, Schumann); and all my works (Opp. 15, 16, etc.) of the youthful period were written for her.[37]

The poems of Gorodetsky were chosen from different collections, including *Ire, Perun, Wild Will,* and *The Flowering Staff.* Motifs of the beauty of nature and its unfettered power join with Symbolist moods. The Op. 17 cycle is titled *Haltes* in French and *Stops* in English. From the musical point of view, these "poems for voice and piano," which became established in Russian vocal lyrics in the 1910s and 1920s are somewhat closer to Myaskovsky or Gnesin. Manuscript excerpts of the poems (respective of their order in musical example 2.10), "Ground Grains," "In the Excitement before a Lyre Touched by Morning," "Melancholy of a Winter Day," and "Between Hammer and Anvil" give us a glimpse of a rather complex musical language. They also illustrate the use of Interpoint and a scale (not strict) with alternating half steps and one-and-a-half steps.

The composer supplies the musical text with plentiful comments: "inspired by the nursery" (the song "I Began To Dream"), "completely free" ("I Love Womanly Water"), "ominously" ("Unceasing Alarms"), "fervently" ("In A Wild Wood"), "self-profound" ("It Must Be That Life Has Broken"), and so forth.

As in Petrograd, composition ran parallel with classroom studies at the conservatory. Years later Tcherepnin was disinclined to attach any serious significance to these studies, so we know no details—only the names of teachers, about whom some things must be mentioned. The professor of the piano class, Tamara Ter-Stepanova, studied under Paul Pabst and completed her studies at the Moscow Conservatory in 1897, earning a silver medal. The same year she returned to her native Tiflis, working until the end of her life in the city's music school and, after its transformation, in the conservatory. Her class was one of the best. Tcherepnin also wrote about Thomas Hartmann in the pages of *The Caucasian Word* (even prior to the start of his studies) and demonstrated a close familiarity with his background and work. Hartmann, unknown today, had studied composition with Anton Arensky, counterpoint with Sergei

V. "Хлеб перемолот"

Pensieroso

X. "В волнении до утренней коснувшись лиры..."

XXXV. "Меланхолия зимнего дня"

XXVIII. "Меж молотом и наковальней..."

Меж мо_ ло_ том и на_ ко_ валь_ ней

Example 2.10

Taneyev, and conducting with Felix Mottl, and subsequently worked at the Munich Opera.

> During a stay abroad, Hartmann becomes acquainted with new trends of Western-European music and grows fond of the French Impressionists—both musicians (Debussy, Ravel), and painters (Gauguin, Van Gogh).... A choreographic poem (based on Anatole France's plot *Sacred Satire*), where Hartmann's talent is freed from the influences of his school, crowns the end of this period. Here the composer's independent face appears.[38]

Further, at the end of the decade 1900–1910, Hartmann, together with the dancer Alexander Sakharov, created and performed a work to accompany the artist Vasily Kandinsky's *Yellow Sound*. Hartmann's compositions, at first reflecting the influence of Mussorgsky, are written in the musical language of the twentieth century, displaying varied use of percussion along with a mastery of polytonality, polyrhythms, and instrumental opulence. By 1912 Hartmann had already published an article titled "On the Use of Percussion Instruments in the Orchestra."[39] In Tcherepnin's First Symphony percussion would become one of the important subjects of the composition.

In 1921 the Red Army occupied Tiflis. Tcherepnin later remembered the last weeks of Caucasian life and his departure from the city:

> [After the Red Army conquered Tiflis] the artists and musicians organized themselves to form a union. At one of the rehearsals of the Opera, my father corrected the playing of the trombone player. The passage . . . had to be repeated—the same mistake occurred. My father addressed the orchestra: "Gentlemen, I will have to repeat the passage until it goes as it should." At this, someone in the orchestra screamed out, "The 'gentlemen' have all run away to Batum; there are only 'comrades' here." My father threw away the baton and left.
>
> Not that my father was bossy, nor that he had any political hatred toward the union. It was the usual way to address the orchestra, "Gentlemen"—no conservative mind was attached to this word. But my father had [a] quick temper. He was upset in his artistic feeling: it was not the question of "regime" but the question of orchestra discipline—my father could not tolerate interference with his responsibilities as a conductor and took the riposte . . . as a personal offense. He never returned to the [Tiflis] Opera.
>
> In Batum . . . we had just enough money to buy our passage as far as Constantinople. . . . The customs officer opened our bags. All was okay with my mother's—which contained a few pieces of clothing, the same with mine, which contained music manuscripts, but when my father's bag was opened, the customs officer discovered a program of the Coronation Gala of the Ballets Russes in London in 1912—my father had conducted . . . his ballet *Pavillon d'Armide* and treasured this program, printed on silk. [The officer] grew red and confiscated the entire bag, which contained letters to my father from Rimsky, Prokofiev, and his numerous musical friends! [I] wonder what became of my father's bag? I hope it fell into the right hands, and that all the epistolary material . . . found its place in some library or artistic archives of the Soviet Union.
>
> [We left Georgia on the Mongibello], a small steamer—I guess somewhere around three thousand tons. Late in the afternoon it started to move slowly. I noted how gradually the port and the chain of mountains vanished in the fog: once again it was a departure from my homeland. "Why?" I asked myself. "Will I ever see it again? Is there any excuse for one to leave his country, especially when his country is in distress, to leave the community to which one belongs by birth and education?"[40]

The twenty-two-year old composer, pianist, and writer who would become one of the most outstanding musicians of the Russian emigration, was departing Russia and Georgia forever. Born and bred in the Silver Age, and deeply familiar with the newest Russian art and poetry, Tcherepnin aspired in his own way to "new shores." He would soon arrive not on the banks of the Neva, nor the Kura, but the Seine.

3   Air and Bread of Emigration

The Tcherepnins arrived in a "country" that appeared on no map and yet extended across many states of Europe, Asia, North and South America, and Australia: Expatriate Russia. Russian speech was beginning to sound in hundreds of cities, and Russian-language newspapers and magazines began to appear. In his 1956 book, *Russkaia literatura v izgnanii* (Russian literature in exile), Gleb Struve, an outstanding scholar of nineteenth- and twentieth-century Russian literature, formulated the idea that "expatriate literature is a current temporarily diverted from the broad flow of Russian literature, which at a certain point will rejoin this common stream.... We can oppose this theory of a 'single stream' to the Soviet theory."[1] He also made an important terminological distinction: "The word 'emigration' in the usual sense does not fit.... I prefer such terms as 'Russia Abroad' or 'Expatriate Russia.'" Struve's book began to penetrate the USSR in the mid-1980s. By that time an enormous wealth of expatriation literature, philosophy, and historiography was entering and broadening Russia's cultural and spiritual life.

A huge dictionary compiled by Wolfgang Kazak, recently translated into Russian, attempts to consider all aspects of twentieth-century Russian literature in a single work,[2] and several other works on the diverse cultural heritage of the Russian emigration have been published in Russia.[3] Yet a comparative study of the musical literature created at home and abroad—a realization of twentieth-century Russian music as a whole—has yet to be written. The musical culture of the Russian expatriation remains little known and under investigated.

A deceptive paradox arises here. Are Rachmaninov, Stravinsky, Medtner, and Chaliapin indeed poorly researched by Russian scholars? Certainly for many years even these eminent musicians were forbidden, and their heritage returned in fragments. But their music returned nevertheless, even if Rachmaninov's church music and the creations of Prokofiev and Stravinsky abroad were only accepted much later. Culture, however, consists not only of the highest peaks, and, in Russia, serious musical scholarship fails to extend beyond these few names. In Mark Raeff's excellent book on the Russian emigration, a sort of encyclopedia of the "first wave" of the emigration, only 6 of the 415 people named in the index are musicians.[4] In a sizable collective monograph edited by professor Karl Schlögel, only about 10 of the more than 1,000 individuals cited are musicians.[5] Among those composers often overlooked are not only the "émigré" Glazunov, who worked in Paris for about eight years, but even such prominent figures as Alexander Gretchaninov, Nicolas and Alexander Tcherepnin, Ivan Wyschnegradsky, Nicolas Obouhov, Arthur Lourié, Nicolas Nabokov, and Vladimir Dukelsky, not to mention representatives of different generations of subsequent "lines": Igor Markevitch, Joseph Schillinger, Lazare Saminsky, Yuri Pomerantsev, Thomas Hartmann, Alexandre Winkler, Feodor Akimenko, Avenir Monfred, Pavel Kovalev, Georgi Catoire, and many others. A list of similarly neglected musicians both world renowned and more modest would occupy dozens of pages. Numerous music scholars and critics suffer similar neglect.

Some chronological milestones and patterns of the Russian emigration are clear. The 1920s were characterized by a gathering of forces and a hope for a return to Russia, whereas the late 1920s and early 1930s featured a revival of creative life and the desire for the creation of a full-fledged "Russia abroad."[6] This was followed in the late 1930s by two developments that are the gradual and inevitable tragedy of emigration: the conflicting desires for assimilation and preservation.

It is conventional in the literature to consider the "first wave" of emigration in the chronological framework of the interwar period. It is true that the Second World War radically altered the situation. Subsequent waves of exiles or refugees had no comparable connection to the continuation of "Russian life" or the fulfillment of the cultural mission which the first wave had embraced and borne with honor. Yet the start and end dates given by many researchers and chroniclers (1917/1918/1920 and 1939/1940/1941) do not reflect the essence of the multifold cultural and creative phenomena. One could say that the culture of the "first wave" lasted as long as its representatives, who lived into the fifties, sixties, and seventies, and preserved certain "patrimonial" characteristics. They were children of the Silver Age, and remembered the pre-revolutionary Russia they had absorbed with their mothers' milk.

Geographically the path of the Tcherepnin family was quite typical—Constantinople, then Paris (others went to Prague, Sofia, or Berlin), and finally the United States. Nicolas Tcherepnin completed the route only as far as Paris, but some years after Nicolas's death in 1945 Maria Albertovna joined her son in the United States.

Lily Chou drew the following biographical sketch from Alexander's reminiscences:

> Finally, on June 27th, after a passage through the scenic Bosporus, the steamer landed in Constantinople. Never did a *lull kebab* taste more delicious than on that first evening. Touschkan, the dog, was terrified by the highly belligerent cats in the streets of the Galata district, where the Tcherepnins had found an inexpensive hotel, and more than once Alexander had to carry the animal in his arms. The family's immediate concern was to establish contact with Nicolas' friends in Paris, for Georgia had been totally cut off from the Western world. In the meantime they provided for survival by giving concerts, one at the YMCA and another at a club called "The Russian Lighthouse."[7]

A 1921 newspaper clipping from a Russian newspaper in Constantinople bears an inscription by Marie Tcherepnin. The unsigned article, titled "Theatre and Music: A Celebration of N. N. Tcherepnin," reads:

Example 3.1

> The latest symphony concert of the YMCA under the direction of Thomas
> Hartmann turned into a celebration of the composer N. N. Tcherepnin, re-
> cently arrived in Constantinople . . . Tcherepnin, who was sitting in the audi-
> ence, was welcomed by the orchestra and public with a triple fanfare and ap-
> plause. The second part of the concert was devoted to Tcherepnin father and
> son. First the charming Adagio from a [Nicolas] Tcherepnin quartet was per-
> formed by a string ensemble, and was warmly received by the public. Then
> Tcherepnin-*fils* played a number of his piano works. Alexander Tcherepnin
> amazes us with his pronounced individuality. The wealth of harmonies and
> rhythms is coupled with an extraordinary, spontaneous creativity that touches
> the listener, never leaves him indifferent, and thus wins him over with the
> force of such talent. The young composer has just completed a piano concerto,
> which will likely be presented at a forthcoming YMCA symphonic concert."[8]

This was Alexander's first review abroad. The author is probably Hartmann, for
who else knew Tcherepnin so well? Moreover, the opinions expressed are similar
to the Tiflis articles penned by him.

One more thread appears from Constantinople: a page containing a musical
excerpt titled "Notes of a Constantinople Organ-Grinder 1921" (musical example 3.1). The accompanying footnote reads "use either for a refrain or to
make breaks, simulating the organ-grinder."[9]

This musical note alludes to urban Georgian folklore (the organ pedal point,
transposed a fifth).

Many recent Tiflis acquaintances and schoolmates reappeared in Constantinople and naturally began reaching out to one another. Anna Markozova wrote
Marie Tcherepnin from there:

> It would be splendid if it were possible to organize a Russian conservatory in
> Paris headed by Nicolas Nicolaevitch. I am sure that he would not forget me.
> I read in the papers that Alexander Glazunov has received permission to go
> abroad—I think he will not return. . . . In Constantinople a conservatory is go-
> ing to be opened, and Streicher promises to arrange a position for me. . . . But
> all the same I would prefer somewhere else. When I am Russian in my heart,
> and love Russia, and am homesick for it as much as all of you. . . . In Serbia
> there is a society of "Patriots of Russian Music," who as far as I know are form-
> ing a conservatory and music schools in Belgrade. Feofan Pavlovsky is chair-
> man (I don't know who he is) and, besides him, there is a violinist, violoncel-
> list, and a whole family of musicians: the Zlatins (from Kharkov). But it is
> better to write to Pavlovsky.[10]

In her next letter Markozova continues:

> Are you considering going to Russia, as the Streichers told me? Will you really take the risk? . . . I, too, am very homesick, but I don't even consider returning. Let's see what the Genoa conference will say, will they really recognize the Bolsheviks—what horror awaits us then? I personally would not return for anything.[11]

Lily Chou recounts the tale of the Tcherepnin family.

> They received funds from their faithful friend Wyschnegradsky, and after waiting six weeks for red tape to be cut, they finally procured a French visa. This period, though nerve-wracking, gave the receptive mind of the young Tcherepnin a chance to savor Constantinople, which he later considered one of the most entrancing cities he had ever visited. The lore of its Byzantine past, the fantastic large Orthodox cathedral—the Aya Sofia, the little Aya Sofia, the ruins Rumelia Hissar—left an indelible impression on him. The visit of the Patriarch of Constantinople—so modest, so human, so kind—also touched him; the whole climate of the Patriarchate was unpretentious, non-aggressive and unceremonious. The liturgy in the Greek Orthodox churches interested him tremendously. Formally, it was like that of the Russian Orthodox churches, but the hymns, the singing, and the psalmody of the priest were quite different, and much more Oriental.
>
> No less interesting was his discovery of the Turkish past of Constantinople, revealed in its palaces, cemeteries, and ancient buildings. A visit to Skadar, on that side of the Bosporus opposite Constantinople, stirred Alexander's historical imagination: here the old Turkey was still intact and reminded him of the Tartars' settlement in the Crimea that he used to visit in his teens.
>
> At the beginning of August the Tcherepnins finally received their French visa and, on August 4th, they embarked on a small Spanish freighter, the San Jose, with Marseilles as their destination. As on board the Mongibello, they were deck passengers; but this time they traveled in relative comfort, camping beneath the open sky in the stern. They even had a table at their disposal, and both father and son joyously wrote music at it. The trip took them through the Marmara Sea, the Dardanelles (upon which the remnants of Russian White Army camps were easily visible) and the Aegean and Mediterranean Seas. The Greek islands, Messina, brightly lit at night, and the Strait of St. Bonifacio between Sardinia and Corsica, were by no means the only picturesque features of this voyage.
>
> The steamer reached Marseilles during the night, and the passengers awoke on August 13th to the sight of the French landscape and its islands, with the many ships in and around port, and the hustle and bustle of traffic on shore even at that early hour: trains speeding in and out of short tunnels, cars and trucks, smoke streaming from tall factory chimneys, planes buzzing noisily overhead.
>
> After so many years of austerity, it was overwhelming to see such abundance: the Cannebière was swarming with people, large department stores were stocked with goods, food shops overflowed with products. There were numerous boulangeries with the enticing smell of good French bread, many tempting candy shops. It must have been a relief to hear a tongue that was rea-

sonably familiar to them, and to see well-dressed, well-fed, contented and busy people milling around under the sunny skies. Nicolai, like many Russians a great lover of fish, treated the family to a bouillabaisse luncheon.

Then it came time to board the night-train to Paris. With the help of a porter, they squeezed their luggage into a crowded third-class compartment. Young Tcherepnin was fascinated by the speed of the train and stayed in the corridor late into the night looking through the window: Avignon, Valence, Lyon, Dijon and then—early in the morning—Paris! Tcherepnin wrote that he wished he had had a camera to photograph their arrival at the Gare de Lyon: his father, mother, himself all strangely dressed, Touchkan sniffing the scent of his French colleagues at every street corner, and their battered luggage. "I was dressed in a suit too small for me, given by an American YMCA, had a strange round hat on my head and Georgian (Caucasian) national slippers." The first item on their agenda was to find a roof. A short walk around the Gare de Lyon brought them to the City Hotel on the Rue de Lyon, and this small, old-fashioned establishment condescended to accept them. Their room on the third floor, with a large bed for the parents and a small one for Alexander, had no running water; but the hotel was clean, the price reasonable, and they considered themselves fortunate to have so quickly found adequate living quarters "for the duration." Not for a moment did they suspect that their emigration was final. Alexander's father felt that his stay in Paris would be similar in some way to his prewar tours: that he would be asked to conduct and to compose for the Diaghilev ballet, that in the meantime the international situation would somehow clear up, and that he would be asked to return to his homeland.

The manuscripts in Alexander's suitcase soon found welcome markets, not with one, but four Paris publishers—thanks to the recommendation of Isidore Philipp, who had become his piano teacher. These sentimental souvenirs, output of teenage days and his stay in Georgia, turned out unexpectedly to be a gold mine. He first considered the title *Primitives* for these pieces, but Philipp—who always addressed his six-foot-four student as *mon petit*—advised against it. So it was that these *bloshki* were sold in small groups under various other names: Bagatelles, Episodes, Suites, etc., and the proceeds, augmented by concert engagements and some help from Wyschnegradsky, were enough to live on for approximately three years.

There is an irony, cruel in some aspects, in this tale of emigration. Alexander left Russia and Georgia much against his will. He did not fear a new political experiment during the upheavals of either 1918 or 1921; in both cases he was taken from extremely satisfying professional milieus. He had enjoyed the St. Petersburg Conservatory; he had enjoyed even more the musical life in Tiflis, where he was, in effect, a big fish in a small pond, scoring a string of solid successes as a theater composer, a concert pianist and even a music critic. Leaving all this behind troubled him deeply.

Yet Alexander's art and career flourished in the West as it probably never could have in the Soviet Union. Here, he had a chance to test his compositional muscles by pursuing music in the most abstract terms, something that would have been frowned upon in Russia, even in the relatively relaxed climate of the 1920s. More important, he had the opportunity for world travel. His later work in China and Japan would have been out of the question for a Soviet national. This world-class musical citizen in fact needed to expand virtually into the whole world if he were to serve his talent to the fullest. The exile that Alexander endured with such reluctance was in reality a golden passport to international success.

Nicolas Tcherepnin, by contrast, was leaving what in his eyes was a world with no immediate promise. Although he had long been a well-loved composer in his native land, and had achieved solid international success a few years before, he could not see the continuation of his career through and beyond the revolutionary disturbances. He was anxious to get to the West where a "normal" musical climate prevailed and he could return to the real business of his life. Yet in Paris he found that Diaghilev had abandoned him, and Western audiences did not treat a permanent Russian émigré the same way it treated a "Russian ambassador." Pavlova continued to commission works from him, but these alone could not sustain an important career. The normal business of his life needed, after all, the Russian integument in which it had flourished. Back in Russia, he would certainly have been put in charge of a major ballet orchestra. In the West, he never procured a regular position as a conductor; and while the occasional engagements he received often had a prestigious aura about them, they did not succeed in bringing his career as a performer back to life. Gone was the middle-class security he had known in St. Petersburg. In Paris he was sometimes unable to earn enough to support his family, and had to rely on the bounty of his far more successful son in order to make ends meet. The emigration that Nicolas embraced with such alacrity was, in fact, little more than a passport to neglect and obscurity.[12]

These judgments, made many years later, may appear excessively rigid. Nicolas Tcherepnin had a tremendous reputation, not only within the Russian community. He composed, conducted, directed, and taught at the Paris Russian Conservatory, and served on the Advisory Council of Mitrofan Belaieff's publishing house. It is equally true, however, that he lost out substantially in the emigration.

Vladimir Scherbachev, a former pupil of Nicolas whose first symphony was performed in 1916 by Ziloti, lived in Germany during 1922–23. Hoping to find work there, he wrote long letters to his wife from Berlin and Dresden, often discussing Russian musicians. "It is extremely difficult for our compatriots to find steady work because of the 'patriotism' of the Germans.... Germans do not recognize [Medtner] at all ... he is in a foul mood."[13] Concerning the Tcherepnins, he wrote: "Recently read in the newspapers that Sasha Tcherepnin had a big success in London with a concert where he played only his own compositions ... Sasha is very talented and writes somewhat like Prokofiev."[14] Scherbachev's words about the elder Tcherepnin are completely different: "the unfortunate Tcherepnin has become quite old and ill, and lives very poorly. When he arrived in Paris, he was of course entirely forgotten there, which had a terrible effect on him."[15] Prior to this letter, Tcherepnin's Petersburg classmate, Ivan Wyschnegradsky, had visited Scherbachev. This may have reinforced his impressions of Nicolas's plight.

The sober and practical Prokofiev assessed the position of Russian musicians at home and abroad in a letter to the musicologist and writer Peter Petrovich Suvchinsky: "I consider your idea to go to Russia this fall in pursuit of 'life with art' to be a mistake. Right now the whole face of art there is distorted by famine, insults, and tears. As for Paris, I don't know what your connections are like there, in terms of beginning any independent activity. Everyone who arrived with a clever brain and an empty pocket has remained the same: Balmont, Shoukhaeff, Gress, Schloezer—all penniless. Borovsky scrapes by. Only Koussevitzky and . . . the tenor Smirnov have found a niche."[16]

A clipping from an article by George Adamovich was pasted by Marie Albertovna into a family album that she titled "K. D. Balmont's 70th birthday." It nostalgically describes the spiritual side of life.

> Balmont did not write verses, Balmont sang songs, and his exuberant voice was heard by all of Russia . . . It is impossible to forget the wave that seemed to carry Balmont on its crest and promised the entire country a "spring" that each interpreted in his own way. All this is far away, as is the brief Russian spring, as are the dreams of "life transformed," as are the first dances of Isadora Duncan, as is Repin's student with the coed in the middle of the river while the wind ruffled their hair and scarves. . . . How does Balmont live now, in emigration? . . . All the songs that excited him half-a-century ago probably help him to survive, eating the "bitter bread of exile."[17]

Nicolas Tcherepnin had written his marvelous *Fairytales* to Balmont's verses, and his friendship with the poet continued in Paris, where the Balmonts lived nearby. Notes and invitations to performances were exchanged, such as the invitation from Elena Balmont to attend an evening with "the best French Sanskritist and Hinduist Sylvain Levy, who has just returned from an entire year in Tahore, India."[18]

In the early years of emigration, Alexander Tcherepnin remained within his family circle. During his later travels, he maintained a tight connection with his parents through daily letters. His activities, interests, and moods were inextricably linked to Nicolas Tcherepnin and the family sphere, including "Grandfather Bertie" and "Uncle Shura" Benois.

The family was extraordinarily amicable and warm, the relationships among them intimate and gentle. Their correspondence shows a surprisingly unified tone, including words and expressions unique to the family. Alexander's parents supported him in personal and professional matters, while he provided them with love and hope. The family considered this wholeness to be their greatest wealth. Describing his previous day's activities in characteristic detail, Alexander notes: "ha-ha, my dearest little ones, it gives me such pleasure that, because we three are so close, everything that concerns one of us concerns the others. And one lives so happily feeling such a strong foundation, my darlings."[19] On another occasion, Nicolas writes, "Today we woke up in a very good mood because we both saw you in our dreams!"[20]

Such displays of affection are so natural and unchanging that they seem neither excessive nor sugary. In letters to Sasha, Marie Tcherepnin uses the diminutives "Sashurochka" and "Sashunichka," and refers to his father as "our

А	лю_	би_	тель	я	боль	шой	до	Вань_	ки	ключ_	ни_	ка
А	е_	ще	ко_	го	люб_	лю? —		е_	го	а_	вто_	ра
И	же_	ну	е_	го	люб_	лю		и	пле_	мян_	нич_	ка
И	дай	Бог	им	всем	ско_	рей		вмес_	те	сви_	деть_	ся
На	премь_	е_	ре	по_	си_	деть		нам	на	Ва_	нич_	ки!

Example 3.2

lovely one" or simply "ours." For Alexander, his parents are "beloved little dearest darlings."

The family was responsible for preserving everything "Russian" amid the international environment, beginning with language. Their correspondence preserves not only the lexicon but also the poetics that the language irrevocably lost in the later USSR. Over time, however, Gallicisms and Anglicisms inevitably entered their speech.

Opera and the search for librettos constituted an important theme in the creative dialogue between Nicolas and Alexander. Having never before turned to the operatic genre, the elder Tcherepnin wrote two operas on the cusp of the thirties: *The Matchmaker* (also known as *Svat,* and based on the Ostrovsky play *Poverty Is No Crime*) and *Vanka Kluchnik* (based on a Sologub text). Choosing librettos took time. "Daddy," writes Alexander in one letter, "before finally setting aside Avvakum, let's wait a little bit. I will bring you three books of materials about him and the events surrounding him. He emerges as a courageous, ideological, cultural person, whom I would not trade for Vanka Kluchnik, who is after all a stereotype and more a 'buffoon' in opera."[21] Although the final decision fell in Sologub's favor, Alexander still admired Nicolas's new piece during its composition and beyond. On the steamship *Homeric* in the Atlantic, he recalled recent impressions of the August 30, 1928 performance of *Vanka:*

> There is so much freshness in it, so much life, endless new techniques, and all this in truly good music; and alongside the amusing and cheerful, so much that is deeply human.
>
> I joyfully recalled the sounds of Vanichka and thought that a new musical essence exists and will exist.[22]

Marie Tcherepnin was a musical authority for both father and son. Nicolas writes her, "Spent all day today architecturally reconstructing, with some apparent success, the second tableaux of *Vanka Kluchnik* which you found less pleasing. Merci for your impressions."[23]

Marie writes her son about a visit by Prokofiev and several others to the elder Tcherepnins in Paris following a November 5, 1928 concert of the works of both Tcherepnins.

> The Great [Prokofiev] was charming, for he has a most warlike and yet cheerful appearance, and always wants to stay close to us! He really likes *Mystère* [A. T.'s Op. 37, No. 2] and thinks it's a new direction for you. He also sincerely likes *Vanka.* He ranks it above *Matchmaker,* and finds that it contains a

lot of new music, and a new approach to opera. . . . As for himself, he is now re-orchestrating *The Gambler,* having gotten all his old Mariinsky material from the Bolsheviks. He also said that your works, Sashunechka, are often performed in the Bolshevik reign, and that he has contributed in no small way to this! In general he impresses me as a very active and self-confident person, but free of impudence.[24]

Contact with Sergei Prokofiev's family was quite regular. Prokofiev writes Marie Tcherepnin: "Dear Marie Albertovna, today at a quarter to nine we successfully gave birth to a son, which I wanted to tell you right away. I kiss your hand. Please forgive the brevity of this message. Your loving S. Prkfv."[25] A letter from Prokofiev's wife continues the familial theme: "Serioja works a lot. I am happy that I started singing again, after a year of silence. Maria Grigorievna has recovered and feels quite energetic. The little one is blossoming, growing, laughs loudly, holds his head up high, and proudly sits on his throne. . . . Serioja would like to know how the composers are doing and what new things they are inventing."[26]

Prokofiev writes Nicolas Tcherepnin in March 1925: "Greetings from Monte Carlo. Returning after [*Love of Three*] *Oranges*. . . . Thank you for the letter and the congratulations on becoming king. But what the hell kind of representative of the famous Esipov school am I? After all, I quarreled with it more than I learned from it. I saw Sashenka—he is blossoming. I embrace you and the hands of Mar. Albrt. I kiss you. S. P."[27] Other letters include invitations to performances, "I am sending you a ticket to see Koussevitzky, who will present my new symphony [No. 2]. Perhaps you will come to the final rehearsal on Friday at 9 AM? I will be at the artists' entrance to the Opéra at 5 m. to 9. I embrace you. Heartfelt greetings from Linette. Yours, S. Prokofiev."[28] Other collegial requests follow: "I shall be very grateful, if Nic. Niclvch. will send me the program of the concert where my symphony will be performed, and also any press that might appear in a familiar language."[29]

One more striking note to Alexander dates from 1923: "Most esteemed colleague Alexander Nicolaevich. On the night of our meeting I lost the parts to my violin concerto and was so distressed by this that I could not go anywhere but to lost-and-founds. So until now I have visited neither you nor your dear parents. However, if you could give me a list of suitable times again, I would be delighted to visit you. Intimate greetings. S. Prkfv."[30]

Dialogue among Russian musicians abroad was an integral part of their musical culture. Reaching out to one another was especially frequent in the 1920s, when the desire to locate and help other émigrés was strong. Some letters are like cries for help. The burdens of life—material, professional, moral—were well known in the Tcherepnin home. Tcherepnin's former student Alexander Torletsky wrote from Zagreb, seeking help after the death of his wife.

There's been a lot of water over the dam since our last meeting in the spring of 1914. . . . During the revolution I escaped, but lost everything. . . . Before me lies a terrible precipice of complete poverty. . . . My mother is dying of hunger and cold. . . . I cannot find work. . . . If you cannot help me, ask others on my behalf. . . . Perhaps Felia Litvinne will want to support the husband of "Siegfried's daughter," perhaps Prokofiev (mother's relative through Ekaterina Grigorievna Raevsky), perhaps Sasha Ziloti. . . . I place in your hands the life of your former pupil Shurik. . . . Knowing "Pavillon d'Armide," one cannot fail to trust in the kindness, generosity, and purity of its composer.[31]

Judging by later correspondence between Torletsky's mother, Baroness von Stepel, and Marie Tcherepnin, the latter was able to organize some help. This was just one of many dramas that crossed the Tcherepnins' path.

As part of his responsibilities when, in 1923, he became the director of Paris's Russian Conservatory, Nicolas Tcherepnin received a large number of job applications, requests, and offers. Most of these had to be rejected, and the names of many highly qualified applicants sank into oblivion. In the fall of 1922 Peter Saburov, a graduate of the Petersburg Conservatory who had studied with Liadov, Tcherepnin, and Steinberg, had to take a job as a pianist in a movie theater; he later gave private lessons in harmony and counterpoint in Geneva. Saburov had asked Prokofiev for help finding a post in Paris when the composer visited Geneva in December 1923, but Prokofiev had deflected the request, answering that he lived outside the city. The musician wrote to Tcherepnin, offering to teach any theoretical subject, but especially harmony of the Rimsky-Korsakov system: "Since the Russian Conservatory in Paris opened under your expert management, I have read about it in Russian newspapers, and heard about it personally from Nikolai Kedrov."[32] One wonders what became of him, and a host of others.

Another applicant for the position of professor at the conservatory was the singer Feofan Pavlovsky, who, as opera director and teacher of an opera class in another music school, was at least better off.[33] A request came also from Sergei Trailin, a famous Petersburg musician whose compositions had once been recommended for publication by Balakirev. Writing from Constantinople to Marie Tcherepnin, he explained, "My affairs are in disarray, somehow I keep breathing, and I have not performed for ten days because the Garden is closed; but musicians keep arriving."[34] Trailin later became remarkably active in Prague, establishing the "Russian Oxford," which became a center of the Russian emigration. He also helped tremendously to consolidate musical forces and establish communication with the "Russian Musical Mecca" of Paris.

This process of forming different circles and communities developed rapidly. Various associations from Petrograd, Moscow, Volga, Voronezh, Crimea, Odessa, and so on, were active in Paris during 1921–22. These included the Union of Russian Students in France, the Union of Russian Writers and Journalists, the Russian History and Art Society, the Literary and Art Circle of Youth, the "Russian Center" club, the Russian Theosophical Society, the Scientific-Philosophical Society, the powerful Russian Student Christian movement, the Union of Russian Lawyers Abroad, the Russian Legal Society, the Union of Russian Officers, the Parisian Jewish Aid Society, the Society of Russian Doctors, and the Russian Gymnastic Society "Falcon." And no association could do without organizing concerts—usually with Russian performers and Russian repertoire—thus ensuring a steady demand for both composers and performers.

The Union of Russian Musical Figures was founded in February 1921 under the leadership of Baron von Drizen and began immediately to organize concerts, lectures, and meetings. Efforts were also made in music education. Marie Olènine d'Alheim, an outstanding interpreter of Mussorgsky's vocal compositions, began offering courses in Paris in November 1920. A year later the *Poslednye novosti* contained an announcement for "the Petrograd Philarmonic Society in Paris under the direction of Mr. Zaslavsky. Departments: music, drama, opera and ballet."[35]

The Russian Conservatory, which opened in 1923 with Nicolas Tcherepnin as director and professor, was named in honor of Rachmaninov. In 1931 stewardship of the conservatory passed to the newly founded Russian Musical Society Abroad (RMSA). Alexander would also teach there during the 1930s and 1940s.

Materials about the Paris activities of these institutions are rare, but fortunately, many were preserved in one place: Czechoslovakia. Thanks to the efforts of remarkable Russian figures, several institutions—the archive of the Russian Musical Society in Czechoslovakia, part of the Russian Expatriate Historical Archive (RZIA), and also the Cultural-Historical Museum in Prague—became true treasuries of materials about the Russian emigration. Leo Tolstoy's former secretary Valentin Bulgakov, who headed the Prague Russian Museum, wrote to Marie Tcherepnin in 1937 to thank her for the donation of several of her father's paintings to the museum. Bulgakov calls Albert Benois' watercolors "the charming creations of an outstanding artist" and the gift "invaluable." Bulgakov remembers visiting the Tcherepnin house, and his acquaintance with Marie and the "greatly esteemed Nicolas Nicolaevitch.... Regrettably lack of time did not allow me to visit other outstanding Russian musicians in Paris or the Russian Conservatory.... In six months to a year I shall visit Paris again and will by all means visit those persons whom Nicolas recommended, and shall carry out his instructions regarding collection of data on émigré activity."[36]

Tragically the archival materials in the RZIA were taken from Prague in 1945, dismantled, and scattered across different "departmental" archives in the USSR, where they were long closed to scholars. Nevertheless the RZIA documents about the activity of the Russian Conservatory and the RMSA were preserved and are accessible today.[37] In late 1931 and early 1932 Russian musicians living in Czechoslovakia began to organize a Russian musical society in Prague and requested the charter, educational programs, concert programs, and so on, from their Paris colleagues and friends.[38]

By July 1, 1931, the membership of the Parisian RMSA numbered 1,260 people—"fans of Russian musical art of all nationalities." Alexander Konovalov, a former imperial minister, served as president of the society. The composer, conductor, and teacher J. Pomerantsev, who had been a pupil of Taneyev, was vice president. The Board of Directors included well-known musicians such as Ivan Galamian, Thomas de Hartmann, and Leonid Sabaneyev. Meanwhile, the

Administrative Council, which included Felia Litvinne, Albert Benois, Nikolai Kedrov, Ida Rubinstein, and Prince Sergei Volkonsky, was headed by Princess Altenburgskaya, who had played a similar role in the Imperial Musical Society in Russia. The list of honorary members (honorary membership, with certain benefits and duties stipulated in the charter, had existed even in the Imperial Russia Musical Society) is no less interesting. In addition to stars such as Alexander Glazunov, Alexander Gretchaninov, Feodor Chaliapin, Serge Koussevitzky, Sergei Rachmaninov, Nikolai Medtner, and Alexander Ziloti, one finds an amazing list of foreign musicians whose imposing appearances demonstrate sympathy for Russian musical culture abroad. The roster includes Fritz Kreisler, Maurice Ravel, Leopold Stokowski, Richard Strauss, Arturo Toscanini, Bruno Walter, and Felix Weingartner. The RMSA charter reflected this unusual "Russo-foreign" makeup: the society is described as a "union of musicians and music lovers who find themselves abroad," whose purpose is "to improve the moral, legal and material conditions of life for Russian musicians abroad . . . to develop solidarity among them and strengthen support for Russian musical tradition and culture outside Russia's borders."[39] For this purpose the RMSA organized concerts, performances, meetings, lectures, music libraries; maintained publishing activity; organized competitions, and so on. Surviving programs show how actively the RMSA carried out these tasks, especially in the mid-thirties.

The fate of the Russian Conservatory, which, as noted earlier, was later taken over by the RMSA, is complex. In its early years the teaching staff was especially brilliant. The syllabi of courses on individual instruments, basic theory, harmony, research materials (a subject that had existed in the Moscow Conservatory before the revolution), opera, chorus, eurhythmics, instrumental ensemble, music history, and aesthetics indicate an obvious orientation toward the Russian conservatory tradition. Even the textbooks used were the same. Unfortunately, over time, an insufficient number of well-prepared and professionally aspiring applicants forced the conservatory to gradually lower its entrance requirements. Thus it was transformed into an educational institution for students of all levels, many studying solely for their own enjoyment.

But even into the late thirties, both the RMSA and the Russian Conservatory maintained positions of prominence, and honorably met the purposes declared in their charters. The secretary of the Russian Conservatory was Yuri Poplavsky, a cellist and good friend of Tchaikovsky. In the fall of 1931, while sending educational materials to Prague and inviting Russian and Czech musicians to study in the Rachmaninov Conservatory, he stated:

> Three currents, in the sense of educational direction, exist in our conservatory, namely, Muscovite, Petersburgian, and Viennese. Thanks to the concentration of the most famous professors in the musical-pedagogical arena, the Russian Conservatory in Paris is the main musical center of all Russian emigration, proudly preserving the great precepts of the original Russian school, now so glorified worldwide.[40]

Prague came to be considered a "filial branch" of the RMSA. In the charter authorized by the Zemsky Urzhad (its text is in both Russian and Czech), the purpose of the society is stated as follows: (1) To support and develop Russian musical culture in the Czech Republic; (2) to unite Russian musicians and Russian music lovers living in the Czech Republic as well as current Russian musical organizations and circles; (3) to promote "Czech–Russian–Slav rapprochement and solidarity in the field of music."[41] The organization of the society (e.g., division into active and honorary members, formulation of rights and duties) was modeled upon the pre-revolutionary Imperial RMS. But there was also a special feature, born of emigrant life: a dedication to the promotion of Russian music among children. Sergei Trailin headed the RMS in the Czech Republic. The board included the historian B. A. Evreinov and the philosopher and music author Ivan Lapshin. The society conducted concerts of Russian classical music in which even young composers and performers participated.

The musical society in Belgrade, called "The Russian Musical Society in the Kingdom of the Serbsko Horvatsko," was similarly organized and managed. In Latvia, the composer Joseph Vitol, a former schoolmate of Nicolas Tcherepnin, likewise requested materials about the RMSA and the conservatory.

The constant desire to maintain contact with Russian musicians in other countries was manifest. For example, in connection with Rachmaninov's sixtieth birthday, the "Russian Unified Émigré Organizations in Czechoslovakia, Incorporated in an Emigrant Council" addressed the composer with these words: "In you we honor not only a great artist but also an outstanding Russian individual who deeply loves his suffering native land and ardently responds to the needs of Russian people, both those tormented by the Bolshevik yoke and those scattered all over the world."[42] In 1933 they learned of Rachmaninov's aid both "there" and "here," something many Russians discovered only half a century later.

Alexander Glazunov responded to birthday congratulations from the Czech RMS by writing, "Expressed with strong and simultaneously touching words, your greetings have made a deep impression on me. . . . My physical health is not the best, but my spirits are quite high, and I am not bereft of ideas. And even my technical command has not waned."[43]

Immediately following Glazunov's permanent relocation to Paris, Nicolas Tcherepnin, already an "old" Parisian, concerned himself with his colleague's employment and material sustenance—and, especially, the publication of his works by Belaieff. Under the management of Nikolai Artsybushev, whom Tcherepnin referred to as "the Barin"[44] in private correspondence, Belaieff Editions and the related Advisory Council had significantly reduced their publishing activity. Tcherepnin attempted to counter this as best he could. In an August 1928 letter to his wife, he noted:

Yesterday . . . visited Glazunov in the afternoon and brought him some Russian books to read, which pleased him very much. His health is still unsatisfactory . . . but his mood is good. . . . On his table lies a letter from Auer, who is now in Paris [and] asks Glazunov to visit him, since he cannot venture out. This means that these old friends will not manage to see each other, although they have much to reminisce about. . . . I managed to convince the Barin as well as Olga Nikolaevna of the necessity of putting together a life for Glazunov in Paris: to allow him to search for opportunities, on the one hand, and to satisfy his needs, on the other; and to immediately grant him an adequate monthly stipend from the accounts of the Belaieff Publishing House!!![45]

A week later Tcherepnin senior wrote his son:

The conservatory is receiving tons of application letters, and an absolutely new sort of student appears more and more frequently—already solidly prepared, or having completed this or that educational institution in another country. . . . Was with the Barin at Glazunov's place, where we found him in good form, and whatever one might say, it was very pleasant for me to see him, and, it seemed, for him, too. . . . Leaving Glazunov, I took the Barin to a coffee shop and in the most categorical terms told him he must print all [Glazunov's] new and existing compositions with an advance honorarium, a proposal that received his approval [sic]. Let us say that the Belaieff Publishing House is once again becoming a publishing house—God willing![46]

Tcherepnin also supported his old Petersburg friend Feodor Akimenko, a pupil of Rimsky-Korsakov and Liadov, who had in his time taught Stravinsky. In the second half of the 1930s, Akimenko wrote Marie Tcherepnin, "Sweet Mashenka, thank you for the funds, which I chronically need"; "just in case, I am sending you five tickets to my concert. Perhaps you can manage to sell them to people interested in my music."[47]

Throughout the twenties and thirties Russian music was often performed both in large Parisian halls (where the already well-known Rachmaninov, Prokofiev, Alexander Borovsky, Vladimir Horowitz, and Jascha Heifetz appeared) and in other venues such as small theaters, educational institutions, and salons. The first known Paris performance by Alexander Tcherepnin took place on December 9, 1921: "An evening of Maria Kuznetsova to benefit the school of U. Ozarovsky, with the participation of Grigori Pozemkovsky, V. V. Abazes, and other performers, as well as the composer Alexander Tcherepnin (in the apartment of Maria and Mikhail Tsetlin)." One could fit up to a hundred people in the Tsetlins' luxurious literary salon. There, for example, the committee to help Russian writers held an evening tribute to Ivan Bunin. On July 2, 1922, Alexander Tcherepnin participated in a concert-lecture by the composer Lazare Saminsky titled "About the Music of Peoples of Russia (Armenians, Georgians, Tatars)."

Subsequently Tcherepnin's appearances became increasingly frequent and took on the character of composers' concerts. The Sonata No. 1 in A Minor, the Little Suite, and Slavic Transcriptions all figured on a November, 4, 1924, program. Reviews appeared in leading Russian-language dailies. One was by Viktor Walther, a violinist and musical critic trained at the Petersburg Conservatory, who had already published numerous brochures, manuals, and articles in *Russkaia muzykalnaia gazeta, Rech'*, and *The European Bulletin* (he had also directed the music department of the Brockhaus-Efron Encyclopedia, and in Paris was both a professor at the Russian Conservatory and one of the best-known music critics). Walther wrote:

> In his concert A. Tcherepnin showed that he is not only a consummate, brilliant pianist but also one of the most interesting young composers. The foremost piece on a program composed entirely of his works was a new Piano Sonata. The bases of the composer's creativity are perhaps especially clear in this sonata. Tcherepnin is very modern, not only in the novelty of his harmonies and propensity toward complex counterpoint construction but also in his approach to music. His great temperament is always subordinated to strict compositional precision, his musical construction always clear. Themes are distinct, very original and expressive. But such expressiveness is not unpleasant—one does not find sugary sentimentality in his works. . . . It is tempting to note one more feature of Tcherepnin's creativity: it is deeply national. His arrangements of songs ("Ey, uchnem," "Down on the Mother Volga," etc.) are very original. The arrangement of "Ey, uchnem" is powerful and horrifying; it seems to me that such an arrangement before the revolution would have been difficult. Alexander Tcherepnin undoubtedly deserves to be included among the most important Russian composers.[48]

In 1924 Boris de Schloezer also attempted to identify Alexander Tcherepnin's place in the environment of the Russian emigration and to examine it in the context of broader Russian musical culture:

> I have already written about the composer A. Tcherepnin as one of the most talented representatives of Russian musical youth. Of those who now work in Russia we know too little, and most of it secondhand. But as far as we can guess, despite having lost contact long ago with Russian musical centers, young Tcherepnin nevertheless maintains a connection with the creativity of Moscow and Petersburg youth, its striving for pure music, and its search for a neoclassical style.

A year later another interesting and detailed article provided an important perspective:

> We assert that, despite nearly a century of existence and continuous development, impoverishment does not threaten the Russian musical school—a term extensive enough to include both Stravinsky and Myaskovsky, both the senior Tcherepnin and Gnesin. A new generation already comes to replace the older one, which is still in full bloom. Its representatives still experience the influence of their senior comrades. But they also declare themselves on their own. This change, this movement, sometimes even struggle, is interesting. Recently we still lumped together Sergei Prokofiev with those just starting out. We saw in him a young man with a still unformed musical personality who accepted and refracted the influence of the grown-ups—Stravinsky, Scriabin. . . . But it turns out that Prokofiev, in his turn, already exerts a tremendous influence on his juniors, for whom he plays the role of "maître," his style being copied

and assimilated. . . . It is precisely to Prokofiev, in turn, that one would like to compare and link the young Alexander Tcherepnin, since they are congruous. I have in mind the lyric Prokofiev, the Prokofiev of the last two, three years. . . . Alexander Tcherepnin's music carries you away and charms you with its spontaneity and absence of premeditation or rationality—exactly as the creativity of a young man should be. Carefree, light, rich in inspiration, lush, similar to a flowing stream in springtime . . . The spontaneity of his creativity—its "impulsiveness"—results sometimes in banality, that "raw" passion or sensitivity which can so spoil Tchaikovsky. However, I do not think that this danger truly threatens Alexander Tcherepnin: in his soul, as in Prokofiev's, the musician dominates the psychologist. His works are, first of all, systems of sound, and the listener definitely feels that the composer enjoys the play of his sounds, their dance, and their irregular architecture.

Other characteristic features of A. Tcherepnin are a tendency toward multi-voiced constructions and an ease, clarity, and freedom of polyphony. . . . Critics have a predilection for classifications. . . . But I cannot pin down A. N. Tcherepnin at all. . . . Sometimes he writes very simply, almost fondly, sometimes he amazes with the freshness and refinement of his harmonic turns, the whimsical breaks of his melodic lines. Shall we label him, along with Prokofiev, a Neoclassicist? Anyway, much can be expected from him."[49]

Schloezer would continue to monitor Alexander's development closely, later publishing reviews in the French musical press. While Tcherepnin had little in common with neoclassicism in its mature stage, this portrait of the composer is otherwise apt. Such appraisals of the younger Tcherepnin were typical of the music critics of the Russian emigration.

Let us return to the musical life of "Russian Paris" and other notable evenings in which Alexander participated. A concert at the Russian Conservatory on March 6, 1926 included an opening address by Schloezer and compositions by Prokofiev, Stravinsky, and Tcherepnin junior. On June 9, 1926, another performance took place devoted to Russian émigré composers, including Wyschnegradsky, Dukelsky, Lourié, Nabokov, Stravinsky, Prokofiev, and Tcherepnin, the latter performing his own composition. November 12 of the same year found Tcherepnin (as well as Viktor Walther and Nina Kotshetz) performing at a student benefit concert in the Russian Music Hall Trocadero. On December 18, 1927, Tcherepnin, together with Walther and the cellist Paul Grümmer, performed his own compositions as well as those of Myaskovsky and Prokofiev at the Russian Conservatory, as part of a lecture-recital by Walther. Presenting himself as a Russian composer within the framework of the Russian concerts was an important form of self-identification, although Tcherepnin's "European" phase was simultaneously burgeoning.

After 1918 Russian classical music continued to spread throughout Europe and North and South America—partly owing to the efforts of émigré musicians, for whom this dissemination was a vital aspect of their mission. New compositions—especially the works of Stravinsky and Prokofiev—were certainly performed in the best halls, and by the greatest musicians. A notable force in this regard was conductor Serge Koussevitzky. Together with Ziloti, Malko, and Emil Cooper (who likewise emigrated), Koussevitzky had been one of the best conductors of pre-revolutionary Russia. Abroad he created an orchestral series called the Koussevitzky Symphonic Concerts, which consistently presented new Russian compositions alongside classics from around the world and contemporary Western music. Thanks to Koussevitzky, audiences heard nearly all of Prokofiev's works, Lourié's First Symphony (later conducted by the likes of Stokowski, Munch, Furtwängler, and Mengelberg), compositions by Alexander Tcherepnin, and much more.

Nevertheless the basic repertoire of émigré musicians was national classics, which splashed onto opera stages and concert halls throughout the Russian diaspora. The original manuscripts of Cooper's memoirs reflect this steadfast commitment—although it should be noted that the first, abridged, 1988 edition of the memoirs omitted the emigration period. Cooper had been a conductor at the Imperial theaters and in Diaghilev's *Saisons Russes* (Russian seasons) in Paris, leading the 1908 production of *Boris Godunov* with Chaliapin, and later the first performances in Western Europe of Borodin's *Prince Igor* and Mussorgsky's *Khovanschina*. After departing Russia, he traveled first to Buenos Aires, where in 1924 he conducted *Boris Godunov,* and then to Riga, where he worked between 1926 and 1928. He wrote, "I clearly gravitated toward Russian art, and consequently both in Riga and in Kaunas I rather assiduously insisted on presenting the Russian repertoire."[50] In Riga he staged *Prince Igor,* Anton Rubinstein's *Demon,* two Mussorgsky operas, and two Tchaikovsky works— *Onegin* and *Queen of Spades.* He also conducted some Rimsky-Korsakov, including *Legend of the Invisible City of Kitezh,* a piece with an unusual fate. A late masterpiece of the composer, a sort of "Russian Parsifal" saturated with deep religious feeling, it was banned from Soviet stages in the second half of the 1920s, when it could only be heard outside Russia. In 1926 Cooper would conduct *Kitezh* on the stage of the Grand Opera in a concert for Prince Tseretelli's company. From that point on the destiny of the work would remain linked with the remarkable private Russian Opera, an artists' collective to which Tcherepnin was closely connected.

In addition to other classic Russian operas, *Kitezh* was produced in a run of performances at the capacious, oft-sold-out Champs Elysées Theater. Each evening a large-format program was available, featuring color reproductions of scenery and costumes by Konstantin Korovin, Ivan Bilibin, and other well-known artists, photos of soloists and directors, and quotes from reviews of the premiere by the French press. Critics directly linked the quality and success of the performances to two factors: the tradition of the Russian Imperial Theater, where nearly all the soloists as well as Cooper himself had worked; and Parisians' still vivid memories of the *Saisons Russes.* One of the numerous reviews stated:

> With *Legend of the Invisible City of Kitezh and the Maiden Fevronia,* the Russian Private Opera has completed its cycle of productions for the current season. On the whole this was a feat of great significance. We Russians enjoyed

the iridescent vision of the Russia of olden times, which continues to live on. In *Snow Maiden,* pagan Russia passed before our eyes; in *Prince Igor,* the Russia of Kiev; fantastic Russia in *Tsar Saltane;* and, lastly, mystical-religious Russia in *Legend of the Invisible City of Kitezh.* But even foreigners valued the spectacle of an unfamiliar gem with obvious admiration, and the performances of the Russian opera garner constant applause.[51]

This Russian opera troupe was organized thanks to the initiative and financial support of Maria Kuznetsova-Massenet. When she was still Kuznetsova-Benois, she was the first to play the role of Fevronia at the Mariinsky Theater. Returning to this role in Paris, she also sang the parts of Yaroslavna and the Snow Maiden there. Maria Kuznetsova-Benois, who had married Albert Benois after his divorce from Marie Tcherepnin's mother, was Alexander Tcherepnin's aunt.

Besides Kuznetsova, many other singers already famous in Russia performed on the operatic stages of the world, including Dmitri Smirnov, Grigori Pozemkovsky, Eugene Sdanovsky, Maria Slavina, Felia Litvinne, Maria Davidoff, Tartakov, Kajdanov, Sadoven', Zaporozhets, Mozzhuhin, Antonovich, and Kurenko. Indeed, the pinnacle not only of Russian opera but of world operatic art was Feodor Chaliapin, who performed both in Kuznetsova's ensemble and in theatres around the globe.

Another event linking *Kitezh* with Nicolas Tcherepnin occurred outside Paris. The article "Kitezh in the Czech Manner" by Vladimir Pohl discusses a production mounted in honor of the fiftieth anniversary of the Brno Opera Theatre, with the theater's own artistic forces. It was "an event of remarkable musical significance, especially valuable for us Russians. . . . A picturesque balalaika orchestra was put together—a touching detail—from among Russian students training in Brno." Speeches preceded the performance, including one by "the notable pupil of Rimsky-Korsakov, the composer Nicolas Tcherepnin. . . . Having journeyed to Brno at the invitation of the director of the theater, and at the request of Alexander Glazunov and Nikolai Artsybushev (his colleagues at the Belaieff Publishing House), Tcherepnin carried out two weeks of dedicated, fruitful collaboration at rehearsals of *Legend.* The success of the premiere was quite extraordinary. . . . Many Czechoslovakian, Austrian, and German stages have become seriously interested in *Kitezh.* . . . Nicolas Tcherepnin completely confirms the strong, positive press response to the talented conductor Zdenek Halabal, to the remarkable director Dr. Branko Gavello, and to the actors."[52] The performance was designed by Ivan Bilibin, who had also been invited from Paris.

It is impossible to list all the outstanding instrumentalists who performed in Paris on these concert series and individual evenings. Pianists Alexander Borovsky, Vladimir Horowitz, Alexander Brailowsky, Ania Dorfmann; violinists Jascha Heifetz, Mischa Elman, Ivan Galamian, Léa Luboschits; and the cellists Gregor Piatigorsky and Raya Garbousova in no way exhaust the list of performers. Russian music was their signature, and they enriched concert practice worldwide with the fruits of the Russian performing school. Vocalists often gave solo concerts in both large prestigious halls and smaller halls, and for various societies, also appearing alongside chamber musicians. Pre-concert lectures continued the educational tradition of concert life from pre-revolutionary Russia, as did "historical" performance cycles. The first such cycle had been undertaken by Anton Rubinstein, initially in Russia and later in the United States. Noteworthy in a similar vein was a series of nine performances in 1923 by the well-known singer Aleksandr Aleksandrovich at the two-thousand-seat Champs Elysées Theater. The first concert was devoted to national song, the second to music before Glinka, and so on, and the series concluded with Stravinsky, Prokofiev, Gnesin, and Nicolas Tcherepnin.

But these public performances were not the only opportunities in which one could hear Russian music in the host countries of émigrés. The year 1920 saw an endless succession of events such as "Thursdays" of the Russian Artistic Society and "Musical Mornings for Russian Youth." Lev Menuhin's four-volume *Chronicle* describes a charitable evening on May 4, 1930 to benefit Russian refugees, with the participation of Maria Kuznetsova, Dimitri Smirnov, the renowned Russian dancer Ida Rubinstein, and Sarah Bernhardt.[53] Not only Russians but the cultural elite of the host countries took part in these Russian evenings and circles.

Scattered, incomplete information about these events in different foreign cities further testifies to the widespread occurrence of this phenomenon. Presentations included a production of *The Golden Cockerel* staged by the Russian Theatre Studio (perhaps an amateur troupe), which was extremely well attended (Helsingfors, 1933), and a concert of the "Bayan" Society in memory of Rimsky-Korsakov (Riga, 1933), along with a variety of anniversary programs commemorating the deaths of Glinka, Tchaikovsky, and Mussorgsky.

Many performers of Russian song and gypsy music achieved "star" status, as did balalaika ensembles. These included the renowned Nadejda Plevitskaya, who recorded with Rachmaninov and was later implicated in a lurid NKVD [USSR secret police] plot to assassinate émigré ex-generals; Alexander Vertinsky, who had tremendous success performing for émigrés from Shanghai and Harbin to Bucharest, Warsaw, and the United States, as well as in the Russian restaurants of Paris; the equally popular Yuri Morfessi; and the Gypsies Nastya Polyakova, Michel Wavitch, and Anna Shishkina. Often they had to adapt their presentations in order to attract a wider audience, but emphasized the "Russian presence" abroad. They satisfied the demands of Russian and—perhaps even more so—foreign audiences.

Choral art is richly developed in—and inseparable from—Russian musical experience and deserves special mention. Many choruses performed both secular and sacred music, singing in churches as well as on the stage. These were the only performances of the emigration in which the repertoire was perforce exclusively Russian, so naturally Russian choral art became better established in Slavic host countries. In Prague a monthly "Russian Choral Bulletin," devoted to Russian choral life abroad, was published by Alexander Archangelsky, who also issued collections of Russian choral music. Archangelsky had been well known in Russia as a Petersburg precentor, organizer of a remarkable chorus, composer of original works, arranger of national songs, publisher of choral literature, and teacher. He died in 1924, shortly after leaving the USSR, but during his few months in Prague Archangelsky made significant contributions to Russian choral culture abroad.

Another well-known figure was Nikolai Afonsky, a former pupil of the Kiev Spiritual Academy. Working as church precentor throughout Germany, and later in the Alexander Nevsky Cathedral in Paris, he created the Mitropolit Choir, which gave concerts of both spiritual and folk music, and toured Europe and North America. After 1950, during the last two decades of his life, Afonsky was overseer of a cathedral in New York. Other choirs directed by Viktor Kibalchich, Aleksei Malchevsky, and Titov performed frequently, as did the Kuban Army Chorus. But among these groups it was surely the Don Cossack Choir, directed by Sergei Jarov, that enjoyed the greatest worldwide renown. Jarov, a graduate of the Moscow Synod School of Church Song, had fled Russia in 1921 after the defeat of General Vrangel's army, re-creating his chorus first on the island of Lemnos and then in Bulgaria. During years of touring, the choir gave more than eight thousand concerts, delighting not only Russian common folk but the likes of Sergei Rachmaninov and Her Royal Highness Princess Maria Pavlovna, who addressed an eight-page letter to the choir in 1935 on the occasion of their three thousandth concert.

Another cultural phenomenon of major importance for consolidation of the Russian emigration, and inseparable from music, was the presentation of Russian Culture Days. These were celebrated around Pushkin's birthday, and both Tcherepnins would occasionally participate in them. The tradition was established by Russians in Estonia in 1924 and expanded to Prague in the fall of that year, within the context of the Council for the Struggle against Russian Denationalization. Within a year "Culture Days" had also taken place in America, Bulgaria, Germany, Latvia, Poland, Turkey, Finland, France, Switzerland, and Yugoslavia. In a collection devoted to these celebrations, one Professor Shmurlo discussed the danger of "loss of sensitivity to the native country." A Day of Russian Culture, he wrote, "sets itself the task of refreshing in some, and sowing anew in others, a consciousness of our 'Russian-ness,' to concretize those eternal riches that belong to us."[54] Naturally, Russian music was an integral part of celebrations. From the many educational music events that took place over the years we can cite a lecture by Prince Sergei Volkonsky on "Pushkin and Russian Opera," copiously illustrated with musical examples. Another concert, "Works by Russian Composers Inspired by Pushkin's Genius," was part of a major anniversary observance in 1937. Celebrated performers of Russian opera presented fragments from the operas of Tchaikovsky and Mussorgsky, and the Kedrov Quartet performed Gretchaninov's *Monument* and Nicolas Tcherepnin's *Three Melodies.* In the concert's second half, Pavel Kovalev performed Nicolas Tcherepnin's *Fairytale of the Fisherman and the Fish,* for which the writer Aleksei Remizov read the Pushkin text. To conclude the event, Serge Lifar himself performed the Dance of the Vityaz from *Ruslan and Ludmilla.*

Much of this was witnessed firsthand by Alexander Tcherepnin. Such events—in which he or his father or both might participate—would influence the evolution of his creative work. But one must also not forget the Benois family—Grandfather Albert and Great-Uncle "Shura." Albert, who was awarded the Légion d'Honneur in 1936, lived rather modestly in a sanatorium. Whenever possible he was supported (as described by the family) by "small handouts" from his brother Alexander. In the United States Alexander Tcherepnin tried to sell his grandfather's watercolors but met with only limited success.

Alexandre Benois participated in many major theatrical events and also maintained his literary activities. He had published a regular series of "Artistic Letters" in the Petersburg newspaper, *Rech'*, and continued these under the same heading in the leading Parisian Russian daily, *Poslednye novosti.* One "letter" was an obituary devoted to his brother—part memoir and biographical sketch, part family record, and part critical discussion of art. Here we see Albert Benois portrayed as a talented musician and pianist-improviser, a Russian-European who always remained true to himself. His art, especially the early works, "will always captivate, as does all in art that is sincere, direct, expressed fully from the heart, with the confidence and ease given only to artists who know the business of perfection."[55]

During the 1960s and 1970s a Russian living in Buenos Aires named A. Kalugin created a four-album "Necropolis" out of clippings from newspapers of different countries, which is now kept in Moscow in the Library Foundation's "Russian Emigration" collection. In the foreword to the first volume, he bitterly observed, "the history of Russia is written in sovereigns, the history of the Russian Orthodox Church in Mitropolits and Patriarchs, and the history of emigration in obituaries."

The "Russian Presence" in Paris, which came to be a significant cultural phenomenon, was recognized as such by its members, although until the 1930s many people "sat on their suitcases." In 1927, when the tenth anniversary of the October Revolution turned gazes once again back to the homeland, the most popular magazine, *Illustrirovanaia Rossia,* printed these verses of Leri:

> A day will come, and it is closer
> Than one could have expected
> We will no longer be in Paris,
> We shall return home again! . . .
> And many pleasures will be strung
> We in this long-awaited hour . . .
> But did you ever think
> What will become of Paris,
> When Paris loses us? . . .
> The Russian coutures will close,
> There will be no Russian cooks,
> No more "Days of Culture,"
> Nor Russian evenings.[56]

Such were their dreams.

An essay by a leading expatriate musicologist, Leonid Sabaneyev—"Musical Creativity in Emigration"—is almost the only article to tackle the difficult topic encapsulated in its title. Sabaneyev had been one of Sergei Taneyev's most favored pupils. He studied harmony, musical form, counterpoint, and composition with his teacher and graduated as a highly trained professional musician. He went on to do his most important work in the areas of musical science and criticism. Beginning in the 1900s he was associated with the magazines *Muzyka, Muzykalny sovremennik,* and, later, *K novym beregam.* His books about Scriabin, both monograph and memoirs, retain their value even today. After moving abroad in 1926, he published a book about Taneyev, wrote actively for newspapers and magazines, and taught at the Russian Conservatory.

The previously mentioned article was published in the late 1930s in an authoritative émigré magazine, *Sovremennye zapiski.*[57] Another article, titled "The Creative Crisis in Music," appeared in the same journal a year later.[58] The link between these articles becomes clear if one considers that the composers who left Russia not only entered another world—with different priorities, predilections, and attitudes toward the composer and the function of music—but also entered a "foreign" stylistic epoch. Fundamental changes in art had begun in the 1910s and gripped some Russian composers. These changes were embraced in the homeland by the "young avant-garde"—who, however, were quickly cut off in the following decade, as information about new compositions and explorations found its way into Russia more and more rarely. Émigré composers, by contrast, found themselves in the European "melting pot," where confrontations between old and new were especially bright and unconstrained. This had both positive and negative effects.

With the exception of Stravinsky and Prokofiev, the leading and best-known members of the Russian compositional corps abroad had matured during the lifetimes of Tchaikovsky, Rimsky-Korsakov, and Taneyev and, in fact, directly continued their traditions. The names of these senior composers were not simply associated with the Russia left behind but also embodied musical "Russian-ness" for émigré audiences. Their place in Russian music history was already clearly defined. Like Bunin or Kuprin, they continued writing and remained true to themselves. They were not blind to the changes happening before their eyes, but they could not and did not want to become participants.

Sabaneyev belonged to that generation but was not at all conservative. For this reason his opinion of the musical creativity of emigration at this historic border of artistic epochs is especially interesting. Much of what he writes seems self-evident today. But in the context of its time and place, it bears valuable witness. He does not question the evident crisis of musical creativity: music, one of "the most sensitive barometers of culture," must inevitably reflect the conditions of public and artistic consciousness; "everywhere . . . a heightened interest in creating art for separate, narrow particulars . . . the growth of separate fabrics of music . . . a growing rift between those who create music and the audience has been noted."[59] Using examples from Debussy, Scriabin, Strauss, Stravinsky, Hindemith, and Prokofiev, Sabaneyev asserts the rebirth of the world of "acoustic reflections"—their complication, deformation, and then the regeneration of relevant musical language and all its elements.

Examining his topic against such a troubling background, Sabaneyev considers the names of Stravinsky, Rachmaninov, Gretchaninov, and Nicolas Tcherepnin.

> These are also relative youngsters. . . . But an authentic new generation is in truth absent, and that is why thinking about the musical destiny of the expatriation evokes such tragedy. However, let us not reflect too much, for we already approach the limits of life of any emigration, after which it is either absorbed back into its country or assimilated into another.[60]

From the problematic need for a newly composed music, other fundamental obstacles arose: the weak financial position of the four émigré Russian musical publishers, who issued new compositions in rare and small editions; and the problem of audience—a public which simply had no money to attend concerts. Sabaneyev read the spectrum of Russian émigré music from "right" to "left": Medtner to Rachmaninov to Gretchaninov—and to Stravinsky, with whom his sympathies did not lie. He accepted Stravinsky's worldwide fame but considered him a cold, calculating master, made of "psychological material completely different from that of the entire series of previous Russian composers," someone who denies "the primary expressiveness" of music.[61] He did not discuss Prokofiev for "formal" reasons, since his return to the USSR in 1936 removed him from the category of émigré.[62] In his book *I Carried Russia Away with Me,* Roman Gul explains this fact as "natural extravagance" of the musician, who had acquired a "loud global name" as a composer and a "storming success" as a pianist. This act by Prokofiev, in the opinion of Gul, whose books were published after the composer's death, had pitiable artistic and biographic consequences. In his article Sabaneyev, however, characterizes Prokofiev's "flight" as a response to the hard conditions of life for Russian musicians in emigration: "Even he lacked air and Russian understanding, even he wanted an audience. After all, the Russian world of musical 'understanding' was and is huge and completely original, and as equally deserving as the European. Indeed, it had a deep, long-lost European national ethnic resonance."[63]

Speaking of the "younger generation," Sabaneyev first names Alexander Tcherepnin, "whose portfolio contains a multitude of compositions," and remarks about the influence on his music of "new German composers and Prokofiev." The music itself is described as active, vigorous, polyphonic, mobile, but thoughtless, and directed toward "the search for and discovery of curious, extravagant sound combinations."[64] Similar reproaches are addressed to Nicolas Nabokov, another young composer. Sabaneyev's conclusion is rather significant:

> If it comes to pass that expatriate musical effort does not have resonance abroad—that the emigrant community wants only memories of a glorious past rather than efforts to create beauty in the present—then it will mean

that the purpose of composers abroad is merely conservation—to preserve the remnants of free musical culture abroad, until they can be poured back into the general reservoir of a newly unified Russian culture.[65]

How did Alexander Tcherepnin answer these and other serious questions? What response did his music receive outside "the emigrant environment?" Was his music, as well as the music of other young expatriate Russian composers, addressed only or primarily to this audience? How was his *European* destiny formed?

4   European Destiny: The Paris School

Expatriate Russia was, of course, a concept, not a country. Those musicians who never ventured beyond its aura—usually members of the elder generation of musicians—were decidedly conservative. Within the context of emigration, their work had a special function. It channeled the Russian canon of their predecessors, but it bore little connection to the further development and evolution of music.

Through family, friends, schoolmates, colleagues, and the Russian diaspora in general, Alexander Tcherepnin belonged to "Russian Paris." But he quickly entered broader Parisian musical life. He continued his education at the Paris Conservatory as a student of Isidor Philipp and Paul Vidal. Philipp, a French pianist, composer, and music critic of Hungarian origin, had graduated first in his class from the Paris Conservatory. He went on to teach at the conservatory for thirty years and published numerous didactic works. These include *Daily Exercises,* with a foreword by his teacher, Camille Saint-Saëns, and an anthology of early and contemporary French music. Philipp also wrote for the magazine *Le ménestrel.* He believed in Sasha Tcherepnin from the start, and helped publish some of Alexander's piano pieces, which he also edited. Paul Vidal, a composer and conductor who had graduated in the same class as Philipp, was deeply involved in theater. In addition to teaching, he headed the orchestras of the Paris Opéra and the Opéra Comique. His works include ballets and comic operas, and Tcherepnin studied both composition and counterpoint with him.

In a 1967 interview for the magazine *Soviet Music,* given during his visit to Moscow, Tcherepnin recalled his studies at the conservatory.

> Incidentally, my teachers in Paris never suspected that I was both performing and composing. Philipp was very surprised when he found out about my compositions, and kindly introduced me to a publisher. This was very important at the time, because I survived for the next three years thanks to those French publications of pieces I had composed in Russia. Then Anna Pavlova commissioned me to write the ballet *Ajanta's Frescoes,* about the story of Buddha's abandonment of worldly life. This was staged in Covent Garden by the choreographer Clustine, and the set was designed by Allegri.
>
> So you can see that by the time I left Russia in 1921, I was already fairly accomplished in music theory and composition, as well as in piano performance. . . . In France I kept my distance from the Russian émigré community. I met more often with French and English musicians than with my compatriots. But I remained a Russian composer, and was so to an even greater degree; because I wasn't really under the influence of any one master or school, I felt the weight of all of Russian musical culture.
>
> People associate me with the group known as "The Paris School," which in

the 20s consisted of the Czech composer Bohuslav Martinů, the Roumanian Marcel Mihalovici, the Hungarian Harsányi, the Swiss-Frenchman Arthur Honegger and Swiss-born Conrad Beck. We were great friends. Our views were similar, but we didn't adhere to any particular aesthetic.

However, the name "Paris School" had a certain symbolism. You see, Paris is remarkable in that an artist or composer who arrives here from another country is not assimilated; on the contrary, he quite often becomes more fundamentally and aesthetically linked to his native land. It is no accident that Nadia Boulanger, who taught composers from many countries, emphasized this principle: Be What You Are. Yes, the Parisian artistic climate helped you think in your native language, encouraged you to aspire to national originality. And I must say that, having lived in France for over thirty years, that helped me remain a Russian composer.

A certain pull toward compressed forms, economy of means and simple writing drew me to French composers. These features are generally characteristic of French musical thought. Even the density of texture in Messiaen is only superficial, and doesn't obscure the clarity of the musical idea (the way it sometimes does in Schoenberg), even in his "avian" compositions. By the way, this birdsong "folklore" is a most interesting subject. I had started collecting this material even before Messiaen. I used it in the finale of my [first] cello sonata.

I never cease to strive for succinctness. I prefer to remove material, to clarify things to an extreme. Prokofiev said that it is impossible to perceive more than three themes simultaneously. From this arose the method of "Interpoint," which I had already created in Tiflis and use frequently—a kind of polyphony in which, to be brief, voices are joined not according to the principle of "note against note," but "note between notes." But in practice it is much more complicated.[1]

Describing the Paris School, Tcherepnin imprecisely lists its members. However, this is truly not an inaccuracy but rather a direct product of the fluid and informal ties which bound the musicians. Although he names Honegger, who was not part of the group, he omits one of its steadiest members, the Polish composer Alexander Tansman. In his biography, *Child of Fortune: The Life and Times of Alexander Tansman,* Janusz Cegiella paints a picture of Paris in the 1920s and reminds us of the major characters in the musical arena:

> From the beginning of the 1920s Paris was the largest center of musical art in the world, and during that time (alongside Vienna with Schoenberg, Berg, and Webern), it was a hub for new music. Claude Debussy, the great reformer and creator of musical impressionism, had died in 1918, but his memory was ever present. Camille Saint-Saëns had reached the venerable age of 85, Gabriel Fauré was 75, and Vincent d'Indy, 68. Maurice Ravel, aged 45, played a leading role. Paul Dukas (aged 45), Albert Roussel (aged 51), and Florent Schmitt (aged 50) all received well-earned respect. The famous writer Jean Cocteau used his pen to support the irrepressible young avant-gardists who called themselves "Les Six": Darius Milhaud, Arthur Honegger, Louis Durey, Georges Auric, Francis Poulenc, and Germaine Tailleferre. In France's capital, dozens of young composers from all over Europe searched for fame. It was

precisely here that artists such as Igor Stravinsky, Sergei Prokofiev, Alexander Tcherepnin, Marcel Mihailovici, Bohuslav Martinů, and Tibor Harsányi, along with elders such as Manuel de Falla, became renowned. . . . The intensity of musical life in Paris was really stunning in those years.[2]

Even more interesting for us are Tansman's own memories of the "École de Paris," quoted by Cegiella:

It was not a school in the normal sense of the word but rather a group of composers from Eastern and Central Europe. We were bonded by deep friendship as well as an attachment to France and its culture. Certainly our interests were closely tied to the period of our youth, but we never built ourselves "a little shrine," nor did we present ourselves as an artistic group united by a technical or aesthetic slogan. Each of us—whether Mihailovici, Martinů, or Harsányi—went his own way. A sort of "École de Paris" had always existed, for the capital of France served as a constant magnet for artists. They drew on French sources and enriched their own, unique ethnic contributions. One thinks of Lully, Gluck, Albeniz, de Falla, Modigliani, Picasso, Chagall, Apollinaire, Hemingway, and even, in some sense, Stravinsky and Prokofiev. For Paris is capable of giving artists a superb feeling of balance, without taking away their individuality.

What primarily connected our group, as well as our senior and junior colleagues, was the very concept of the phenomenon called music, its evolution and purpose, both actively created and passively perceived. Music is by nature spontaneous, almost biological. It is transformed by the activity of single individuals and their mysterious talents into an organized art. It is guided by its own internal laws and requirements. . . .

The evolution of expressive means is necessarily and inextricably linked with individual epochs. However, in my opinion, an attempt to reduce these passive or active components to a mere combination of sounds leads music down a path immeasurably narrow in its autonomy and potential development . . . and leaves only the curious, unexpected, shocking—which quickly becomes rather dull, and atrophies. Here the question is not about concepts of the avant-garde, or the impossibility of understanding between two generations, etc. Each generation has its own avant-garde, and it seems ridiculous to argue that you still belong to it in 1967 when you already belonged to it in 1920! Not that it is impossible—anything is possible! It is rather a question of honesty, which does not allow you to freely ally with new currents because that would be artificial. It certainly does not exclude the chance to enrich one's trade with new expressive tools, which brings new opportunities. But it is not necessary to abandon the foundation, i.e., that which forms the actual purpose of creativity. Even the most interesting expressive means cannot become ends in themselves.[3]

Most striking in Tansman's words, and closely comparable to Tcherepnin's destiny in the 1910s and 1920s, is the theme of "two waves of the avant-garde," canceling out or complementing each other.

Returning to the description of the Paris school by Tansman's biographer, one sees a remarkable similarity to that of Alexander Tcherepnin above. Cegiella writes that, on his first trip to Paris, Tansman was already drawn to "The Six," making friends with Milhaud and Honegger. He even received an offer to become the "seventh." But he preferred independence and refused the honor, considering the affiliation to be a somewhat artificial phenomenon. Around 1923 Tansman joined a different group, where "there was no common stylistic orientation, and the group was not monolithic in its musical attitudes." It consisted of composers "who had chosen as their place of activity not Berlin but Paris."

> The name "École de Paris" arose directly from this, invented once again by a magazine. Their names appear in dictionaries and encyclopedias under this designation. In addition to the Pole Alexander Tansman, it included the Russian Alexander Tcherepnin,[4] the Czech Bohuslav Martinů, the Romanian Marcel Mihailovici, and also the Hungarian Tibor Harsányi.
>
> Their ties lay more in maintaining creative communication and reviewing one another's compositions. If one had to identify a common stylistic feature, it would probably point to folklore.... The group's headquarters was the Café du Dom on the Boulevard Montparnasse. The "École de Paris" did not "arise from protest" against something, nor did it have its own Jean Cocteau. It simply did not aspire to appear in print.[5]

It is interesting that different sources cite different composers as members of the Paris school. For example, Henri Prunières, the highly knowledgeable music critic, also includes in its ranks Stravinsky, Prokofiev, Igor Markevitch, Nikolai Obouhov, Conrad Beck, and Gregory Fitelberg.[6] A biographer of Martinů's "French Period" names the Austrian Alexander Spitzmueller in addition to the Russian–Polish–Roumanian–Czech foursome.[7] The two-volume encyclopedic *Dictionnaire Larousse de la Musique* simultaneously considers the École de Paris in both a limited and broader sense. Those who are placed within the framework of a "school," although without a uniform doctrine, are "some young foreigners living in Paris and seduced by French aesthetics ... the Swiss Conrad Beck, the Hungarian Harsányi, the Czech Martinů, the Romanian Mihalovici, the Pole Tansman, and the Russian Alexander Tcherepnin."[8] But in a broader sense, the author of the entry, A. Girard, chooses to include in the ranks of the École some thirty composers, nearly all of them foreigners—Russians (Prokofiev, Lourié, Obouhov—but not Stravinsky!), Americans, Britons, Austrians, Italians, Bulgarians, Finns, Greeks, Norwegians, Canadians, Portuguese, Swiss, and Yugoslavs.

In a farewell written after Alexander Tcherepnin's death, his Paris colleague Marcel Mihailovici would say:

> Ah, what a person we have lost! ... Tcherepnin possessed a rare kindness, rare generosity, he did not know the word envy.... He has written a huge quantity of scores, and turned, frequently with great success, to all genres, all forms of our art. Alongside Milhaud, Hindemith, and Martinů, he was one of those composers whose diligence reminded us of the great creative minds of the last century.... I knew Sasha for more than fifty years. I can almost name

the date of that evening when I first saw him. It must have been 1925. Tcherepnin had just won the Schott Prize in Germany for his Concerto for Flute, Violin, and Chamber Orchestra. One evening I was leaving the Salle Gaveau with Ravel and the Honeggers. Ravel had wanted to go to Graff, a pub near Gare Ste-Lazare. We sat down at a small table in the back. Andrée Vaurabourg, Honegger's wife, suddenly said: "There's Tcherepnin!" Ravel asked whether this was the Tcherepnin who had just won the Schott prize. Vaurabourg nodded. Ravel suggested we invite Tcherepnin to join our table. Tcherepnin approached. He was handsome, tall, trim, with long fair hair and blue eyes. A real prince! ... He was beyond fashion—he did not carry a hat, and wore his tie untied around the unbuttoned collar of a dark blue shirt. He never opened his mouth, never uttered a single word that evening, I even wondered if perhaps he was mute. But when he left, he said, "Thank you. Good-bye." So he was not mute.

Sometime later, with the help of Tibor Harsányi, with whom Tcherepnin was close, and who was also my friend, I gradually got to know him. I saw more and more of him. He even joined our group, which music critics at that time had christened "the Paris school" (Martinů, Harsányi, Beck, and I). The name was borrowed from the fine arts: beginning in 1910 it was said that artists and sculptors working in Paris belonged to the École de Paris. Foreign musicians living and working in Paris also had the right to belong to this group. This included musicians at Notre Dame Cathedral during the Renaissance, and later Lully, Mozart, and Wagner. Not to mention Chopin, Falla, Enesco, Honegger, Stravinsky, Prokofiev, Copland, and certainly our old colleague Alexander Tansman.[9]

Another important reminiscence, by Tcherepnin himself, concerns his meeting Bartók during the first years of his Paris life. He recalled having been invited to drop in on composer Karol Szymanowski and violinist Paul Kochansky before they proceeded together to the reception.

After a brief talk, we all went together to the home of Henri Prunières, the director of *Revue Musicale,* [where] according to Szymanowski, I was to meet *tout Paris musical.* The reception, incidentally, was given in honor of Béla Bartók—and, indeed, just as Szymanowski said, *tout Paris* was present. At the piano, Poulenc and Jacques Février were playing jazz. The few rooms were overcrowded. Prunières and his wife were busily circulating, yet failing to introduce anyone to anyone else—for, of course, *tout Paris* was supposed to be well acquainted.... Every one was chatting; everyone seemed to enjoy the party.

Being shy, I was pushed by the crowd towards a corner—finding myself near ... another wallflower, [like] myself completely abandoned and looking [forlorn], as if he were saying, "Why am I here?" For a long time we stood near each other without saying a word. I do not know who ... was the first to break the silence—I guess it was [he], because the language [we spoke] was German, in which I would have hardly approached [anyone] in a French gathering.

It happened that the man with whom I was speaking was Bartók. Nobody paid attention to the "guest of honor"—so we had an hour-long talk. The theme was folklore: Bartok spoke of his interest in Hungarian, Roumanian,

Bulgarian folk [music]; learning that I was Russian, he inquired about the rhythmic and modal aspects of . . . Russian folklore, and seemed particularly interested in what I was able to tell him about . . . Georgian folklore, and about the first inversion of a triad built [of] fourths, which is the basic Georgian chord. We spoke also about [the relationship] of language to music, specifically about rhythmic correlations of language and musical phrases. . . . At that time the music and even the name of Bartók was entirely unknown to me; undoubtedly . . . Bartók [knew just as little about] me. But this long, friendly conversation, the exchange of names and . . . addresses, aroused our mutual interest in each other and in each other's music, which was to show itself in the future in many a way.[10]

A sad memory of Martinů is recounted in a May 2, 1968, letter to Vasily Kiselev:

Although I knew Martinů well, and together with him formed part of the École de Paris group of composers, I lack material of interest for a memorial article. . . . I know that he, like myself, never ceased to love his homeland and aspired to see it. His last unfulfilled dream was to celebrate his seventieth birthday in his native land, for which he had prepared in advance, and which was more or less secured. In August 1959, when I was in Lugano, I wrote him in Basel that I would come to visit him. . . . I arrived to find him in a coffin: he had died precisely on the day of our planned meeting.[11]

Yet however convincing the professed absence of a united platform or aesthetic program, the union of this group of international composers indicates at the very least some shared challenge of survival in a foreign environment. Each aspired to preserve the features of his culture, and succeeded. But all were carried by the same European stream. Tcherepnin testified that although he had been severed from the changes taking place in Western European music by historical cataclysms, upon arrival he found that he had been moving in the same direction. Tansman was influenced by Stravinsky and Ravel. He combined Polish folklore with a neoclassical orientation, and prominently used both polytonality and free tonality. The musical language of Mihailovici likewise combines native Roumanian features as well as classicist inclinations, and a tendency to "free" the twelve-step scale. . . . Tcherepnin's unpublished letters to Messiaen, Florent Schmitt, Marc Pincherle, and others contain interesting details of the dialogue between him and the Paris musicians close to him.[12]

As a Russian, indeed a Petersburger in Paris, Tcherepnin faced striking, historical turns. By 1914 the presentation of music by Mussorgsky, Borodin, and Stravinsky (especially the *Rite of Spring*) in the Diaghilev *Saisons Russes* had already left a powerful impression. The French, bewitched by Petersburgian, Russian sonorities, set about transforming the source. Alexander had processed these influences by the time of his arrival, but now these forces reached him refracted by the French musical environment. Indeed, during their formative years, the Mighty Five themselves ("Les Cinq," to whose name "Les Six" alluded) followed not the Austro-German but rather the French musical tradition. Their idols were Berlioz and Lizst, who had themselves imbibed so much of Paris. Tcherepnin fit very naturally into Western European musical life. At the same time, with the possible exception of Hindemith, who is strongly yet perhaps unintentionally reflected in Tcherepnin's music of the twenties and thirties, Alexander's influences were predominantly French.

In early postrevolutionary Russia there was also great interest in the French, specifically "Les Six." We find an example of this in the small but significant article by Darius Milhaud printed in 1923 in the first issue of the magazine *K novym beregam.* Soon after that, Milhaud visited Leningrad and met musical contemporaries as well as musicologist Boris Asafiev, whose book on French contemporary music would appear in 1926.[13] Despite the subsequently extensive scholarly literature on this subject, even in Russia this little book turns out to be very useful, for it speaks with the voice of the epoch, the voice of Russia and Petersburg. Asafiev's descriptions of French composers are remarkable vis-à-vis Tcherepnin. It is useful to remember Honegger's comparison of German and French composers in their sensitivity to the artistic environment, in particular the brevity of the latter.[14] Honegger's early music is characterized by a combination of strong rhythmic and polyphonic texture, and the development of the major-minor system through a synthesis of chromatic tonality with so-called twelve-tone diatonicism (in natural modes), while simultaneously preserving tonal support. Asafiev identifies all this as also characteristic of Tcherepnin's music.

Contrasting the fundamental features of French and German music, Asafiev hardly knew that his thoughts would also be relevant, albeit with some changes, to two Russian compositional schools. "German symphonism," he wrote, "grew out of dramatized contemplation and leads to psychological analysis; French symphonism is directed outward, toward figuration, demonstration, pantomime, and the picturesque."[15] In Asafiev's judgment, "the surmounting of emotionalism,"[16] "the persistent striving" of French music "to be expressive in the concrete, through representation,"[17] is also linked with formative processes. "Even in large compositional forms of French instrumental music, the suite as principle and the suite as scheme play an important role."[18] Unwittingly this also describes the Tiflis Tcherepnin and the Paris Tcherepnin. Asafiev's characterizations of Auric and Poulenc, "mobility . . . laconicism . . . the thirst for clarity, naïvete and primitiveness of formulation,"[19] likewise apply to Tcherepnin. Compressed forms and contrast, rather than development (characteristic of Milhaud), are also peculiar to Tcherepnin, as demonstrated by his eight-minute-long, three-movement Piano Trio Op. 34, which dates from 1925.

Gennady Rozhdestvensky, who was a friend of Tcherepnin and conducted his symphonic compositions, told the author of this book that the composer's work could be linked most vitally with "Les Six." Nevertheless Alexander's first European successes were connected with England. His first composer's concert after emigration, which included a performance of the *Bagatelles,* took place in London to great acclaim in November 1922. Half a century later Tcherepnin would write Grigori Shneerson from the British capital, "Celebrated the fiftieth anniversary of my western debut—performed my violin sonata with Yehudi Menuhin at the BBC, also some piano pieces, interview, etc."[20]

In September 1923 London would see the great ballerina Anna Pavlova perform the ballet *Ajanta's Frescoes,* which she had commissioned from Tcherepnin junior. Ironically it was partly in anticipation of commissions from Pavlova that Tcherepnin senior had relocated his family to Paris. His *Pavillon d'Armide* had first revealed Pavlova's dramatic talent to audiences in St. Petersburg, and later in Paris at the first Diaghilev Season in 1909. For Alexander, the commission challenged him to compose in what would become one of his most important genres. Pavlova had decided on the ballet's plot during her wide travels. Along with printed examples of Indian music, she gave the young composer an image of an Indian temple in which the life of Buddha was depicted, including an episode of his renunciation of the world. For Tcherepnin this was a novel encounter with the East—no longer the Caucasus but not quite the Far East. After the successful Covent Garden premiere, Pavlova took the production to the United States, and as a result Tcherepnin's name would become known in the U.S. three years before his own first American visit.

A major step on Alexander's path to becoming established as a "European" composer was his 1925 victory in a Mainz competition organized by the well-known music publishing house Schott & Sons. He had submitted his *Concerto da Camera* for flute, violin, and chamber orchestra (future Op. 33), and received the following letter from the publisher:

> Please allow us to add these written lines to our telegraphed congratulations. We were delighted to remove the cover of anonymity and read your name. That your work was chosen and awarded this prize from among 103 submitted to our competition says more about your work than any critique. Let us add that we sensed inspired originality in your noble and broad compositional style, and we are proud to have the opportunity to present your piece in our catalogue.
>
> We hope that the relationship which has begun in this way will continue. In any case we would be grateful if you would give us the opportunity henceforth to become acquainted with your newest works.
>
> Incidentally, you will be interested to know that your "Nine Inventions for Piano," which was issued by our Paris representative Max Eschig and Co., has been acquired for Germany. So your name is already represented in our catalogue.
>
> In addition, kindly send us a photo with a short curriculum vitae as soon as possible, since we need this in order to publish the results of the competition.[21]

Press responses soon followed. The leading *Allgemeine Musikzeitung* reported,

> Thanks to his talent and creativity, Tcherepnin definitely towers above the commonplace. Admittedly I have a great mistrust of major-minor harmony with simultaneously sounding major and minor thirds.... This dissonant illness spoils most of all the first movement (in a–b–a form), with its ingenu-

ous principal theme in eighteenth-century style, which has recently become popular again; the middle section (b) is beautiful and refined but unfortunately very short. The major-minor tonality is more advantageously used in the Andantino, a sort of canzona; the cadenza, with *pp* strings, is especially attractive from the point of view of musical timbre. The quite fresh and vigorous scherzo is probably the most successful movement.... This Concerto, which won the prize at a 1925 publishers' competition, is a noteworthy creation.[22]

The premiere of the *Concerto da Camera* at the Donaueschingen Festival was conducted by Hermann Scherchen. Among the very positive reviews was this one: "The Russian composer Alexander Tcherepnin is a musician of European caliber.... His name will appear alongside Stravinsky and Hindemith."[23]

The Concerto entered the repertoire. In 1926 the piano-accompanied version was performed in Paris. A short review in the leading publication *La revue musicale* was written by the renowned Raymond Petit. It is valuable not only for his repeated attention to Tcherepnin's music but also for this observation:

> This is one of the best works by a composer who is, unfortunately, very uneven; but his music is frequently filled with finesse and brilliant eloquence.... The Concerto is charming, light and lively in its fast movements, languid in the Andante.... All the same, the structure of the work is not always sufficiently condensed; but from the standpoint of rhythm, I see not a single weakness, not a single error.[24]

Alexander's former teacher, Victor Beliaev, was present at the Donaueschingen Festival, and communicated with his erstwhile pupil. A long article by him soon appeared in the Soviet press. This was the only domestic coverage of Tcherepnin other than responses to the 1967 concerts and the quote cited earlier. Because the composer had been excised from the cultural life of his homeland, the article was forgotten. However, it actually represents the best analysis of the composer's music in the mid-twenties. Its perceptiveness stems from the author's profound expertise in modern Russian music, which Western critics could not fully share. Tcherepnin found the article interesting and astute, as he admitted to Beliaev many years later:

> Your article about me—the first article about me—was simply providential: you guessed forty-two years ago what until this day few have understood, and what even I did not recognize in myself but only gradually learned to understand. You pushed me out of the "slip," like a boat being launched into water, foreseeing and predicting where and how I was going to sail![25]

The depth and insight of the article, its nearly complete unfamiliarity to the modern reader, and the composer's high opinion of it led to the decision to append it unedited to the end of this chapter. Beliaev views his hero in the context of the Petersburg musical tradition, the New Russian school (i.e., the Mighty Five), and the contemporary musical reality of Western Europe, and yet emphasizing Tcherepnin's independent path.

The composers of "The Six," especially Milhaud, repeatedly testified to the ubiquitous misunderstanding of their musical language, particularly in the tonal sphere, owing to its abundant dissonance. The Chamber Concerto appeared just as "new" and alien, even more so to German audiences. Note the following newspaper commentary issued by a representative of Schott Publishing Company on February 4, 1929, in connection with a performance of the concerto in Hildesheim, led by Fritz Lehmann:

"Modern music is not only an art but also a science. Anyone who becomes acquainted with Alexander Tcherepnin's ultramodern composition can be sure of this," writes the reviewer. Having attended the dress rehearsal that morning, the author declares Tcherepnin a "Russian innovator with a real future ahead of him" and launches into an often outlandish description of the experience of hearing the Concerto.

> The *Concerto da Camera* in D Major for Flute and Violin Op. 33 stunned, indeed frightened, anyone who heard it for the first time. At times the first movement involuntarily suggests the voices of animals. But never mind! In the evening, on hearing it a second time, the ear already responded better to what it heard. . . . The score indicated that we have here a new nine-step C-major scale. This certainly provided an opportunity for refined dissonance, so-called cacophony. These harmonies, which at the dress rehearsal seemed devoid of any melody, but with a rough rhythm and consistent style, became increasingly clear during the concert. The theme, which is still hard to discern in the first movement, felt like a symbol of death in the second movement, the Andantino. The likeness was to a funeral march, from the sound of bells to weeping mourners. In the third movement (*Vivace*) there is something like a dance of death, like Saint-Saëns' *Danse Macabre*. An ominous scale grows stronger almost note by note. Nearly to the point of madness! The dead seem to be gathering in hell. They are met by the awful exultations of infernal phantoms! Piercing chords, like screams! Again, something strangely like the pealing of bells. The solo violin and solo flute seem like zealous leaders of dreadful welcome songs in the orchestra. And in the fourth movement, just as brief as the others (fortunately!), a mad group dance begins in truly devilish colors, with rhythms made only of skeleton bones. This similarity to a Witches' Sabbath ends with submersion into emptiness, nothingness.

The reviewer finally concludes ingenuously, "That this work of Tcherepnin is valuable in itself is clear from the fact that so clever and courageous a musician as Fritz Lehmann chose to perform it."[26]

La revue musicale evaluated the Sonata in G for Cello and Piano in a survey of recent editions that included Tansman's Sonata for Cello and Piano, Honegger's Prelude and Blues for Harps, and pieces by Vincenzo Davico: One could reproach this piece for not really being a "sonata," and not really being "in G." And these are not simply the remarks of a fussy purist. This work sins first of all by its tonal organization and insufficient, unclear structure. Nevertheless, Tcherepnin shows real gifts of life and musicality. His machine-gunfire, the use of high and low pitches in shaping the subject, two-part counterpoint, and persistent three-note repetitions reveal true individuality.[27] Both tonally and formally, in an un-sonata-like way, these were not weaknesses but rather inherent characteristics. Responding to two newly issued editions of *Four Preludes* Op. 24 and *Four Romances* Op. 31 for Piano (published by Durand in Paris and Universal in Vienna, respectively), Raymond Petit writes,

> I find that the *Preludes* considerably outrival the *Romances*. In the latter, the author allows his facility free rein with too much abandon. However, the first and last Romances are pleasantly melodic. On the other hand, the *Preludes* are Tcherepnin at his best; though they tend somewhat toward the harsh and nostalgic as opposed to the light and joyful, the author cultivates both tendencies with equal happiness. The stormy passages are rather overloaded with scales abounding in leaps of a tone and a half. What is more, Tcherepnin resorts here, as in many other works, to imitations on each note of the chord built on the augmented fifth. This seems not always to be successful. But the second prelude, which is very slow, contains excellent linear combinations and would sound wonderful on the organ. Sometimes the influence of Milhaud becomes subtly visible (for example, in the second, two-voiced prelude). Might it be to this that Tcherepnin owes a certain taste for ambiguity between major and minor, which makes him often conclude his works with a perfect double chord that contains both major and minor thirds? Otherwise this sounds just right, and leaves the soul like a question, which is perfectly in keeping with the character of these brief but very expressive pieces.[28]

La revue musicale forms a kind of chronicle of the composer's early endeavors. Despite the reproaches one expects from scholars, it is important to quote these texts sufficiently in order to give readers a sense of some of Tcherepnin's lesser-known works. They broaden the context of his creativity, and testify to the rapid and successful development of his career, of his European destiny. Since the authors of these articles were renowned and talented critics, it is not surprising that they correctly identified the important features of Tcherepnin's music of the twenties and early thirties: freshness; immediacy; spontaneity of expression (on which, however, the composer sometimes relies too much); uniqueness of expressive language, especially in the sphere of harmony and polyphony; rhythmic drive (although sometimes phrases descend by inertia); compactness of form (although sometimes insufficiently developed). Note this additional review by Raymond Petit concerning the performance of *Georgian Rhapsody* for Cello and Orchestra Op. 25 at the Concerts Colonne:

> This work demonstrates all of Alexander Tcherepnin's qualities: the acts of youth, rhythmic momentum, the freshness of invention suddenly mixed with doses of seriousness and nostalgia; and nevertheless it is not this work among the author's oeuvre that earns our preference. One has the impression that his ease runs a little too freely here, and without any checks. You only rarely feel the dense fullness that distinguishes the Second Concerto for Piano, for instance. The themes, inspired by rather than borrowed directly from folklore, are pretty, of course, but sometimes lack accent. The solo instrument (cello) is excellently exploited, supported by an orchestra of often exquisite invention; but this concerto form leaves little room for the contrapuntal combi-

nations in which Tcherepnin excels. What a delight whenever he can slip one in! Hence the charming chase, lasting but an instant, of the flute and cello! An element that does not weaken is the rhythm—nervous, frenzied, or languorous and always full of invention. From the light drum-beats, unaccompanied by other instruments, the most wonderfully whirling episodes begin, and I challenge anyone to not have some trouble remaining quietly in his seat at that moment.[29]

The second most important critic at *La revue musicale* after Henri Prunières was the Russian Boris de Schloezer. The brother-in-law and close friend of Scriabin, de Schloezer had published articles and books about him as well as Stravinsky. In *La revue* he regularly published large analytical, aesthetico-philosophical surveys and individual reviews. His article on Tcherepnin's two piano concertos contains important insights and observations:

> The First Concerto (in F), composed nearly two years ago, was played by Mlle Pelletier with the Lamoureux orchestra; the Second (in A), which has only just been completed, was performed by the author himself at one of the last concerts of the Société Nationale de Musique in an arrangement for two pianos. . . . The comparison offered by these two concertos heard several days apart reveals just how far Alexander Tcherepnin has come.
>
> I really like the beginning of this First Concerto where the harmonies of fifths and fourths, obstinately beaten out, explode at the piano in a neat, vigorous first theme with broken rhythm. There are more very pretty episodes in the development; but the somewhat facile and cowardly pathos of certain phrases bothers me, as does the abundance of brilliant passages in octaves that one feels are "veneered" over the work. Alexander Tcherepnin loves the piano, he knows its capabilities, and its technical character interests and entertains him for its own sake. But he sometimes ends up allowing the instrument to dominate him, and then one feels his music gush, so to speak, from under fingers trained in scales and exercises. Composed in the strict form of a sonata allegro, this First Concerto appeared nevertheless diffuse and a little long.
>
> From this standpoint, the Second Concerto demonstrates undeniable progress: lasting almost as long as the First (about twenty minutes), it seems a lot more concise and collected, although the sonata-allegro form is now freer, as the author introduces a series of variations on his second theme into the development. But the reason is that *remplissage* is absent from this Second Concerto, and the purely technical passages are integrated into the very body of the work. The author's critical sense and taste have become purer, and he no longer allows himself to fall into verbiage and colorless sentimentality: his themes, his melodies, have instead a very clean, very personal shape. The harmony is always tonal and often fresh, although the author somewhat abusively uses the interval of a tone and a half; and the bounding rhythms that animate this music of youthful gaiety lend even his polyphony an elegant and light gait.
>
> This work, certainly one of the best concertos of Russian musical literature, resembles directly the neoclassicism of Serge Prokofiev, whose influence on the young Russian school is becoming more and more evident.[30]

Another article by de Schloezer, regarding a June 9, 1926 concert by Russian composers mentioned in the previous chapter, places the event within the context of French music criticism:

"Contemporary Russian Music" is the title Spinadel has given to a series of evenings of Russian music this winter in which he presented the works of Russian composers now living in Paris: Vladimir Dukelsky, Arthur Lourié, Nicolas Nabokov, Alexander Tcherepnin, and Ivan Wyschnegradsky, as well as Prokofiev and Stravinsky. . . .

The works by Tcherepnin included in the program have been heard before. *Two Arabesques* for Piano (performed by Mme Ravenet) and the Sonata in D for Cello and Piano (Mme Clément and Tcherepnin himself) exhibit power and rich melodic and rhythmic imagination, if sometimes seeming a little garrulous and uncontrolled.

While the young Tcherepnin has felt Prokofiev's influence, Dukelsky could not escape the same fate; an agreeable melody is heard in his *Triolets* (Mme Vajewska). Meanwhile, the works of Nabokov and Lourié bear the mark of Stravinsky. Nabokov's melodies are close to Glinka, and even pre-Glinka traditions are restored to life by the efforts of the composer of *Mavra;* as for Lourié's Toccata for Piano (M. Claudio Arrau), it obviously entered the world under the sign of Stravinsky's Sonata, but Lourié does not copy—he invents. His Toccata, written in a single breath, presents a brilliantly constructed and polished composition with individual melodies specific of him alone, whose harmony is founded on a firm tonal foundation, since harmonic unity is constantly determined by encounters and interweavings of various tonal moves.[31]

There is no doubt that Alexander read these reviews attentively. Reproaches for insufficient musical organization in his composition probably coincided with growing changes in his musical thought. The entire state of music in Europe prepared him for this, for Paris was also open to "other," for example, Austro-German, music. Hindemith and Schoenberg were constantly performed. Their music was discussed in the press, along with theoretical questions of atonality, polytonality, and musical language in general. These discussions appeared in journals alongside reviews of Tcherepnin's works.

The half-step/one-and-a-half-step scale, as the reviews indicate, had been heard but not yet accepted as a principle.[32] It is impossible to establish exactly when Tcherepnin first formulated and demonstrated his principles, but his strict, rational use of them began during these Paris years. Later, interviews or accompanying notes to recordings or publications hardly ever appear without a description of the composer's language.

The prize-winning *Concerto da Camera* Op. 33 characterized Tcherepnin's "technical" inclinations, as would several subsequent opuses. But prior to these later works he composed *Three Pieces* for Chamber Orchestra Op. 37. Alexander's parents were fond of this set, especially the second movement, *Mystère,* for cello and chamber orchestra. This piece is often performed separately and is indeed the best of the three, perhaps even one of Tcherepnin's greatest works. It is full

Example 4.1

of broad, emotional, continuous melodic expression, unconstrained by strict ratio. An excerpt from the exposition (musical example 4.1), demonstrates the second statement of the theme of the second subject.

In Op. 37 the young composer demonstrates an uncommon mastery of formal construction. The first movement—Overture—combines fugue and sonata forms in a manner reminiscent of the first movement of Taneyev's *Johann Damaskin* (with a mirrored, condensed reprise). This is especially notable in the development of material, the polyphonic techniques, the numerous effects of instrumentation, and what might be called "thematism." Concerning the latter, an example can be seen in the second movement, at rehearsal number 230, where elements of the main subject theme are found in the lyrical melody of the second subject.

* * *

In 1926 Tcherepnin married Louisine Weekes, a wealthy American socialite. The marriage lasted a little more than ten years, spanning both Europe and the United States. He crossed the ocean often, traveling to the Old World for tours, opera, and ballet productions, and visits to his parents in Paris, after which he would return to an apartment in New York City and his wife's home in the suburb of Islip, Long Island. It was in Islip that Tcherepnin composed his First Symphony. Numerous works in a variety of genres preceded the First Symphony: the opera *Ol-Ol*, two string quartets, *Three Pieces* for Chamber Orchestra Op. 37, the small orchestral piece *Magna Mater*, and preparations for his next opera, based on Hugo von Hofmannsthal's *Wedding of Sobeide*. But this symphony was a milestone for him. It may also be considered an important example of European symphonism.

During this period (1927–28) Alexander began a process of creative self-examination in his letters to his parents. Almost immediately upon his arrival in New York Tcherepnin mentions the new work: "My head is exploding with musical ideas. And I have plastered ten pages (small ones) with musical figures.

Apparently the design and kernels of a future orchestra piece are being planned and discovered."[33] Still the word "symphony" does not yet appear, and will not for quite a while. Three days later, on April 23, he writes, "the *Wedding of Sobeide* has distracted me a bit from my orchestral ideas, but I'll work on these first, since I already have some germinal ideas—thank goodness!" A few days later comes a longer comment:

April 26.
> Worked very productively yesterday, managed two contrapuntal passages and got the first movement to a certain point of completion, i.e., about one-sixth of the expected length. The main thing is that this time I want to avoid paltriness. So I'll work quietly and with concentration, so that the form will be symphonic and spacious, even at the cost of less focus. And since I don't have to rush, my mind is clear, and themes are developing with various techniques; so I hope that with enough endurance and patience I can create a truly symphonic work, instead of the meager chamber pieces assigned to large orchestra, like *Magna Mater*. And such a big undertaking really inspires me now, and I feel free of all my reservations; I've thought about the form and now am gradually investing it with meaning. And after getting to the end of the first section yesterday, I got to New York in a relatively quiet state of mind. . . . Already some things are in my head—many ideas were buzzing around even during the car ride.

Tasks defined beforehand, technical solutions, as well as the initially unclear term "investment of meaning" seem to indicate work with "thematism" or whatever was intended to carry out this function. The slow progress of the work, to which the next letter testifies, is tied to intellectual efforts, such as the rejection, or perhaps loss, of spontaneity, but moreover with problems of formal construction.

April 28.
> All day was spent in front of music paper, and after eight hours I overcame a difficult twenty-six-bar passage. Today I will add a level of counterpoint to it. This will probably be even more difficult than the tasks I had yesterday and the day before yesterday, but more interesting. More and more orchestral tasks and opportunities are coming to mind; work with Grümmer on Reger and on my own stuff has awakened in me a desire and love for nuance, so that what I am doing now has a much wider horizon compared to what I did earlier.[34]

The May 1 entry concerns only technical questions but is quite representative.

May 1.
> Yesterday, as expected, the whole morning was spent finishing a difficult passage, and now I have some doubts about it: everything is divided into three groups, the first has four voices; the second, six or seven voices; the third, five. In the middle of each group the part writing is clean and complete within itself; but when placed on top of each other, this creates some parallel octaves. However, truth to say, these are the only parallelisms, since I avoid them. But I don't want to distort themes and alter the harmony in

order to get rid of them, and so I don't know what to do. I may leave it as is, because, after all, success in each independent group is already a certain achievement. And generally speaking, how are sevenths, seconds, fourths, thirds, or fifths worse than octaves? Dad, what do you suggest?

May 2.
Yesterday labored over and tinkered with the cancrizans music. Spent the whole day on it, and got so wound up that at night I continually woke up with solutions for one or another passage. Alas, the results were not so brilliant. To be honest, the form of this passage is well thought out, but whatever music I add ends up sounding trite. It either relies again on traditional forms and the canon, or else resembles a unison with the accompaniment.

Tcherepnin would continue to struggle against inertia:

May 3.
Worked very hard all morning yesterday and finally overcame the most difficult spot, even without the help of fugato or similarly automatic substitutions.... So today, after two weeks' worth of work, I am more than halfway through the first movement.... A lot of work still remains to be done, plus this is only a sketch; so a lot of time will have to be spent on the orchestration and the layout.

It is notable that, for the composer, orchestration is a separate step that belongs to a subsequent stage of the work process. This is also confirmed by his sketches. They are the skeleton, or the line drawing awaiting color, but are not directly connected to the composition, as is the case, for example, with Tchaikovsky.

May 6.
Spent all of yesterday working on my piece and, after completing an easy passage, managed six more pages. Now everything is clear until the end of the first movement, although much remains to be revealed—there is a week's worth of work left on the rough draft alone. Having mentally listened to the three-fourths which is done, I am still rather pleased both with the music and the length. It seems to last about eight minutes, the entire movement will have a fast tempo. It will not slow down even once, and on the contrary will continuously accelerate, which is unheard of for me. That is exactly the task I had set myself—not to be paltry. Besides, all eight minutes are pure development, since the themes are stated one by one in the first eight bars. Everything follows from them, and there are no repeats. The modulational and rhythmic planes are also developed, so I am generally pleased with the work so far and hope to complete a rough draft of the first movement within a week. I also have many ideas for the second and third movements but haven't started thinking at all about their development.

This struggle against paltriness and its conquest through special techniques testifies to a natural gravitation toward the miniature. Most striking is the constant combination of the intuitive and the conscious, with one or the other prevailing in different cases, and at different times.

May 11.
>   Gave it my all yesterday and at last completed a rough version of the first movement of the orchestra piece. Unfortunately I can't bear to think of playing through it since everything is written on small slips of paper and notes, and I can hardly even imagine it without interruption. But all the same, I take some satisfaction in the fact that I achieved what I wanted and followed through on what I had intended, that is, I realized my idea. Now I will get to writing out the full sketch of this movement and start thinking about the next one. When doing the sketch I think I'll simplify the texture, because I have built such skyscrapers in my dreams that you can't even tell which floor an idea is on! And in the end, all this is good, as it enlightens or deepens the thought, instead of creating a barely understandable mishmash. Among my small sheets of paper I have marked three spots where sophistication obscures meaning, and when I make the full sketch I'll fix them.
>
>   But yesterday I was in a very strange mood. I finished composing at about 3:00 o'clock, and from 4:00 on, no matter what I did, some sort of music kept rustling around in my head. I would remember it from time to time as though I were in a perfumed room, and I would be pleased. This lasted until late that night, and my head is still swimming from it, but not a single note of it is left, nothing solid remains! . . . Perhaps it was subconscious reflection on the next movement.

In the finale of the 1924 cello sonata, we find the use of bird sounds as "musical material." This may be the first time such sounds were ever used or, at any rate, one of the earliest occurrences. These appear again in the "history" of the First Symphony, and although they are not directly incorporated into this composition, their description is worth noting:

May 13.
>   Yesterday worked a lot on the second movement. Quite a few ideas have accumulated, and form begins to be clarified; but this will perhaps involve even more work than the first movement, because I want it [the second movement] to be interesting, well-constructed, and simultaneously filled with constant surprises. The birds of Islip are a big help to me, especially with the rhythmic aspect. I became acquainted with several, having overheard them yesterday. . . . What seduces me most in their art and language is that at the end of each phrase they reach some sort of rhythmic, melodic cadence—a punctuation point. Indeed the number of rhythmic interruptions before the cadences sometimes varies, though rarely; but the cadence always remains constant and signals the ending. And what is curious is that when you hear familiar ones, their rhythms are identical. Generally speaking, the second movement is moving along with the help of the birds, but this is only preliminary headway. Did not yet start writing the full sketch of the first movement.

The early development of the orchestral piece that would become the Symphony was repeatedly complicated by the distraction of *Wedding of Sobeide*. Tcherepnin was abridging the Hofmannsthal text to create the libretto.

> May 15.
>
> Yesterday was very unsuccessful. Spent all day at my writing desk, but ideas realized on paper brought only disappointment. And having written down what I had composed, I concluded that such music better suits the entr'acte to the third act of *Sobeide* than the central movement of the Symphony.

The same theme recurs in the next day's letter.

> May 16.
>
> Yesterday expended enormous effort on the second movement, and here is the diagnosis: having read too much *Sobeide*, I am probably instinctively under the influence of its plot. Consequently my brain operates on a whole different wavelength. It is like a river that has broken through a dam and flows in a completely different direction. . . . And yesterday, before looking at the *Urplan* for the second movement, I decided to finish it according to the form I'd kept in mind all along. To my surprise I became convinced that it is the entr'acte to the third scene of *Sobeide*. After lunch I sat down to work diligently on the old plan for the second movement, worked out some principles, then my mind started wandering again, and I ended up composing the beginning of *Sobeide*. Afterward I took a walk with Madame to the sea, which is unpopular here, to get some air. After we returned, again a whole page of music and materials for *Sobeide* emerged, instead of the second movement. So, after weeks of work, plus yesterday's significant achievement, I now have more than ten pages written, which are now in a special folder labeled "Sobeide." As for the second movement, I remain as far from its realization as when I started.
>
> Just before dinner, for the first time I had a breakthrough in the second movement and . . . finally established a plan: three paired counterpoints, counter-pointing among themselves, and each pair containing the largest possible distance between the voices. Formally this will be accomplished through successive statements of these themes. So I am now preoccupied with finding this threesome, consonant among itself in its disagreement, and once I establish them together, that is, discover their final form, I shall tackle the use of each one independently.
>
> The final solution is far away, certainly, but I'm glad I found enough self-criticism to realize that my work was headed down the wrong path, so I can reject something I had composed with passion but which belongs elsewhere.

This idea, which seemed abstract, was, in fact, executed as planned (musical example 4.2).

On May 18 a potential distraction arose, as Tcherepnin began contemplating a sextet for winds and strings. We will hear more about this never realized project, particularly in the discussion of Tcherepnin's Piano Quintet later in this chapter.

Example 4.2

The letters to his parents chronicling the birth of the Symphony betray the systematic implementation of Interpoint and the nine-step scale, although the composer does not explicitly declare this to be the case. On May 21 Nicolas Tcherepnin's reply to Alexander's May 1 letter arrives, and the younger composer responds:

> May 21.
>
> Dear Dad, what you write me about parallel octaves is very interesting. Unfortunately, looking at each level as a unison is not necessary, because each level is not a melodic line imposed on harmony but rather a common mechanical porridge. Yet I think that in the notion of horizontal logic, there is already something which undermines vertical verification; that is, it is preferable to leave a voice horizontally logical rather than to alter its logic with useless distractions that spoil the melodic structure and are, moreover, unnecessary for the ear. So I think I'll leave my layers untouched but will think about whether there are any unnecessary supporting voices that obscure the meaning; and if I find any, they shall be destroyed!
>
> Now I'll dig into the second movement. Different solutions are already spinning around in my head, and I hope to make progress.

> May 22.
>
> Tonight I'm writing to you again, to tell you that I attacked the second movement this morning and have now finished sketching it out. I played it through and howled with delight, because the whole thing is completely finished. It was clearly right to toss out the haphazard plan and resurrect the older one. . . . When I returned home I began thinking about what comes next. I already have ideas for the last movement; but since this thing is now becoming a symphony (!), it seems like it wouldn't be a bad idea to make an intervening link between the first and second movements—a fast, scherzo-like interlude, which will generally deepen the content of the second movement. This idea has already occurred to me many times since I decided to go back to the old plan. Now it has crystallized in the form of a scherzo for solo percussion: drum, cymbals, two small drums (with snare and without), a tambourine, castanets, and tapping on the body of a violin. The question now is whether it will be possible to sustain this material for a minimum of three or four minutes. If I can, I will do it; but if not, I'll have to let it go, because I don't want it to sound too contrived. The entire question is whether I will be able to find enough variety of combinations.

These and subsequent entries show a growing awareness that the composition being born was a symphony. Also evident was a conscious intention to include an interlude for percussion. Nicholas Slonimsky, the chronicler of twentieth-century music, remarked of Tcherepnin's first symphony: "Among his innovations, one movement of the Symphony in E (1927), written for percussion instruments of indeterminate pitch, outstripped Shostakovich and his interlude for percussion from the opera *The Nose*. The use of special performance techniques for the string instruments, especially with the stick of the bow, gives this symphony its experimental character."[35]

In his written reflections, Tcherepnin also comments on the pacing of the composition, a concept of artistic time that will remain essential to all his remaining works.

May 23.

It is only morning here, but I've already been working for an hour and have covered six pages for the new rhythmic percussion interlude, which I find very enjoyable. I think I'll manage to get it to a size befitting a whole movement without damaging the ear! Even strings are involved, hitting their violins with their bows! . . . I am sitting down with my score. . . . Spent the morning very fruitfully, work on the percussion movement goes well, only I'm afraid of resolving it in a way that is too improvisatory. So as not to rush, and thus risk infusing the movement with temperamental rhythmic filler when the music ought to be no less thoughtful than the adjacent material, I started simultaneously working on the fourth movement—a developing rondo—and unearthed a bit of material. All during breakfast at Mme Peters' [his mother-in-law] my head was full of the rhythmic movement, and I came home quite wound up. Now I've put down on paper what I was afraid I would forget. . . . Now I can get on with the work.

May 24.

Yesterday before supper worked on the percussion movement and accomplished a lot. It is now two minutes and forty seconds long, and I don't know how to lengthen it further—whether with a second trio or by expanding the coda. Today I'll think about that and start laying the groundwork for the fourth movement. Now, with it two-thirds finished, work proceeds more cheerfully. Plus the fourth movement should be lively rather than profound. And having burned myself out on the second movement, the joyful brusqueness of the fourth makes me especially happy.

The following entries complete the chronicle. They concern mostly the finale, as well as the Symphony as a whole.

May 25.

Yesterday worked persistently on the fourth movement. Set aside the percussion movement to ripen for now. After a whole day's work, successfully formulated the initial statement of the first theme. It's quite amusing. Also interesting that many things which I arduously crafted earlier, such as Interpointed themes, have now taken such hold of me that they flow out naturally. Managed to write a clever ending for the first theme, with syncopations. It serves simultaneously as an introduction to the second theme.

May 26.

Yesterday worked until dinner but not so successfully. . . . Nevertheless I produced some notes and plans, and reflected a bit on the manner of modulation, in order to better tie up some loose ends.

May 27.

Yesterday was spent like this, my darlings: in the morning I worked on the fourth movement, and after enormous effort, achieved development for the second theme. By virtue of its structure, the theme lends itself to development. Here it is:

Example 4.3

> Because it's so fanfare-like, the theme itself is too bright to be repeated a
> lot, but the accompaniment offers many opportunities. So after all my at-
> tempts to repeat it, I became convinced that it is best not to repeat but
> rather to develop. I have developed it into a sixteen-bar phrase. Where to
> go next has become much clearer, so by lunchtime I had found the central
> thread of the entire movement. Now all that's left is to work patiently along
> the charted plan.

Clearly the quickly conceived second movement is already inseparable from
the symphony as a whole. From this point on, all four movements are clearly
mentioned. Yet "squareness" is also described, usually with a negative conno-
tation.

> May 28.
> Worked all day yesterday and even after supper till about 10:30 on the
> fourth movement. Completed the second theme as planned out the day be-
> fore yesterday, finished the second statement of the first theme, and in the
> evening worked on the third. This last theme is quite square but necessary
> to counterbalance the irregularity of the first and second themes. But while
> working on it, I feel like I am solving math problems with rulers, mea-
> suring and joining staves. And since my head is swimming with this work,
> at night I dreamed that I was actually taking measurements to cut wood!

May 29 and 30 describe work on the coda of the finale, where the "struggle
against inertia" takes place in a characteristic way.

> May 30.
> Worked very intensively all day and got the last movement up to the coda.
> And since the coda should be a reprise [the fourth] of the first theme with
> something added, I was on the verge of rejoicing. But after thinking some
> more, I became convinced that such a solution for the coda would be a big
> mistake and would dampen its effect. So I tackled construction of a new,
> complex, syncopated coda.

The next day marks the end of the first phase.

> May 31.
> Yesterday applied myself to the syncopated passage and after lunch fin-
> ished a draft sketch of the whole symphony. Still it remains to be found
> whether it is possible to lengthen the percussion movement, [or] to alter
> one modulation. Then I will start filling out the full sketch. This will be
> rather difficult, since I will have to study some spots very critically and per-
> haps rework them. But when all is said and done, the first phase of work

is complete—the piece exists. But it is still, one could say, surrounded by scaffolding. This must be carefully removed, and then it will be possible to judge the entire building. So now the plan is this: I'll fill out the sketches, reflect on the sextet, read *Sobeide* now and then in order to collect material (for *Stenka* as well, as a distant future project), and beyond that, keep my fingers in shape.

The mention of the sextet, as noted above, never written, testifies to Tcherepnin's simultaneous involvement in numerous creative tasks.

June 1.

Yesterday . . . having spent an hour or two on ideas for the sextet, I started to write the sketch. Alas! I immediately realized that this entails not only copying out slips of paper, but a full processing and reworking of the musical threads! The first weaving of counterpoint turned out to have been hasty, written by the brain instead of the ear. I spent the afternoon and the entire evening until eleven laboring over it, accomplishing nothing. I shall continue today. But I already see quite clearly that everything is only in the planning stages, and the real work has just begun. This is even before the orchestration. Having realized this, I believe that to spend my energy on the sextet would be a mistake—the sextet will be bad and the symphony will continue to be rough. From now on I intend to work seriously and single-mindedly on the symphony, so that the full sketch will be complete with voice-leading, etc. The more effort I invest now, the easier it will be to orchestrate. . . . The work ahead is even more critical and creative. . . . I am rather happy about this, because dissatisfaction is the source of progress; and I think I have enough skill to produce a complete, well-made creation.

Although Tcherepnin continued his daily reports, he did not indicate progress until the following citation from June 5. This purely technical description represents a unique example of the focus of his conscious and purposeful compositional work.

June 5.

I was finally freed from the place where I had been stuck for five days. The difficulty was that I had composed a three-voice counterpoint and then had automatically doubled each voice at the major sixth, but stacked so that doubling went across three octaves. What emerged was a six-story building, where the voices either ran over each other or missed each other by such a distance that suddenly two stories were empty, etc. All this was set over a moving, quasi-ostinato bass that also got in everyone's way.

First I considered the three basic voices to be unchangeable, but this was the very mistake that forced me to struggle for so many days. Yesterday, however, I called one of the voices into question. And I began to work from the idea that only two voices were unchangeable. This turned out to be very effective. In the upper part were the three independent voices in two octaves, in counterpoint with one another, based on the first unchangeable voice. On the bottom was the second unchangeable voice with its counterpoint, first doubled and then alone in a diminuendo, with undoubled counterpoint; and between these layers a new fellow entered in a slower tempo—with the theme *en ralenti.* The bass could stay the way it was, without getting in anyone's way, and as a result the passage turned out to be a lot more complex than it had been but faultless in its voice-leading and structure.

Is this not a page from a composition textbook? Two weeks later, the elder Tcherepnin's "criticisms" arrived.

From among the numerous entries in this "Diary of a First Symphony," one entry contains doubts about the genre:

> June.
>
> From its chaotic appearance, the symphony is starting to take on musical outlines.... I am convinced that the label "symphony" hardly fits here. Even if the scope is symphonic, the material is insufficiently deep; or, more precisely, operates on a plane different from that of a normal "symphony." It's more like an expanded concerto grosso, for large orchestra. So I am thinking of calling it: "Concerto for Orchestra," with sections titled Toccata I—Toccata II—Adagio—Rondo. That will first of all be more appropriate and, second, will save me from the instinctive fright of publishers and conductors!! Also, true sonata-allegro form basically doesn't exist in this work. Ideologically this piece is more connected to the Chamber Concerto than to any symphonic tendency.

The following entry shows how a twentieth-century composer is helped by theoretical-harmonic analysis of a composition in progress.

> June 10.
>
> The initial sketch (more or less finished) is ultimately not too bad but has a casual character. It might have been otherwise. In order to avoid this sounding accidental, and to make it definitive, it was necessary to find some other approach, some other criteria. And having battled all morning without finding it, in the afternoon I discovered a starting point.... I did a harmonic analysis of the busy violin section, and calculated the possibilities for expression of the themes. Having done that, it became quite easy to add on or, more precisely, to select a version for each little theme. And now, in my opinion, the whole thing became convincing and logical. Yesterday I bought scores of Beethoven's Sixth and Eighth Symphonies for study.

Despite all the apparent, rational construction of the work, there are also sudden, spontaneous intrusions. During a conversation with his wife's visitors on June 13, Tcherepnin was flooded with musical ideas for a potential fifth movement.

> June 13.
>
> But since I would need bells for this, I'm afraid, if I follow through on this idea, that I'll make this symphony un-performable once and for all, and bury it. Besides, I'm also afraid I will change the style. But just in case, dear Daddy, what kind of bells can one expect to find in a normal orchestra? The idea is basically this: to balance the overall form after an andante, it wouldn't be a bad idea to also have a concertino similar to the percussion

one. And since I wish to similarly use "special" instruments for this, I am in fact wondering if here I shouldn't use a glockenspiel, that is, bells, campanelli, perhaps celesta (for speed), timpani, tam-tam. But this is still far from decided. Because such a movement would be a real departure from the style, and especially since I wouldn't use all these instruments anywhere else, I think I'm not likely to do it. But just in case, Daddy, please still tell me the range and notes for normal bells. And one more thing: is it possible to tune the low timpanum (G) up to B? In order to have B–C–D?

This sonoro-dramaturgic idea did not last.

June 14.
Yesterday I applied myself to editing the third movement, and by 11:00 PM had worked the whole thing into the sketch. But, to be fair, this was because I was much more careful than when I was composing the first movement. So the editing involved no more than a correction of voice-leading in two spots, and all other corrections were made while writing. So three-quarters of the entire thing is already in a clean sketch, and I hope by next week to be finished with that. . . . and then comes the orchestration. After deep reflection I rejected the idea of a fifth (fourth) "bell" movement as too out of character. And an entire second concertino would make it sound too deliberate, whereas the percussion movement poured out as naturally from the musical materials and the thought process as did its neighbors.

Five days later, on June 19, after several days of laborious editing of unsatisfying passages in the draft sketch, Tcherepnin wrote, "I shall start on my score. I cannot wait to finish the sketch and get to orchestrating. Have some doubts about the strength of the coda, which ends a little unexpectedly. Maybe I'll change it."

In a lengthy report the next day, the composer describes his attitude toward orchestration as a kind of "coloring in": "Now orchestration will not be so difficult, mainly because every note of the sketch is believable. And the task of orchestration shall no longer be to adjust what was composed but to make the composition more vivid and convincing" (June 20, 1927).

Alexander described the process of orchestrating to his father, whose knowledge of the orchestra as both conductor and composer was masterly.

July 3.
This morning I will try to concentrate my full attention on orchestrating. Two weeks have passed since the completion of the sketch; that was how long it took me to orchestrate *Magna Mater*—but I'm still only at the beginning. The first passage was solved by dividing all the strings (except for contrabasses) and assigning them an eight-voice counterpoint. Against this background the woodwinds play the main idea—flutes and oboes in octaves and clarinets with bassoons. For the sake of unity the second bassoon played the bass note, and then began to move at the same time that the first bassoon landed on the following bass note, but supported by the tuba. The French horns had their own figure—a sustained note with rhythmic character. And by the end, everyone except the tuba let go of their held notes

and cadenced via light counterpoint into the next key. At the same time the muted cornet, with accents on each note, cut through this fog with an independent voicing of the theme *en ralenti*. Trombones were not invited to participate at all. Small problems nevertheless emerged—the oboe ends a little unexpectedly; the fourth horn ends with a contrapuntal jump a sixth above the second horn. These are all questions for you when you look at the score. What disturbs me much more than these things, which are after all just details, is the layout of the unison with which it all begins. Here it is, Dad. Please tell me whether this beginning is convincing:

In this unison I eliminate the first octave in the woodwinds in order to allow the theme its characteristic jump.

At the same time I don't give the brass the first unison in order to reserve freshness for the answer in the French horns. The first and second violins are in unison in the second octave for more strength, and I don't move them higher, so that the opening will feel more natural and secure. Finally, I don't continue to lower the cellos and contrabasses, so the unison will retain a lighter, more luminous character. I don't fundamentally doubt this reasoning, but have great doubts about whether it will be convincing enough for the ear, and whether such a beginning might sound thin and rather weak. So I ask you, dearest Dad, to tell me whether such a unison will be brilliant in *fortissimo*, and whether such an orchestration will be consistent with my ideas! And, if not, point out to me where I have made a mistake. . . . Considering the significance of this oeuvre in my catalogue, I shall not blanch at the long process necessary to complete it, and I'll do the following: I will now write out the score as honestly and fully as possible. I want the orchestration to correspond completely to the content, and I want the music to be vivid.

The next day another veritable treatise appears—on orchestrating different sorts of compositions (chamber versus symphonic) and on the "experience of self-knowledge":

July 4.

Linear counterpoint, when it doesn't rely on a harmonic foundation, as in Wagner, produces the poorest and least interesting orchestral music. When uncomplicated, it produces doublings or pallid sounds; when complicated and multi-voiced, it sounds like an organ. Emphasizing the voices by doubling is boring and unpersuasive. In music like that, the different registers of the instruments can be colorful, but these achievements are usually sacrificed to linear logic. The result is that such music fares best in chamber style. It is very difficult to find techniques that will convey a growing counterpoint texture for a symphony orchestra, which has outgrown chamber style by its very nature. The technique for making such music interesting is to find alternation of groups where the musical content can provide a temporary chamber form, as a counterbalance to the tutti flowing out of the content—in a word, to use all possible light and shadow effects.

But as soon as the music turns from being contrapuntally linear to contrapuntally thematic, i.e., when themes are developed rather than stated, entirely new opportunities open up. And all at once it becomes very

Example 4.4

Example 4.5

easy, i.e., such music suits a symphony orchestra quite well. . . . In brief, I have prepared my sketch in the same way that Premazzi would complete a watercolor, having delineated every blade of grass, every leaf. I am convinced that assigning my sketch to an orchestra is as inappropriate as painting theatrical scenery with Premazzi's techniques.

And it is precisely this contrapuntal completeness of the sketch (nothing added, nothing taken away) that makes the orchestration even harder than if the completion of the chaotic material were directly orchestrated with full consideration for each instrument.

But the very idea of this symphony was, so to speak, a return to the Chamber Concerto, a return to pure music, in contrast to *Mystère, Message,* the Second Quartet and *Magna Mater.* This pure music is complicated by

Example 4.6

the techniques used in these five pieces, but its task is essentially only musical, organic. Therefore the difficulty of the first movement in particular
stands in complete contrast to the difficulty of my works from the previous
year and a half. But having completed this symphony, I am making a point,
so to speak. I sum up the techniques in order to go further, since destiny
seems to be pulling me in other, more natural directions. One might say,
"the cold storage before *Sobeide!*"

The orchestration of the First Symphony was finished on July 18 along with
several minor changes to the coda. In spite of his vast documentation about this
symphony, the composer never mentions his working according to a "system."
Still the use of *Interpoint* and the nine-step scale serve as a key harmonic foundation, and underlie the content and development of the entire work. Note the
final chord (musical example 4.6).

Despite the laborious process of its creation, this twenty-five-minute-long
symphony—contrasting, dynamic, and fascinating—creates the impression of a
work that was written "in one breath."

The premiere, which was conducted by Gabriel Pierné, took place in 1927 at
the October 29 Colonne Concert. It is surprising that the Paris public, already
accustomed to so much, was shocked. Thanks to the help of Dr. A. Lichké this
author received a copy of a review by René Brancourt in *Le ménestrel*. The reviewer finds that the work "not only does not belong to the art of music but appears to be its absolute negation." He continues:

> I speak of Mr. Tcherepnin's "Symphony in E"—although I should not have
> thought that this work belongs to any key at all. I am convinced that the com-
> poser, some smart aleck, wanted to make fools of the respectable public. In-
> deed, several dozen snobs bravely took the bait, repeating after the model of
> Lucas in *Le médecin malgré lui* "this is so good that I cannot understand any
> of it." But the adventurers were unable to carry with them the greater part of
> those present, who had come to the Châtelet to listen to music.
>
> However, everything is shaped by place and time: the first movement,
> for instance, would be remarkably suitable for a play about a revolt in a
> madhouse. . . . The second movement is essentially a concerto for percussion
> interspersed with sounds produced by the wrong side of the bow. This move-
> ment, which could undoubtedly be included in the repertoire of some fair-
> ground spectacle, is not without considerable refinement and elegance. The
> remaining two movements are, unfortunately, not so entertaining. I suspect
> that the composer found it necessary to display his inner poet, which mani-

fests itself in the love duets between the passionate oboe and the highly moral trumpet, and also in the endless solos, now on the violin, now the double bass, which recall two reptiles filled with a desire to put an end to their fruitless solitude.... In conclusion, we can thank the composer for so successfully stigmatizing cacophonous music through his deliberately exaggerated caricature—although it will not help him win a place on this well-traveled road.[36]

La revue musicale certainly did not ignore this musical event:

This symphony, aside from the protests of a certain public—the one which always suspects youth and novelty of being nothing but the expression of rowdy youngsters—earned some calm and measured reproaches. These emanated from critics, or composer-critics, who cannot be suspected of taking a stand against all modernism. Thanks to his gifts, his accomplishments, his ingenuity, and his verve, Mr. Alexander Tcherepnin has certainly often been considered, even here, as one of the hopes of the current school. For him we did not economize on respect and encouragement. This work still bears, from start to finish, the trace of great compositional care, veritable asceticism (as some think), powerful orchestral coloring, guided usually by large-scale plans lacking details and frivolous embellishments, and nevertheless curiously combined with an entirely sudden harshness of timbre. A seething polyrhythm full of youthful allure alone directs the development of an entire movement, treated like a concerto for percussion instruments. But all the same I see a rhetoric in this manner of expression deliberately encumbered with a multiplicity of classical counterpoints; others have given us examples, they were merely men, not orators. I notice, and this is a more substantial point, some ostentation in the audacity, often naïve and with the seams showing, which disturb me. And as there is so much promise in this work, one listens to it with mixed feelings. It seems to me that the author would benefit from composing less than he does at present. I have already remarked on his excessive fertility; one cannot force the ripening of real music, but in any case it is also essential to think it through sufficiently.[37]

Alexander's parents regularly sent him numerous reviews that appeared in the press. In the 1970s Tcherepnin wrote Shneerson:

In 1927, after I created the second movement of my First Symphony without defined pitch, and assigned it to only percussion instruments and violins tapping on their instruments with the wood of the bow, its first performance took place at the Colonne Concerts in Chatelet, conducted by Gabriel Pierné. It caused a memorable scandal. The majority of critics pounced on me, but even sympathizers didn't realize that in the percussion movement I had reduced the theme, figures, and motives of the first movement to their purely rhythmic, untempered essence! I simply wanted to free myself from the purely conventional division of the octave into twelve semitones and from certain tempered sounds, and to create music "beyond good and evil," i.e., without pitch. Now, with the expansion of the concept of music, the problematical character of this movement has disappeared. What had seemed so daring now appears quite well founded. Perhaps that is why this symphony has been performed more and more frequently in the last ten years. I even conducted it in London at the request of the BBC, and several years ago at the behest of Berlin Radio. Stuckenschmidt told me then that, to his knowledge, no symphony before mine had ever contained such a movement for percussion, and "a cappella," and he actually gave me a fake "diploma" for being the first![38]

Even in his last years Tcherepnin included the First Symphony in draft programs, including those devoted to the "Tcherepnin Dynasty."[39] A diary entry from 1967 recounts, "in the morning a lecture about my 'composing kitchen,' titled, for some reason, 'Intropoint.' More people than at the first one. But Monti did not manage to arrange a good performance of my First Symphony."[40] The site of the talk, somewhere in Europe, is not specified, but the mention of the First Symphony is notable.

The First Symphony Op. 42 was preceded by the Second String Quartet Op. 40 (1926) and followed by the Piano Quintet Op. 44 (1927). In genre, style, and even language, these latter two compositions reflect Tcherepnin's creativity during these years. The composer wrote a series of liner notes intended for phonograph recordings, which are in fact creative documents that characterize not only the compositions but their creator. His annotations convince the reader, from the composer's point of view, that perception of a creative composition is the task of the listener, through his perceptive abilities. The task of the composer is to make music, so his musical composition contains nothing but musical notes and accompanying marks—merely some equivalent to the flow of music and an explanation of how it should be performed. These liner notes provide insights into the epoch as well as the author. The firsthand comments reliably characterize in detail other chamber works unknown to the reader— presumably pieces from the second half of the forties. Tcherepnin actually prefaces the notes with a brief and relatively simple description of the "system," which sheds some light on this.

> From earliest childhood, when I composed instinctively and was not yet trained in traditional harmony, I had a propensity for modal sounds, which combined major and minor; and in the four-note, major-minor chord (C–E♭– E♮–G) I felt a completeness and finality similar to that which classical composers attributed to the major triad. The major-minor sequence—step-and-a-half, half-step, step-and-a-half—was then extended and created a hexachord: C–E♭–E♮–G–A♭–B–C.[41]

Describing further all the possible combinations—ascending and descending motion, different combinations and transpositions—the composer gives a picture of the major-minor foundation of the nine-step scale with three tonics. Later in the same note he characterizes another important aspect of his compositional system.

> As opposed to impressionism, which was considered vanguard in the teens of the century, I searched for clarity in my compositions, and still do today. In Tiflis, in the late 1910s, I already felt that polyphony was a means of ridding music of pretentiousness, saccharine qualities, and harmonic fogginess. . . .

Gradually my original type of polyphony, which I called *Interpoint,* was developed. In contrast to classical counterpoint, which has notes against notes, *Interpoint* has notes between notes. *Interpoint* can be vertical, i.e., truly note between note, or horizontal, when the bar line is different in each voice, it can also be esoterically mixed by varying the duration of contrapuntal phrases in different voices.

The nine-step scale, *Interpoint,* clarity, conciseness of forms, these were my musical baggage, my musical credo, when in August 1921 I got off the Marseilles train in Paris at the Gare de Lyon and, after three years in Georgia, settled in Paris.

In Tiflis, after an infatuation with pianism, I found chamber music to be the most suitable form for realizing my musical tasks. . . . The most complex in texture and the last chamber piece in this group is my Quintet Op. 44, composed in the fall of 1927 immediately after the First Symphony, whose premiere in the Colonne Concerts conducted by Gabriel Pierné caused a memorable scandal and produced contradictory press responses.

Quintet in three movements.

1. *Allegro* in sonata form. The two-bar piano solo comprises the "kernel" of the first theme, melodically based on a sequence of three notes: B♭–B♮–G. This opening is later developed on many levels. The second theme, in contrast to the first, is broad, melodious, and expansive. It begins in the low register of the cello, passes to viola, to second violin, and ends in the high register of the first violin, with constant support from the piano and the strings not charged with playing the theme. The piano accompaniment and short coda continue to develop through elaboration of uneven rhythms in the piano, whereas the first theme, which is in horizontal *Interpoint* between the instruments . . . develops through expanded rhythm. After a climax in eight-voice *Interpoint,* the development proceeds by stages. The piano develops the theme in eighth notes, in 7/8 meter; unison strings develop the inversion of the same theme in quarter notes, in 7/4 meter. Then the strings divide, and while the violins stay in quarter notes, the viola and cello sound the theme in its basic form in half notes, i.e., in 7/2 time. To counter this, the basic theme moves to an even more extended meter in the left hand of the piano, in notes equal to seven eighth notes; then meters (rhythms) begin "narrowing," first to 5/8 in horizontal four-part *Interpoint* in the strings against 5/4 in two-voice horizontal *Interpoint* in the piano; then 4/8 in the strings against 4/4 in the piano; and, finally, 3/8 in the strings against 3/4 in the piano, resulting in a very short recapitulation compared to the exposition. The ending extends into a new coda, with pianissimo strings playing a regular quarter-note pulse, which serves as background for the gradually emerging themes in the piano. The coda ends with an eight-voiced chord reiteration of the first theme in the piano, to which the strings answer with the "missing" ninth voice (G).

2. *Allegretto.* The theme is first played by pizzicato cello, with the piano in *Interpoint.* The *Interpointed* voice follows this initial statement first melodically and then harmonically in the piano, while the strings create a new *Interpoint* to the existing one. The texture becomes very complex in the middle of the movement, where the strings in four-voice horizontal *Interpoint* are vertically opposed to the piano in four-voice horizontal *Interpoint.* The thematic mate-

rial develops freely and leads to the coda, which ends with a piano fanfare in *Interpoint,* answered by the cello. Strings play pizzicato throughout.

3. *Allegro.* This movement is monothematic: the theme is first stated in its entirety; then the end of the theme is played cancrizans, i.e., backward, which creates a second theme; after that, the beginning of the theme is also played in retrograde, which creates a third theme. A diverse rondo as well as a broadly developed coda is built on these three "versions" of the same thematic material, using all manner of vertical, horizontal, and esoteric *Interpoint.* Tonally the quintet is based on the nine-step scale.[42]

In a first perusal of this exclusively "technical" description of the quintet, it is useful to note some key concepts: "thematic," "melodic," and "harmonic" development, and "tonality." Based on a nine-step scale that is written out each time in the sketch, the musical world of the quintet does not betray the slow, laborious work that produced it, nor the quite rational complexities of its construction, evidenced by the composer's comments. Its Hindemith-like motoric quality promotes the dynamic expansion and energetic pressure of the first movement, which is as long as the next two movements combined. The middle movement has the character of an intermezzo, beginning and ending with an expressive dialogue between piano and cello. In the finale, the composer's efforts result in tonal cohesion and density. Here we also find Tcherepnin's inherent attraction to music full of motion and unexpected contrasts.

The quintet had originally been prompted by circumstances which Tcherepnin shared in a letter to his parents:

> An American magazine has announced a big music competition in Philadelphia, open to all nationalities, for composition of a chamber music work for ensembles of three to six instruments. There are three prizes of $5,000, $3,000, and $2,000, with a January 1 submission deadline. The jury consists of local composers whose ideals range from Debussy to Wagner, so the idea of applying doesn't seem promising to me, but why not try for it after all? Last night I had the idea of a sextet for flute, English horn, French horn, viola, contrabass, and percussion. Such a grouping would give a very original, dark color to the piece, and at the same time allow me to use many techniques of larger orchestration and counterpoint over many octaves, which currently occupy me. But the only question is where to find the time, because I'm tied up with the orchestra piece until July, then comes 'Sobeide' and preparation for concerts. And yet it would be really fun to write such a sextet. (May 19, 1927)

This sextet remained unrealized, but after the completion of the orchestra piece, which became the Symphony, Tcherepnin reported to his parents on the progress of the quintet in letters from September to December of 1927. Since the summer months were spent near his parents, the early stages of the composition are not documented in correspondence. Despite very slow progress at times, the composer did not abandon the idea of sending the quintet to the competition. "I'm becoming more and more convinced that I cannot complete the quintet. It's really a pity, although my chances of a prize are very small, since my sort of music does not easily arouse enthusiasm. All the same, it is a pity!" (November 6, 1927). That same day Cassado, "the owner of a Stradivarius," came over to play through some of the piece. From November to December 1927 the chronicle of the Quintet is rather extensive. With the deadline as stimulus, Tcherepnin works madly to complete the piece.

> December 23.
> Yesterday I spent from 10 in the morning till 11 at night entirely on the quintet. There is so much to do there, but I was able to finish the second appearance of the second theme, its transition, the first return of the first theme, as well as the return of the second theme from where I had stopped before. All this I managed to enter into the rough draft. Today I shall try to work on the coda, without worrying about details. But I have nightmares just thinking about how much is still not clarified, and that a week from today is the final deadline for sending a clean manuscript plus all the parts!

On the 28th the composer describes his emotional attitude toward the piece:

> Dec. 28.
> I work tirelessly, or, I should say, I'm getting tired but not getting any rest. The day after tomorrow I absolutely must send it off. It's now 8 o'clock in the evening and I am approaching the coda of the finale, and, on the way, I am really falling in love with the Quintet—much of it is very convincing.

Finally, two days later, he writes:

> Dec. 30.
> By midnight yesterday everything was done—a remarkable tour de force, since the writing of the clean manuscript began only on the 25th! That is, the entire business took five days. *Interpoint* is my motto here. There are *Interpoint* themes, so the motto also clarifies things. And to prevent my being recognized if by chance someone on the jury knows my music, the major-minor scale is renamed "scale of three linked tetrachords." This, by the way, is much more correct terminology and allows its essence to be grasped better and more quickly. . . . God Speed, though I am quite convinced that this music is not for an American jury. . . .
> But in the course of this forced revision of the Quintet and its fast clean up, I learned to really love this opus, which is truly a quintet with *Interpoint* texture, in which each instrument performs an individual task and has its own face. And furthermore the form is broad and well developed, i.e., a step forward after the scantiness of the Trio.

The premiere of the Piano Quintet would not take place until 1930 in Copenhagen, where it was performed by the composer and the Vienna String Quartet. Alexander recalled that at the performance the leader of the quartet, Rudolf Kolisch—a pupil and relative of Schoenberg—opined that Tcherepnin's system was essentially similar to dodecaphony. However, the genesis of the system as we know it, and the reality of its sound, shows that this is not the case.

At the same time, composition of *The Wedding of Sobeide* proceeded full steam ahead. Reflecting on the experience of working in the piano, chamber ensemble, symphonic, and theatrical genres, Tcherepnin arrived at some generalizations. An important fact, in his opinion, was familiarity with his father's opera *Vanka,* which was notably far removed from the complexities of Alexander's own musical creativity and that of his European colleagues. Perhaps a kind of artificiality began to manifest itself owing to a lack of connection between what he had accomplished and his individual character as a composer.

> In the business of *Sobeide,* it is now certainly too late to change the three whales on which it stands.[43] But one can surely see that four different genres— the symphony, the quintet, *Message,* and *Sobeide*—all affirm my idea. The difficulty I had composing this piece perhaps reflects the exceedingly small range of possibilities to which I limited myself. *Vanechka* [*Vanka*] has certainly played a role in this understanding. And after the completion of *Sobeide* I will take a break from composing in order to search for additional whales, free of the weight of these compositions. Then my work can take on an element of freedom and enjoyment that it now lacks. (September 11, 1928)

"Earth and Fate," as a line from Pasternak says, would propel him forward.

Appendix

Contemporary Music and Alexander Tcherepnin
VIKTOR BELIAEV

Though Russian music is still very young as a national music, it has nevertheless already managed to pass through several stages of development— stages that are clearly and precisely identified. One of these, the so-called New Russian school, ended before our very eyes with the era of Glazunov. Like any historical period, its ending was characterized by a culmination of style and an attainment of technical skill not reached previously. Because of inertia, the latter is, in itself, still capable of developing in ways that are foreign to such a movement. One example is the work of Nicolas Tcherepnin, foreign to the New Russian school but connected to it by succession. Although his work developed in the tradition of the New Russian school, it decisively broke away in search of new artistic ideals. Breaking with this school, however, did not cause Tcherepnin to sever his connection to its tradition of mastery. He saw his new creative mission as the engineering of more complex, refined composition, whose essential elements he borrowed from [that tradition]. In this respect, on the one hand he was a child of these musical fathers, and on the other he was responsible for the overthrow of artistic foundations on which his early creativity was based. But his act of overthrowing produced a negative rather than a positive effect, for he was unable to tear himself completely away from the old traditions, and only partially "discredited" them aesthetically through his later creative work.

What Nicolas Tcherepnin did not manage to achieve, the younger composer

Igor Stravinsky achieved brilliantly. Stravinsky began composing within the bosom of the New Russian school but then followed Tcherepnin's footsteps by breaking away through technical complexity and refinement. But he did not stop along the way as Tcherepnin did. Indeed, he went further and arrived at the creation of a new style, whose main feature was rejection of complexity and a turn toward primitiveness. This must be unequivocally considered the style of our new musical epoch.

That primitivism is the style of our epoch is abundantly clear from a whole series of phenomena. The birth of a new musical style during this time is extraordinarily interesting. As contemporaries, we cannot understand all its details; but we can nevertheless ascertain that it is an epoch of palpably rougher musical tastes and ideals, particularly in Western Europe. I believe I am not mistaken in saying that the sense of true depth in musical creativity is now lost in modern Europe. Its striving for musical primitivism expresses hope of respite from the creative pressures of the previous epoch, but at the same time it is the result of a desire to forget ourselves amid the harsh, unstable conditions of postwar life. Thus modern European primitivism acquires a hedonistic character, distinct from the serious primitivism of Stravinsky. If we look more deeply at modern European primitivism, however, we find that it contains various national shades that do not change its essential character.[44]

The work of Russian composers now living in the USSR [1925] lies in a completely different direction from the work of Stravinsky and his contemporaries. The music of living Russian composers is predominantly psychological. They take their inspiration from the depths of the mind rather than from a desire, like that of the Western-European primitivists, to represent the world in a different form. Having dug deeply into psychology and introspection, Russian composers now disregard the development of musical form. In this regard they follow trails more or less blazed by their predecessors. For their European colleagues, however, formal and constructive questions stand perhaps in the very foreground of art. The hedonistic musical outlook equates creative ease with levity, which is then renounced. This notion is completely alien to Russian composers.

We find the following state of affairs in modern music: on the one hand, inertia, expressed by growing complexity and the deepening of old traditions, and, on the other, a desire to create a new style by rejecting these traditions, even though the new style is evolving from elements of the old. The latter tendency characterized the younger generation of composers, to which Alexander Tcherepnin undoubtedly belongs. In recent years, not only has his stature grown, but he has taken a notable place among European composers.

... [Alexander] Tcherepnin's compositional talent appeared at a very early age. By the time he was admitted to the conservatory (where he would not stay long), his "portfolio" contained no less than six piano sonatas and a proportional number of smaller works. The works he has authored since then include an opera (*Ol-Ol*, on the plot of *Days of Our Lives*), a ballet (*Ajanta's Frescoes*), two concertos for chamber orchestra, two piano concertos, two [piano] sonatas, and *Georgian Rhapsody* for Cello, violin sonatas,[45] [cello] sonatas, as well as songs and other piano pieces.[46] In all, about 130 works.

From the very beginning of his career, he declared himself an adherent of a new direction in music. He refused to follow in his father's footsteps, and rejected the "psychologism" peculiar to many Russian composers. Staying in Europe helped him identify his creative ideals much more clearly, and he began to cultivate his own simple, naïve style. Although this style belonged to the new epoch, it was deeply tied to the artistic ideals of previous epochs. Yet its expressive manner is distinctly different.

Tcherepnin, unlike his father, did not go through a period of rebellion against established traditions. Nor did he, like Stravinsky, go through an evolution from an old style to a new one. It is as though he were born already in the new style, which is why it seems to be a natural part of his creativity. Not having experienced the temptation to refine his style or render it more complex, he did not introduce elements of the past directly into his work. Tcherepnin did not experience the tragedy of rejecting the old, and he did not accept the idea of "innovation in principle." At the same time he came under one of the most integral and vital influences—that of Prokofiev, who exuded all the positive qualities that distinguished Russian composers from foreign ones. Exposed to this healthy influence, Tcherepnin did not lose the spontaneous or childlike qualities of his writing, which contains a Haydnesque or Mozartean element of innocence. But the Russian influences on Tcherepnin are not limited to Prokofiev. His music reflects some influence of Mussorgsky, and, although it may seem strange at first, of quite conservative composers like Medtner. These diverse influences created an interesting situation for Tcherepnin, who imparted to Western European music some Russian musical ideas that would not have taken root in their original form.

Being a Russian composer in essence and a primitivist in manner of expression, Tcherepnin is linked through his musical language with new European composers, with whom he also shares the task of solving technical and formal problems. These common interests do not reflect emulation. On the contrary, they derive both from features of his own creative persona and the conditions of modern music that we now observe. Identical needs bring about identical results, and identical purposes bring together artists in identical fields.

Tcherepnin's position as a composer connected modern Russian music with that of modern Europe. What are the personal features of his work that distinguish him from other Russian composers? In his first forays into composition, one notices some lack of experience in musical structure. This might be construed as an inherent lack of feeling for form, if seen primarily from the viewpoint of older, traditional structures, which demanded "solid" works and "solid" sizes. But, in fact, what might have once been a handicap could now be considered an advantage in the new "primitive" style. In Tcherepnin's early efforts one can already observe tendencies that became fully developed in his later work. Even in larger works such as chamber concertos, he uses only the simplest forms and treats them with great skill and originality. This resembles the practice of the earliest German classicists at a time when form was more flexible and not yet so crystallized.

Along with the rest of the modern musical world, Tcherepnin turned to the classics. This marked a return to a new starting point, which was the only way to achieve the goal of musical progress. Indeed, where did the systematic development of Wagnerian or Straussian principles bring us, if not to the complicated, *ne plus ultra,* enormous orchestral device which we now possess? But must musical progress really turn from quality to quantity? Will not this progress, after a certain point, no longer be progress but regress, a reduction of musical content in favor of the physiology of sound? A new direction in music, primitivism, definitively declares its refusal to participate in the quantitative progress of music. It declares the slogan of today and the near future to be the struggle for qualitative progress of music. Its starting point is not sonoric luxury but an interest in the intrinsic value of the musical idea itself, regardless of its musical embellishment.

In step with this wave, Tcherepnin does not renounce his native artistic beliefs in the realization of his principles and remains very original. One of the most distinctive features of his music is its harmony, characterized by an extreme simplicity that truly distinguishes him from other modern composers. The modern position on harmonic creativity is very complex. The contemporary crisis in harmonic thinking has brought to life the widespread use of two terms, unknown before our time: "polytonality" and "atonality." These, however, do not in themselves exhaust the complexity of modern harmonic tasks. Almost all modern composers can be assigned by critics and the public either to the group of polytonalists or that of atonalists, depending on the complexity and harmonic singularity of their works. To be a tonal composer today means to be unmodern, obsolete, lagging behind the century and the era. However, Tcherepnin manages to be simultaneously both a modern and tonal composer, and in this respect is a rare and happy exception. Unafraid of primitive Haydnesque or pre-Haydnesque forms, (a very arbitrary description of Tcherepnin's forms), he does not shy away from simple harmonies or typical modulations. He uses them with extraordinary spontaneity, which results in tremendously fresh impressions. In addition to Tcherepnin's lack of fear of simple harmonies, he is also unafraid of minimal sound, and frequently limits himself to two- or three-voice construction. In contrast to his polytonal and atonal contemporaries, Tcherepnin almost exclusively uses the nine-step, major-minor scale of his own invention (D–E♭–F–F♯–G–A–B♭–B♮–C♯), and most often ends with a D tonality. This scale, extremely simple in its construction, is also extremely fruitful in an artistic sense. Through his versatile and skillful use of it, Tcherepnin once again proves that the sonic vision of the Russian composer is quite distinct from that of his Western-European colleagues. Indeed, where the latter see harmony as artistically worn out and stale, and thus direct their thoughts toward a circle of clichéd harmonic relations, the Russian composer finds an abundance of harmonic treasures. It seems to me that this phenomenon is the foundation of Stravinsky's innovations. Where Schoenberg lacks sound combinations made of all twelve half-steps of the octave, Stravinsky achieves new effects through simple two-voice combinations.

The basic psychological tone permeating all of Tcherepnin's works is a deep artistic innocence and spontaneity that allows him to approach creativity in an entirely new way, from unexpected points of view, which are completely different from those of "serious" musicians. He builds upon a strong foundation in the traditional use of musical tone but interprets this in a gallant, "secular" sense. Tcherepnin's songs are not heavy, German, through-composed Lieder (i.e., songs with a semantic musical task carried out from beginning to end) but rather are light and gentle watercolors that capture fleeting, simple, graceful feelings. There is even something Korsakovian in them, if one removes the formal and emotional dryness inherent in Rimsky-Korsakov's abstract song style. Tcherepnin's piano pieces are extremely picturesque, with tender, seductive intimacy. This intimacy is not the intimacy of a secret revealed by the composer and of revelations from the depths of the heart, but rather it is the result of a natural sociability and naïve frankness. Tcherepnin is no anchorite or hermit hiding from others in the depths of his creative feelings but instead is a pleasant and brisk interlocutor who proves even more brilliant in the society of numerous friends who surround him. This contributes to his being fresher and more impressive in forms such as the concerto and brilliant compositions for the stage than in works that are more closed in character. Here he is both brighter and braver, with the courage of a talented novice who is not yet affected by automatic reflex or life experience, and is strong by virtue of his natural gifts.

The freshness and spontaneity of Tcherepnin's response to the world are the positive qualities of his creative persona, as are his remarkable and unique talent, inquisitive pioneerism, innocent artistic "fearlessness," and elegant, refined musicality. All this allows him to adeptly navigate modern life.

Antithetical to Russian composers who use their work to resolve psychological problems, Tcherepnin expands the range of Russian musical creativity to unconditional and unobscured musical optimism. We are indebted to him for this critical and precious contribution.

November 22–27, 1925, Moscow

Nicolas Tcherepnin, during Alexander's childhood, St. Petersburg.

Alexander and Ming Tcherepnin with two of their sons, Serge and Ivan.

Tcherepnin with his wife, Ming, and singer Chow Shiao-Yen, after a concert of contemporary Chinese music, London, 1946.

Tcherepnin with composers Yenin Yuasa and Akira Ifukube, Tokyo, 1936.

Alexander and Ming
Tcherepnin with Igor
Stravinsky and Aribert
Reimann, Berlin Festi-
val, 1961.

Alexander rehearsing his violin sonata with Yehudi Menuhin for the BBC's fiftieth anniversary celebration of Tcherepnin's first appearance in London.

The Tcherepnin family gravesite at Sainte-Geneviève-des-Bois Cemetery on the outskirts of Paris, France.

Historic plaque on Rue de Furstemberg in Paris, marking the building where Tcherepnin lived.

5   The Four Corners of the Globe

This Near Far East

> After a fortnight's voyage from San Francisco, aboard a transpacific liner, you approach the coast of Asia. The Yellow Sea, colored by the mud of one of the world's largest rivers, has really turned yellow: picturesque fishing boats, with typical eastern sails, begin to surround you; in the distance there is a faint line of land—your first glimpse of China. The coast grows more distinct. The steamer at last enters the broad estuary of the Yangtze.[1]

Thus began Alexander Tcherepnin's description of his travel to China in 1934. This trip was planned as a dizzying tour: China, Japan, Singapore, India, and Palestine.

It was not his first tour to distant countries. In 1931 Tcherepnin had visited Egypt and Palestine. His interest in Eastern music, ethnography, and history continued to grow, and was tied to his Eurasian ideas. Such an interest had already appeared in letters to his parents in the late 1920s. In May 1927 he wrote, "Spent two hours on a history of China. Very interesting and I shall write about some of these things."[2] While reading Ivan Sakharov's book, *Travels of Russian People to Foreign Lands,* Tcherepnin copied out, for a letter to his parents, a large fragment from the 1468 diary of the merchant Afanasii Nikitin about the exoticism of India and its inhabitants (August 31, 1928). On June 25, 1927, he described how an artist-friend of his wife's "began to talk about her travels to China. . . . She brought many things from China and Siam that have sparked my interest in traveling there." The next morning Alexander went to look at her paintings of her travels.

Elsewhere in the article about the 1934 trip (in which he was accompanied by his first wife and stepdaughter), Shanghai appears as a city with "American-built skyscraper hotels" but filled with music displaying national rhythms and sonorities.

> Chinese native music is based on the natural pentatonic scale, is melodious, lyric, and highly varied. . . . Chinese popular songs are monodies. When they are accompanied by an instrument, the accompaniment is built up horizontally—the instrument playing the melody from start to finish, and the voice joining in unison with it at the most important spots. Even in the more complicated instrumental music, no deliberate attempt is made at harmonizing the melody or at building up a contrapuntal combination of any kind. In native Chinese music, there is no harmony or counterpoint, as we understand it. But in an orchestra each musician has to play the same melody according to the capacities and register of his instrument. This results in a "false doubling," which, together with the variety of the often syncopated rhythms played by the percussion instruments, creates a sort of native polyphony peculiar

to Chinese music. The form of a native tune consists in perpetual variation of the same melody; a musical phrase is never repeated exactly, the melody always progresses, a change in the fundamental tone replaces modulation. Ingenuity in melodic invention seems never to cease, and when, toward the end of a piece, the movement grows faster and faster, the melody adapts itself to the new rhythm. There is a fascination to this type of "everlasting" melody. It is a device that should prove useful, on occasion, to our composers.

Shanghai, Tcherepnin reported, was the only city that had a symphony orchestra, and the only one with a conservatory, newly opened. "So far only four students have graduated, the first of them being the gifted pianist and pupil of Mr. Zaharoff, Miss Lee Hsien Ming." Here lay his destiny: future wife, mother of his sons, and devoted proponent of his music. As the composer describes it, music education in this conservatory, and in the music department of Peking University, was based on Western models.

Shanghai had a large colony of Russian émigrés, among them Boris Zaharoff, a friend from Petersburg. The composer and teacher Aaron Avshlalomov also spent many productive years in China, ending in the late 1940s. He composed numerous works on Chinese themes and texts, into which he incorporated traditional instruments such as the pipa and erhu. Symphonic scores were transformed by his use of these native sounds and musical genres of his adopted country. The Tcherepnin archive contains clippings from several Russian newspapers in publication during the period of his visit. One of them, undated, is titled: "The Composer A. Tcherepnin Speaks about His Work. A Special Interview for the *Shanghai Dawn*." After describing the life of "the renowned Russian composer," and his successes in Europe and the United States, the reporter inquires about the purpose of the visit.

The composer reflects for a minute. "I would like you to carefully consider what I am about to say." He finally says, "I traveled here because my work required it. A long time ago, when I was still a child, I remember listening to village singing with my father, true national song in which the national soul is so clearly reflected. In this simple, innocent singing there is something that can endlessly inspire our work. In it is the source, the beginning, the basis of any music. Unfortunately such simple music is almost impossible to find today, when composers don't write how they feel but only how they were taught, when layer upon layer of artificial culture obliterates the essence of our spirit. Now in most cases the city prescribes songs to the village, which the villagers then obediently repeat. I wanted to find a place where people still sing in their own way, with the internal voice of the soul. I believe that I will be able to do this here, in the Far East, where I have arrived in pursuit of a dream. I have already heard fragments of some primitive melodies. . . . I have written these down and perhaps they will form the basis for a new phase of my artistic development. I don't know, perhaps I will be disappointed, or perhaps I will find a new path, waiting to be discovered. . . . There's one more reason why I came to search for this in the East," he continues in the same thoughtful tone. "I do not want to label myself Eurasian or any other ready nickname which still cannot reflect my deepest beliefs. I just want to say that, in my opinion, we Russians are not really Europeans, no matter how much some of us may object to this. Russia has not banished Mongols. She threw off their yoke and assimilated them."

Tcherepnin's activities in China and Japan reached far beyond the concert hall. Despite breaks of one or several months, he stayed over a period of three years, from April 1934 until April 1937. Inspired by artistic, pedagogical, and educational ideas as well as projects, he contributed enormously to the development of the national schools of both countries. Thirty years later he would speak of this work to a Russian friend:

When I was in Shanghai for the first time, i.e., in 1934, I was struck by Chinese traditional music. I was saddened by the fact that when Chinese composers began composing for internationally known instruments (piano, violin, orchestra), they composed music that derived nothing from Chinese national or traditional sources. To encourage them in this direction I set up a competition for piano compositions that reflected Chinese traditional music or folklore, open to all Chinese composers. I arranged this with the Chinese National Conservatory, through their director Hsiao Yiu-Mei, with whom I had become friendly in Shanghai. Pieces were submitted under pseudonyms. The jury included Hsiao Yiu-Mei, Huang Zi, the provost of the conservatory, the pianist Boris Zaharoff and, I believe, the theorist Aksakov in addition to myself. The first prize was unanimously awarded to the piece *Buffalo Boy's Flute,* whose composer turned out to be He Luting [in those years transliterated as Rodin Ho]; second prize was awarded to *Shepherd's Pastime,* composed by Lao Chih-cheng; and, in addition, an honorable mention was awarded to the still very young, fledgling composer Liu Xue-an, for the piece *Crazy.* I especially admired the piece of He Luting, a two-voiced invention whose structure resembles fine brick masonry. I recorded it together with Lao Chih-cheng's piece for the Victor record label. I tried to find a publisher for the pieces. But at that time nobody in China, or even abroad, was interested in modern Chinese music, and my attempts were not crowned with success. So I founded my own publishing company, under the name Tcherepnin Collection. Since it was difficult to find an engraver and note printer in China, I had [the sheet music produced] in Japan. The first composition issued was that of He Luting, and I chose a figure of a young shepherd sitting on a buffalo while playing a flute as the logo for the publishing company, which corresponds to the title of the piece.

I maintained the publishing company until 1937, and in four years issued more than forty works of modern Chinese and Japanese music: songs by Liu Xue-an, piano pieces and songs by He Luting, and chamber works by Lao Chih-cheng. (The Chinese did not write orchestral music at that time.) I also published the works of numerous modern Japanese composers. Among these were scores by Ifukube and Matsudaira that had won prizes in [my] competition for orchestral works by Japanese composers, piano pieces and songs by Bunyah Koh, Yasuji Kiyose, Yoritsune Matsudaira, Kojiro Kobune, Toshitsugu Ogihara, Tadashi Ota, etc., and the traditional *Etenraku,* transcribed for orchestra by Hidemaro Konoe.[3]

I performed piano compositions of Chinese and Japanese composers throughout China, Japan, America, and Europe. I also assigned the American distribution of my publications to the Schirmer Company, and the European distribution to Universal Editions. Everything in Japan was lost during the war but copies of most of these works are still available here and there. . . . Both in appearance as well as concept, I was imitating Belaieff Publishers. The names of the pieces and the composers were written in three languages on the cover: Chinese (or Japanese), English, and Russian. The covers were gray, just like Belaieff's.

In Japan and China I also worked in earnest to help educate young pianists and composers. I devised a piano method based on the pentatonic scale, which helped teach Chinese and Japanese musicians to remain true to their own heritage.

Regarding my pupils, as far as I know, He Luting is now director of the Shanghai Conservatory. Ting, who studied with me after the war in Paris, is also a professor at Shanghai Conservatory. Ifukube, Matsudaira, Ogihara, and Kiyose have earned international recognition and are respected composers in their native land. So this work has not been in vain.

During his stay in China and Japan Tcherepnin worked on a second act for Mussorgsky's fragmentary opera *The Marriage.* He finished it and performed the two acts for the Russian Society "East." He often played Russian music—from Bortniansky to Stravinsky, including his own piano concertos. His involvement with the cultures of the Far East yielded important results for Russian, Chinese, and Japanese musicians.

The instructional pieces for piano (Op. 53) received wide circulation for many years, along with other, more complex concert works—such as *Hommage à la Chine,* which Tcherepnin often included in recitals. As late as 1945, still full of the Chinese aesthetic and musical atmosphere, he composed *Seven Songs on Verses of Chinese Poets* Op. 71. He translated the texts into French and Russian himself. And in the mid-1950s he arranged seven national songs at the request of the Chinese singer Si Yi-gui.

Upon his return to China after one of his trips to the United States Tcherepnin again gave an interview to a local Russian newspaper, which ran under the headline, "Europe Takes an Interest in Chinese and Japanese Music." The interviewer writes that "the talented Russian composer A. Tcherepnin will write an opera based on Chinese life."[4] This opera was actually composed in 1945 and revised in 1952. Comprising two scenes, it lasts only three-quarters of an hour and yet represents a complete, staged work. Based on the Chinese text *The Nymph and the Farmer,* it has only two characters. Along with *Hommage à la Chine,* it is the most impressive of the "Chinese" works and contains exquisite music. An aria sung by the nymph is also one of the best examples of a "continuous" melody in Tcherepnin's work.

In the above 1936 interview, Tcherepnin speaks of Western interest in music of the Far East. "When I performed works of Chinese and Japanese composers in numerous concerts in Germany, France, England, Holland, and the United

States, the public's reaction clearly showed that the novelty and freshness of Eastern creativity will quickly take root in musical circles there."

Besides the compositions mentioned previously, the ballet *The Woman and Her Shadow* (with a libretto by Paul Claudel, influenced by Japanese Noh theater), evokes traditional Japanese music, and the Fourth Piano Concerto (*Fantasy*) is a sort of suite whose individual movements correspond to a Chinese poem.

In the Far East, just as in Georgia, Tcherepnin was the first Russian composer who did not simply visit or pass through but lived there long enough to digest national life and national art. The result in both cases was an organic assimilation of characteristic features of both the musical language and the broader musical thinking, wonderfully "concurrent" with historical tendencies and individual aspirations.

Numerous articles and dissertations, most of them by Chinese scholars and musicians, are devoted to Tcherepnin's activity in the Far East. His name and legacy remain deeply respected, and both the composer's music and his treatise *Basic Elements of My Musical Language* testify to the deep influence of Eastern experiences on his work.

This internationalist phenomenon had many antecedents in European culture, both recent and distant. In 1829 Goethe wrote an article titled "More on World Literature," which built on his earlier piece "About World Literature" and asserted the necessity of mastering the artistic ideas and forms of all humanity.[5] The question lay not in the negation of national literatures but on their elevation and globalization, the inevitability of which Goethe linked to the increasing effectiveness of "means of transportation." Nor did Goethe limit himself to Europe—"world literature" is not an inaccurate formulation; already in old age, he still learned Persian, wrote the *West-East Divan,* and took a great interest in Chinese literature.

The first example of European musical Orientalism appears in the mid-nineteenth century. Valentina Konen analyzes the link between European musical Orientalism and a new phase of music history. She cites two names in particular, Mussorgsky and Debussy, who fundamentally transformed European musical thought, especially in the harmonic sphere.[6] Both these composers and the cultures that produced them—Russia and France—had a direct influence on Tcherepnin.

We have already discussed Tcherepnin's ties to the Orientalism of the Mighty Five. But he was also familiar with a whole galaxy of composers besides Debussy, such as Ravel, Roussel, Dukas, and Milhaud, who all appreciated musical exoticism. A natural comparison can also be made between Tcherepnin's and Messiaen's compositional systems. Messiaen, however, was less influenced by Japanese music and not at all influenced by Chinese music. Indeed, his major Orientalist work, the *Turangalîla* Symphony, was composed in the last half of the 1940s.[7]

Other Tcherepnin sources flow from the culture of the Russian Silver Age:

the poetry of Balmont and Gumilev, the art of the Diaghilev Seasons, and the World of Art group in general, such as Leon Bakst's costumes and decors, not just its music. Some of these influences did not represent the highest level, such as the work of Sergei Vasilenko, who was friendly with Nicolas Tcherepnin and Sergei Gorodetsky, and in 1916 wrote his *Exotic Suite.* Arthur Lourié's *Japanese Suite* and certainly Stravinsky's *Three Japanese Lyrics* were also sources. Nevertheless, among not only Russian but European composers generally, Alexander Tcherepnin was the first to delve into the fundamental properties of Far Eastern musical thought and language, rather than treat these as merely exotic local color. "You have managed to connect East and West in your art, as in your life,"[8] wrote Milhaud, in an anniversary catalogue issued for Tcherepnin's seventy-fifth birthday, which contained greetings from many leading international musicians.

On Both Sides of the Atlantic

When Alexander Tcherepnin left for the Far East, he was already famous as a composer and pianist. He often performed Russian music, especially his own, and his popularity in Europe was reflected in frequent newspaper reviews. Existing recordings (especially a compact disc of two of his piano concertos) confirm his excellent and original pianism. His popularity in Europe is reflected in plentiful press comments.

Tcherepnin's ballets were widely performed. His operas were also staged in Europe as well as in the United States, although the *Wedding of Sobeide* was produced only in Vienna. His first opera, *Ol-Ol,* enjoyed substantial success, as evidenced by responses to one performance in Zagreb in 1933, where it was shown in a single evening together with *Bird-Maiden,* which Nicolas Tcherepnin called *The Bewitched Bird:*

> Alexander Tcherepnin, the young thirty-four-year-old Russian composer, is a fighter, a representative of the avant-garde musical movement. Yesterday his one-act opera, *Ol-Ol,* received a very sympathetic response, indeed fanatical recognition, among our youth, who uphold Osterc, Kogoj and Bravničar as their musical examples. . . . Alexander Tcherepnin is closely linked with Prokofiev, and we know that he leans on *Love for Three Oranges* and on Mussorgsky's *Boris Godunov* for support. . . . He has vast technical experience in Asian-Slavic styles, a developed and vivid imagination, and the ability to create powerful contrasts of musical color. If in the sphere of pianism he is a great performer, and a composer rich in ideas for compositions, in his opera *Ol-Ol* he is original, magnificently colorful, and as deep as an Eastern philosopher. Words take priority in this opera. . . . A central aspect of *Ol-Ol* is the recitation, a certain realistic spoken singing. Only the chorus of the students, one aria of the despairing Gluhovtsev, the "last word" of the officer Grigori, Olga's (Ol-Ol's) final statement and the final chorus of the students are constructed of sung melodies.[9]

After its premiere in Weimar in 1928 and performances in Leipzig, Dresden, Stuttgart, Prague, and Belgrade, the opera crossed the ocean in 1934. Here it was performed for the first time in Russian, in New York, mounted during a season of Russian opera at the Casino-Theater, together with Tchaikovsky's *Iolanta*. This was actually the American premiere of both operas. The reviewer compared the plot of *Ol-Ol* to Puccini's *La Bohème*.[10]

From the mid-1920s until his final days, Tcherepnin's life unfolded on both sides of the Atlantic. In his consciousness and musical perception, Europe and the United States did not get along well with each other. Until the 1950s, especially while his father was still alive, the composer gave unconditional preference to Europe, especially France, and adjusted with difficulty to the language, culture, and psychology of America. To a certain extent this attitude persisted until the end of his life. "Paris for me," he wrote in the 1970s, "is perhaps the most 'natural' city to live in; each turn is familiar, close, dear for the memories of all that was lived through there, all that was felt, where I feel absolutely at home."[11]

During his earliest stay in the United States, in 1927–28, the composer felt especially isolated and distant from his environment. He wrote his parents in July 1927, "I dream of stepping, one month from now, onto sweet, native French soil" (July 12, 1927). He wrote about a visit to a school in Boston where someone from Lousine Weekes's family was studying.

> Having walked through the school, we then watched a game of baseball. The game is rather complex. Something in me always protests against sports and physical pastimes. Looking at these young idiots gamboling in the fresh air like piglets—people having the opportunity thanks to material means (these are all children of rich families) to contribute something to the spiritual part of the country, and instead destroying any concentration, any idea with foolish, low-bred displays of physical, forceful instincts—watching this game, in many respects I understood the reasons for such a low cultural level (in the sense of creating cultural values). (May 8, 1927)

He attended a production of a Robert Browning play in a New York theater and felt that "the drama was not very convincing (seventeenth-century Rome), and was terribly performed with growls, gestures, and unnaturalness surpassing any bounds. It all resembled a farce, a parody. Americans are only able to present thrillers, but when some transformation of the epoch or work of the writer is required, they do not feel at all at home; compared to them, the Comédie Française is a miracle of naturalism!" (May 23, 1927). An American Revue aroused these impressions: "Instead of grace there is force; instead of dances, gymnastics; instead of singing, whispers; instead of wit, foolishness" (July 28, 1928). Most damningly, he writes, "the maximum dose of America for the cultured person is two months" (June 28, 1927).

The contrasts softened over time as life in America changed. Enjoying home with Lee Hsien Ming and the children, being afforded recognition as a composer in the United States, and especially teaching at DePaul University in Chicago, his attitude altered significantly. And yet he was still somewhat hesitant, as the following diary entry from September 1975 attests:

> Yesterday I took the biographies of Smetana, Bruckner, Mahler . . . and the stories of Faulkner out of the library. At home that evening, flipping through Faulkner, I somehow clearly felt how little interest or attraction I have toward America, and how all that is American, including music, seems trite to me. Why? I do not understand it at all. After all, I love America, have seen a lot of the good and the kind here (but also enough of the bad and unkind), and I am grateful to America for having enabled me to find my financial footing. I have grown linked to America, i.e., our children became Americans. . . . Faulkner, however, I did not read but only looked through. But I began to read the biography of Smetana. And here I felt again how little connection I have to the Czechs. . . . Again I do not understand why. I saw a lot of goodness from Svoboda, from Kubelik, was such great friends with Martinů, liked being in Prague, in Brno before the war. And among all the Slavs, Czechs were the closest brothers of Russians; and cultural exchange with them by Russians was the most interesting; so many good Czech musicians were active in Russia—Suk, Napravnik, the director Paleček, etc., etc., and the love was always mutual. On the contrary, and also mysterious, is my love for Austria. Today when I started reading Bruckner's biography, sobs rose in my throat, after simply encountering the names of Austrian villages, provinces, and cities.[12]

But visiting a country and living there are quite different, and on the threshold of the 1950s, as Tcherepnin began permanent residency in the United States (later receiving U.S. citizenship), much changed. The diaries of his American years reflect an ever widening circle of interactions in the New World. Naturally former Russian ties were renewed, but new and close ties also emerged and strengthened. Thus, arriving in New York on November 20, 1961, Tcherepnin stayed for several weeks in the empty apartment of Elliott Carter. On a subsequent day he visited Leopold Stokowski: "He said that he had first perceived *Georgiana* [Tcherepnin's Orientalist orchestral suite quarried from his contribution to the 1945 collaborative ballet *Chota Rostaveli*] as a purely folkloric creation, but after having studied it, delved into and performed it, he recognized me in it. Similarly it was a big success with the audience."[13] In those days the Tcherepnins organized a reception in honor of Virgil Thomson. There were many such encounters and friendships with American and European musicians.

Most important, the work of the Russian composer was in demand. He received many important commissions, and his works were being performed. In one of his letters to Grigori Shneerson, with whom he constantly corresponded, Tcherepnin wrote:

> The Fourth Symphony Op. 91 was composed in 1957 as a commission from Charles Munch and premiered in Boston in 1958. Since then it has become one of my most performed works, appearing on programs in Europe, both

Americas, and Australia. I even conducted it in Manchester last summer. In the middle movement there is a misprint of the metronome marking—it's supposed to go twice as fast as the indicated speed.

Symphonic Prayer was composed in 1959 for the opening of the American Festival in Chicago. The premiere was conducted by Eleazar de Carvalho, and the piece was repeated on closing night. I was not in Chicago at the time, and the directors of the festival changed the title without my permission, listing it in the program as *A Prayer for Peace*. As a result, I learned from the press and witnesses who reported to me that the performance at the closing concert was accompanied by a peace demonstration. This is also one of my most often performed pieces.[14]

Tcherepnin enjoyed teaching. His diaries after 1949 record daily preparations for lessons, including the study of Ludwig Bussler's works. A 1949 entry notes that, for a counterpoint exam, his student Robert Muczynski presented "inventions on my themes," reflecting the influence of Tcherepnin's musical language.[15] Another pupil, Phillip Ramey, who also had close contact with such leading American composers as Copland and Bernstein, has written extensively about his teacher.[16] Enrique Arias, author of the previously mentioned bio-bibliography of Tcherepnin, attended Tcherepnin's music classes at De-Paul University. He wrote about Tcherepnin's symphonies and musical style for various publications,[17] and also recorded his impressions of the composer in his book.

His classes in music history were a joy. Tcherepnin used to lecture in a small but crowded classroom on the fifth floor of the building that housed the Music School, right in the center of Chicago's business district. He would enter, drape himself over a desk at the front, sitting at an awkward angle. After asking how far he had gotten the last time, he would proceed with his narrative, always from memory but always full of facts and specific citations. It was not so much a lecture as a story, a story of major composers, important works, styles, and forms. He spoke simply and slowly in his own brand of curious English with a noticeable Russian accent. All our notes reflected his style of lecturing. But no one had difficulties understanding what he said nor what he meant, for his illustrations were always to the point.

Whatever the subject of discussion, he was at home with the material or composer. To this day I am surprised at the width of his interests. However, he was at his best when he came to the later nineteenth and twentieth centuries, especially the Russian school. Then he spoke with the special authority of one who not only read history, but lived it.

There were certain points of view that he emphasized as being his own. For example, he felt there were two major composers of the nineteenth century who prepared for the revolutions of the twentieth: Liszt and Mussorgsky. Liszt, he noted, was evolutionary, growing out of the tradition of Schubert, Beethoven, Bach, and earlier; Mussorgsky was revolutionary, creating an individual harmonic style and sense of form. Tcherepnin always mentioned the Coronation Scene from *Boris Godunov* with its overlapping dominant seventh chords and augmented fourth apart, as the classic instance of Mussorgsky's innovations. Beethoven, he would say, resolved his dominant harmonies in a linear, logical manner, but Mussorgsky put dominants on top of each other, thereby creating thick, dissonant structures. Yet Mussorgsky and all those like him were also a part of a tradition, a tradition of Russian liturgical music. Tcherepnin explained that the Russian fondness for modality and non-functional chord progressions mirrored what liturgical composers did as late as the eighteenth century. Church music in Russia never became completely tonal the way western church music did in the time of Bach. Instead it contained older scales, speech-like rhythms, and quasi-improvisational chord progressions.

He found Western music sometimes too structured, too concerned with systematic procedures. Bach's *Well-Tempered Clavier* was a magnificent accomplishment; but it stood for tonality and for equal temperament to a dangerous degree. Although Tcherepnin admired Schoenberg's music, he felt the serial technique restricted. Tcherepnin preferred Mussorgsky's approach, with its freedom to explore the possibilities of the moment.

All of these views were a result of Tcherepnin's avid interest in culture and general history. Throughout his life he was an expert book collector, amassing an impressive number of unusual books, particularly in Russian. Also he made it his business to study the culture of the place he was living in—Paris, the Orient, and Chicago. He contributed to that culture by organizing concerts of younger composers' music, by working with the established artists of the area, and by encouraging the development of gifted musicians.

Tcherepnin's impact on the musical life of the Midwest was tremendous. During his DePaul years, he was an active member of the Midwest chapter of the International Society for Contemporary Music. He gave frequent performances and lectures throughout the area and came to be identified as the resident spokesman for contemporary music.[18]

In the late 1950s Tcherepnin resumed teaching in Europe and went on to give numerous international seminars. In April 1962 he wrote in a letter to Schneerson:

> I shall now stay in Chicago until the end of May, will be in Paris in June, and then will teach composition again at the International Academy in Nice in July, then in August at the Mozarteum in Salzburg. In both cases I teach in four languages: French, German, English, and Russian; and pupils come from all over the world. I used Russian to teach Serbs, who did not know French. I would be happy to accept any young Russian composer who would like to be in my class: it is easy to arrange a grant. (A stipend is given for tuition and living expenses.) If you think there is interest in this, I will send you brochures for both schools.[19]

But, alas, for obvious historical and political reasons, no Russian composers ever appeared in Tcherepnin's classes.

Alexander continued living "on both sides of the Atlantic" for the rest of his life. A third site was added to the two regular sites of Chicago (later New York) and Paris: Marlowe, England, on the Thames.

Alexander Tcherepnin often sought out nature, both during periods of intense work and on his brief and rare vacations. He sent descriptions of these places from different ends of Europe.

> Rest in the Pyrenees! A long-desired respite. I write you from a door that opens onto a wide balcony—marvelous air, pure, dry; a view of mountains covered with green bushes. In the distance one sees Mount Canigon, with traces of snow on its peak; one hears an orchestra of cicadas, birds in the morning, and a chorus of frogs in the evening. Peace and goodwill! I am composing children's pieces for the piano. Already handed one to the publisher who commissioned it, and others are "for the future," for "new beginnings." These are like small blocks that can be rearranged, repeated, or omitted at will: aleatoric moments and formulas, a game of registers, from contrasting musical phrases to pauses of precise duration, pieces with codas that one can lengthen or shorten at will, etc., etc. I am greatly enjoying this and have now written eight pieces at a technically simple level, accessible to children. They prepare the young pianist for problems of musical notation. So much needs to be done in this direction. Inexhaustible opportunities.[20]

Living at the home of the pianist Margrit Weber in Bäch, Switzerland, while composing his Sixth Piano Concerto, Tcherepnin writes:

> A quiet lake, reflecting the sky; a hilly coast that turns green on one side and is dotted with white houses. Spring and the peal of bells are in the air. Nature awakens from the dead, comes to life, and grows. It is bright and cheerful food for the soul. This landscape is accompanied by a diverse "score" which contains sounds of all sorts of divine creatures who inhabit that world, especially birds.[21]

Another letter from 1968 describes his new Marlowe abode:

> For the first time I am spending the summer in an English village, and I am very glad to be here. A small but cozy cottage is surrounded by a not very large, unpretentious garden. I take many walks along the Thames, along footpaths, through fields and woods. There are marvelous centuries-old trees here. . . . Everything makes me well disposed for work. In the early morning there are exclamations and roulades of birds.[22]

In his correspondence Tcherepnin never fails to report the piano's manufacturer: Bechstein, Steinway, etc.

Ships, trains, letters, telegrams, and long-distance telephone calls all played a prominent role in Tcherepnin's life as he straddled the Atlantic. One must also not forget the radio. His comments about listening to music on the radio and his notes about sound transmission quality are captivating. They betray a curious enthusiasm, an almost mystical attitude unimaginable today, that simultaneously sheds light on the creative process. Back in 1928 he noted:

> Mommy dearest, you wrote splendidly about the radio. I am of the same opinion, and this increased influence that music has over ordinary life knows no bounds. It is especially true because this instrument is cheaper by com-

parison than any other, and yet has the greatest variety of potential uses. Undoubtedly its biggest influence will occur only when it is considerably improved. But the mere fact of these musical vibrations and this unité of our globe are already something profound in what I would call a religious sense; and the inspiration for Schumann's *Fantasie,* taken from Schlegel, seems particularly appropriate here:

> Durch alle Töne tönet
> Im buntem Erdentraum
> Ein leiser Ton gezogen
> Für den, der heimlich lauschet.

> [Through all the sounds that ring out
> In earth's multicolored dream
> One quiet tone persists
> For the one who listens in secret.][23]

And music turns from an abstract art into a physical, tangible vibration. What I have always felt, which I think all composers share, is that from among many choices we have opted to find particular relationships. And what we experience sometimes, when for days or weeks we nearly kill ourselves struggling over one passage or one interval, is the moment when our construction does not respond to this radio-reality.[24]

Tcherepnin was frequently called a musical citizen of the world. He surely deserves to be called a musical citizen of the twentieth century.

6   In the Composer's Workshop

This chapter, like Tcherepnin's *Basic Elements of My Musical Language* in appendix 2, is addressed to readers knowledgeable about music theory. Widespread familiarity with these materials would lead to their inclusion in the canon of important theoretical texts on twentieth-century music. They can also serve as useful tools for those interested in researching the creative process. For this reason I have allowed the composer, wherever possible, to speak for himself about his aesthetic views, specific works, and compositional phases.

> In my opinion, the composer conveys in music what he receives from the society where he lives; his mission (though not prescribed) is service to society. Certainly service should not be understood in the sense of echoing bad taste but the expansion of "taste."
>
> The composer's means of expression are limited to a certain extent by the cultural standard of the society in which he lives and to which he belongs. . . . The composer's mission seems similar to that of the preacher: it is positive and has as an objective the union of people through art. Art in modern society has replaced religion, especially music, which is somehow connected to sound waves (those accessible and inaccessible to human hearing) of the universe.
>
> When I start to compose, I "hear" nothing at first, I only feel, just as a pregnant woman feels the presence of the child conceived in her. Only gradually does the "material" arise that seems to me to transpose the "unheard" soundings to the sphere of the heard—and only then does truly conscious, constructive compositional work begin.
>
> On the one hand, the universe is the source of creativity; on the other, society is the source. The distant and the near, which is why the near acquires a deeper sense. In my opinion, there is no music of the past or future (in the sense of an approach to modern creativity); there is only music of the present, a sort of thermometer of the state and cultural development of a society. The composer, true to people and to his mission, builds "in time" and also "characterizes" his time. Thirteen and a half minutes of Bach's *Passacaglia* record forever thirteen and a half minutes of Bach's epoch. In the same way, thirteen and a half minutes of the first movement of Schubert's *Unfinished Symphony* have forever recorded thirteen and a half minutes of Schubert's epoch. And they painted a picture true to the original, because they live and continue to live.[1]

For his compendium, Benjamin Folkman assembled the following collection of Tcherepnin's remarks on compositional creativity, culled from various sources, including the maestro's autobiographical typescripts, lectures, interviews, essays, and correspondence.

There are Sunday painters; but there could not be Sunday composers. Borodin was probably the only exception. . . . But, as it is said, the exception confirms the rule. . . .

✳

In a pattern (or theme) there is an embryo of its growth, just as in a human seed there is an embryo of the future human organism—blood, bones, arteries, etc.

✳

I know nothing; I feel.

✳

Creative ideas are in the air and we composers are antennas. We pick up these ideas and somehow prove their validity.

✳

A composer or performer never has to stay where he does not want to stay; his field of action is unlimited and his "home" travels with him. . . . Homesickness is unknown to one who loves people, is at peace with himself, and feels that he has a mission to fulfill.

✳

People are more united by music than by any other art. You go to an exhibition and look at pictures and it's an individual experience; at a concert we are sharing a common interest and feeling.

✳

Nobody really understands music. Technique? Yes, maybe. But music? Never. It can only be heard and felt. Without that it is nothing. It is completely meaningless unless it is played.

✳

People like to say they can tell about a composer's moods or his state of health and such things from his music. I am always suspicious of such claims. I have devoted my life to music, and, personally, I do not believe that such a direct relationship exists. If there are exceptions, they are probably intentional.

✳

A composer composes whether he is commissioned or not. It helps, of course, if he can count on some remuneration. He must live, after all. But his real reward is in the performance of his work.

✳

The masterpieces of prewar music are still with us: "modern" yesterday, "classified" today. But the general tendency has been revised. The ideal of the 19th century was to be strong and profound. The ideal of the first half of the 20th century—to be new. We have inherited the aim of the first and the language of the second.

✳

The music which fixes the present is the music that will live in the future.

✳

Art must reflect its epoch, as Van Gogh reflects his time and Picasso reflects his. Yet art must stand apart from the movement of the epoch or suffer the stigmata of localism instead of universality. The very crux of the problem is that the artist remains stable through it all, and how then can he reflect an unstable epoch?

120   *Alexander Tcherepnin*

At each epoch of musical history there were limitations in musical speech due to the standard of the composer's cultural environment. But there were and are no limitations to the deepness of a composer's thought.

*

I always preferred city to countryside. It is the city and human beings that inspire me to work and not the chickens, cows, and trees.

*

I can only compose when I "have the itch." My work is much more intuitive than calculated.

*

I wish the day [were] twice as long and my gray matter twice as alert.

*

Good music is good, no matter what the means, and bad music is boring.

*

Serialism is a means to an end, and to that extent is valid. . . . Unfortunately it can act as a cover for mediocre talents that have little natural inspiration but can construct a perfectly logical, and therefore defensible, serial composition.

*

Personally I accept every medium of musical expression—it is not the medium that "makes" the composer but the composer that makes any medium acceptable by writing good music.

*

I never had a continuous perfect pitch—at some moments, especially when composing, I . . . enjoyed perfect pitch, while at certain other moments the color of the tonality often escaped my attention and I heard everything in a relative pitch.

*

A composition method is useful: everyone can become a composer: the only important thing is the right approach. What is usually considered as "gift" is the right approach plus work.

*

Anyone who understands English should be able to write a letter in that language; anyone who can read music should be able to compose it.

*

The greater the talent, greater must be the work to materialize the potential that it has.

*

A composer is to a certain degree a computer. You see, if you put a program in a computer it will produce music according to that program. And in order to produce a new composition, the composer has always a kind of technical program in mind that he will use. Now the difference between the mechanical computer and the composer computer is perhaps that what the composer computer does is a compromise between this program and his ear and way of thinking. . . . Now to tell you honestly and truly, in some pieces I forget what the program was after I become accustomed to the music . . . and when I am playing these I am not thinking of the program that produced them but

mostly of a kind of sentiment or inner content of these pieces that I am trying to project while playing.

*

I believe in the "reality" of music, in its "existence," in the world of music
that is just as realistic a world as the visual one. The visual we can "touch" by
seeing it; the musical one we can "touch" by hearing it. Sometimes, when in
my attic I am deeply sunk in composing, the reappearance of the visual world
in the form of an opening of the door and a dear person entering seems to
me like a "ghost"—so different are the dimensions. Scares me and gives me a
shock. So I am sure that the world of music "exists" and that a composer has
to "listen" and to take the "existing" material to construct with it, just as an ar-
chitect constructs houses, churches, orchestra halls, and bars out of "existing"
stones or wood or whatever else.

*

When guiding my imagination toward composition of a new symphony,
it came to my mind that all my compositions starting from the mid-thirties
became more and more homophonic, and that it was time for me to look for
a new polyphonic approach—via independent "plans," further development
of *Interpoint,* "non-imitative" thematic work. On days when my imagination
was not working, I wrote "polyphonic exercises"—sketches.

*

Pedagogy is a sort of exodus for creativeness: teaching to compose or to
orchestrate exhausts, to a certain degree, the compositional imagination . . .
teaching piano fills one's head with compositions of others; there are a thousand pretexts to escape the effort of composing.

*

You can only teach the technique of composing, not the composing itself.
That depends entirely on talent, instinct, and temperament.

*

For more than a hundred years, I think, the conservatories all over the
world have taught the musical language as a historical language, not even as a
living language, mostly as a summary of what was already acquired . . . in classical and Romantic times—not even so much Romantic. . . . The composer . . .
was aware that nothing of what he was taught could be used as such in his
compositions. . . . It was not the same in classical times; for instance, whatever
Mozart was taught he immediately used. Beethoven also studied with Haydn
and Albrechtsberger in order to acquire a technique that he could immediately use.

*

Analyze all the Beethoven sonatas, for they will teach you all you need to
know about composition.

*

The student's work should begin with monodies, melodic and rhythmic.
Next step: to find their *Interpoint.*

*

Avoid the ostinato; it is the Achilles heel of modern music.

*

The university is too late to begin specialized and concentrated work on music. Much talent is lost or dissipated for having been discovered or attended to too late.

*

Learn to think in silence and learn the beauty of the music of silence. In our modern times we are surrounded by too much noise. We stand the chance of losing all the inner beauty by the intrusion of too many extraneous sounds. Choose quiet living quarters, patronize silent eating places, and, occasionally, dynamite the music machines.

*

One should not flatter the bad taste of people but also should not indulge in bolstering one's own ego by producing puzzles.

*

The older I am, the more difficult it is for me to concentrate, to respond by the work to the inner urge for creation. And the most difficult thing is to "start," and to arrange my schedule drastically in order to keep the desire to compose alive.

*

My father and I had an arrangement: It was his ambition to compose an opera, and we agreed that when I had written a thousand *bloshki,* he would compose an opera. I never did reach a thousand—just two hundred. . . .

*

When Cui asked my father to complete and orchestrate Mussorgsky's *The Fair at Sorochinsk* . . . and my father . . . found no time . . . I did the orchestration of the whole opera . . . in secret . . . and was proud to present my father with the completed score. The good intention was handicapped by my lack of skill in orchestration. I do not know what became of the score—probably it was left in Petrograd. . . . It had, of course, nothing to do with the version of *The Fair of Sorochinsk* that my father did in 1922. . . . [nor did it have anything to do with the ballet version of *Sorochinsk Fair* that Alexander himself did in Paris in 1940.]

*

When a composition is completed I cannot imagine that it could be different from what it became. And never have the urge to change the music, which somehow becomes as definitive as an incarnated child. The only thing that I often have the urge to change—and am changing—is the orchestration. Here I am often dissatisfied with the balance and am urged to revise it (and often do so). Another thing that is subject to change is the dynamics and the tempi. Here I feel that I . . . should carefully edit practically all my compositions of the early period. Wonder if I ever will accomplish it.

*

I feel that every good piece, old or new, has one thing in common—a "vertical" spontaneous impression on the listener. It has something that catches our ear, sticks in it, gives us the desire to hear it again without our realizing at first why and how this is so. Provided we have felt this vertical action on us, we become intrigued to find out how it was produced. We start to analyze it. Sometimes, as a result of such analysis, we find out that we have been fooled. At other times the close analysis shows us the presence of great "order" and as we go deeper into the piece, we discover that it is a masterpiece. The virtue of a piece is a combination of vertical projection plus internal order. Vertical projection without internal order is of no value and fades away after close analysis and after repeated hearings. Order alone without vertical projection is a still-born piece of music.

*

Never has the composer had the opportunities that he has today; at the same time, never has he had so many responsibilities. A bad composer in Mozart's time would just be a bad composer and nobody would ever know his name. But a bad composer today—especially one who is also a bad teacher—might spoil the taste of a generation.

*

The folklores of all countries have this in common—they represent an objective musical truth.

*

While the diatonic scale can normally be "natural" or "well-tempered," the nine-step scale can only be "well-tempered." The accidentals . . . are simplified, and related mostly to the major-minor accidentals if taken from the same tonal center: therefore, they have practical rather than theoretical value, and there is no difference between, let us say, A♭ and G (and so on)—even after displacing the tonic and naming the note differently according to accidentals.

*

Gradually I think our chromatic language is becoming as well organized as the classical language—diatonic language—was after we passed from modes to major and minor scales. Now I think we are proceeding in a kind of synthesis of many chromatic approaches [to] the formation of a new language that will be the same for a composer in New York as for the composer in Tokyo or the composer in Paris; and it will be rather a question of what they will say and not how they will speak, because how they will speak will already be established as well as it was established in Classical times.

*

When I first got to Paris, Boris Schloezer, whose sister was the second wife of Scriabin . . . became interested in my compositions, particularly in the theoretical basis of them. For his information I wrote down the system of hexachords, the nine-step scale and, as illustration, copied for him some of my two-voice inventions. He told me of his intention to write an article about my musical "speech" and my musical ideas. . . . He did nothing of the kind. However, the writing down of a sort of small treatise about the hexachords, the nine-step scale, and the rhythmic approach to . . . polyphony consolidated the results of my personal approach and made it even more conscious and pushed my mind toward further research.

*

I feel that the process of composition is, for a professional composer . . . not a pleasure, but a heavy responsibility, a continuous effort resulting from the urge to create. The "pleasure" comes only when the composition is completed and I am writing down the completed version, or see the completed score. Therefore I compare the process of composition to the state of a pregnant woman. There is no pleasure for a woman in pregnancy—on the contrary, lots of unpleasant and uncomfortable moments. The joy comes only when—after the delivery—the mother has the child brought to her, lying near her in a berceau [i.e., cradle]—alive and born.

Who does not like to make love? But how many women would prefer not to have the act result in pregnancy. So the "amateur" composer to me seems like a lovemaker who has none of the troubles of pregnancy as a result.

The amateur composer takes pleasure in composition; but . . . composition produced in this way fails to give pleasure to the listener; while the professional composer does not take pleasure in composing, but the composition that comes as a result of his urge and of his effort projects his message to his fellow human beings and might become a source of their pleasure.

So difficult to have the will (at least for me) to become pregnant![2]

Tcherepnin's propensity and ability to reflect on his compositions constantly prompts him to reflect on personal experience. This reveals itself in his writings and the compositions themselves, creating a portrait of the master in his workshop.

Another previously unpublished text concerns the period when he taught at DePaul University. We find a prologue that is followed by notes about melody, rhythm, and other pedagogical matters.

The Composer can be recognized by the desire to compose. Composition cannot be taught. The composer should reach everything himself, and the task of the tutor is to place before his pupil a set of elementary problems, whose solution the pupil can achieve by logical thought.

Creativity is similar to meditation. The creator should strive toward isolation from external impressions and listen only to himself. The first stage of creativity is improvisation. It is possible on any musical instrument, and can even be done without an instrument. Improvisation is a stream. It bears with itself dirt and silt but can contain a stone or a particle of gold.

The composer studies in order to be able to find this stone or particle and record it. When many such recorded bits have been collected, the composer can start constructing something out of them, by comparison and combination, as a child builds a small house out of blocks. Improvisation develops the taste of the composer, and the use of what he finds for construction develops his logical thinking.

When the improvisational path creates many works and the composer learns to compare the found bits in various forms, the composer can total up what he has done and analyze his own taste. He will find rules specific to him, the result of his intuition, and will begin compositional work. By improvisation he has discovered a little part of himself. His task is to release intuition from self-repetition. Having divined her [i.e., creativity's] laws by observation, he will learn to do at will what was earlier done subconsciously. He will save up intuition for further development.

His creativity is transformed from a self-sufficient subject to the object of his will, and instead of gluing together discovered scraps he can now develop a found particle via logical thought—to find its innately organic development. In this phase the composer can tackle any task—any problem that is no longer assigned but instead strongly desired. The creative sanction to take on any compositional task constitutes the schooling of the composer.[3]

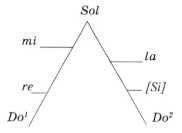

Example 6.1

It is abundantly clear that Tcherepnin describes his own experience here. Another pedagogical section shows that Tcherepnin transmitted to his pupils not only his experience of the process of composition but offered a system of composition, which later became his *Basic Elements*. It was not an official syllabus course at DePaul but rather a sort of individual practicum or seminar.

> The repeating scale. Relationship of the notes out of which the scale is composed, their relationship to the root.
>
> An understanding of a scale as a triangle.
>
> The root and the relation to it of the intervals: unison-octave, second-seventh, third-sixth, fourth-fifth. Fourth-fifth is at the top. Third-sixth and second-seventh are at the sides.
>
> The concept of the root as the base of a triangle, fourths-fifths as its peak.
>
> *Temperation of melodies.* Position of a given melody over various scales—Chinese, European, nine-step, chromatic:
>
> Finding the tonic
>
> Finding the missing note
>
> Ending on the root
>
> Ending on the missing note → concept of surprise
>
> *Rhythmization of melodies.* Position of a given melody over various rhythms:
>
> Ending on strong pulse
>
> Ending on weak pulse
>
> Variation of rhythms
>
> Repeatability of rhythm
>
> Non-repeatability of rhythm
>
> *Rhythm.* Problems: 1) Find temperation for a given rhythm.
>
>   2) For a given temperation find a rhythm.
>
> Infinite melody
>
> Infinite rhythm
>
> Repeated melody
>
> Repeated rhythm
>
> Song with accompaniment (the two-part form)
>
> Rhythm with accompaniment[4]

Tcherepnin's articles, lectures, letters, and diaries powerfully illustrate the marked attention he gave to the language of art and to its creation in the twentieth century. Russia resisted the exploration and experimentation of mod-

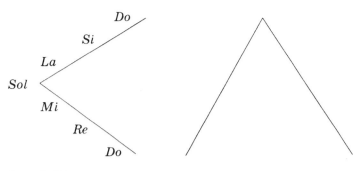

Example 6.2

ernism for much longer than other European cultures. From the 1930s on, this was partly the result of official policy; but it was also part of a cultural tradition in which the poet was more than just a poet, the composer more than just a composer, and where the "what" was more important than the "how." Boris Schloezer wrote repeatedly about Tcherepnin and immersed himself deeply in the artistic life of the West. While reviewing Boris Asafiev's series of books about Russian composers, despite the esteem in which he held them, he made the following observation: "I have one very serious criticism of Glebov's characterizations, analyses, and opinions: they fall entirely in the field of psychology. The author speaks at length about what Tchaikovsky's art expressed.... But about how all this is expressed we hear nothing."[5]

It is clear from published texts that Tcherepnin was acutely aware of the higher purpose of art as well as what is traditionally called "content." But his interest in the language of music, and especially in extending its limitless opportunities for expression, was quite profound. He was not alone in the belief that progress in art is vital, and he took remarkable interest in all that was new— electronic music, musique concrète, and "under-privileged" instruments, as he called them.

Several of Tcherepnin's writings relate directly to these ideas. From our perspective thirty years later, we may not necessarily discover anything truly new, but these texts contribute enormously to our understanding of Tcherepnin's life.

The World of Sound (1964)

Invisible rays. Inaudible sounds.
Rays that we can see. Sounds that we can hear.
The colors that the painter uses are only a little fraction of the infinite variety of colors of the light spectrum.
The sounds that our ear is able to perceive and to differentiate are only a little part of the infinite variety of sounds that are vibrating around us.
And of these sounds only a minimal part is accepted as "musical."
Western music came finally to the arbitrary division of an octave into twelve equal semitones.

Chinese, Hindu, and Arabian music uses an equally arbitrary although different organization of the so-called "musical" sounds.

The poetic meters, the pulsation of dance rhythms, as organized in music, are only a few relative to the infinite number of possible time subdivisions.

In our epoch the Eastern and Western musical languages finally became acquainted, mutually influencing each other more and more and enriching the conventions of one by the conventions of the other.

Stimulated by science, the music of today is trying to liberate itself from the conventions of East and West—thus penetrating deeper into the world of pure sound, becoming nearer to nature, richer in means of expression, freer from the limitations of "musical conventions."

The incubation period of composition is a mysterious one.

From where and by which way does the initial idea, which is to become the seed of a composition, come to the mind of the composer?

In my case, when I start to work on a new composition, I do not hear it. I feel it. I experience the urge to "tune in," to become a "converter" of inaudible vibrations into audible sounds.

What follows is but a partial materialization in forms of sound that even in this stage stay free from conventions of pitch and of meter.

Another effort is needed to bring the idea into what we call "music" and to start the actual work on a "musical" composition.

Since my early youth I dreamed of the liberation from conventions. It is for this reason that I conceived the second movement of my First Symphony (1927) for percussion instruments a cappella, thus achieving the liberation from pitch. For a similar reason, even earlier, I ended the piano piece *Message* by knocking on the wood of the piano the meter of the principal theme, thus reducing it to its purely rhythmic value.

It was also in the twenties that I used in my compositions what I called then the bird folklore and introduced the rhythms of insects, [and] the irregular meter and intonation of spoken language in [to my] music.

The other way to escape conventions was by color: a sound color of the harp, of the harmonica, of accordion, of tuba or of so many other instruments that are still winning their place under the sun and are in need of being served by the composer.

The musical coexistence that soon will result in a happy marriage of East and West, the rise of percussion group as such and as a fourth group in our orchestra, the appearance of electronic devices of sound production, and the introduction of scientifically conceived new musical instruments are of primary importance to the development of music and open an entirely new way for a composer of today.

I am fascinated to live in our epoch and to see the art of music becoming the true art of sound.[6]

The following article by Tcherepnin was published in the periodical *L'Age Nouveau*. A special issue of this literary and artistic review was devoted to the theme "Music and the World of Sound." It appeared alongside articles by Henri Dutilleux, Pierre Henry, Maurice Jarre, André Jolivet, René Leibowitz, Frank Martin,

Alexander Tansman, and Edgard Varèse. Notably Tcherepnin's contribution was written in the early fifties. Although it seems axiomatic today, when the article first appeared his ideas were quite new and fresh.

Percussion: Is It Musical? (1955)

One cannot deny that contemporary composers, in their works, reserve a particularly important place for percussion. This fact has attracted the attention of critics, and some have seen percussion as a means of liberating music through a procedure whose emotional value is foreign to that of music itself.

As for me, I would not know how to separate the emotional value of percussion from that of music in general. Percussion is only one of the means that a composer uses to express his musical intentions. On a purely emotional level, a melody sung pianissimo by a flute in its low register can communicate more emotion to a listener than an obsessive rhythm assigned to timpani playing fortissimo. The emotional value of music is implicit not in the means it employs but in the message it contains.

Why does contemporary music accord so considerable a place to percussion? I see numerous explanations for this phenomenon.

To begin on the most simplistic level, a comprehensive exploration of color leads to the use of all suitable means of obtaining colors. Percussion is one of those means at a composer's disposal.

Note must also be taken of the ever more extensive relations between the dance and the great part of contemporary music. Has ballet not tended to become a new form of musical expression?

Finally, there is the eminently justified desire of the composer to transcend the limited extent of sounds considered "listenable"—the development of the piano, which is a percussion instrument by its very construction, has represented this attitude.

In my case, the use of percussion represents my attempt to liberate rhythm from tempered sound.

The seven-and-a-half octaves of organized pitches that we consider the sole standard musical sounds constitute only a minimal part of a sound world which is, I am sure, as real as the visual world.

This sound -world, which we can sense thanks to our hearing, extends beyond the seven- and-a-half octaves but remains infinitely restricted in comparison with the world of sound waves that traverse the universe. Like a painter who reduces what he sees in placing it on a canvas infinitely smaller than the real extent that his eye perceives, a composer reduces what comes to him from the world of sound in the form of sound waves as he integrates it into the range of audible (listenable) sounds.

The impulse to compose, instinctive in origin, generally comes to me as a sensation of the presence of sound waves. I feel the existence of these, which, however, are not audible. Little by little I succeed in expressing them in the course of transposing them into the domain of audible sounds. At least, it seems that I have succeeded in doing so in certain cases. Sometimes, however, I feel betrayed by the means that are considered musical: in any case they do not offer me any of the equivalents I am looking for. It is then that percussion helps me escape from the cage of the seven-and-a-half octaves. Yet I am only looking for an extension of sonic means. I would not dream of executing a musical structure confined to noise. I do not believe that noise per se is capable of being music. If it becomes music, it ceases to be noise.

I should like to stress that percussion belongs to the realm of music and not of noise, and to discuss extra-musical explications that have been applied to the use of percussion. These are not lacking. I would answer by saying, however, that I do not know whether percussion engages the spirit or the senses. I would not presume to establish a distinction between the one and the other. Why not ask if percussion addresses the right ear or the left ear of the auditor? The senses cannot be felt without the spirit's consciousness of sensation. Conversely, how could the spirit perceive sounds, how could it speculate upon their meaning if the senses did not communicate their vibrations to it?

Interpretation, extra-musical again, sees in the use of percussion the demonstration of a need to astonish. Has a composer ever wished to astonish indiscriminately? True, I was personally accused of wishing to shock the listener when I entrusted the scherzo of my First Symphony to percussion alone. The first performance of that symphony provoked numerous commentaries. To tell the truth, my only objective was to liberate rhythm from the conventional sound of our standard notes. No one, at the time, noticed that the rhythms that I used in the scherzo were merely reductions, to their purely rhythmic value, of themes of the symphony's first movement, which precedes the scherzo.

Continuing to parry extra-musical judgments about percussion, I will say that its use corresponds neither to a composer's desire or need for excess, nor to any bellicose plan of his to suffuse the listener with self-destructive impulses. It is not a means of gratification for the masochist.

It is a fact that the composers of my generation show a tendency to accentuate the percussive character of instruments. I mentioned, above, the case of the piano, which, by its construction, is a percussion instrument. I myself have a tendency to make different instruments of the orchestra alter from "melodic" to "percussive"; in my Suite for Orchestra, the rhythm introduced by the percussion instruments at the beginning of the second movement is immediately reprised by the strings, and by the winds; in the final analysis, the orchestral instruments are used like percussion, with rhythm dominating the construction of the work.

This observation takes away nothing from what I affirmed at the beginning of this article: to achieve his ends, the composer has a certain number of means whose use is always legitimate if that end requires their use. Percussion is only one of those means. It is but one of the colors on a palette. It could not conceivably be made an end in itself. There is not music and percussion. There is only music.[7]

After the completion of his First Symphony, Tcherepnin's interest in novel sound possibilities continued to grow. In 1930–31 he composed a concertino (Op. 47) for twelve solo instruments, in which two violas da gamba were combined with modern strings and piano [later recast as the Triple Concerto for Piano Trio and Small Orchestra]. In 1939 a series of works for unusual instrumental combinations appeared, including a sonata for bassoon (or saxophone, Op. 63), an andante for tuba (Op. 64), and his Sonatina for Timpani and Piano Op. 58. The latter (like the others) was composed "on commission from a publisher for pedagogical use in American colleges." Tcherepnin added, "It is performed a lot, and is available in a version for timpani and orchestra."[8] Several years later the composer wrote to Shneerson about a festival in Zug, Switzerland, devoted to the "rehabilitation" of the gamba, discussing new musical possibilities for the instrument, including chromatic writing. Tcherepnin then composed Sonata da Chiesa for Viola da Gamba and Organ Op. 101.[9] Other unusual works include several pieces for accordion; the Concerto for Harmonica Op. 86; and *Diatonic Caprices,* a four-movement suite for Celtic harp. The following excerpt reveals Tcherepnin's thoughts on this subject as he pursued his pedagogical activities in Chicago.

Let Underprivileged Instruments Play (1962)

In 1949, DePaul University in Chicago engaged my wife, the Chinese pianist Lee Hsien Ming, and me as members of the faculty. Since then, of course, my home has been in Chicago, and I have had the privilege to participate in the musical life of the country, not only as a composer and pianist, but also as a pedagogue, lecturer, and orchestral conductor. I am fascinated by the intensity of the musical life in the States, by the eagerness of young people to study in order to become accomplished musicians. In teaching young composers, I am trying to help them to discover themselves, to find their own individualistic approach to composition.

I am also trying to draw the attention of young composers to the various musical media in which a new work will be welcome. While piano, violin, cello, string quartet, and symphony orchestra have been well served by the great composers of the past, and continuously provided with new compositions of high merit by composers of the present, so many other instruments and various other ensembles are in need of adequate literature.

There is tremendous opportunity for a young talented composer if he chooses to compose for the "underprivileged" instruments. Certainly compositions, let us say, for tuba, for accordion, for harp, for band, for brass ensemble, for saxophone quartet, for marimba, for percussion—are lacking, and it is the young generation's job to fill the need for compositions which would give new virtuosos a chance to shine via good music. And there is the great coming musical medium—electronics!

When I imagine music, I am not always able to find equivalent sounds in the well-tempered scale. There is always a kind of "transposition" I have to make when writing down the composition. In electronic music such compromise becomes unnecessary: every sound in every color at any volume on any pitch can be obtained. Here what we call "musical sound" becomes enriched and practically unlimited!

No doubt the future of music will be associated with all these new ways of producing sound. The door is open to a new world of musical expression. We are living at the most exciting and revolutionary time in music.[10]

The subsequent excerpt discusses the twentieth-century theme of electronic music which he mentioned above.

Electronic Music and Other Matters

The artist is not someone living in an ivory tower. He must absorb everything around him and give it back in the form of his art. It is his duty to serve people, to say something to humanity.

Then, some of you may ask, what about electronic music? Are some ivory towers charged with electricity? And has the wiring gone bad?

It is very difficult, even for an experienced musician, to find out the construction of electronic or serial music, until he realizes that it asks nothing more of us than to open our ears. Most of us [need to] have our ears and minds "shocked" open; only in this way are we able to concentrate on the sounds of the present, musical and otherwise, instead of the sounds of yesterday.

Why should we limit ourselves to the sounds of a piano, for example, when cymbals and drums offer overtones that a piano cannot? So many more varieties of sound are made possible with the addition of new instruments. Since Beethoven's time the piano keyboard has grown in both directions—a fifth above and a sixth below. Since the time of Liszt, nothing has been added.

In the field of sound experimentation, I have a great respect for the work of Henk Badings, the noted Dutch composer. He has written in every genre with a style of romantic modernism but is also experimenting with four-track tape, his use of which is truly great by today's conception of the sounds. But this musical speech can go only as [far] forward as the musical standard of the audience, which wants to be given a language that it understands. A few new words can be added gradually, but a totally new language such as electronic music is initially disturbing and unacceptable at first to the majority.

The musical scientist searches for new worlds of sound and time. The message, his spaceship, is self-expression in terms of his time and culture. New sounds, fed to the audience in the proper amounts, constitute new fuel for the journey.

In 2700 BC the Chinese emperor established certain pitch restrictions. They still exist. True, we are experimenting in an epoch where there is a tremendous need for research in every direction. A musician cannot be a ghost of Canterville and refuse to fit into his own epoch. The composer must go as far in research as is necessary to project his ultimate message, which he may sense but not realize fully himself. The research in electronic music—foreign to our ears and perhaps mystic[al] in message—is the means: the act of composing is mystic[al] in itself.

When I listen to music and compose, I am not hearing the music actually as it is. First, I feel music and hear nothing. There is a tremendous world of vibration, only a part of which can be heard. Our powers of perception need to be developed. Perhaps there are inaudible vibrations that are sensed or felt. It is common knowledge that a dog can hear higher vibrations than the human ear.

The higher pitches of electronic music are fantastically clear, while the lower seem to have less sound value. There is too much tremolo in the low pitches, which one day must be stabilized. But the point should be made that all sound-producing instruments should have a literature, whether the medium be human or mechanical.

There is a strange situation in which we are lionizing pianists, violinists, and cellists. The eternal "lion" is the singer, also the most conservative lion. The underprivileged instruments, however, must also be given a chance to roar—the percussion family, the harmonica, the accordion (there are 3 million players in the United States alone), recreational instruments, i.e., those lacking a broad serious repertoire. Composers have written largely for the established lions. More music is needed—good music—for the neglected cubs, instead of an overabundance of the same for string quartets and other accepted forms. Serious composers must permit all the lions to roar!

Now there will always be the "high brow" serious composer who looks down on the lighter mediums, the cubs. I know who will be on the mantle piece tomorrow, but whose music will be heard tomorrow? Quarter-tone music was written by Abbe Vogler in the time of Mozart! It is not the great complication that survives but the simplification. Bach gave us wonderful polyphony and Schoenberg simplified it. Will oversimplification survive?

The composer always serves a certain milieu surrounding him. Snobbism cannot control the outflow of the artist. Although the creator must give the community the music it needs, it is also his kharmic debt to contribute to the progressive experimentalism so necessary for the perpetuation of the art form.

There is, incidentally, a terrific parallel between the human body and the simple folklore that has survived. The folklore in music is similar to [human] anatomy. The great artists of all time have elaborated upon the simple and beautiful basics that are everlasting. Michelangelo used the lines of the body, magnifying their complexity. He represented deepness of spirit. Da Vinci displayed passion; Raphael expressed celestial proportion; Delacroix, battle scenes; Picasso, eternal lines; and the like. Anatomical music survives; there are superficial changes only.

I cannot say that electronic music, as we know it just now, is anatomical; but a time is coming when revolutionary simplification will [shape] its life-cycle. And our ears will have to remain open. Electronic music involves new tone color not necessarily related to known timbres. Who knows how the futuristic electronic lion of tomorrow will roar?[11]

Certain general tendencies emerge from the composer's reflections on the evolution and progress of twentieth-century music. His unusual classifications are all the more interesting given that he was a Russian composer abroad. His voice is the voice of an actual participant in this evolutionary process.

I personally knew Webern. Life in conservative Vienna was not easy for him. He could hardly have foreseen that his works would serve as the starting point for the ideology of postwar Western composers, and that they would contribute to the development of Western European music. In an epoch when science stimulates art (just as in its time music was stimulated by literature, philosophy, and painting), his creativity is especially significant and compatible with modern (West European) ideology.

For the modern generation he is a classic; yet music has certainly advanced much further. Indeed, as my sons Seriozha (Serge) and Vanya (Ivan) pointed out after last year's sessions in Darmstadt, post-Webernists such as Stockhausen and Boulez are no longer at the forefront; and music has left behind not only Webern but also the composers of Darmstadt and Cologne. . . . It seems to me that we live in an extremely interesting epoch. What we call music, and the assumed limiting of music to organized "musical" sounds, was expanded. The contemporary composer has all "musical" sounds at his disposal—conventional and unconventional. The palette of sounds is expanded, the composer no longer needs to make concessions to his internal ear, and he has the means to notate accurately what he hears inside his head—whether it be tempered or untempered, coordinated or unmatched, in all possible divisions of pitch and rhythm. And what is notable is that the experience of modern electronic or abstract music (assuming lack of prejudice) does not demand traditional musical training, and consequently is more accessible to the masses. After all, a course of harmony is not needed to enjoy the song of a nightingale, the sounds of nature, indeed, sound as such. Music that stems from tradition, i.e., from accumulation and continuation (as with Webern, Boulez, etc.), is accessible to a relative few, while electronic and abstract music bring a new "primitivism," accessible to all those with ears and the desire to hear.

Broadly speaking, I see the following basic currents in modern music:

1. Traditional—Webernist, post-Webernist—the music of the "elite," inspired by musical evolution and science, full of complexity.
2. Vanguard—electronic, aleatory—inspired by the science of acoustics.
3. Dynamic—deriving from emotion (from jazz, which has become a "national" art), but more complex (Gunther Schuller, etc.).
4. Soviet—deriving from musical tradition and inspired by the construction of a new society.

And all these currents reflect and express modern life, which differs considerably from the life of previous millennia. Thus arises the search for expression through art. We managed to be born in such an interesting, animated epoch but also such a complex and difficult one! In a hundred years it will be deciphered. But meantime our business is to work honestly and tirelessly, to believe in what we do.[12]

In the late 1960s Tcherepnin had a brush with electronic music and described the experience in another letter to Shneerson:

I have been commissioned by the BBC in London to compose music for Lev Tolstoy's fairy tale about Ivan the Fool (which has long attracted me). . . . Douglas Cleverdon will write the libretto, preserving Tolstoy's text as much as possible. It will be part sung, part spoken, with musical accompaniment. It will last an hour. The orchestra, singers, chorus, and dramatic actors are all under my direction. Ivan the Fool's role will be performed by my cousin Peter Ustinov. A recording will be made in London in August. Simultaneously Ustinov will record Blok's *Twelve* in his own translation with my music.[13]

A year and half later Tcherepnin wrote: "With the help of Seriozha [Serge Tcherepnin], I composed five minutes of electronic music for *Ivan the Fool* and learned a lot. God willing, I hope to employ this means of musical expression further."[14] However, Alexander never again returned to electronic music.

The door to the workroom of some composers is very tightly closed, whereas others leave an extensive paper trail of compositional sketches, multiple versions of pieces, and observations about the creative process. This always depends on the historical epoch and the personality of the individual. In comparison to extant research on Bach, Mozart, Beethoven, Schubert, Tchaikovsky, Taneyev, and Prokofiev, the creative process of composers of the second half of the twentieth century is quite under-investigated. At the same time the observations of composers from Honegger to Webern and Boulez (and, among the Russians, Edison Denisov)[15] bear witness to the fact that the modern epoch introduced much that was new, and was linked with new artistic results and principles (for example, sound structure).

As a composer who not only described the process of musical composition but recorded it in detail through daily correspondence and diaries, Alexander Tcherepnin is a unique phenomenon. Only one comparable example can be found, in Scherbachev's letters to his wife from Germany, where he reports his work on his Second Symphony day by day, accompanied by musical examples. Medtner also accompanied his musical sketches with extensive commentary.

Tcherepnin's First Symphony is far from the only one of his works documented in this way. Among numerous other chronicled scores (including late ones), one finds some remarkable documentation concerning the opera *The Wedding of Sobeide.* Most of these documents are located in the Paul Sacher Foundation archive.

One problem in working with this material is the difficulty of comparing verbal notes with musical manuscripts and final editions, as well as with actual performances, which have until lately not been frequently recorded or broadcast on the radio. It has already been noted that without a composer's notes, many modern compositions cannot ultimately be understood. The intellectualization of music, and, accordingly, of the compositional process, has greatly increased in the latter part of the twentieth century. Tcherepnin demonstrates the mechanisms and nature of this development. The combination of the intuitive and rational is perhaps the most central and interesting motif of his epistolary and diary notes.

In a remarkable 1975 diary entry, the composer himself admits to this, after yet another bout of self-reflection.

> After almost seven years of relative and later complete barrenness, it is not so easy to return to creating. This, in spite of the fact that everything here is ideal for concentration. . . . I work daily, without time limitations. But I face two enemies: reservations about beginning to work and premature criticism. . . .
>
> I start with an approach, a compositional means. My approach always stemmed from source material. Then, after a certain amount had been accumulated, construction began. The search for material is an intuitive, subconscious process. Construction is rational, conscious. The selection of material is dictated by musical taste; creation, by cognitive logic.

In the Composer's Workshop   135

Material is a seed with potential for growth, whereas construction is the process of growth. The vital element in my approach was (and is) to like the material, and then to search for balance in its construction. When all had transpired and the piece of music was complete, it was sometimes unclear why the search for balance, for final rendering, had taken so long, and was sometimes so painful. Why had so much time been required to find what in the end seemed self-evident? And the next piece would again pose the same problems and the same long search for balance.

And things are no different now. After two months of work I have seven notebooks of sketches—searches for material. One notebook contains the beginning of the work—three-and-a-half completed minutes of music, which have yet to be added to, developed, and perhaps refined. And this is only one section of a movement that I vaguely expect to have five sections.

For the second section I plan to use what I composed last summer in Marlow, which revolves around a constantly repeated A♯. The third section, on which I am working now, has thematic material set to the rhythm of "Trouble Is a-Coming, People." After that I am contemplating a slow section composed in 1970, on which I would impose quite different, freely counterpointed material. And in the final, fifth section, I would return to the material of the first movement but mixed with all the others. . . . This is all very well, but all the material is somehow "routine" as dear Daddy would say, and is forced to emerge without any inner fire, without an organic desire toward expression. I shall not try to overcome this nor try to notate it. When I am ready to work, I will search throughout to find what is compatible with my creative beliefs.

And, as always, while collecting material, there are concurrent discoveries that can be applied to something else, probably individual small pieces. But there is not only this. I have another parallel task. Since I arrived here, I have been reading Dickens's Pickwick while lying in bed before going to sleep. I've realized that the *Notes of the Pickwick Club* form a unique sort of comic novel. I know of nothing similar. And so, as sometimes happens when the notion of composing seems disgusting, unnecessary, and useless, it occurred to me to compose a comic symphony, and initial material for the beginning, as well as an approach, came to mind. I have stopped there for the moment, however, and returned to the material on which I had been working. But I have not quite completely returned, because from time to time the initial ideas for the "Pickwick Symphony" germinate, and there are already quite a lot of these sprouts. So I hope it will be possible to perform both tasks simultaneously—one for the Chicago Symphony Orchestra, another for the Koussevitzky Fund.[16]

Another two years of daily work lay ahead. This process, recorded in the diary, enables us to compare Tcherepnin's creative process in the 1920s with his process half a century later. The initial material, entitled "For the beginning of the cheerful Pickwickian Symphony" (musical example 6.3) later appeared in one of the pieces of Tcherepnin's very last "cycle." We learn from an August 1975 diary entry that, "the thought occurred to me to record in a notebook what I have composed—short fragments here and there, *opivochki* [little remnants] . . . unrelated to the symphony but poured out, so to speak, 'from the heart.'"[17] Later, on January 1, 1976, he projects this goal: "To continue 'little

Example 6.3

remnants,' and together with the piano pieces composed in 1969, consider assembling them into one grand work, perhaps some kind of modern *Gradus ad Parnassum.*"[18]

This collection of about forty short pieces (Op. 109) still remains unpublished.[19] The date of each composition is in the left margin, and the duration is always noted at the end. The shortest pieces last twenty-five to thirty seconds, and the longest one lasts one minute and twenty seconds. There are suggestions for dynamics, metronome markings, and other notes. A common feature is the absence of any key signatures (some pieces are atonal) or meter changes. To a certain extent, the musical examples shown in example 6.4 are comparable to the early, Tiflis piano "trifles," although everything here is more calculated, unimprovised, and remarkably more concise.

Throughout decades of compositional activity, Tcherepnin's creative process certainly changed and evolved. Beginning in the latter half of the 1920s, rational, technical work grew in importance. Nevertheless, we see from the composer's records that basic terms remained essentially the same. The synonymous "kernels," "ideas," and "material" can be understood as thematism in the traditional sense.

In Tcherepnin's diaries he frequently wrote instructions to himself regarding the composition of future works. These often appear in the sketches as well. The following is a music notebook entry dated October 20, 1928:

> A basic plan for the next opera (try to use in *Sobeide* as well)
>
> 1. Sustained melody over punctuated rhythm.
> 2. Recitative within musical development.
> 3. Recitative on top of main melodic material, for example:
>
> To preserve expression—minimum in the orchestra, and maximum in the voice.[20]

The general ideas described above usually also contain specific instructions— "27.I. When Sobeide enters, have a nervous rhythm in the percussion alter-

Example 6.4

Example 6.5

nate with strings across three octaves, and two or three-voices singing sus-
pensions . . . 20. III. When Sobeide goes to kill herself, only strings." Planning
augurs the composition. Long before he finished the outline, Alexander made
a note, "End the opera with an instrumental solo," and later followed through
on the instruction. The first measures of the overture as well as the final measures of the opera are shown in musical example 6.6. They illustrate the consistent use and predominance of E major-minor tonality, especially in contrast to
the First Symphony.

Sometimes the idea can be structural or constructive, even abstract. The
diary entry for February 15, 1928, reads: "Last night considered the essence of
the entire first scene (not the first act, just the scene) of *Sobeide;* it will be very
picturesque and engaging, but the notes aren't coming to me, that is, the material just isn't there yet. But what is interesting, of course, is that the principle
is there, i.e., the method. It's only a matter of execution, which is to say, it's a

Example 6.6

question of patience, technique and time."[21] But if composition is a question of technique and time, what is the role of inspiration? The composer mentions this in an earlier letter to his parents. "After supper worked on the rough draft of the quintet. The third movement still lacks a second theme and, alas, inspiration has not yet come to me. After a week of work, I have only twenty-one measures finished."[22]

But spontaneity constantly reappears, not only at the initial stages. A diary record from July 12, 1970, states: "Worked in the morning and afternoon with a little more energy. This is the third day I have spent preparing material for the wind quintet instead of the symphony—and many ideas are coming to mind."[23]

The slow rate of work is salient. It is due not to lack of talent but to the demands the composer placed on himself. However, it is difficult to compare compositional speeds, since many highly talented composers simply never tracked how long they spent on particular works.

Technique is directly related to the genre of the piece. The Sobeide chronicles abound in reflections on the psychological aspect of certain scenes, as seen in this letter to his parents:

> The entire resolution of the opera hinges on the central movement, which is now approaching. I want to make it as strong and concentrated as possible . . . scenes are no longer divided as they were in the beginning of the act but flow into each other, constantly increasing in intensity and leading us forward. Ganem and Sobeide, first loving, then abusive; then Shalnassar, Gulistana, a wild orchestra, a general scuffle and quarrel, Sobeide's hysterics at the climax, and, finally, the cold ending. This enormous growth of temperament must be considered as calmly and cold-bloodedly as possible. Only then can I allow myself to freely carry out the plan. (October 20, 1928)

In the Composer's Workshop   139

In order to understand the composer's following comments we need to summarize the plot of this now little-known, early play by von Hofmannsthal. The playwright was quite popular in Russia in the early 1900s, and Alexander's enthusiasm for *The Wedding of Sobeide* began even before emigration. He would later profess his appreciation for the work on numerous occasions, once discussing it with Hofmannsthal in person. The play was also published independently many times, and in 1907 and 1908 it was staged by Meyerhold at the Vera Komissarjevskaya Theater, with Komissarjevskaya herself in the lead.[24]

To rescue her ruined father, young Sobeide marries an elderly rich merchant. She admits to the groom that for a long time she has loved Ganem, Shalnassar's son, but cannot marry him because he is poor. The noble merchant releases Sobeide. Having come to Shalnassar's house, Sobeide learns that she was severely deceived: Ganem and his father are rich and conduct a wayward life. Offended by this, and by the way she is received, Sobeide returns to the merchant's house and ends her life by jumping out of a high tower. The last dialogue—the merchant's declaration of love and the death of Sobeide—is a compressed final scene, characteristic of twentieth-century opera. The scene of the heroine's death, with its rhythmic pulsation of bells in octaves which toll out the last minutes of her life, are reminiscent of the ending of Prokofiev's opera *Fiery Angel*, although Tcherepnin could not have known this score.

> Thought both in the morning and afternoon about the characterization of Sobeide. Thanks to previous explorations, ended up, by evening, in possession of enough material . . . to be able to begin developing it as Sobeide's answer in her dialogue with the Merchant—her first "speech" and the first brief conversation. This is now the task closest at hand, and if I complete it this week, I will be very pleased. If the Merchant is mostly calm and quiet in character, Sobeide is certainly a contrast. Her material is based on rhythm and her themes are rough and nervous. Since I have had little experience with such music (something similar can be found only in the second theme of *Magna Mater*), I expect to have a lot of difficulty. . . . At the same time I notice that half-deliberately and half-intuitively, I return from "spatial" music to "true" music, as though in the tradition of Russian opera. This is also because I have seen and heard too much "spatial" music, which was the goal of *Ol-Ol*. I became convinced that with love for and faith in the libretto, there is only one way to truly express the psychological makeup of the characters. But one must not put them in straitjackets, where their personalities will become colorless.
>
> Since I truly love *The Wedding of Sobeide* as a libretto, its characters are dear to me, and it matters to me how various words are conveyed. Hence this or that melodic figure in the musical development cannot replace the truthful dramatic accent hidden in a word. And since I love the libretto, I constantly reread it. That's how I found what I believe is an effective place for the ballet section, since it must reflect the dialogue. (February 27, 1928)

The last of many notes to his father earlier that month reveal an interesting allusion to cinema and Tcherepnin's propensity for compositional fragments.

Spent all of yesterday on *Sobeide*. The idea is there now, and I have chosen separate passages, clearest to me in their psychology, and am realizing them. As in the filming of a movie, when a director uses the presence of a given person to shoot all scenes connected with him, I am now busy with the Merchant. Having initially chosen his first speech to Sobeide, a rather formal one, but psychologically interesting, I think that until I really understand the character of Sobeide, I will continue working on separate ideas for the Merchant. (February 18, 1928)

This tendency to work simultaneously on two or more tasks is an important characteristic of Tcherepnin, which he himself often recognized.

Yesterday did a lot of work on the violin piece, and after enormous effort, completed it, and began to write it down. By supper I had notated half; after supper did not return to writing in order to occupy myself a bit with the piano. . . . [Today] finished writing down the violin piece by breakfast time, played it through and was still quite pleased. First, it is not paltry—five minutes is a lot for such a piece; second, it has good development; third, it's melodious; fourth, it modulates freely, so it's more varied. So having played it after breakfast, I was able to pat myself on the back and say: "Now, Alexander Nikolaievich, it's time to get down to orchestrating. You can resolve additional violin pieces in your spare time, because this manner of accumulating material, such as for Impromptu, which has been gathering for a whole month, brings better, more creative results than when the development is forced." And since a huge orchestration task lies ahead, such unhurried creation of small pieces is the best rest and recreation. . . . With the week starting tomorrow, it's time to begin the score. (June 26, 1927)[25]

By comparing his compositional impulses to his written impressions of "other" music, Tcherepnin was able to characterize his own philosophy and work process. This happened frequently, but his impression, for example, of Puccini's *Turandot*, almost on the eve of *The Wedding of Sobeide*, shows what the composer had saved in his acoustical piggy bank.

Attended an evening premiere of *Turandot*. In terms of music, there is much of interest, many unisons, impressionistic techniques, numerous ostinatos; but the singing is always harmonious, even when performed against a complex harmonic background. Personally I enjoyed it: 1) Dances are performed to the singing of three mandarins, who criticize the dances—this scene lasts a quarter of an hour—the mandarins sit motionless, verbally quarreling, while the dancing continues. As a device it is very convincing. 2) Rhythmic accompaniment to the recitatives. 3) The scene from the third act, with the death of Liù, the girl who loved prince Calaf and deciphered the riddle of Turandot. In addition to that, I enjoyed the constant use of the chorus, and some instruments play in their extreme registers (the horns go to E). This intensity exists throughout the orchestra (but the orchestration is by Alfano), and there are constant ostinatos. But the libretto is excellent, and with this opera Puccini acquires a tragic character. Having attained such great popularity, he refuses to rest on his laurels, and shows more than ever that he is a first-rate musician. Thanks to the quantity of unisons, uneven rhythms, modulations down a step, and convincing exchanges between chorus and instrumental voices, *Turandot* has a very Georgian character. By the way, it is very interesting that Puccini often uses voices alone, without accompaniment. This is very impressive." (February 27, 1927)

Impressions and influences are also drawn from other sources and included in the compositional process.

From Reger's biography I gathered that familiarity with the great masters *kommt in den besten Familien vor* [happens in the best families]—so at the age of thirty-five I first became acquainted with Wagner's scores, and slightly earlier with the quartets of the masters. I am very encouraged: it's never too late. And I have decided to take an absolutely new approach to my pianism, namely, to learn to play in different clefs and to think in many voices while sitting at the piano, i.e., to create combinations that I had tried to create on paper. Sometimes I waste tens of pages trying to find one right polyphony. But sitting at the piano would save a lot of time. (May 13, 1927)

Certain concepts and constantly repeated phrases shed light on the creative process. Why does he write initial notes on separate slips of paper? Does this not result from an internal recognition of them as fragments which will later be joined with other "building blocks," with other fleeting thoughts? The recurring "fasteners" suggest this—a lot of material is composed, but the ideas are not yet tied together. Certain notes made during the orchestration process also seem to imply an attitude in this direction, much like the "coloring in" of a drawing. One of numerous examples appears in a pair of letters to his parents, dated February 17 and February 19, 1927, describing work on *Magna Mater*, after the sketch has already been finished. "I shall get down to my envisioned orchestration; it is surprising how this pans out in the score. Many of the seams turn out to be volumetric shadows, which, when underlined by color, receive their formal raison d'être."

There is an evident typology for the stages of notating a composition. First there are "sheet notes" with "material" and partial development (for the First Symphony, two hundred to three hundred pages of notes are mentioned). After that comes the "rough draft" . . . at first fragmentary, eventually complete in two parts. Next is the "clean draft" of the composition or its completed portion—a two- or three-part version, sometimes with intended instrumentation (a type of "short score"). Finally comes the full score, with and without changes.

Quite frequently, even as early as Tiflis, the main musical line or, less often, two lines contain the scale that becomes the basis for a composition or movement. One sees the composer immersed in tonal design plans and delineation of space within the framework of his system. Tcherepnin turns to the piano at different stages of composing, both to search and to verify.

Balancing the work of composing with the work of performing was often problematic. Various letters from the *Sobeide* period confirm this. "Even if the business of composing is quite slow, in the area of the piano I see the first results after three weeks of work, in spite of the fact that I almost never practice more than two hours per day." "Yesterday I complained to you, my darlings, that composing had slowed down and piano was doing better. Today the reverse is true—yesterday my head was so filled with a scene from *Sobeide* that I practiced very inattentively. But the scene advanced significantly."

The rationality of Tcherepnin's work mode is exemplified in the precise scheduling of his work throughout the day, often for more than ten hours (composing—practicing piano—rewriting what had been composed). Indeed, he makes a conscious attempt to understand where his time and energy goes.

Having invited us into his inner workroom, Alexander Tcherepnin generously presents rich material to future researchers and historians of Russian twentieth-century music.

7 The Russian Composer

How does one remain a Russian composer abroad? In numerous annotations to published editions and recordings, as well as in newspaper, magazine, and radio interviews, Alexander Tcherepnin is characterized as a "musical citizen of the world" (*Musikalischen Weltbürger*), a composer who belongs to many countries and cultures. Willy Reich first used this formulation as the final words of his monograph on Tcherepnin, identifying the composer with "the universal humanism connected to understanding the true mission of the artist."[1]

Benjamin Folkman cites an expression with which Tcherepnin describes himself. It is less literal and more existential than it appears:

> Russian composer
> Georgian composer
> Composer of the School of Paris
> Chinese composer
> American composer
> Is this a handicap or an advantage?
>
> > I once calculated that in the twenty-one years between the two world wars, I spent two onboard ship, on trains, planes and in cars. My home was where my table and my sheet music were. Another full year of travel could be added for the period after the Second World War. I wandered around in forty countries, was at home everywhere and really felt at home nowhere. My only home is in my inner self, which remains the same and follows its own development.[2]

Tcherepnin's sense of migrancy, "homelessness," and absorption in his own world were the consequences of emigration followed by long and distant wanderings. Although his biographer, Willy Reich, received firsthand materials (diaries, letters, articles, and numerous other documents), many of these remained trapped behind a "Great Wall," that is, the Russian-language barrier! Reich could not fully appreciate the neo-*Kuchkist* genesis of the composer's musical system. Neither could he recognize, except in the most general way, the folkloric sources of many compositions. Moreover, the 1970 publication of Reich's biography could not possibly cover the last years of Tcherepnin's life, which comprised active correspondence with compatriots, a visit to the USSR, and the creation of two choral cycles—folk song and liturgical.

Compared to the above excerpt, Tcherepnin describes himself quite differently in his later correspondence. "My fate has been to lead a life abroad; and although the French consider me one of the composers of the École de Paris, émigré Georgians consider me a Georgian composer, the Chinese consider me a Chinese composer, and Americans consider me an American one, I feel like a Russian composer. I continue to think and to compose in Russian."[3] Indeed, this book serves to substantiate such a fundamental perception.

Writing his parents about preparations for Independence Day festivities in 1927, Tcherepnin observed, "Americans set off fireworks and, most important, petards, whose sounds, so similar to gunfire, remind me of Petersburg in 1917 and Tiflis in 1921!"[4] April 15 of the same year he wrote from the steamship *Majestic*, en route to the United States:

> Today, my wonderful darlings, is Easter Saturday, of course, and reminds me of how we spent this day in Peter [familiar name for St. Petersburg]. What a marvelous time that was! I remember it as if it were yesterday—the big silver basin in the Alexander Nevsky Cathedral, the service with a double chorus, and myself with you, dear Dad, and the figure of Uncle Kolya making his way toward us, and then our walk through the cemetery, all three together. I would so much love to visit there again and spend an Easter Saturday this way. May God grant it! Today I read in the steamship newspaper that the Hangchow government has arrested Borodin, so it looks like it's the end of the Bolsheviks there.[5] Could it be that even in Russland things will get better some day, and that we could manage to travel there for even a month each year, if not move forever? And think how many opportunities such trips would permit: the Public Library with all the books one could ever imagine, the Singing Chapel Library, the Petersburg Conservatory Library. What an enormous selection, what possibilities for native materials and the deepening of the national foundation! I dream that this will really come true some day. (April 15, 1927)

In the summer of 1928 Tcherepnin visited the Baltic countries, part of the former Russian Empire. His letters from late July and early August arrived from Riga, Tallinn, Narva, Hapsal, and Pechora.

> Yesterday spent the entire day enjoying the Russian landscape—small villages, carts, women in bandanas, roads full of puddles and virgin woods. Riga felt entirely like Russia. At the station only Russian speech could be heard, and one could see St. Petersburg horse-drawn cabbies. . . . It was so entertaining here to feel the reality of Russia and to be three hundred kilometers away from St. Petersburg after ten years!

> Little Russian churches give the landscape a more native feeling. . . . From high up on the quay there was a divine view of Narva and Ivangorod.

> Visited a small chapel under an oak with a miracle-working icon and the cemetery of the Northwest (Yudenich) Army. . . . Such contact with "native ground" is both very pleasant and nostalgic, and it induces much reflection.

> And on the road from Pechor, Great Pskov with its white bell-towers; and houses could be seen on the coast. My heart ached at being in my native landscape again after ten years. How I wish I didn't have to leave Izborsk for any place else, and could simply say: "Well, we've arrived home." (July–August 1928)

Russian language, and even spelling, was central to the Russian environment, especially within the Tcherepnin family. The Soviet reforms of orthography, although long overdue, were summarily rejected in most émigré publications, which adhered to pre-revolutionary spelling. In 1928 Alexander ordered a typewriter with a Russian font from the United States. "Alas, the spelling turned out to be Bolshevik—the Я and Ъ are missing," he wrote, and sent the machine for alteration (November 11, 1928). Four days later he proudly reported that "the Bolsheviks are expelled from my typewriter," and followed this with several common words printed in the old style, "I never thought these characters would be so full of native charm" (November 15, 1928).

Despite having quite naturally and successfully become part of the musical communities of various countries, France foremost among them, Tcherepnin remained an unquestionably Russian musician. This was true to his sense of self, to his undeniable history, and even to the way his contemporaries perceived his music. He took part in activities of the Russian diaspora. In 1927 he wrote his parents, "Upon request from [Viktor] Walther, I put together a suggested program for a chamber concert/lecture on the theme of 'New Russian Chamber Music.' Walter can speak about the development of a chamber style in Russian music and about its three directions: emotional (Myaskovsky), experimental (Prokofiev) and structural (myself)" (December 9, 1927). In 1958 *Russkaya mysl* reported: "The latest work of A. Tcherepnin is his Fourth Symphony in E minor for large orchestra. The Belaieff Committee awarded Tcherepnin the Glinka Prize for the work. The first performance of the new émigré Russian symphony will take place in the upcoming Boston Symphony season, conducted by Charles Munch. The previous Glinka Prize was awarded to composer Nicolai Medtner, who died recently in London."[6] Feodor Aivaz, a native Russian, worked at the Brno Opera Theater, directing operas by Tcherepnin and many other Russians. He wrote Nicolas Tcherepnin, who had helped Aivaz stage *Prince Igor* and *Legend of the Invisible City of Kitezh,* asking for the score to the Glazunov concerto and Alexander's sonata, on behalf of the Viennese violinist Lilli Ziber: "after all, your son, Glazunov, Rachmaninov, Stravinsky are for us an embodiment of that Russian culture which we have always loved so much, and which is beginning to be known and loved abroad only now."[7]

Even in emigration, Tcherepnin did not abandon his work as a music critic. This was not unusual among Russian composers—Lourié published many articles as well as a book about Koussevitzky; Dukelsky wrote about Diaghilev, Prokofiev, and Koussevitzky; Nabokov left not only memoirs but numerous articles. The émigré periodical press was generally remarkable in both quantity and quality.[8] In addition to a few specialized music journals, music was invariably featured in the most popular daily Russian-language newspapers. Among dozens of major authors who wrote brilliantly for the papers were Alexander Amphiteatrov and Vsevolod Pastuhov (*Segodnia*, Riga), Hermann Lowtzky (*Rul'*, Berlin), and Valerian Svetlov (*Vozrozhdenie* and *Rossia i slavianstvo*, Paris). A notable collection of newspaper clippings related to music is in the archive of the Union of Adherents of the Purity of Russian Language, in Belgrade. Here some of Alexander's writings can be unearthed. Others are found in the Russian emigration department of the State Russian Library. Although not as plentiful as documents that date from the Tiflis years, these publications are important nonetheless.

Tcherepnin was most often published in the Parisian émigré newspaper *Poslednye novosti*. His articles from the late 1930s reflect a turn away from avant-garde aspirations, experimentation, and complicated technique to formal simplicity. These "Musical Notes" are impossible to date precisely but are likely from 1938–39. They contain reviews of a series of concerts of the Pasdeloup and Lamoureux Associations, and of other national and private concert societies. Most of their attention is devoted to new music.

> The works of contemporary composers featured significantly in the programs of many concerts. . . . It is possible to recognize, it seems to me, that the dominant tendency of modern musical creativity tends toward the creation of the serious, the genuine, rather than a search for the new or unprecedented. The "Heroic" period of modern music has passed [and] successful experiments have become convention; they are classifiable, and in many cases serve as the foundation for a tradition that is imperceptibly arising. At the same time our era appears especially inclined to give credit to what had formerly passed unnoticed, lost amid the struggle for the new in its own time. Somehow one has a clear sense that anything that was ever done (or is done today) with talent, with true creative temperament, is viable, irrespective of the style in which the composer's talent expresses itself.[9]

Further on in the article, the reviewer comments on individual pieces by Henri Barraud, Alexis Roland-Manuel, and Jacques Ibert.

The brief article "Russian Music in the Lamoureux Concerts" offers a vivid depiction of Russian musical life in Paris. "Sunday's concert program included Balakirev's seldom performed overture *Rus,* composed in 1862 for the unveiling of a Novgorod monument to the millennial anniversary of Russia's founding. The composer intended to present in music the three elements of Russian national evolution: paganism, the Moscow princedom, and the primeval beginning. For these elements Balakirev used the themes of national songs which he collected himself. Dear to us in this work is the desire to express what is native, to display the direction that created the National Russian school." Unequivocally linking the Russian school with the Mighty Five, which is no surprise, Tcherepnin speaks astutely and sincerely about Tchaikovsky, whose Sixth Symphony was conducted by Eugène Bigot: "If in listening today to Balakirev one somehow involuntarily hears him in historical perspective, then in listening to Tchaikovsky one forgets all preconditions—so strong is his creative genius, so powerfully one feels today . . . the need to join that melodic world to which we are introduced through his creations."[10]

Another article on musicians of the Russian emigration opens with one of Tcherepnin's favorite ideas, which reappears on numerous occasions: "The more national a piece of music, the more international is its value. Russian music only became a cultural export when Russian composers realized their native elements and recognized in it a basis for their creativity." This is a rather common idea but one that may surprise us coming from the lips of this "musical citizen of the world." Tcherepnin also characterizes his junior Russian colleague, Igor Markevitch—then only barely known as a conductor and not at all as a composer. Speaking about his new work, *Le nouvel age,* Tcherepnin concludes, "Having grown up in emigration, Markevitch creates deep, truthful—and at the same time constantly evolving—Russian music."[11]

Still another striking article concerns a concert by Rachmaninov. This document becomes all the more significant considering that Tcherepnin, in his early Parisian years, had evaded a request to introduce his elder compatriot at a concert of Russian composers where they both were to play. Alexander later recalled, with some shame and embarrassment, that he had done so because he felt the great master was obsolete. However, writing many years later in 1938, Tcherepnin had begun to take a different view:

> As things happened, everything important and vital in pre-revolutionary Russia was forced to continue outside Russia. Almost all of Stravinsky's works were written in France, the better part of Prokofiev's oeuvre falls in his Parisian period, most national works of Nicolas Tcherepnin were created in emigration. Akimenko, Gretchaninov, Medtner, Hartmann, Paul also live and create in emigration, and the tombs of the last representatives of the national Russian school—Lyapunov and Glazunov, as well as Diaghilev . . . have become holy sites for the Russian emigration. Note further that precisely that which was the most national has emigrated; and the very fact of emigration not only failed to interrupt this national direction of émigré composers but indeed has strengthened it. Sergei Rachmaninov is first of all a great Russian artist; wherever he may live, whichever nation he may belong to, and all that he creates will forever remain the heritage of Russian music, Russian culture, Russian people.[12]

Most important here is not to dispute the discrepancies in the descriptions of Stravinsky and Prokofiev but rather to pay close attention to the ideas expressed here, as Tcherepnin is essentially talking about himself. His thoughts about composers who preserved and even intensified their "Russian-ness" abroad and their work, which remains "the heritage of Russian music," are very important for us.

Although music criticism did not become a major part of Tcherepnin's career, writing about music was part of his professional plans. In 1927 he wrote from New York:

> I think it wouldn't be a bad idea to add a third activity to my current dual career of pianist and composer: that of writing about music from aesthetic and historical perspectives. I have accumulated quite a number of books, enough to become a "specialist" on the history of Russian music, and I have thought an enormous amount about matters of technique and compositional ideology as well as aesthetic principles. Under such circumstances, this third aspect of my skills could in many respects direct my activity in a more serious channel, rather than just giving recitals, and will tie in with my compositional work even better than pure performance. (June 3, 1927)

The propensity for writing that is evident in the diaries and letters did not result in regular activity. But Tcherepnin did once appear as a specialist in Russian music history, when he prepared his *Anthology of Russian Music,* which contains eighty musical examples from the pre-Glinka era, beginning with extracts from folk and church music.[13] Although published many years after its creation, in the mid-sixties, this volume nevertheless gave Western readers much new information about early Russian music. Tcherepnin presented a copy to the Glinka Museum during his visit to the USSR. In a letter to Viktor Beliaev Alexander writes:

> The Belaieff Publishing House in Bonn recently printed eighty copies of my *Anthology of Russian Music,* along with my commentaries about the source material which predates the beginning of the nineteenth century. I gave this work to the publisher in 1938, but nothing was done about translation until after the war. Only now has the book finally been published. I assume you received the copy I asked the publisher to send you. I am very interested in hearing your opinion. My sources were various church books, beginning with Razumovsky and Mesentz, and various monographs. Some materials were found in the Italian libraries in Livorno and Bologna, some here and there around Europe. Among Soviet books the only ones then familiar to me were the *History of Russian Music* by Findeizen and Preobrazhensky's *History of Devotional Music.* Since then, Soviet scholarship has produced magnificent works with examples from the history of Russian music of all epochs, some of which I have been able to acquire. So if I were to embark on a similar project now, I would have an abundance of valuable examples. But, unfortunately, I had no such thing in 1938 and had to make do with what was at my disposal. Russian music since Glinka is well known in the West, but the earlier periods are only known by hearsay. Hence I limited my work to the time before Glinka, and even now, despite all its limitations and likely flaws, it may still shed light on earlier Russian music for foreign readers through the examples given. Indeed, it is the first such work to provide examples rather than simply recount a story (in German or English).[14]

As a pianist, Tcherepnin was an unrelenting proponent of Russian music. He made and performed his own piano arrangements of choral compositions by eighteenth-century composers (e.g., Bortniansky, Berezovsky) and later published his own editions of pieces by Glinka, Borodin, Liadov, Tchaikovsky, and others. He often played the works of his father, especially the *Esquisses sur l'Alphabet Russe.* This kept a constant "aura" of Russian musical intonation in his ear. Later in life he made recordings of Russian songs by Borodin and Balakirev with Boris Christoff, issued on two LPs, and also performed and recorded his father's songs with Nicolai Gedda. Still he most often played his own compositions.

The textual content and plots of vocal and theatrical works, such as those in Nicolas Tcherepnin operas, remained an important means of self-identification for Alexander. The elder Tcherepnin had also made an orchestration of Sokolovski's opera *The Miller—Magician, Swindler, and Matchmaker,* which, when it was performed in Paris in 1929, was probably the first eighteenth-century Russian opera that foreign audiences had ever seen staged. Nicolas even produced an edition of Mussorgsky's *Sorochinsky Fair,* having added a lot of new music, which was followed by Alexander's own completion and orchestration of *The Marriage.* Arthur Lourié had published vocal plays in Russian, based on Pushkin, Mayakovsky, Kuzmin, and Akhmatova, and he remained true to these authors abroad. In 1935 Lourié wrote a two-act opera called *Feast during the Plague,* based on a minor tragedy by Pushkin, and almost quarter of a century later it was staged in Paris. It was followed by another work in three acts, *The Moor of Peter the Great,* but this was neither published nor mounted. Even composers who had left Russia as children or teenagers sought out Russian themes, plots, or texts. Nicolas Nabokov earned fame for his ballet-oratorio *Ode,* inspired by a Lomonosov ode called "Evening Reflection," staged by Diaghilev in 1928. Twenty years later he composed the elegy *Pushkin's Return,* the opera *Rasputin's Death,* five poems for voice and orchestra with verses by Akhmatova, and four poems based on Pasternak's verses from *Doctor Zhivago.* Vladimir Dukelsky chose a Pushkin plot for his opera *Mistress into Maid.*

The link with Silver Age poetry was especially strong, for poetry held a prominent place in the culture that gave rise to these émigré composers. In Tiflis Tcherepnin had already composed numerous songs to Sergei Gorodetsky's poetry, and a quarter-century later he turned to Alexander Blok. The artist, illustrator, and designer Yuri Annenkov, who had designed Alexander Tcherepnin's version of Mussorgsky's *Marriage,* wrote eloquently about the Russian emigration in his memoirs, *Diary of My Meetings: A Cycle of Tragedies.* He devoted an entire chapter to Alexander Blok, whose poem, *The Twelve,* he had illustrated for a classic 1918 edition. In the last lines of the chapter he observed:

> In 1945 the composer Alexander Tcherepnin wrote some music for a chamber orchestra, set to the words of Blok's *The Twelve.* I first heard it in 1947, in Paris, during a musical festival devoted to Tcherepnin. The well-known actor Pierre Brasseur read the poem in a French translation by Gabriel Arout. I attended a second performance of this musical setting of the Blok poem in autumn of 1960 in the Salle Gaveau, where Paul-Emile Deibert narrated. The poem had found its acoustical expression, musical setting, and depth. "Music" with a capital M.[15]

Blok's exhortation to "listen to the music of the revolution" was unexpectedly embodied by Tcherepnin—in the rhythms and intonations of the poem he heard, and the authentic songs of the time, which he included in the fabric of the piece.

Extremely close to his father, Alexander was always familiar with Nicolas's creative works and plans. This had a considerable impact on Alexander's musical world, and thus it is worth examining some unpublished archival materials relating to Nicolas. In early April 1925 the elder Tcherepnin wrote to Vladimir Ivanovich Belsky, an important colleague of Rimsky-Korsakov and the librettist of *Tale of Tsar Saltan, Legends of the Invisible City of Kitezh and the Maiden Fevronia,* and *The Golden Cockerel.* Responding to the unexpected letter, in which Tcherepnin asked how Belsky was doing in Zagreb, Belsky answered:

> I feel as if it [the letter] opened a window to the lovely past. I saw you at the piano and as conductor, listened again to your resounding music, from the graceful *Pavillon d'Armide* to the *Fairy Tale of the Fisherman and the Fish,* which I feel is already a classic work of Russian music. I heard again your church music, your last "pre-Raphaelite" liturgy, and your quiet and modest conversation about great hopes and ambitious plans. I recollect your intentions to write an opera based on a Russian apocalyptic plot.

Belsky thanks Nicolas for taking care of his copyrights:

> However miserly the fee, it would do me a great service in my emigrant life; but this is highly improbable. I shall refer to *Golden Cockerel,* which is being staged or was staged in Berlin, Antwerp, New York; but no one considered himself obliged to pay anything to the emigrant deprived of his civil rights. . . . I am depressed by my separation from the cultural world and friends, and only dream to move, at any cost, to another place—if not Russia, then Paris.[16]

A second Belsky letter from August 1925, written in response to another unpreserved letter by Tcherepnin, indicates that Nicolas had made some successful efforts concerning Belsky's copyrights:

> Everything you have told me about yourself further arouses my curiosity about you as a composer. With all my heart I share your enthusiasm for Georgian folk music. I always had a romantic predilection for this ancient people, and what I myself had the fortune to hear in Guria and Ajaria encouraged this even more. Your religious-national musical bent also links your musical contemplation with mine. I likewise sympathize with your attraction to Leskov, and find the "Perambulation of the Virgin" that you have in your plans to be a marvelously touching poem. . . . I would work with you both with excitement and complete trust, but I cannot view the conditions of this collaboration optimistically. For a poet and musician to cooperate fruitfully, it is necessary for them to be in such unison that all your intentions would be mine, and mine yours . . . and how could we achieve this sitting in different corners of Europe? Besides, I have no access to materials here.[17]

After a visit by Belsky to Paris, the discussion turned to librettos, not only for Tcherepnin-*père* but for *fils* as well.

> Every free minute I spend remembering my dear Paris friends, their domestic coziness, the heartfelt kindness of the gracious hostess, the wide friendly embrace of the owner, as well as the magnificent musical emanations from your house. . . . I think of the construction of operas for the Tcherepnins, and have to admit that, although I had thought more of the father, I have moved toward thinking more of the son. The task itself is easier.[18]

Further correspondence reveals that, regarding Alexander Tcherepnin, "the ending of Posadnik is finished, and if this drama still interests him, then after writing for the father, I shall also work for the son." This unknown plan failed, as did the joint project for Nicolas Tcherepnin and an opera, *The Hour of God's Will* (based on Leskov), which could have been a continuation of *Kitezh.*

Alexander Tcherepnin's explorations of "Russian" librettos were constant and inseparable from his reading. He often mentions these in the correspondence and diaries preserved at the Sacher Foundation. Especially numerous are comments about the acquisition of books by Pushkin and about Pushkin, as well as books about Dostoevsky and other classic authors. Tcherepnin was purposefully gathering a Russian library, and he tended it until his final days.

> Yesterday was still reading Saharov, enjoying the language; finished Astronomy, and began to read Rovinsky's *Survey of Icon Painting in Russia.* This last book is very instructive and would certainly teach me to distinguish icons, at least approximately, if I only could see the related samples it discusses. And these are kept in Russian churches, museums, and collections! So once again, as with Old Russian music, I encounter the same problem: from outside nothing can be learned, nothing mastered—one must be 'there'. (August 31, 1928)

> Before going to sleep, I read Radischev. It seems to me, that . . . the eighteenth century is closer to us than the nineteenth . . . a different kind of people, more whole, sitting upright in a chair. In the nineteenth century this chair begins to splinter, and in the twentieth century we are already on something altogether different—a toilet seat. . . . Reading Radischev, who stood on the boundary of these centuries, comforts and interests me more than the eight volumes of Maikov lying nearby. (January 22, 1928)

The use of Russian history for opera plots repeatedly arises in Tcherepnin's plans. He receives from the USSR, perhaps by request, Chapygin's new book, *Razin Stepan,* which was approved by Gorky and was long considered the high point of the Soviet historical novels.

> Read Lazhechnikov and Chapygin's *Stenka Razin. . . . Sten'ka* continues to anger me with its Bolshevik coloring. However autocratic, seventheeth-century Moscow had culture and unity, and Chapygin's paean to the dark, uncivilized beginning of Cossacks and broad masses is quite ridiculous and jarring. If these masses had won, rather than the Moscow autocracy, Chapygin would probably be not only illiterate but would live in the woods eating grass and raw bear flesh. The idea of a state, when it means achievement of the highest cultural level or internal unity, is always higher than the idea of uncivilized unruliness. To spit on seventeenth-century Moscow means to spit on that which made possible the existence of the Russian state as a state. If this can be forgiving of some Demian Bedny [Stalin's poet laureate and perhaps his aesthetic hatchet man], who has remained indifferent to the cultural level of the country, then Chapygin ought to think twice before driving a stake into history. (June 13, 1928)

The idea of using the novel as a foundation for a libretto was set aside.

Steeped in the tradition of the Mighty Five, Tcherepnin could not avoid

Example 7.1

Example 7.2

turning to folklore. The new attitude toward folklore, embodied by Stravinsky, was also familiar to him from his youth.

Perhaps the first evidence of folk song can be found in the vocal suite for tenor and orchestra, set to Gorodetsky's poem "1914."[19] This score, dated August 1916, is not mentioned in biographies, bibliographies, or notographies. It has two movements: "Prayer of the Soldier" and "Woman Soldier." In this World War I era of Petrograd, the seventeen-year-old composer had not yet entered the conservatory, but he used a large orchestra, including trombones, contrabassoon, tam-tam, and piano. Note the rhythmic structure of the folkloric poetry (8 + 5 syllabic pattern) in measures 3–6 (musical example 7.1). Borodin's aria for prince Galitsky is rhythmicized exactly the same way, with the addition of doubled voices, as in the original folk song, "Masha Went for Mushrooms." The precise rhythm of the folk song (7 + 5) gives a Russian character to the theme of the second movement, although its harmonic element is not based on characteristic intervals of thirds and fourths (musical example 7.2). Another vocal piece set to Gorodetsky, which deals with a war theme, is "At the Kazan Railway Station"[20] (musical example 7.3). Undefined fifths remind us of the device used many years later by Prokofiev in his "Russian" movement, "The Field of the Dead" from *Alexander Nevsky.*

In *Basic Elements of My Musical Language,* the entire ninth section is devoted to "Use of Folkloric Material," comprising a list of pieces where folk songs were used. The inventory of Russian, Georgian, Armenian, Tatar, Czech, Chinese, and Japanese songs, dances, and separate themes is quite extensive. In the tenth section ("Some Additional Thoughts") and in *A Short Autobiography,* the problem of folklore is considered from a theoretical viewpoint and, most im-

Example 7.3

portant, in connection with his own evolution. Indeed, in the 1966 letter to Beliaev cited earlier, Tcherepnin wrote:

> I must first congratulate you on the development of your work, which has brought you international recognition; and I must express my gratitude for the article you sent about folk music and its history, which appeared in a Hungarian musicological journal. I, too, have been much occupied with folklore: Arabian, Chinese, Japanese, Dalmatian, and, of course, Russian and Georgian, and consider the folkloric "cure" to be the best medicine against abstruse abstractions. In my opinion, the study of folklore is as important for a composer as the study of anatomy of the human body is for an artist. The lines of the body are the lines of life, and the folk song, which lives through rhythm, is the lifeline of music. Folklore for the musician is a true source of "eau de vie"—inspiring, healthy, able to serve as the foundation for a young composer, capable of reviving the strength of the composer who is floundering amid the tenets of abstract theories.[21]

In both his *Short Autobiography* and the theoretical *Basic Elements*, Tcherepnin explicitly links the beginning of this "cure by folklore" phase to the late 1920s, and to ideas regarding Eurasianism. This complex and multifaceted concept is associated with the philosophical works of Lev Karsavin, Sergei Trubetskoy, and Pavel Suvchinsky. But, as far as we know, Tcherepnin was not connected with the representatives of the Eurasian movement. When he speaks of a Eurasian worldview, it is an act of self-identification in terms of personality and art. This becomes evident when tracing his creative biography, for example, the influence of Kuchkist "Russian Music about the East," the Scythianism of Prokofiev and Stravinsky, and, most important, the formation of his personal musical language from an amalgam of sources, including various "Eastern" influences. In this context Richard Taruskin's renowned book about Stravinsky, in which the problem of that composer's "Eurasianism" is considered in great depth and detail, is germane.[22]

To understand the ripening and systematizing of Tcherepnin's opinions, it is useful to examine a lengthy article about him in the leading journal *Deutsche Musik-Zeitung*, which relied entirely on the composer's words and explanations. The article was published in 1933, and, because of its original materials, it provides an important window into both the musician and the epoch.

> As for Tcherepnin's musical language, it is necessary to remember the deep reflection in his nature of the blood and character of the Russian people, whose son he is and wants to remain. He has already once expressed an idea which for us Germans has now become second nature: "All that has arisen on a firm ground of national, ethnic identity simultaneously has a tremendous right for greater international recognition. Every creator should speak in his language and involve his audience in the culture to which he belongs by nature."
>
> Modern Russia, which belongs ethnically to the Slavic peoples, has an indigenous population of European type, to which Asian elements have been added as a result of the Mongol invasion and their three-hundred-year domination. . . . The most popular Russian works of even the most seemingly Slavic Russians contain a considerable percentage of Asian spirit. Rimsky-Korsakov's *Scheherezade*, Borodin's *Polovetsian Dances* from *Prince Igor*, Balakirev's *Islamey* and *Tamara* are typical in this respect. . . . And Tcherepnin similarly considers the synthesis of Europe and Asia to be the ideal and original essence of Russian music. Hence it becomes clear why he titled the duet for violin and cello, recently issued by the Berlin publishing house Benno Balana, *Euroasisches Heft I* [Eurasian Notebook I]. In it he tries to apply this connection of musical styles of Europe and Asia. Russia for him is Eurasia. . . . If one analyzes the music of Tcherepnin, whose unusual charm is nevertheless subordinated to rules, one arrives at specific technical conclusions about his formation of a melody (due to a special scale, rhythmic elements, and elements of harmonization of themes).

In subsequent paragraphs the article describes Tcherepnin's musical language and analyzes it in detail, noting musical techniques gleaned by the composer from Eastern music, as well as his debt to the old traditions of polyphonic technique. The reviewer asserts:

> It is hardly necessary to emphasize that the technical elements of music present for Tcherepnin not a cold-blooded game of construction but a living intuition. . . . This explains many oddities in the composer's musical language, which, nevertheless, always rivets the listener's attention. . . .
>
> Undoubtedly, through all of Tcherepnin's works runs a single line, as is always the sign of a strong artistic phenomenon. Unquestionably this line is not German but precisely Russian. But this "Russian-ness" has nothing in common with today's Bolshevik Russia, but rather reminds us of his deep national connection with Mussorgsky, the slightly passive Christianity of Tolstoy, and Dostoevsky's manner of depicting the world as it is.[23]

Example 7.4

In the time of Dostoevsky and Mussorgsky, "Eurasianism" as a concept did not yet exist. But Russian thinking was intuitively gravitating toward the idea, as one sees with "In Asia lies our salvation" from Dostoevsky's *Diary of a Writer*. This gravitation intensified during late Imperial times. Another composer quite distant from Tcherepnin but deeply embedded in the Silver Age—Lourié—wrote in his diaries, "read Khlebnikov last night. Youthful memories flooded over me and the Asian wind blew softly again. How I loved this wind in bygone years! Everything European is for me death, decadence, bifurcation, disintegration, doubt, skepticism, and lack of will. Everything Asian is alive, truly vivid, cheerful and bright. What a strange vision: Christ in Asia!"[24]

It is not possible to disentangle the Orientalism of the Mighty Five from Eurasianism in Tcherepnin's music. In numerous autobiographical comments he links *The Wedding of Sobeide* with Eurasian tendencies. This is a convenient example with which to demonstrate the amalgamation of Eastern rhythms, generalized Easternness, and folklorism into a personal language. Indeed, the opera's second-act sequence, "Dances," offers a striking example (m. 410), where two sets of percussion, onstage and in the orchestra, produce a polyrhythmic effect typical of the Caucasus, combined with the sound of the tsurn.[25]

In "Dances" (scene 2, mm. 541–544) the melody of the top voice is similar in its modal structure to the third voice of Armenian religious music as it was preserved in the nineteenth century (musical example 7.4). In close proximity (mm. 550–569) the rhythm of the Georgian dance *Lecuri* is clearly heard. The same scene includes "Eastern" sounds and rhythmic relationships between drum and tsurn (from m. 416) (musical example 7.5). Harmonic intervals of fourths and fifths appear repeatedly throughout the opera but suggest no specific tonal reference—not even a Georgian one. The nine-step scale is used virtually throughout the entire composition.

The synthesis of Eurasian ideas is unevenly spread among different compositions. One of many examples is the Sonata for clarinet and piano (1939). It has only one movement and contains elements of cyclical forms—a frequent combination for Tcherepnin. This laconic sonata shows the collision of constructive-urbanistic imagery and nostalgic memories of the Mighty Five, resulting in a vigorous union of "European formalism" and temperamental "Asian sensuality"—alluding to the *Polovetsian Dances* but expressed in the composer's distinctive language.

Example 7.5

Tcherepnin did not simply "turn" to folklore but "was turned" to it, both by his exposure to national tradition, and the obvious link between his musical language and folklore. At the same time he did not rework examples of folk songs or strive to reach their archaic layers as Stravinsky did; instead, he treated them in a compositional way that avoided novelty. He also drew from many collected editions, including those of Evgenia Lineva, which he brought from Russia.

Included in Tcherepnin's list of his own compositions that draw on Russian folklore are the masterly piano pieces *Slavic Transcriptions,* where Russian and Czech themes are organized into a kind of suite created for his own performances. Much more significant among such works, however, are the *Russian Dances* for Orchestra Op. 50, where the feeling for Russian folk dance is enriched by exposure to musical sounds of the Far East. These are, moreover, loose adaptations. The composer emphasizes the general sound environment and infuses the kernel of the dance with diatonic-pentatonic scales. Here we find themes of dancing, of the soldier, the wedding, all based on examples that are difficult to pinpoint and that were probably never specific to one piece. In the fourth movement a limerick is intertwined with the "Kamarinskaya Dance," the latter sometimes played by three trombones in unison, and the former, by flutes and clarinets. This suite unmistakably demonstrates that Tcherepnin took with

Example 7.6

him from Russia not just collections of songs but a musical instinct formed by the *Kuchka* and enhanced by vivid impressions of Stravinsky's *Petrushka* and *Rite of Spring*.

The opera *Ol-Ol* (1924–25) is based on the play *Days of Our Life* by Leonid Andreyev. Tcherepnin turned to Andreyev's works on other occasions, such as for the scenario of his ballet, *The Abyss*. *Days of Our Life* was staged in St. Petersburg by Kommissarjevskaya, in Moscow at the Korsh and Malyi Theaters, in Odessa, Riga, Kiev, Saratov, and abroad (1910 in Vienna and Berlin, etc.). This drama was one of the most sensational plays of the pre-revolutionary decades, overcoming prohibition by censors in both Russia and Germany. It is striking that Tcherepnin, who was so far from Russia, chose this particular subject. The composer drew on the songs of the city, of modern life. In general, *Ol-Ol* is an opera about Russian life, and its sonic structure is unusually melodious for Tcherepnin. Nationally colored speech and aria-filled material prevails. But the melodies are expressively biting, particularly those of the character of Olga, a quality partially attributable to the composer's use of the nine-step scale (musical example 7.6, Overture to act 1). The name of the play is taken from a song popular among students in the 1900s, titled "The Days of Our Life, Fast as the Waves."[26] Quite naturally Tcherepnin chose to use the melody in the opera. Four choral voices are accompanied by the orchestra playing ostinato-like seconds in octaves, which creates an effect of "simultaneous contrast" (musical example 7.7). The simplicity of a later aria, sung by Onufry (rehearsal no. 80), contrasts with the intensely expressive musical language heard elsewhere in the opera.

The rondo finale of the Orchestral Suite Op. 87 (1953) opens with a folk-loric melody that is difficult to recognize as a direct quote. One can identify simple, short folk-song motifs, and further on (three measures before rehearsal

Example 7.7

no. 390) the theme contains clear elements of "Ey Uchnem" (musical example 7.8). Again, the composer is more interested in the general style rather than in an authentic reproduction of specific material.

Tcherepnin's closest approximation of his native symphonic tradition is probably found in the *Russian National Suite for Small Orchestra* (1941).[27] Only two songs here are identified by name—"Duckie" and "Korobeiniki" [Peddlars]—and they are reproduced exactly. Others, such as "Kamarinskaya" and "The Moon Shines," are easily recognizable and coincide with the development and expansion of the music.

Tcherepnin identifies his ballet *Stenka Rasin* as being infused with folkloric material.[28] This forty-minute ballet was written in 1937 to his own scenario, with choreography by A. Eltsov. In measures 9 through 12 of the Overture, the rhythm of the basses in octaves seems to correspond to Borodin's "The dark wood rustled, the dark wood hooted," in counterpoint with the same theme but condensed (musical example 7.9). Full of "Eastern" atmosphere, this is one of Tcherepnin's compositions most indebted to the Mighty Five. Despite being complex, harmonically dissonant, and steeped in *Interpoint,* its "Dance of the Gypsy," "Feast with the Shah," and slave-dance episode, as well as "Dance of the Tsarevna" on the deck of the boat, clearly reflect the Orientalism of the Mighty *Kuchka.*

It is not clear why the ballet *Trepak,* created by the composer and Sergey Sudeikin, did not make it onto Tcherepnin's folklore list.[29] The first production, which used soloists and an entire choir, was choreographed by Michael Mordkin, one of the stars of émigré ballet. Although the work still does not reproduce songs in their original form, it does mix actual song excerpts with stylized fragments, and alludes strongly to Silver Age and even Acmeist aesthetics.

Example 7.8

The three-act ballet contains the following scenes.

Act 1:
1. Introduction
2. Story of war
3. Round dance
4. Fight among the muzhiks
5. Competition of the Kamarinskaya dance
6. Dancing all together

Example 7.9

7. Marching
8. Delegation of veterans
9. Training of the novice
10. Military trepak
11. The bride's farewell
12. Departure

Act 2:

13. Zealous prayer
14. Kheruvimskaya [angel dance]

Act 3:

15. The construction of nature
16. Dance of the birches
17. The white dove
18. The devil and the white dove
19. The white dove and little devils
20. Dawn
21. Black-clothed clergy and the white dove
22. Religious procession
23. Return of the soldier
24. Pas de deux
25. Final dancing

Tcherepnin was most likely attracted to the trepak as a type of collective folk-dance, such as the kamarinskaya or the Ukrainian analogue, the gopak. It is even referenced in Pushkin's *Eugene Onegin* and in Tchaikovsky's *Nutcracker*, although in the latter's piano pieces Op. 72 the trepak works almost like a "code." In Tcherepnin's own ballet, *Trepak*, elements of the folk dance appear

Example 7.10

Example 7.11

in scenes 4, 6, and 8, and develop the themes and fragments reproduced here (musical example 7.10).

This ballet is also colored by the modal nature of the many themes that gravitate toward the pentatonic. *Trepak* was written after the composer's second trip to China and Japan, and the combination of major and minor pentatonics is an organic result of his visit to the Far East.

The textual part of this ballet recalls both liturgical verse and the poetry of Khlebnikov and Zabolotsky. One is immediately reminded of Tcherepnin's and Sudeikin's participation in Vassily Kamensky's evenings of futurist poetry in Tiflis two decades earlier. This is evident in the lyrics of "Kheruvimskaya" (scene 14), whose theme is similar to that of the previous number (musical example 7.11). The fusion of national-spiritual and Silver Age aesthetics is most notable in scenes 13 and 14. The scene entitled "Voices of Nature" is even reminiscent of Scriabin's lyrics, especially his *Preliminary Action*.

Trepak is one example of how émigré composers remained Russian abroad. Another Russian endeavor from the late 1930s and early 1940s was Tcherepnin's work on Mussorgsky's unfinished operas. Following in the footsteps of his father, who edited Mussorgsky's *Fair at Sorochinsk*, Alexander composed a second act for *The Marriage*.[30] The collaborative result was first heard in Shanghai and, later, on the radio in Bern. In 1939 it was performed by Russian musicians on a "Russian Culture Day" in honor of the Mussorgsky Jubilee, and was later staged by numerous theaters around the world.

Even in his late years Tcherepnin turned to Russian themes and folklore.

However, this was now linked to a new period in his life, one in which he felt he was coming full circle.

On the brink of the 1960s Alexander began receiving letters from the USSR. He answered joyfully, willingly, and at length. He renewed correspondence with Beliaev and Shaporin, and formed new ties with Kiselev, Shneerson, Khrennikov, and Bernandt. This sparked new "Russian" impulses and gave proof to his recognition.

During these years international tours by Soviet musicians were on the rise. They frequently featured contemporary domestic repertoire, and Tcherepnin attended whenever he could. He wrote to Shneerson in January 1970 about a concert he attended in New York conducted by Kiril Kondrashin. Expressing enthusiasm for David Oistrakh's performance, Tcherepnin continued:

> After intermission was Shostakovich's Eighth Symphony. What touches me more and more in Shostakovich is the humanity of his art, the breadth of his form—which seems to answer the immensity of our native land and embody it in music—and the authenticity of his creative genius. From beginning to end one listens to this symphony, lives it with unrelenting excitement caused by its inner message and deeply human significance. One feels a certain unknown essence inherent in works of musical genius. It transforms a set of musical sounds into a masterpiece. A joyful and deep impression. Kondrashin's inspired performance allowed the music to touch the hearts of the audience, to bring them spiritual renewal.[31]

Here Tcherepnin betrays a vision of Shostakovich remarkably different from that expressed in earlier comments.[32] This new view of his colleague reappears later in a letter written upon Shostakovich's death, where we also find a thought Tcherepnin frequently expressed: the immortality of the artist whose work bears the mark of his era.

> The death of Shostakovich is an irrevocable loss for the entire musical world. It is ineffably tragic. Of course I immediately sent my deep condolences to his wife. Physical loss is painful and difficult to bear. But the music of Shostakovich will never die; he will remain with us, and with the many that shall follow him. . . . His music captured his experience of reality and preserved it for future generations.[33]

Tcherepnin's library and reading were enriched by books he received from Moscow. He especially delighted in materials on the history of music. "The letters and diaries of Tchaikovsky are my favorite reading. Just before going to bed I am right now re-reading the first volume of his letters to his relatives," Alexander writes to Kiselev. He confesses, "The reading of letters, diaries, and writings of composers is more interesting to me than any fiction. They provide a picture of real, rather than reshuffled life."[34] In 1968 he mentions Tchaikovsky again:

> The day before yesterday I conducted a concert of Russian music in Manchester— Tchaikovsky's *Voyevoda* . . . my Divertimento, and Rimsky-Korsakov's *Sche-*

herezade. I have literally fallen in love with *Voyevoda:* so much music, lyricism, emotion, and dramatic feeling. The concert was a great success with the audience, and the orchestra enjoyed it as well. I don't understand why Tchaikovsky wasn't happy with it and destroyed the score! How fortunate that, thanks to Ziloti, it was preserved.[35]

Tcherepnin helped the Tchaikovsky Home and Museum obtain copies of autograph scores from French archives. After receiving an edition of the sketches for the Sixth Symphony from Klin, he wrote about the anticipated pleasure of studying them.

Enclosed with it were postcards showing the museum. Only in Russia could a landscape so dear to my heart, so calming to my soul, be found.... Yes, in such surroundings one can concentrate on work. I feel I belong to this world, in spite of the fact that my life is unfolding under absolutely different conditions, foreign to my nature.[36]

These renewed contacts inspired him to return to composing music to Russian texts, as revealed in the previously mentioned letter to Yuri Shaporin in 1960:

I have received an opera commission. Initially thought to use a Chinese libretto, but that idea has now become hateful to me. I don't know how much time I have left in this world, but I don't want to leave without having composed an opera in sympathy with the ideals of the Russian people.[37]

He makes similar comments elsewhere:

The longer I live, the more deeply I understand my connection to our common roots; and I would like to express this not only in words but also in music. It has already been a while since the Koussevitzky Foundation commissioned an opera from me. Originally I thought of using a Chinese plot—a drama by the sixteenth-century poet Li Yu, which was translated into English especially for me. But the more I thought about it, the less I was attracted to this plot.... Something epic, with large choral scenes, lots of movement, and dramatic moments would be much closer to my heart.[38]

Although this opera was never written, the intention itself was already significant, especially in light of Tcherepnin's positive assessment of Shaporin's *Decembrists:*

I would be delighted if Yuri Shaporin wrote me. Tell him that I often read his scores of *Kulikov Fields* and *Decembrists* in my rare free moments and always tremendously enjoy the breadth of scope, the majestic inner calm, and the Russian-ness of his work. These are truly the "large canvasses" of which Prokofiev dreamed when he returned home.... So I hope to be able to hear both these works and much else that is being created in the homeland but has not reached here yet.... From conversations with some foreign musicians who have visited the Soviet Union, I have the impression that the young generation is fond of dodecaphonic music (performed by a circle of "amateurs"), and is composing serial music, but that all this stays within rather narrow circles and doesn't get published.[39]

The libretto and composition of *The Story of Ivan the Fool,* based on Tolstoy, affords us another example of a "folk" variation on Russian subject matter. In the fall of 1967, almost immediately after his return from the USSR, Tcherepnin considered a Saltykov-Shchedrin "fairy tale," *The Story of How a Muzhik Fed Two Generals,* but he rejected it.

> Tolstoy's fairy tales are close to my heart.... I feel that it can somehow be adapted into a folk-theme production with numerous songs, choruses, and a lively plot. Although as I imagine it, much of this fairy tale seems utopian, a utopia that is sweet. And the moral—that work is the foundation of life—as well as the notion of dishonor through betrayal, is dear to me.[40]

Although *The Story of Ivan the Fool* has a folk aura, Tcherepnin uses ethnic material quite freely. "Ivan's Song" is based on melodic intervals of thirds and fourths but again does not derive from a specific example. In this case the songs that interest the composer are city songs, songs of the soldier, and limericks: "Ever since yesterday for some reason I keep hearing in my head the theme of the soldier song that I heard in my early childhood, 'Soldiers, Brave Fellows, Where Are Your Cannons?'" Having notated the exact melody, he writes Bernandt, "If you are familiar with this song, could you quickly send me the correct music as well as the complete lyrics? It would be a huge help!!! (I suspect that this song is 'pseudo-folk', but for the given purpose that is irrelevant)."[41] In the archive we find a complete set of manuscripts of this radio play along with the complete lyrics for "Soldiers," as well as metrically free interpretations of "Who among Us Is Good?" (which Tcherepnin altered to "Who among Us Is Pretty?") and other songs such as "We Make Beer."

The trend toward city songs is not accidental. Tcherepnin explains in a 1970 letter to Shneerson, "Just received a commission for a cantata for chorus and orchestra on Russian folk themes. I would like to use city songs and limericks as the basis! Unfortunately I don't have any."[42]

Writing to Russians about his completion of the "circle of life," Tcherepnin often mentions two choral cycles—Op. 103 and Op.104. He wanted these works to complete his "Russian biography." Indeed, although after 1968 he still lived another nine years and composed more music, he attached great importance to these particular compositions.

> Composing to Russian texts brought me great joy, and even though I am no churchgoer, seeing the Book of Prayer, Obyhod, and Gospels on my table brought me inner calm. Only yesterday I finished the works and today brought them to the publisher. Alas, in Russian they [one word indecipherable] and will be translated into English![43]

He later writes in a letter to Bernandt:

> I am also sending you ten a cappella choruses that I composed in New York in the fall of 1967. Six of them are sacred and four are secular, folk-influenced. All are set to Russian texts but were published late last year only in English translations. My delay in sending them to you was precisely because of this—

only now have I found time to add in the original Russian texts. As you will see, all the sacred works are set to liturgical texts and are freely composed. Only in the Hallelujah, as it approaches a brisk tempo, is the treatment influenced by the famous *Rospiev* [ancient style of Russian Orthodox church singing]. Two of the folk compositions use only one folk theme, but the two others—"Sorrowing" and "Fable"—combine two folk themes. I am very interested to hear what you think of them. These were the first things I composed after returning from a visit to my homeland, and I undoubtedly was under the influence of this enormously joyful experience.[44]

Alexander and Ming's trip to the Soviet Union is described in an article published in the journal *The World of Music*.[45] It is also described in Tcherepnin's diaries, but only briefly, because time was scarce. The invitation to visit had been sent by the Union of Composers, and, as five years earlier with Stravinsky's invitation, Tikhon Khrennikov played a leading role. Tcherepnin's only disappointment was a failure to find some of his personal archives. A year before the visit he had written Shneerson:

When I departed Petrograd in 1918, I left all my manuscripts, diaries, and the journal that my cousin Nikolai Benois and I "published" together (by hand) in an old-fashioned iron chest in the attic of the Benois home in Petrograd where we lived (15 Glinka Street). If you have a chance to find out what became of this chest, and locate it, I would be especially interested in my diaries (started in 1906), which span the period 1906–1918, including the first seasons of the Ballets Russes in Paris (1909, 1910, 1912).[46]

These materials, invaluable to both Tcherepnin and his biographers, were undoubtedly lost in the cataclysm of the revolution or the blockade.

The Op. 103 and Op. 104 cycles are not among Tcherepnin's best works, nor do they approach the heights achieved by other contemporaneous sacred music or folk-song arrangements. However, their composer considered them important and remarked on the symbolism of their creation as the result of a return from a visit to his native land. The reason for his partiality seems to lie in the choice of an a cappella choir. In spite of many unconventional and exotic combinations of instruments for which Tcherepnin had written, he had turned to an a cappella choir only once, indeed on the eve of his trip to the USSR. It was for one short piece—*Mass for Three Voices* Op. 102 (1966). This simple, classical mass was composed upon request of the prioress of a convent in Duluth, Minnesota, where Tcherepnin first gave a concert and later spent time. Comparing the convent to St. Scholastica College, where he stayed with his wife in July, the composer added: "In gratitude for hospitality, and stimulated by what I had experienced and seen, I composed a mass for three voices a cappella and presented it to the convent at the time of my departure. It is a typical mass: *Kyrie, Gloria, Credo, Sanctus, Benedictus, Agnus Dei;* but it is in English instead of Latin, which is now required! This unexpected project brought me great pleasure—for the first time in my life I composed for the Church."[47]

It is interesting to note that both Op. 100 and Op. 101 are linked to the world of sacred music. The sound of a female chorus without accompaniment was vivid in the composer's mind at the time of his trip to Russia, and he had not forgotten the centuries-old tradition of Russian musical culture, especially the Orthodox service. Op. 103 and Op. 104 were likely symbolic of this "return" to his personal and artistic consciousness.

Among the six sacred choir songs there are only faint allusions to choral tradition. Tcherepnin's individual style dominates. Only two of the songs end tonally, and the polytonal/sometimes atonal sound is frequently dominated by chords in fourths and fifths, which overpower traditional thirds. An abundance of chromatic and other peculiarities also differentiates these pieces from domestic tradition, as well as from the work of Nicolas Tcherepnin. One additional characteristic of Alexander appears in this liturgical cycle, which is his love for conveying motion, imagery, gesture, and the everyday sound environment (e.g., the ringing of bells in the coda of the "Angel Song"). Often, when young Russian composers decided to return to sacred music, their creations would reveal something in common with Tcherepnin's works.

The four pieces of the folk-influenced Op. 104 for mixed choir are substantially based on original samples that Tcherepnin had available, although some are closer and some further away from the original sources. The first, "Mountains," is a musical transcription taken from the collection of Evgenia Lineva, a common national choral practice of the postwar years. The second, "Shali-Vali," is a variation on the theme "As on Thin Ice." This melody is in the character of a round and overflows with pentatonicism. The third song is the most directly linked with tradition, especially of the Mighty Five. Its melody appears in major mode, then in its relative minor, and then alternates major and minor. The song is based on two national themes: a round dance and "Ey Uchnem" by Lopatin-Prokunin/Lineva. Such combining and merging of folk songs was also standard concert practice in the USSR after the 1920s. As we have seen, "Ey Uchnem" had already appeared in Tcherepnin's oeuvre, particularly in his ballet *The Abyss*. But in the case of Op. 104, he makes reference only to the melodic theme. Free "compositional" treatment, as well as the interpretation of a song as a small scene in itself, is characteristic of this work, probably the best in the cycle. The fourth and final song in the suite, "Fable," also has two melodies: one suggestive of a dance tune from Lvov-Prach and another from a collection of Balakirev but with different lyrics. In both cycles, however, something from Tcherepnin's "French" period still remains. The song "Fable" echoes the musical Impressionists in its use of harmony and texture.

In chapter 2 we discussed the significance of émigré contacts and other influences on Tcherepnin's work, especially in his first decade abroad. It is interesting to follow these threads here. Some dissolved in emigration, whereas others remained vital and continued to reflect his musical consciousness as well as the direction in which his life turned. The biographical materials in the Sacher Foundation illuminate this theme, as do other unpublished collections such as the archives of Sergei Koussevitzky and Arthur Lourié.

Particularly instructive are the letters of another "Russian Avant-Gardist,"

Ivan Wyschnegradsky. These letters date from the mid- and late 1960s.[48] On May 28, 1965, Wyschnegradsky left an LP record for Alexander with the concierge in Paris, which contained recordings of his recent works. When he subsequently became acquainted with Tcherepnin's new works, he wrote in October 1968:

> Dear Sasha! Bravo, bravo! Your Divertimento is a remarkable piece and pleased me in every way. It has an extraordinary wealth of musical ideas, bright and expressive, and brilliant orchestration. Despite its length, my interest did not wane for one minute. I would love to hear it again in order to better understand its structure, since such a large and significant work is difficult to grasp the first time through. You say that you now write differently. I would like to know in what sense you mean this; what part of this work belongs to your past, and how much have you changed since then? Three or four years ago I heard one of your new piano concertos . . . which I also liked very much.[49]

Further in the letter Wyschnegradsky describes in detail the conclusion of a large work that had taken him many years to complete, titled *L'Éternel étranger*. It is a staged musical work for four pianos, percussion, chorus, and soloists, and is set to his own lyrics. It uses microtonal techniques which range from third tones to twelfth tones:

> The task is very difficult, as I think of this music (approximately the same in the Prologue and Epilogue) as absolute. . . . I can only add (and this is an important detail) that the action takes place in Russia and that the entire ambiance is Russian. I can say the same about another of my staged works (I only have two): a one-act choreographic work . . . which includes a text I have written (sung by the chorus and soloists "in the orchestra"). It is devoted to the Russian people. . . . In it I express my belief in the Russian people and their great spiritual predestination. . . . I tread a path of revolution. I feel closer to Scriabin, who was the first to destroy dualism—the opposition of mode and harmony, which is absolutely alien to adherents of Schoenberg. . . . I have wanted to write you for a long time, to share my ideas with you. . . . You see, in the end, you and I are now (at least this is what I think) the only two serious Russian composers abroad. (This isn't counting Stravinsky, and I don't know of any others.) Why shouldn't we exchange ideas? And as for friendship, you already proved it a long time ago, with deeds rather than words.

There are numerous other letters which are crucial to understanding Wyschnegradsky's music that cannot be included here. It is important to note that he first identifies himself as a Russian composer, and secondly refers to the source of his own creativity: Scriabin. In the development of national musical traditions of the nineteenth and twentieth centuries by Russian émigré musicians, one recognizes the most significant aspect of their historical mission. Tcherepnin—a Russian composer in exile—served this mission throughout his entire life.

8   Finale

The title of this chapter does not herald any grand intent to summarize the life and work of Alexander Tcherepnin in definitive fashion. His legacy is too voluminous and too little studied to be assessed conclusively at this time. The title derives, instead, from the late diaries and letters of the composer himself, where he strove to understand and sum up his own creativity and life in the twentieth century.

It makes sense to return to Nicolas Slonimsky, whose words began the first chapter.

> Retrospectively, he [Alexander Tcherepnin in 1968] muses on the biographical and musico-epistemological aspects of his pursuits.
>
> His conspectus of these has ten points:
>
> 1. Instinctive period
> 2. How do I do it?
> 3. Piano practice
> 4. Theoretical study of Beethoven's works
> 5. The formation of a sui generis 9-note scale
> 6. The theory of Interpunctus
> 7. Escape from the mousetrap of cultural music into the world of natural art—that is, folklore
> 8. Journey to the East
> 9. Return to the West
> 10. Synthesis
>
> Elaborating on these ten points, Tcherepnin equates the instinctive period with his early youth. The question, "How do I do it?" reflects the first period of self-examination. Intuition was not enough; he had to find the rationale for his music. Piano study and the analysis of Beethoven's works were pragmatic occupations.
>
> The invention of a nine-note scale, however, represents the response to an intellectual impulse. Ever since his first attempts at serious composition he had been conscious of the ambivalence of homonymous major and minor tetrachords and triads, which also fascinated Stravinsky. But to Stravinsky the duality of the major and minor was *res per se*, sufficient unto itself. To Tcherepnin it was the point of departure for a new modality. . . .
>
> The scale has come to be known as the "Tcherepnin Scale," and is classified as such in the august *Musik-Lexikon* of Hugo Riemann. It can be analyzed in many various ways, for instance, as the evolute of three mutually exclusive augmented triads at the distance of a semitone and a whole tone, respectively. Or else it can be described as a chromatic "lipogram," in which the second, the sixth, and the tenth notes (or the third, seventh, and eleventh) of the chromatic scale are excised. In my own compendium, *Thesaurus of Scales and Me-*

lodic Patterns, the Tcherepnin Scale is tabulated under No. I-84, and defined as a double interpolation of the division of the octave into three equal parts. Permutations of the component intervals produce two basic modes, which, of course, can be transposed to any note of the chromatic scale. . . .

In harmony, especially, he employs a variety of structures—diatonic, pandiatonic, pentatonic. Although his melodies often assume atonal shapes, Tcherepnin has never been tempted to join the growing cohorts of dodecaphonic composers. . . .

The theory of "Interpunctus" is simple in its schematic plan, but infinitely varied in its applications. It posits a lemma that a coupled contrapuntal set may enter the vacant interior of another coupled contrapuntal set, provided that the first can be placed within the second without overlapping. The resulting four-part set may in turn enter, as an integral entity, the gaping maw of yet another coupled contrapuntal set, forming a polyphonic edifice of six parts. As far as instrumental, or vocal, ranges can reach, the resulting six-part set can be absorbed in the stomatic cavity of a still more voluminous two-part set, and so on and so forth. . . .

Tcherepnin was never a folkloric composer by intent and purpose, but he needed, as he himself phrased it, the fresh air of ethnic modalities to "escape from the mousetrap of cultural music." This he proceeded to accomplish by a study of folk music of many lands. . . .

At mid-century, during his "American" period, Tcherepnin reached Point 10 of his categorical tabulation, Synthesis. This consummation was achieved in his Second Symphony in 1951 and culminated with the *Symphonic Prayer* of 1959, which embodies styles and techniques that he had found useful and effective. In recent years he has become interested in electronic music. He has incorporated an electronic part in the score of his musical fairy tale, *The Story of Ivan the Fool,* after Tolstoy, written for a BBC broadcast on Christmas Eve 1968. Tcherepnin's lifetime has coincided with an unprecedented change in musical styles, from the innocent ecstasies of Scriabin to the unhinged exhibitions of the latest avant-garde—possibly the most revolutionary half-century in music history. Tcherepnin himself has contributed his share to this cavalcade of sound, revelling in autogenetic dissonances and twisting tonal melodies out of joint . . .

He faced a crucial test of tolerance for new-fangled auricular bombination when his sons, Ivan and Serge, both of whom have ineluctably become composers, joined the avant-garde. . . .

One is tempted to telescope two scenes in the fourth dimension of time: Nicolas Tcherepnin, looking over the shoulder of his adolescent son Alexander and marvelling at his free treatment of unresolved dissonances, and the septuagenarian Alexander surveying with curiosity and pride the manuscripts, in graphic optical notation, of his own sons, and certain that somehow this brave new music signalizes the emergence of a new means for the sonic art of the future. *Tertium non datur,* proclaims an old scholastic rule of logic. But in esthetics a *tertium* may well be found in a viable coalition of seemingly incompatible concepts. Alexander Tcherepnin has opted for electronic music just as his father had to reconcile himself to the prevalence of dissonance. In turn, the youthful advanced guard finds utilitarian merit in the formal symmetry of the language of the classics. The three generations of the Tcherepnin

Family extending through a whole century, demonstrate the historical truth that music is an art in flux, forever returning to its sources to replenish the energies spent in the pursuit of novelty.[1]

This breakdown of Tcherepnin's life into periods is not unique. The archive of Vassily Kiselev contains a typed catalogue of compositions sent to him by Tcherepnin, with an attachment of the following preamble, written in French.

It is possible to break down the evolution of Tcherepnin's music into four periods:

The first, lasting from childhood to the age of approximately nineteen years, is marked mainly by works for piano, and a spontaneous attraction to all things musical. Alongside the *Sonatine romantique* and the First Piano Sonata, the *Bagatelles* for piano, which were composed in his childhood and subsequently became famous, are perhaps the most characteristic of these years.

The second period, which begins in Tbilisi in 1918 and continues until 1927 in Paris . . . opens with his Inventions, Op. 13, and evolves to the First Symphony, Op. 42 and the Quintet, Op. 44, by way of rather complex works. . . .

The third period of his musical evolution, which began under the influence of "Eurasian" ideas (the synthesis of the Russian and Eastern), includes the opera *The Wedding of Sobeide,* Duo for Violin and Cello, and Concerto No. 3 for Piano and Orchestra. In time this phase was transformed by folkloric sources from Russia (Russian Dances, Op.50), as well as from the Middle and Far East (Etudes for Piano on the Pentatonic Scale, Concert Etudes, Op. 52, the ballet *Trepak,* Op. 55). It lasted from 1928 until 1947 (Fantasia for piano and orchestra [Piano Concerto No. 4], Op. 78).

The fourth period, which commenced in 1947 (Second Symphony, Op. 77) demonstrates a kind of synthesis of the three previous periods, and is marked by the creation of Tcherepnin's largest orchestral works, such as Divertimento, Op. 90 and the Fourth Symphony, Op. 91. This symphony, first performed in Boston and conducted by Charles Munch, earned Tcherepnin the Glinka Prize and is his most performed composition.[2]

The catalogue Tcherepnin sent Kiselev runs only until the late 1960s, but the composer continued to compose and perform for another decade and a half, despite long and grave illnesses. His correspondence with Russians and his diaries (where the last entry was made on the eve of his sudden death) paint a detailed picture of a busy life full of dynamism. It included performances as pianist and conductor, lectures, classroom teaching, recordings, and, of course, composing. A catalogue of his very last works includes such interesting pieces as the *Quintet for Woodwinds* and the *Flute Duo.*

On New Year's Eve [1973] Ming and I flew from Paris to Munich, where immediately on January 2 rehearsals began for the recording of my First Symphony and the Symphonic Prayer—two three-hour sessions per day for three days, which I conducted. Between sessions there was an interview on the radio with press, correction of parts, invitations to breakfasts and suppers, etc., from morning until late at night. The next day, after finishing the recording, we flew to New York, which takes nine hours from Munich, but there is only a three-hour time difference. After a meeting in New York we finally arrived home, where a mountain of collected correspondence awaited us, which took several hours to sort out. From morning till night the days are full. Then another flight, to Miami, where the violinist Erick Friedman and I were to perform my Violin Sonata, and again rehearsals, interviews, receptions after rehearsals, and the concert, and a final early morning taped interview at my hotel before our departure from Miami.

Immediately upon returning to New York there were rehearsals for three concerts planned around my birthday, with Nicolai Gedda, Judith Blegen, the violinist Spivakovsky, a string quartet, and the cellist Parisot. In addition to all that, I had an interview on the radio, providing commentaries to broadcasts of my works on various radio stations; and then concerts, receptions—not only in New York but also in the provinces; and all this alongside packing, flights, unpacking, hotels, interviews on arrival and at hotels, rehearsals, receptions, etc. And on top of all that, I need to practice, and learn new music.[3]

Throughout his existence, Alexander Tcherepnin never stayed in one place; and whether we divide his legacy into ten periods or five, his evolutionary artistic journeys are also indubitable. Still there are some constants for this "Russian composer," which we have already identified. This includes his dynamic rhythmic structures, which often emphasize toccata and *ostinato,* as in the work of Stravinsky and Prokofiev. Another is a tendency toward the suite as a structure for the development of a piece rather than sonata-allegro form. Connected to this is a tendency to create impressions using bright contrasts, and to think theatrically, so that even themes take on a character, a "personage." Folkloric sounds and Orientalism form a tonal foundation for a portion of his compositions, under the broad heading of "Eurasianism." Another theme in Tcherepnin's work is the opposition of the personal and the impersonal.

The genres that comprise his output derive directly from his individual style. There are three operas (one "Russian," one "German," and one "Chinese") and fifteen ballets, including one based on the music of *The Fair at Sorochinsk* by Mussorgsky and Nicolas Tcherepnin, and another written together with Arthur Honegger and Tibor Harsányi. Tcherepnin also wrote a total of four symphonies (leaving two additional symphonies incomplete), as well as other orchestral compositions (among them many suites), and numerous works for solo instruments and orchestra. The latter include six piano concertos, an enormous number of piano pieces, and ten cello works, among them three sonatas and a group of twelve preludes. There are also works for mixed instrumental ensembles which include traditional instruments such as woodwinds, as well as works for saxophone, tuba, even accordion. Despite this universalism, there is an obvious emphasis on the ballet and concerto genres.

There is extensive, mainly American, scholarly literature about Tcherepnin's symphonies and certain of his other pieces, particularly works for piano. An exhaustive analysis of Tcherepnin's musical output is certainly beyond the scope of this volume. But in keeping with the historical and documentary intent of this inquiry, let us turn instead to the words of the composer himself.

For me, symphonies are in a way a "thermometer" of my creative state, summarizing what was, opening new paths for what can be, and, most important, expressing in the fullest sense what "is."

My First Symphony registered my temperature in 1927
My Second Symphony registered my temperature in 1947
My Fourth Symphony registered my temperature in 1957
(The Third was compiled from my ballet music and does not count.)
And as for the Fifth—1967 (again a 7!) it should express what I am now and what I would still like to be![4]

We have seen how the creation of the First Symphony reflected the composer's "pulse" and his theatrical approach to music. Like the stringing together of beads on a necklace, it also demonstrates the way Tcherepnin connects contrasting passages to build drama, his use of rhythmic development as a theatrical tool, complex polyphony, and broad, carefully conceived dynamism. This use of rhythm as a dramatic device in Tcherepnin's work should be seen in the context of other works from the 1920s: Stravinsky's *Les Noces*, Bartok's First Piano Concerto, Prokofiev's *Pas d'acier*, and Shostakovich's Second Symphony, whereas his polyphony is similar to that in the compositions of Hindemith, and Myaskovsky's Eighth and Ninth symphonies.

Tcherepnin's Second Symphony is connected with the atmosphere of war and with Alexander's loss of his father in 1945. Both these themes are reflected in the expressive lyricism of the Lento movement. An emotional transition "from darkness to light" can be felt in the succession of movements. Here one observes the stronger, more pervasive presence of Tcherepnin's musical language—its metrical and rhythmic character, and the polyphonic saturation of orchestral texture.

The Fourth Symphony is undoubtedly the best and most Russian of all. Its conceptual depth and epic quality result in part from the assertive development section of the sonata-allegro first movement and the coda of the second, as well as the theme of doleful liturgical chant as a *cantus firmus,* which dominates the finale. The score is also tied to turn-of-the-century Russian symphonism, marked by a synthesis of the Petersburg and Moscow traditions. Numerous examples allude to Liadov (the final section of the first movement, the main theme of the second), Glazunov, and Rachmaninov (the main theme of the third movement, with its narrow melodic range and melodic repetitions). Nevertheless, despite the presence of dramatic moments, particularly in the first movement, the concept of the symphony is not a dramatic one, which links it even more strongly to Russian symphonism.

Russian figuration appears in two folk-song–like themes: the second part of the first movement has tonal, metrical, and rhythmic similarities to the epic song "About the Nightingale Budymirovich"; and a small fragment in the second movement is reminiscent of the chorus of the wives of the Strelets from *Khovanshchina.*

The symphony's Moscow influence is revealed by a preference for particular techniques of musical development. Themes do not recur, and new themes are

Example 8.1

Example 8.2

deduced from initial impulses rather than from the presentation of old themes in variation form. In the finale, the slow church chant theme is foreshadowed from the moment the violas sing the very first note of the movement, at rehearsal number 940 (musical example 8.1). The finale strikes the listener as powerfully reminiscent of something heard in Russia, perhaps by Myaskovsky (musical example 8.2).

From the diary records we learn that Tcherepnin spent a good deal of time composing the Fifth Symphony, which, however, remained unfinished. It was [partially] completed by Ivan Tcherepnin.[5]

Note Tcherepnin's own words about another of his favorite genres, the piano concerto:

Example 8.3

In my opinion, the task of a piano concerto is to provide the pianist an opportunity to reveal his musicality and "apparatus," i.e., the "spotlight" from
start to finish should be on the pianist. An ideal piano concerto (not speaking of the classical period) seems to be Schumann's concerto, where the piano
leads everything, and does it lovingly, not at all aggressively, and without a
hint of "schmaltz." From beginning to end it has marvelous music, without
eccentricities, without games or special effects, without competition for domi-
nance between the piano and orchestra. In contemporary music Prokofiev has
achieved this perfection and balance, though in a far more brilliant realization. The concerto should be interesting, that is, challenging for the pianist,
and quite easy, by contrast, for the orchestra. If in chamber music (such as in
a string quartet) a composer finds a medium for philosophizing and investigation, in a piano concerto such an approach is out of place.[6]

Each Tcherepnin concerto supports these words to some extent. The Second
Piano Concerto is a bright, masterly composition in one movement, with recurring elements. Both in its structure and musical development, it falls in the tradition of the European concerto from Liszt to Prokofiev. Imbued with the musical language Tcherepnin had already spoken about confidently in the early
1920s, it is a graceful and convincing work. This concerto, like its composer,
is a child of the twentieth century, born in the post-Prokofiev era. The non-
virtuosic treatment of the piano as a percussion instrument reveals this, as do
the huge spaces between the bass and the highest notes, a technique Prokofiev
particularly loved. An example from the recapitulation shows the melody in the
piano doubled over the space of three octaves, with the orchestra playing "in
the middle" (musical example 8.3). The lyrical second theme demonstrates use
of the nine-step scale (musical example 8.4).

Like the symphonies, Tcherepnin's six piano concertos—composed between
1918 and 1965—record the composer's "pulse" at different stages. Nos. 1, 2,
and 5 were frequently performed by Alexander and other pianists. The sixth
and final concerto was commissioned and premiered by the renowned pianist
Margrit Weber.

Example 8.4

For Alexander Tcherepnin, whose life was devoted entirely to music, summing up his life involved summarizing twentieth-century music. His "avant-garde" youth had shown that even among the sharpest twists and turns, there were still rules and constants. Although the century began with a crisis in tonal music, the second wave of the avant-garde brought even more radical problems. Many of these were beyond him, but, through his sons, he tried to take part and understand.

Having received a copy of Ivan's new work titled *Rings* in August 1969, Tcherepnin wrote to Shneerson:

> The piece *Rings* for string quartet with contact microphones, oscillators, and two-ring-modulators, is abstruse. No matter how much I read through it, I cannot imagine how it would sound nor understand how it was constructed. I will have to wait until I hear the tape recording made during the first performance in Boston.
>
> Here I amuse myself with recording the sounds of cicada choruses, crickets, insects, frogs, and, especially at night, woodpeckers. When I try to record, it sounds no less abstruse than *Rings;* and this to some degree justifies and confirms the musical approach in *Rings.* In both cases the world of "sound" is more multifaceted than the world of "music," which is limited by pitch temperament and inherited grammatical conventions. This is simultaneously easier and more difficult. The works of contemporary composers respond to progress in the engineering of sound production, as well as to the nature of sound itself. The contemporary composer creates, i.e., searches for, it is more precise to say, a new sound structure and a form appropriate to modern mankind.[7]

Today these processes have become part of history and in many respects are understood. A 1970 Tcherepnin letter is a valuable document of contemporary response to such new works:

How strange is the current musical climate in the West! The latest work of Stockhausen, according to witnesses, consists in his having permitted each separate instrument of a full symphonic orchestra to play one by one some arbitrarily chosen note. Each subsequent performer chooses a note after having heard the previous one, and so on through the entire orchestra, in addition to which Stockhausen sat at the electronic controls and varied the intensity of sonority and filtered its mechanical reception.... On the other hand, "quotations" of the classics in their original form or electronically modified serve as fodder for the music of Berio and many other modern tutti quanti. "Quotations" are also used by pop music—a lot from Bach—both in their original form and with altered rhythm; or altogether altered aleatorically, without a distinct form....

Does this seem strange to me because I am in my seventy-second year of life and, not having noticed it, have gradually become a vestige of the past in the living world of contemporary music? Or is it because of the decadence of modern art?

Anyway, Western youth sees in this art, in the sort of music described above, a concordant phenomenon.... I can't help wondering if it makes sense today to write a symphony, a quintet for woodwinds, etc. And I wonder whether I "hobble behind like a mangy hound," as the Old World is portrayed in Blok's *The Twelve*! Only the need to compose and my love for sound and its organization rescue me from my doubts, and support a belief in the creative instinct, and in the conscious shaping of discovered embryos into musical figures dictated by my ear.[8]

Not infrequent were moments of despair like the one described in this 1976 diary entry:

Tried to work but ineffectually. I long for something touching, intimate, instead of eccentricities. In general, the approach is so unclear. I am so thrown off course by modernity, and at the same time am dissatisfied with my own work. The time has come, as Dad would say (in jest), "to visit Beethoven."[9]

Two opinions expressed in Tcherepnin's reflections deserve our attention: a historicism of thought and an understanding of the inseparability of artistic means from artistic purpose. Certainly he was not unique in thinking about these issues. But it is important for us to know his precise opinions. Another piece of writing from 1965 documents the global changes of the time:

Until the late eighteenth century there was little difference in the means of transportation and the way of life of most people.... Charlemagne went from Paris to Asnières in a chariot drawn by bulls. Paul Revere rode a horse to save the cause of the emancipation of the Americans from Englishmen. Only in the nineteenth century did things seriously change—steamship, railway, gasoline—and in the twentieth century mankind experienced a cardinal change for the first time in its history. Electricity, the automobile, airplane, jet, telephone, TV, records, magnetic tape, electronics—flights into the cosmos.... Amid all this, can art—an embodiment of modernity and a modern society, the modern person—resist moving forward, not only in the sense of mission but also in the means of realizing this mission?

Therefore it seems to me that all modern technological opportunities, including electronic sound reproduction and the release of sounds from restrictions of pitch temperament, can assist the composer. They can be used by him for any purpose but, above all, to realize his mission of serving the people and society in which he lives. And I am happy that my son Serge, at Princeton [University], and my son Ivan, with Stockhausen and Pousseur, are trained in these new "means," which for them will be as natural as church harmonies were for Palestrina, as tempered construction was for Bach, "classical" musical language for classical period composers, folk songs for the Mighty Five, and the language of tone rows for Webern.

And I hope that, armed with these means, they can as honestly serve art and people as did their grandfather, my father, and as I have all my life tried and continue to serve. The young, unknown tribe is coming; it is time for me to decay and for them to blossom![10]

Another diary meditation in Marlow in 1975, after a long break caused by his latest heart attack:

The contemporary development of musical language, and not only language but the entire conception of form and the approach to musical content, has destroyed the approach that was natural. And it is understandable that the development of music seeks full-scale change, change which is far more categorical than the changes brought about by my generation in the period of our youth.

Youth is certainly right, and the freeing of tempered sound by electronic means, the expansion of what we now accept as music, is a completely logical phenomenon. After all, when I was young I dreamed of exactly this, and aspired to it. In the second movement of the First Symphony I freed myself from tempered construction through the use of untempered percussion. And now what I anticipated with such force, persuasiveness, and consistency has come to pass. Everything which follows down the old path is deemed a priori unnecessary, and spurned. One epoch is over. Another begins, and with confidence, despite its uncertain steps, discovers and reveals itself. The challenge is to find my place in all this.[11]

Reflections on the possible destiny of Tcherepnin's life were complicated by his feeling of rootedness in Russian culture.

Is it really possible to trust that one's time will ever come, when it seems to have passed? Time will tell—when I die and am sprinkled with *eau de mort*, will someone ever come to spray what I created with *eau de vie* (as happens in Russian fairy tales)? But in any case, whether what I created is fated to live or die, I shall strive to work until my last breath. I would like very much not to die before I complete the two symphonies I have begun, complete the Swiss commissions, and put my affairs and files in order....

And for the Russian musician abroad, these are now very difficult times. During the transition from the nineteenth to the twentieth century, and in the first half or third of the twentieth century, Russian music won recognition for itself, as did French music, whose compositional approach was similar to Russian. We tried to get away from Wagnerianism, and in general from German music—classical and romantic—which had had hegemony from the time of Bach until the late nineteenth century. The Russian and French beginnings turned out to be an unexpected change of approach, from internal to external, from philosophical to beautiful, sonorous, and folk-influenced. Composers searched for ways to remove German influence (were proud of this, strove toward it). They tried to compose music without choucroute,[12] and derisively called Stasov "Bach." Now much of this music seems like Christmas-tree decoration, whether it is *Scheherezade*, *Daphnis*, *Kikimora*, etc. I don't touch upon Tchaikovsky, who never rejected the German inheritance and used it as an expression of feeling and even Russian spirit. With Schoenberg, Alban Berg, and Webern, German music had its revenge. The strong hand of Boulez again turned the rudder toward intellectual music. And after him, since the sixties, new music—music hand in hand with science—has begun a completely new chapter and successfully leads the way. This new direction was born not from the *Rite of Spring* but from *Prince Igor* or *Godunov;* not from *Daphnis* or *Pelléas* but from post-Schoenbergianism, post-Webernism. And where am I in all this? The First Symphony, the Quintet, etc., perhaps conform slightly to the modern direction, but then everything I have composed derives more from Russian tradition. Perhaps only in Serenade [for String Orchestra, 1964] and Suite for Harpsichord [1966] have I found for myself something basically strong, even if not entirely new. Well, now I would like to move on to new shores, not because it's fashionable but because I feel the need. The question is really whether I can carry out what I feel inside, and avoid compromise.[13]

Tcherepnin tried to sum up his life not only in the creative realm but also in the autobiographical sphere. Writing on the eve of his last year of life, he observed:

I write this diary not as a "chronicle" of the everyday but because I want to record what oppresses me.... You see, I am Russian. And all my psychology is Russian, my thinking, my conscience, my creativity. And why did my parents and I leave Russia? You see, I did not want to leave either Russia or, later, Georgia; and I entirely sympathized with the revolution.... And yet we left. My poor father lived from hand to mouth.... I helped my parents, my grandfather Alik, however I could. Daddy died, having pawned his last watch the previous day. There was not even a clean shirt to put on him in the coffin, so we dressed him in my Chinese pyjama.... In the innermost part of my being I have not ceased to be Russian, and I live an absolutely different life.[14]

Tcherepnin's reflections about the end of earthly existence, about the inevitability of leaving, are very humane and noble, free of fear before the unknown (though he did not share the Christian belief in an afterlife). If it is really possible to be "ready" to leave, he was ready. Or, in any case, he was preparing to depart with respect to his creative life. In January 1977 he recorded in his diary a program of many points that he "must," and others he "hopes to," achieve in the field of composition, publication, and performance of his compositions. He even has sections labeled "Wishes and Hopes," and "Pledges" with numbered bullets, as well as the following:

1) It is necessary to sort through all the manuscripts, sketches, and letters here [in New York], to throw out what is unnecessary, to classify what is necessary;

2) The same must be done in Paris. Especially, to sort out everything related to Daddy, to leave it in order;

3) To classify the entire contents of chests of letters and documents, to put it in order. Also, all the documents and letters of Grandfather Benois;

4) To compile exact instructions in French regarding the Belaieff matter, and in the case of Muraviev's death, about the duties of the post of chairman; . . .

7) To inventory the library in Paris, especially valuable Russian books, so that heirs know the price and do not sell "by weight";

8) In general, to bring everything in such order that when I die, all would be [extremely] clear and the estate would be completely in order.

> Four pages of things that must be done before I die. I must now appreciate each day, must struggle with apathy, pessimism, inertia, and each day fulfill at least a little of what I have planned.[15]

A short time before, in November 1976, a diary entry shows preparations of a different sort at the Sainte-Geneviève-des-Bois Cemetery:

> Paid for the upkeep of Daddy's grave. The monument was repainted and in good condition, but the icon from the cross was stolen. . . . It has become the fate of all the icons. . . . But the cemetery, with its Pskov-like church (built according to Benois' designs) and similar monuments, with the autumn coloring of birches and deciduous trees on a light, partly sunny autumn day, was not sad, reconciling. . . . Maybe it won't be bad for me to be buried together with Daddy. There is room. Also, a young tree has sprouted, like on the grave of Grandpa Benois in Issy de Moulineaux. I didn't have the feeling of greater proximity to Daddy. He lives within me, not in the damp earth.[16]

In accordance with Tcherepnin's express wishes, his body was cremated. Some of the ashes were scattered over the Thames, some over the Seine, and the rest were buried near his father.[17] The ashes of Ivan Tcherepnin were also buried there in 2003, in accordance with his will.

The long wanderings and journeys of Alexander Tcherepnin ended nearly thirty years ago. What was the sum total of his earthly life as "wanderer"? What is his place as a Russian composer of the twentieth century, an artist of the Russian emigration? He himself provided one answer:

> My entire life has been nomadic, and when someone asks exactly where I live, I have to confess that it's mostly at airports waiting to board, on planes in mid-air, and in hotels. And though I have two "official" residences—apartments in New York and Paris—for a long time now I have been accustomed to feeling at home wherever I am. Wherever there is a room with a table where I can write, a bed where I can sleep, and especially when such a room contains a piano and my wife is with me, I have the feeling of being completely at home! . . . I dream that in the coming year, 1969, if I should live to turn seventy, this event will be celebrated in my native Leningrad . . . i.e., if I really dig deeply into my soul

and talk about home, then despite an absence of fifty years, I am truly at home in my Homeland, where I was born and raised, and which I have never ceased to love and keep inside me. I have not the slightest doubt that I am the "product" of my native land. I feel this in my attitude toward life, people, art, and my music. In all this I have a Russian approach, and approach my musical activity not as a manifestation of creative "ego," but as service to the people and society where I have been.[18]

This is not a singular mood but an expression of knowledge that had matured in Tcherepnin much earlier. Although he carried it within himself, he had indeed voiced this before, such as in a 1960 letter to Yuri Shaporin:

So I hope that my creativity will turn out to be suitable [to my homeland]: despite long years of wandering, I have never ceased to feel Russian, to feel I belong to Russian culture and ideology. In my lectures I always defend the idea that the composer should serve society instead of dictating to it. I also try to carry this through in my work.[19]

This book has traced Tcherepnin's contacts with the language, subjects, texts, themes, and folklore as well as church-music sources of "Mother Russia." But much work remains in order to understand how Tcherepnin belonged, if a generation later, to the Russian, St. Petersburg, Mighty Five compositional school. It was not directly with Borodin, Moussorgsky, and Balakirev that Tcherepnin belonged but rather with Stravinsky and Prokofiev, with the evolution and updating of tradition, and the preservation of certain archetypal characteristics. This continuous development of tradition and its merging with new ideas brought by the twentieth century created a whole new tradition: Russian music of this century.

In 1926 the "Russian Parisian" poet and philosopher Dmitry Merezhkovsky was asked this question: "What is emigration? Is it only a path away from the homeland, exile?" He answered: "No, it is also a return, a way home. Our emigration is our path to Russia. . . . [We are] immigrants from a former Russia into the future Russia."[20] The music of Alexander Tcherepnin, alive, very modern, very Russian, shall indeed repatriate to the Russian listener. This book is a step on that very path of return for the composer and his music. In the United States, as well as Western Europe, interest in Tcherepnin's work has waned somewhat, but it will undoubtedly return. For true music is eternal.

Appendix 1
Alexander Tcherepnin about Himself

Alexander Tcherepnin wrote diaries all his life, conducted an extensive correspondence, and continually reflected on his own creative process as well as his system of composition. He also repeatedly penned recollections of his experiences. (Enrique Arias's *Bio-Bibliography* contains a reference to the first such autobiographical text, published in 1928 in Cologne.)[1] In many of his press or radio interviews, and in his program notes for musical recordings, Tcherepnin began with childhood memoirs of St. Petersburg and his family, proceeding to emigration, Paris, and the later phases of his life. With time, the theme of a Tcherepnin "dynasty" enters Alexander's autobiographical sphere. Tcherepnin's stories generally focus on music, its role in society as well as evolution and progress, the mission of the artist, Russia as a "Eurasian" nation, and himself as a composer. Where his opinions or descriptions stray from an objective historical perspective, we will not dispute the matter, but we let Tcherepnin speak for himself.

In the unpublished *Alexander Tcherepnin: A Compendium,* edited by Benjamin Folkman, the preface discusses Tcherepnin's most extensive memoir, which was initially prompted by a commission from Flammarion Press for an autobiography. Tcherepnin responded with a fifty-six-page typescript written in French, completed on August 26, 1947. The publisher, however, who had expected an anecdotal narrative of travels and romance in Tcherepnin's engaging *raconteur* style, was disappointed to receive a detailed, year-by-year analytical examination of Alexander's evolution as a composer. Flammarion refused to publish the text. Yet the academic nature of the document proved invaluable ten years later to Tcherepnin's biographer, Willy Reich, who in some cases needed to do little more than recast Tcherepnin's text into German.

After 1947 Tcherepnin made many additions and revisions to the text, finally bringing it completely up to date in 1962. Other autobiographical texts exist but not all are currently in the hands of the Paul Sacher Foundation. The following essay, reprinted from the Folkman compendium, was written by Tcherepnin in 1964 in English and first published under the title *A Short Autobiography* in the 130th issue of *Tempo* magazine in 1978.[2]

A Short Autobiography (1964)

My father, Nicolai Tcherepnin, was an outstanding Russian composer, brilliant conductor, enlightened pedagogue. My mother had a beautiful mezzo-soprano voice, but because she was extremely timid, she became a soprano domestica, and I was the only one to accompany her singing of the German Lieder, Russian romances, and French songs, which, of course, I treasured.

Music in our home was a religion. I was the only child, and as a result I was admitted to all musical reunions (thus remembering Rimsky, Liadov, Cui, Glazunov, Stravinsky, Prokofiev, Diaghilev, Benois, Fokine, Pavlova, Chaliapin, etc.) and to rehearsals at home and at the concert halls when my father, his friends, or his students were conducting, as well as to concerts, to operas, and to ballets. Admissions also included home discussions of the Russian ballet (Diaghilev, my father, Benois, Fokine, Bakst, Nouvel, Nurok and tutti quanti) during the time of its conception and formative years. I was also permitted to associate via the Benois family (that of my mother) with contemporary painters and sculptors, attended their exhibitions, and met with writers and poets the stature of Gorodetsky, Kamensky, Gumilev, etc.

My father believed in God and loved the Church—he was Greek Orthodox—so I went with him to church services and attended discussions about religion at home with bishops and priests (the late Metropolitan Evlogi was an intimate and dear friend of my father's). I was equally at home in the Roman Catholic Church (my mother was Catholic) and with Roman Catholic priests, Moslem priests, Moslem mullahs, Shintoists, Confucianists, and Taoists—also with various branches of the Christian church—Georgian, Armenian, Syrian, Constantinoplean, Jerusalemian, and Coptic.

This was my background, and it is no wonder that since my earliest childhood music became my religion, my life, my goal, in fact, the very reason for my existence. According to my parents, I was hardly out of my cradle when I took to singing motifs I heard (such as the principal theme of Borodin's B minor Symphony) or motifs freely invented by me. There were two baby grand pianos in our home, and no sooner would my parents leave than I would be at one of them exploring the sounds, trying to find the sounds I heard going on within me. (As a matter of fact, to this day, when I listen within me I can hear sounds—melodies, motifs, harmonies, various sound combinations: music never stops working within me; it is as if music were part of my blood circulation, a part of my system.)

I never dared to improvise or to touch the piano in the presence of my father for fear of disturbing him, but I was less shy with my mother who soon realized what music meant to me. There was plenty of music paper lying around in our home. I observed how my father was writing his scores, and tried to do the same while alone. Noticing this, my mother taught me the secrets of music notation when I was five years old, so it happened that I learned how to write music and how to notate my musical ideas before I learned how to write words—before I learned the alphabet. So it is that even now the most direct expression of my thoughts is by music rather than by words. Yet, strangely enough, no regular music instruction in theory was given to me until the age of nineteen, at which time I had graduated from high school and had entered the Petrograd Conservatory. The only music instruction I had was piano study and even this was done casually. Instruction was initially given me by my mother, then by some old ladies, and finally by Leocadia Kashperova—an elderly woman who studied in her youth with Anton Rubinstein, and who composed and taught privately in her home, having no affiliation with any of the numerous Petrograd music schools. She used to tell me that I am running and that all she can do for me is to move my feet in order that I do not break them by running too fast, and indeed I was running: outside of the pieces she would assign me, I was busy studying classical and modern music of my choice and even had the nerve to perform them [sic] in public without my teacher's control or my parents' knowledge.

The fact is that music, having been my natural language, I always wanted to converse in this language with my fellow human beings. When on the stage I felt as natural and happy as in my home and never experienced stage fright—just the contrary. There was always a longing to be on the stage—a delight in performing at any occasion. This was a feeling begun in my early age and one that has continued until now at age sixty-five! I cannot separate myself from music. It is through music that I communicate with people.

The stage is like a church for me—the exact place where I can serve my religion, which is music, thus accomplishing my mission toward human beings.

As mentioned, during the first fourteen years of my "creative life" in the field of composition, I was left entirely to myself with no instruction, no supervision, no other way of learning the reactions of people and musicians than by performing my compositions on the stage. I must admit that, after nearly every concert that I played up to the age of fifteen or sixteen I would return home and go to bed weeping. Whether it was a reaction after the excitement of playing in public or whether it was because I felt the inadequacy of my abilities or a combination of both I cannot say; yet, it is a fact that after each performance I would hide myself under the bed cover and cry until the fatigue would close my eyes and put me to sleep.

Being very shy when I was young, even with my parents whom I loved dearly, I never confessed my troubles. The idea of shocking or troubling my parents was unbearable to me, so I never admitted my troubles to them and proceeded alone in my artistic development.

It was my wish to see my family happy, in fact I wished for all humans to be happy. Even in my earliest childhood I realized that happiness and unhappiness, joy and sorrow [are always] coexisting and cannot be separated from each other. As childish as it seems, it brought me, in music, to the idea of the combination of major and minor. I had always felt that the major-minor triad of C, E♭, E♮, and G is a "fundamental," "final" chord—therefore "consonant," "stable," and not in search of resolution like a dissonance in the classical concept of this term. I felt attracted to this major-minor chord. I heard it constantly sounding in me, and somehow, even in the early instinctive period of my composing, I used this chord as a final "consonant" chord. Later I realized that one of the reasons my ear protested against this well-tempered pitch, in which the intervals are different from the natural intervals, was because my ear was still hearing the traditional pitch with its traditional intervals rather than the major-minor triad. There was conflict between what I heard within me and what I would be able to reproduce by the conventional medium of the so-called "musical" sounds.[3]

Had I been born in 1949, I most certainly would have turned to electronic music in search of exact reproduction of what I heard in me, but being born in 1899, at the first decade of our century, there was no other way for me than to try by combinations of intervals to give the impression of natural intervals. Instead of searching for new means of reproducing the correct sounds that my ear heard, I had to adapt my ear to the convention of established music sounds. Of course, in my early teens I had no idea about the difference between natural and well-tempered pitch, and blamed my ear instead of blaming the well-tempered tuning.

The acceptance of the major-minor triad resulted in further acceptance of many unorthodox chords. So it came that already in my earliest composition the function of "dissonance" was lost, modes replaced the tonalities, and the self-made musical language, resulting from what was instinctive in me, was the tool which enabled me to materialize my musical thoughts and ideas.

For the entrance exam of the Petrograd Conservatory for which I applied at the age of nineteen, I produced orchestra and choral works, operas, ballets, five piano concerti, twelve piano sonatas, chamber music and vocal compositions that were passed among members of the jury, Glazunov, Liadov, Sokolov, Petrov, Ossovsky, etc. The jury scanned the manuscripts, and I have often wondered what the jury would really have thought if they had thoroughly read them, but such was not the case. I had a good ear and played well and so was admitted to the harmony class of Nicolai Sokolov and for the first time in my life had instruction in traditional harmony. Only then did I realize how different and unorthodox my own way of facing the harmony problem was. I did the required assignments with ease, and studying this problem gave me the idea to analyze my own way of musical methods which until this time was chiefly instinctive.

The 1917–18 season was that of revolution. In August 1918 my parents and I left Petrograd and settled in Tiflis, capital of the then independent republic of Georgia in the Caucasus. We stayed there for three years. While studying piano and concertizing there, I was again left alone as a composer.

I studied the classics, especially Beethoven, his musical language and form, and was attracted by Georgian popular and liturgical music. This, together with the self-analysis that started in Petrograd, crystallized my own musical language.

Superimposing two major-minor triads I discovered that they would fit into a hexachord that reads: C, E♭, E♮, G, A♭, B, (C); the same hexachord reversed and read from the top down would be C, A, A♭, F, E, D♭, (C). Added together they produce a nine-step synthetic scale that reads: C, D♭, E♭, E, F, G, A♭, A♮, B, (C). The major-minor triad is the fundamental triad of this scale. Due to the fact that the two tetrachords forming this scale are joined and identical, there could be only four nine-step scales as to actual sound, each having three modes—which brings the number of nine-step tonalities (or nine step modes) to twelve as to sound. I found that my instinctively composed music leaned toward this nine-step synthetic scale, is based on it, and is explained through it. From then on, what had previously been done instinctively was now done through theory and conscious application.

Meditating about the progress in music and rejecting the traditionalism from my early youth and the vagueness associated with it, I found in my mind that progress would be achieved via clear part-writing and therefore by polyphony. Here again, through analysis of instinctively acquired part-writing technique, I found that I had been naturally following certain polyphonic rules, a procedure I named "Interpoint." The name of this device is self-explanatory: punctus-inter-punctum, (as opposed to punctus-contra-punctum). It can be vertical if taken in the strict sense of the word or it can be horizontal when each of the parts acts as if having its own bar line, its own time; it can be polyrhythmic if each of the parts has its own meter in the form of a rhythmic pattern. It can also be a combination of both or of all three forms. Derived from my instinctively composed works, the nine-step scale and the *Interpoint* now became devices I was able to use consciously, and which were particular to my musical language.

During World War I Russia was completely isolated from the Western world. There was no radio. The only news one would have was through the newspapers which were strictly censored. There were no airplanes. The entire western border of Russia was a line of battlefields; the only directly accessible Western neighbors were Germany and Austria. In the south the Black Sea was dominated by Turkey, who was also in the war against Russia. To travel from Russia to France, one would have to go to Finland, then further via Sweden and Denmark or Norway by ship through the North Sea under the menace of German submarines, to England, and from there cross the Channel, under the same menace, to France. This was the only route of communication with the West. The southern route was too close to Turkey, while the lengthy route via Siberia, Japan, and the United States was complicated by the necessity of crossing two oceans before reaching Western Europe.

[Thus] cultural exchanges ceased. There was no knowledge in Petrograd about the progress of musical trends in the West, and vice versa. Even worse than the occupation of greater Russia by the armies of the German-Austro-Hungarian Empires was the civil war from within Russia itself. No less isolated was Georgia and the Caucasus during the three years of my stay in Tiflis, and even more isolated since early in 1921, when Georgia was besieged by Communist armies coming from Azerbaijan. So it happened (in my case so small compared to the great events around me) that from the age of fifteen until the age of twenty-two I had no communications with the West. In Georgia I had not a single friend with whom I could discuss my musical ideas; whatever I thought about music and its progress, I did in my own private meditations.

When I came to Paris in the fall of 1921, with a suitcase of my manuscripts and a small dog named Tou[s]chkan, whom I picked up on the streets of Tiflis, I found that my way of thinking about the progress in music was somehow identical with the views of the Western composers of my generation. The Western trend toward polyphony, toward organization of chromatic writing, toward using the medieval polyphonic devices, with or without classical form, corresponded precisely to my idea of organization of chromaticism via two hexachords (that could also serve to organize the twelve-tone scale) or via varieties of the nine-step scales, to the search of a new approach to the polyphony that I saw in interpoint. So I felt more at home in Paris than I felt in Russia or in Georgia, and this is probably why I settled in Paris.

If one looks through the score of my First Symphony (1927) one will find the practice of serial thematic construction of the theme and all the medieval polyphonic artifices associated with the use of interpoint. And if one examines the Finale of my First Cello Sonata (1924) one will find birdcalls used as motifs and, above all, the urge to be clear in texture and concise in form. In fact, the urge to get away from the conventional pitch resulted in scoring the second movement of the First Symphony for percussion instruments only, which produced considerable controversy at the time of the premiere of the First Symphony conducted by Gabriel Pierné, at the Concerts Colonne in Paris [in] 1927.

All this happened before the birth of dodecaphonic music, before Messiaen's looking for birdcalls for thematic material, before the esoteric use of rhythmic patterns by many a Western composer, and long before the liberation of music from a conventional pitch that became dear to post–Second World War composers. The fact is that progress in music, the development of new means of sound-making, new techniques in sound organization and sound production, is never due to a single man; rather, the "what next" comes as a continuation of what was before. Whether as an amplification of the "old climate" or an opposition to it, the "new climate" is the logical reaction mostly brought on by a new generation. It is not important who was the first, but more important who was the best. He who succeeds in being congenial with his time, who in Art expresses most strongly the "present," will be the one who will survive by representing the "present" to the "future." In my case, notwithstanding the differences that might exist due to personality, to the way of life, to the belonging to one or another community or country, I feel the affiliation to my generation which came after the First World War: a generation which opposed impressionism in music. Most of the composers of my generation had the same problems, which each of us tried to face and to solve to the best of his abilities.

The ideas that were previously mentioned as being instinctively mine, then consciously used, might have been my own personal ideas as I saw them, but they were also the ideas of my generation. They were "in the air," I felt them, faced them, and tried to use appropriate means to materialize them. I was not alone, and who of us was "first" is of no importance. The essential thing is to be honest and to compose music that one feels to be right. The ultimate value of a composition is the complete balance of the "what" with the "how." The "how" can and should be analyzed. The "what" is extemporaneous and can only be felt, and escapes every cerebral investigation.

I believe that the creation originates in what we call the instinct. How much the instinct is instinctive, I do not know. It might be that a composer is sensitive to non-audible sounds and then further expresses them into sounds that we call "musical." The composer's work consists of expressing the instinctively chosen sounds which are approved by his ear for the construction of a musical composition by adequate technical means.

In the late twenties I started to become tired of my own "technicality" of the nine-step scale, of *Interpoint,* of polyphonic devices, and even of the instinctively found musical material. The life of a composer is a continued drive toward progress, so I looked for a new means, for a deeper meaning of art. I began to reconsider values in order to get nearer to people and to get away from a deus ex machina kind of production.

Born and educated in Russia, I meditated about Russian music, about Russian people, about [the] Russian world concept (Weltanschauung), and [about the] Russian mission in art. This meditation brought me to the Eurasian theory about the Russian race. Old Russia—around a thousand years ago—was geographically situated in feudalistic states not always friendly toward one another. The Mongolian invasion put all these states under the domination of Mongols, so Russia became part of the great Mongolian State extending from the Vistula to the Pacific Ocean. After many centuries the Russians succeeded in defeating the Mongols, [though] the Mongols were never driven away; instead of Mongols dominating the Russians, the Russians dominated the Mongols, and inherited the great Mongolian Empire from the Vistula to the Pacific. There is a French proverb which reads, "Scratch a Russian, and you will find a Tatar." Indeed the Mongols merged with the Russians, and the actual Russian race is in many ways the result of this assimilation.

Hence, Russia is as much a European country as she is an Asiatic one—a true "Eurasian" empire—both geographically and ethnically. Russia is as much at home in the West as in the East; but while in relation to the West, Russia has an inferiority complex due to the superiority of the Western Culture—in relation to the East, she feels an equal. What is more, Russia has a message to bring to the East, while it has a message to receive from the West. To a Russian, the East is not exotic; it is familiar, a part of the Russian nature. Western influence on Russia might be materially important but it is spiritually destructive, while Eastern influence is of great artistic and spiritual value. The influence of Tibetan sacred painting on the Russian icon is obvious and important; the influence of Eastern music is manifest in such masterpieces as *Prince Igor or Steppes of Central Asia* of Borodin or *Scheherezade* of Rimsky-Korsakov, just to mention but a few of many examples.

When it came time to "scratch" myself, I recognized my affiliation with the East, natural for me as a Russian, and I found in the Eurasian Weltanschauung a stimulation, both philosophically and musically. To get away from my own musical formulas, I began to look into musical folklore. I came to the conclusion that what the knowledge of the anatomy of the human body is to the painter, the folklore of the people is to the musician. The lines of the human body are the lines of life, the lines of survival. Michaelangelo, Leonardo, Delacroix, each for his own purpose, studied the anatomy of the human body, and this helped each of them to operate with eternal lines in the production of their masterpieces. So did Picasso—only instead of recreating the image of a human, he used the same eternal lines of the body for abstract constructions, which gave life to his abstract paintings.

The musical lines of folk music are the lines of musical survival, for the folklore of all nations shares the common quality of having lasted through the centuries. In operating with material from folklore, the composer operates with eternal lines—lines for him to use in whichever way he feels appropriate.

I felt that the use of folklore in my compositions would be the right way to get away from self-imposed technical formulas. I started the search for folklore in Egypt and Palestine. I returned to the Georgian, Armenian, Persian, Azerbaijan, and Russian folk melodies that I had known and collected before.

It happened that shortly after the start of this "search," I went on my first concert tour to China and Japan in 1934. The concert tour was to last a few weeks in each country; but entranced by what I saw and heard, I stayed in Japan and China for an entire year; then after my return to Europe, I once again returned to the Orient for another year of concerts, of teaching, and of learning.

In the many compositions that I did between 1933 and 1939 I used various folklore as material, which helped me to find a new way. Perhaps the most important among them are the ballet *Trepak* that I composed in 1937 for Lucia Chase in which I used Russian folklore in a Chinese way, and the ballet *La Femme et son Ombre* that I composed on a libretto by Paul Claudel for Roland Petit's Ballet de Paris, in which Japanese folklore was used.

The war came, and what I—like most of humanity—lived through could not help but influence my art. Everything seemed so small in comparison with the tragedy and suffering that the war brought to everyone. It was no longer possible to think of art for art's sake or to seek refuge in operating with folklore. The most important goal for the composer seemed now to serve humanity, to help unite people by works of art, to try to bring understanding, beauty, and balance to shaken minds.

The first composition that I composed after the war with this idea [in mind] was my Second Symphony. Here I have tried to express my deep feelings of love for and affiliation to humanity, to produce a score in which every note would be "composed," not manufactured, by technique. I consider it [to be] providential that, precisely at that moment of my life, I was engaged to teach at DePaul University in Chicago, that I came to the U.S.A., settled in Chicago, and became associated with the American community.

Now, more than ever before, I realized the responsibility of the composer's mission toward humanity. The high standard of living in the United States provides many millions of people access to cultural values. The composer can converse with humanity through radio, television, and records. Concerts also expose the composer to a direct association with humanity, since music unites people around a work of art. Thus the work of art must be worthy, must bring a positive message to the people via music. The composer absorbs what humanity gives him and gives it back to his community in the form of a work of art.

I feel happy that I have been able to contribute to the life of American music as a composer, performer, lecturer, and pedagogue, and to serve the American community in every way I can to the best of my ability. I love people, I love to associate with people, and I love the American people. It is in this spirit that I have composed during the past fifteen years.

As to the "technical" means, I feel that I came to synthesize the dreams of my youth: the range of what we today consider "musical" sounds is wider and richer [than before]. The non-pitched percussion movement of my First Symphony is no longer a problem, and non-pitch music is cultivated by the post–Second World War generation of composers. The electronic medium gives [one] the chance to reproduce the sounds that one hears [with]in himself, exactly as one hears them with no concessions—thus realizing the urge that I had since I first listened inside myself an urge no longer contested by others. All the species of *Interpoint* as I conceived them in my youth are now audible and present in avant-garde compositions of the new generation, while the chromaticism for which I fought in the early twenties—whether it be in a serial way or in the way of arbitrary scale combination—has become integrated in dodecaphonic musical speech. The aleatory approach that I tried to materialize in the *Sonatine Sportive* for Saxophone and Piano in 1939 is one of the many approaches of the music making of today. What is most important, music becomes more and more a religion in that it serves to unite people by way of participating in the production of a musical composition—an ideal in which I have always believed, an ideal which makes the life of a composer worth living.

I feel fortunate to have survived until the time when music became truly universal, to be able to discard the multi-secular conventions, to create the true art of sound.

Notes

1. Alexander Tcherepnin, "Autobiographisches," Rheinische Musik-und Theaterzeitung (May 1928).

2. Alexander Tcherepnin, "A Short Autobiography," Tempo, no. 130 (1978).

3. An amplification of this point may help some readers. Here are the frequencies of the "natural" and "well-tempered" A major and A minor triads:

	NATURAL		WELL-TEMPERED		
	440	=	A	=	440
MAJOR	550	=	C♯	=	554
	660	=	E	=	659.26
	440	=	A	=	440
MINOR	528	=	C	=	523.25
	660	=	E	=	659.26

In the well-tempered system, the major third is decidedly sharp compared to the natural major third; the minor third decidedly flat compared to the natural minor third. Playing both these well-tempered thirds simultaneously creates the illusion that the "in-between" natural frequencies are being heard—or, at least, that the sharp major third is being somewhat flatted, and the flat minor third is being somewhat sharped.

Appendix 2
Alexander Tcherepnin about
His Compositional Technique

Although composers' theoretical descriptions of their musical language are scarcely a phenomenon unique to the twentieth century, such discussions became far more common after 1900. Some such elucidations took the character of a system offered to all, like that of Schoenberg, which was recognized, in time, as the continuation of the Austro-German compositional culture, and came to underlie the musical thinking and creative practice of countless composers, some of them Russian.

Other masters felt the need to substantiate their own individual compositional systems. Olivier Messiaen published a theoretical treatise whose name Tcherepnin's treatise echoes, *The Technique of my Musical Language* (*Technique de mon langage musicale* [Paris, 1944]). No letters or diaries by Tcherepnin discovered so far testify to his acquaintance with Messiaen's text, but most likely he was aware of it. Indeed, the French composer's text may well have prompted Alexander to undertake his own theoretical exposition of his compositional technique.

But this may also have been the result of a broad tendency of music in the last two-thirds of the century: composers' comments (both explanations and descriptions) devoted not only to their oeuvres as a whole but even to individual works. This was, indeed, a development specific to the twentieth century, since in earlier times, when all European music shared a common basis, theoretical works were devoted to music as a whole. In the new era, a musical language is often specific to a composer and demands the author's explication.

A fundamental fact must be stated immediately: for Tcherepnin, theory followed creative practice. Even in his youthful Tiflis works we not only hear the foundations of the nine-step scale but also recognize his awareness of that base. Many of his early musical manuscripts, and nearly all his later ones, carry a scale written out at the top of the page, which is most likely a basis for the composition as it evolves—although it may perhaps be a post-completion X-ray of the work. In many statements, as in the *Short Autobiography,* Tcherepnin stressed the organic nature genesis of his musical language.

His first attempt to formulate the basic properties of his technique was made at the prompting of Boris de Schloezer in the early 1920s. Burrowing deep in his acoustical world, deep within himself, Tcherepnin continued refining his explanations and descriptions until his last days. More important, in this synthesis of East and West, old and new, professional and national, he soon found a philosophical and aesthetic credo that stretched far beyond the limits of "technique."

Alexander attached great importance to *Basic Elements of My Musical Language,* which was written in English. Both Willy Reich's and Enrique Arias's books devote considerable space to discussions of the nine-step scale, and *Interpoint,* as well as their variants and revisions. With regard to these it is important to note a vast diary entry in Russian, made on October 17, 1976, and dating from Tcherepnin's stay in Marlowe. Marjorie Glock, who was working on an English translation of Reich's book, and essentially became Tcherepnin's second biographer, visited him frequently there, receiving extensive additions, amendments, explanations, and so on, from the composer himself.

A matter of terminology must also be clarified: Tcherepnin names his polyphonic technique sometimes "interpoint," sometimes "intrapoint," undoubtedly proceeding mainly from phonetic opposition to the concept of "counterpoint." The musical essence here is the idea of "the note between notes." When discussing his synthetic scale, Tcherepnin also regularly uses the term "mode," in analogy with the traditional diatonic "white-note modes." Dissonant three-sound verticals based on the nine-step scales he in turn treats as consonant chords (triads).

This author first became acquainted with the treatise via a photocopy presented by Ivan Tcherepnin to the Glinka State Central Museum of Musical Culture on a visit in 1991. The following text is drawn from the Tcherepnin compendium compiled and edited by Benjamin Folkman.

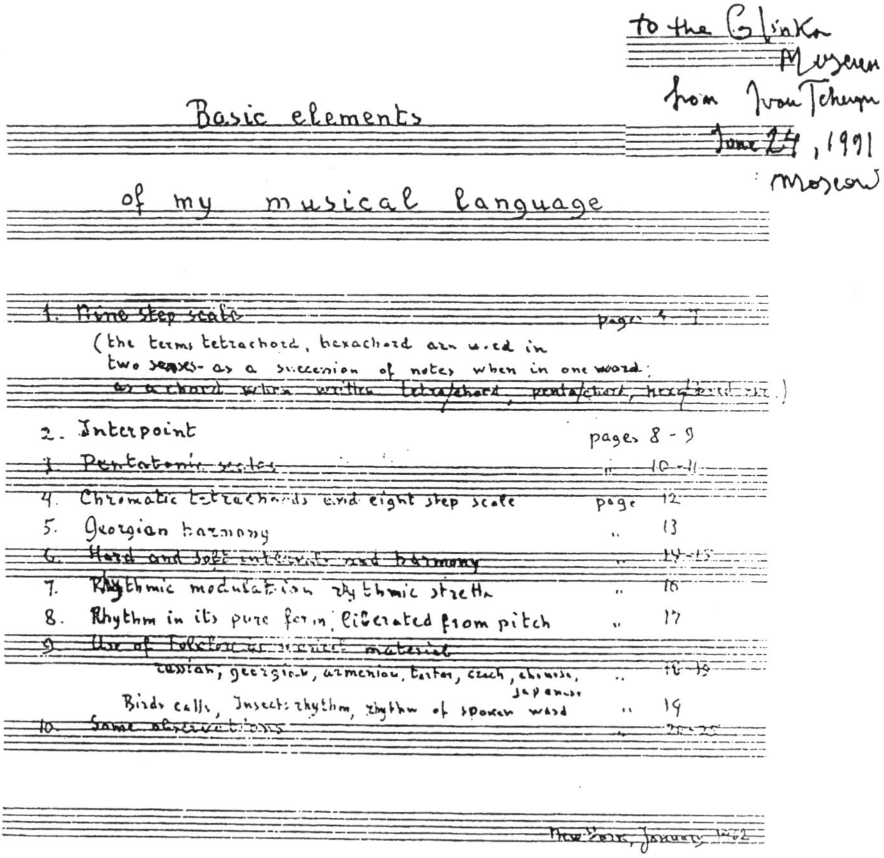
to the Glinka Museum
from Ivan Tcherepnin
June 24, 1991
Moscow

Basic elements
of my musical language

1. Nine step scale — page 4 - 7
(the terms tetrachord, hexachord are used in two senses - as a succession of notes when in one word; as a chord when written tetra/chord, penta/chord, hexa/chord etc.)
2. Interpoint — pages 8 - 9
3. Pentatonic scales — " 10 - 11
4. Chromatic tetrachords and eight step scale — page 12
5. Georgian harmony — " 13
6. Hard and soft intervals and harmony — " 14 - 15
7. Rhythmic modulation rhythmic stretta — " 16
8. Rhythm in its pure form, liberated from pitch — " 17
9. Use of folklore as source material
russian, georgian, armenian, tartar, czech, chinese, japanese — " 18 - 19
Birds calls, Insects rhythm, rhythm of spoken word — " 19
10. Some observations

New York, January 1962

Figure A2.1

I. Nine-step scale

Major-minor tetrachords are constructed within the interval of a major third using two half-steps and one whole-step:

Major-minor hexachords are constructed within the interval of a major seventh using alternations of half-step and one-and-a-half-step intervals:

with one octave added to complete the row:

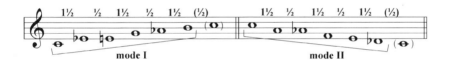

As shown in the example, mode II is the inversion of mode I.

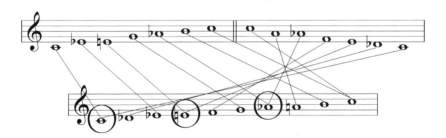

Note that C, E and A♭ are common to both hexachords and that the major third interval between them is the same distance covered by the tetrachord of mode I.

The nine-step scale, which results from the addition of two major-minor hexachords is therefore based on three interlocking major-minor tetrachords and can have three modes:

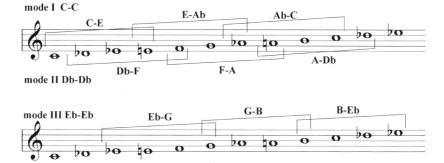

Because the interlocked tetrachords have identical intervals, the nine-step major-minor scale can have three points of departure (three tonics) in the same row, which are indicated by changes in notation (not by transposition).

As each nine-step row can have three modes and three tonics for *each* of the modes (differing by notation), this results in a total of 9 nine-step scales for each row: 3 fundamental and 6 derivative (through change of notation).

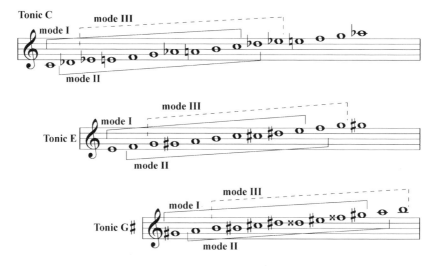

Each nine-step row can be transposed [only] three times in "fixed Doh" terms, [i.e., by a half-step, a whole step, or a step-and-a-half], since any further transposition merely yields one of the four fundamental rows (or scales), with the tonic (fundamental tone of the start) placed a major third above or below.

There can therefore be 4 fundamental nine-step scales, each with three modes (12 scales altogether) and 8 derivative nine-step scales (obtained by change of notation), each with 3 modes each (24 altogether).

This brings the number of nine-step-scale "tonalities" or modes to 36.

THE FOUR FUNDAMENTAL NINE-STEP SCALES ARE AS FOLLOWS:

(notation in ascending fifths)

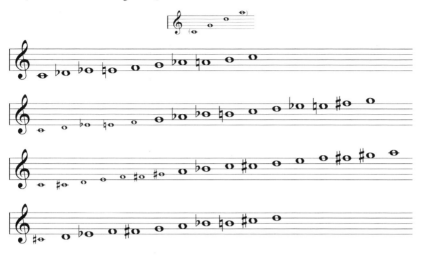

The notation will indicate the position of the point of departure (the tonic) and can be said to indicate the position of the tonal center.

If used in major thirds or minor sixths the scale will keep those intervals *audibly* intact (although some of the thirds will be written as diminished fourths, and some of the sixths will be written as augmented fifths):

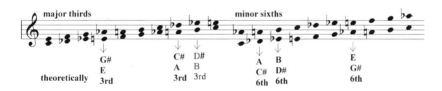

If used in minor thirds or in major sixths, the intervals will *audibly vary* between minor thirds and major seconds (when in thirds) or between major sixths and minor sevenths (when in sixths):

If used in fourths or fifths, the intervals will audibly vary between perfect and augmented fourths (when in fourths) or between perfect and diminished fifths (when in fifths).

If used in minor seconds or major sevenths, the intervals will vary audibly between major and minor seconds (when in seconds) or major and minor sevenths (when in sevenths).

In arpeggiated form, the nine-step scale can be presented in the following ways:

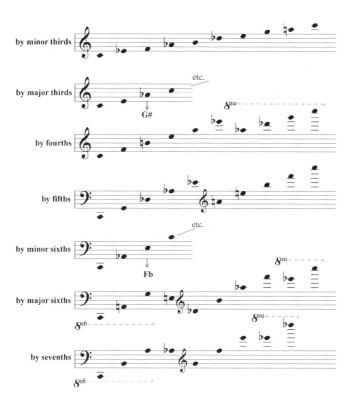

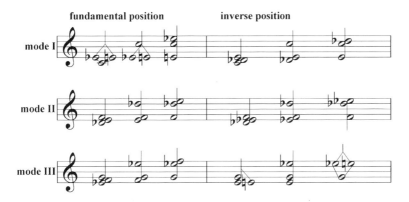

The fundamental perfect chord of nine-step scale harmony is the major-minor tetra-chord.

THE MAJOR-MINOR TETRACHORD AND ITS INVERSIONS:

In five-part settings in which the fundamental tetrachord is considered as stable (and final) any note of the fundamental tetrachord can be doubled; the pentachord intro-duces the element of instability.

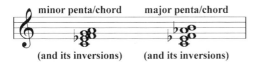

The minor pentachord is tonal in its "resolution":

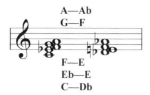

A—Ab
G—F

F—E
Eb—E
C—Db

The major pentachord can effect modulation by nine-step resolutions that arrive at a new tonal center:

Tonic C   Tonic D

In six-part settings the pentachord (major or minor) is considered as stable, while the hexachord is unstable, finding resolution in a pentachord, and so on, up to the point at which—in ten-part harmony—the entire nine-scale becomes a stable chord, with instability provided by an extra tonal appoggiatura (in ten-part settings), two extra appoggiaturas (eleven-part) or three appoggiaturas (twelve-part)

EXAMPLES OF THE HEXACHORD CONCEPTION OF MUSICAL SPEECH:

Feuilles libres, Op. 10, No. 2
Nine Inventions, Op. 13
Sonata for Violin and Piano, Op. 14
Six melodies, Op. 15, No. 5
Six études de travail, Op. 21

NINE-STEP AS EXCLUSIVE TONAL BASIS:

Four Preludes, Op. 24
Canzona, Op. 28
Sonata for Cello and Piano, Op. 29
Sonata for Cello and Piano, Op. 30, No. 1
Four Romances, Op. 31
Concerto da Camera, Op. 33
Trio, Op. 34
Mystère for Cello and Orchestra, Op. 37, No. 2
Training, Op. 37, No. 3
Violoncelle bien tempéré (Twelve Preludes for Cello and Piano), Op. 38
Message, Op. 39
Voeux, Op. 39bis
Second Quartet, Op. 40

Magna Mater for Orchestra, Op. 41

Symphony No. 1, Op. 42

Piano Quintet, Op. 44

Hochzeit der Sobeide, opera, Op. 45

Piano Concerto No. 3, Op. 48 (subordinate theme of 1st movement, entire second movement)

EXAMPLE OF EMPLOYING THE ENTIRE NINE-STEP SCALE AS A CHORD, AND THE USE OF NINE TONE ROWS WITH APPOGGIATURA RESOLUTION:

Symphonic Prayer, Op. 93 (measures 1–43)

II. Interpoint
(punctus inter punctum)

Interpoint can be *vertical* (which is self-explanatory):

EXAMPLE: SYMPHONY NO. 1, THIRD MOVEMENT

can be *horizontal:*

EXAMPLE: SYMPHONY NO. 1, FIRST MOVEMENT

N. B. The accented string rhythms coincide with the strong beats of the measure. Woodwinds establish their rhythm on the second 8th-note (horizontal displacement by the value of ⅛). Horns start on the third 8th-note (horizontal displacement by the value of ¼).

can be *metrical:*

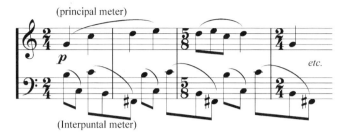

EXAMPLE: EXPRESSIONS, OP. 81, NO. 10 (EXIT)

N. B. Although the patterns coincide vertically, they are of different meters and different lengths.

can consist of various combinations of the three essential trends:

EXAMPLE: SHOWCASE, OP. 75

Combination of metrical and vertical *Interpoint*

MORE COMPLEX COMBINATIONS:

6-part "Formula" (3rd movement of Symphony No. 1, Op. 42)
8-part vertical/horizontal *Interpoint* (Quintet Op. 44, 2nd movement)

EXAMPLES OF *INTERPOINT*

Twelve Preludes for Cello and Piano, Op. 38 (especially Nos. 2, 4, 7, 10)
Message, Op. 39
Second String Quartet, Op. 40
Quintet, Op. 44
Piano Concerto No. 3, Op. 48
Duo, Op. 49
Chant et refrain, Op. 66 ("refrain")
Showcase, Op. 75 (especially Nos. 1 and 3)
Expressions, Op. 81
Eight Pieces, Op. 88 (No. 2, Intermezzo, No. 7, Etude)
The Lost Flute, Op. 89 (especially II. The poet's day)
Symphony No. 4 (especially movement II)

III. Pentatonic Scales

a) Major pentatonic scale and its modes:

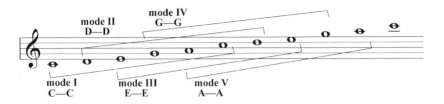

or, if taken from the same tonal center,

b) Minor pentatonic scale:

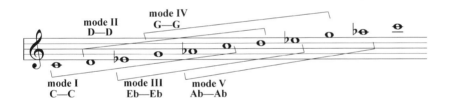

or, if taken from the same tonal center,

Major pentatonic as chord (constructed by using every second step).

of course, also in 3rd, 4th, 5th, and 9-step construction.

Alexander Tcherepnin about His Compositional Technique 201

Minor pentatonic as chord (constructed by using every second step).

of course, also in 3rd, 4th, 5th, and 9-step construction.

EXAMPLES OF MAJOR PENTATONIC

Etude de Piano sur la gamme pentatonique, Op. 51
 No. 1 Première Suite
 No. 2 Deuxième Suite
 No. 3 Bagatelles Chinoises
Five Concert Studies, Op. 52
 Ombres Chinoises
 Luth
 Hommage à la Chine
 Guignol
 Cantique
Technische Studien auf der pentatonischer Tonleiter, Op. 53
Deux mélodies, Op. 68
Seven Songs on Chinese Poems, Op. 71

MAJOR AND MINOR PENTATONIC

Trepak, Op. 55
Etude No. 7, Op. 56
Flute Trio, Op. 59
The Farmer and the Fairy, Op. 72 (also scale as chord)
Suite for Solo Cello, Op. 76
Fantaisie for Piano and Orchestra, Op. 78
La femme et son ombre, Op. 79
Suite for Orchestra, Op. 87 (third movement)
Symphony No. 3, Op. 83 (beginning of first movement)
The Lost Flute, Op. 89 (beginning)
Elegy Op. 82, No. 1 (stated as chord)

IV. Chromatic Tetrachords

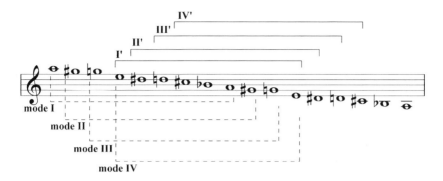

Modes I, II, III, and IV differ through the construction (modes) of the tetrachords.

Modes I′, II′, III′, and IV′ differ from fundamental modes I, II, III, IV only through pitch.

It is possible to produce a variety of scale construction by combining different modes of the tetrachords.

The fundamental chord would be one of the four tetrachords taken as a chord, and its inversions.

EXAMPLES OF TETRACHORD CONSTRUCTION

Symphony No. 4, Op. 91 (middle section of third movement—taken as a chord)
Partita for Accordion (third movement)
Piano Sonata No. 2, Op. 94 (eight-step scale)

V. Georgian Harmony

Fundamental Georgian triad and its inversions:

EXAMPLES OF ITS USE AS A TONAL BASIS

Rhapsodie Georgienne for Cello and Orchestra, Op. 25
Suite Georgienne for Piano and Orchestra, Op. 57
Enfance de Sainte Nino, Op. 69
Georgiana, Op. 92

VI. Hard and Soft Intervals
Hard and Soft Harmony

Hard intervals are major and minor sevenths and seconds, also perfect and augmented fourths and perfect and diminished fifths.

Soft intervals are major and minor thirds and sixths.

Hard-interval triad and its inversions:
a) Georgian triad

b) hard-triad

Harmony in hard intervals is limited to four parts:

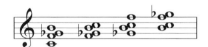

EXAMPLES OF HARD-INTERVAL HARMONY

Piano Concerto No. 3, Op. 48 (exposition of the principal theme)
Suite, Op. 87 (beginning and end of the second movement)
Symphonic Prayer, Op. 93 (second section; also appoggiaturas in hard-interval set-
   ting)
Piano Etude Op. 56, No. 4

ALTERNATION OF HARD- AND SOFT-INTERVAL WRITING

Piano Concerto No. 3, Op. 48

Principal theme of the first movement (hard intervals):

Subordinate theme of the first movement:

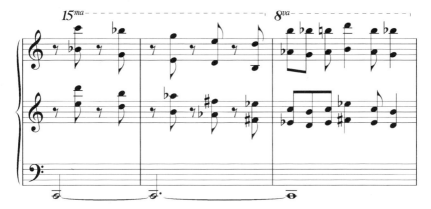

Chords built by thirds in nine-step setting

VII. Rhythmic Modulation

Rhythmic modulation: consists of "transposing" one theme into the meter of another theme or vice versa.

Example of rhythmic modulation: Cello Sonata No. 2, Op. 30, No 1, first movement recapitulation. The principal theme is transposed into the meter of the subordinate theme, the subordinate theme into the meter of the principal theme.

Rhythmic stretto: consists of gradually shortening the length of the measure.
Examples:

String Quartet No. 2, Op. 40, first movement—4/4, 3/4, 2/4, 3/8

Quintet, Op. 44 (at the end of the last movement preceding Coda)—4/4, 3/4, 2/4, 3/8, 1/8

Concertino, Op. 47 (first movement, second section)—7/4, 5/4, 3/4, 2/4, 1/4

Symphony No. 1, Op. 42, from—4/4, 3/4, 2/4, 3/8

VIII. Rhythm in its pure form liberated from pitch

Examples:

Message, Op. 39, last measure—the principal motif reduced to its purely rhythmic value

Magna Mater, Op. 41, coda—pure unpitched rhythm (percussion alone)

Symphony No 1, Op. 42—the thematic material of the first movement reduced to its purely rhythmic value and developed on that basis

The Farmer and the Fairy, Op. 72—introduction for unpitched metallic percussion instruments only

The Lost Flute, Op. 89, movement Va) Calamity—pure rhythm for unpitched percussion only

IX. Use of Folklore as musical material

I a) Russian Folklore

Transcriptions Slaves, Op. 27, Nos. 1, 2, 3, 4

Russian Dances for Orchestra, Op. 50 (Russian and Ukrainian themes)

The Legend of Razin, ballet (Russian and Ukrainian themes)

Flute Quartet, Op. 60, third movement (Ukrainian theme)

The Twelve, Op. 75, for Narrator and Chamber Orchestra (quotation of Russian themes)

Ol-Ol, opera, Op. 35 (two themes of Russian student songs)

Suite Populaire Russe [for small orchestra, 1941]

Songs and Dances for Cello and Piano, Op. 84, (No. 3, Ukrainian song; No. 4, Kazakh song)

Suite, Op. 87, last movement Rondo (Russian songs)

b) Russian liturgical chants

Symphony No. 4, Op. 91 (Requiem theme as cantus firmus in last movement)

Symphonic Prayer, Op. 93 (liturgical psalmody in third section)

II a) Georgian Folklore

Rhapsodie Georgienne for Cello and Orchestra, Op. 25

Suite Georgienne for Piano and Orchestra, Op. 57 (themes "transposed" in nine-step setting)

Concertino, Op. 47, last movement (rhythm of Georgian theme used as rhythm for freely invented theme)

Songs and Dances, Op. 84, No. 1

Chota Rostaveli, ballet, Act II

Georgiana, Suite for Orchestra, Op. 92

b) Georgian liturgical chants

Enfance de Sainte Nino, Op. 69, middle section (psalmody from Georgian liturgy)

Shamkhaz Venache (Hymn to our Lady) [piano], Op. 82, No. 5 (Georgian medieval chant)

III Armenian Folklore

Duduki, from the Episodes

The Legend of Razin, end of Scene 2

IV Tatar Folklore

Songs and Dances, Op. 84, No. 2

V Czech Folklore

Chanson tchèque, Op. 27, No. 5

VI Chinese Folklore

Punch and Judy, Op. 52, No. 4

Chant (liturgical), Op. 52, No. 5

VII Japanese Folklore

Flute Trio, Op. 61, last movement (theme of Tokyo Ondo)

La Femme et son ombre, Op. 74 (theme of Etentuku, theme of Tokyo Ondo)

VIII Birdcalls used as material

Sonata No. 1 for Cello and Piano, Op. 29 (1924), last movement

Entretiens, Op. 46, No. 10

Expressions, Op. 81, No. 9

IX Insect rhythms and calls

Duo, Op. 49, fourth movement

X Rhythm of the spoken word used as foundation for thematic material

Entretiens, Op. 46, No. 4

Enfance de Sainte Nino, Op. 69, middle section

Sonatina for Timpani and Piano, Op. 58, third movement

Expressions, Op. 81, No. 2

X. Some observations

1. The origins of the nine-step scale.

   Since my early youth I had the tendency and the urge to combine major and minor chords. Only a major-minor tetrachord gave me the sensation of finality and of stability. Then gradually I extended the 1½-tone ½-tone 1½-tone row further to reach the octave. By adding the ascending hexachord with the descending one I found the nine-step scale which evidently guided me instinctively before I started to theorize it (the first appearance of the nine-step scale is in the Romantic Sonatine, Op. 4, composed in 1918, while the conscious theorization of it came only in 1922 after the theorizing of hexachords that started around 1920.

2. Twelve Preludes for Cello and Piano, Op. 34 (1925–1926) are written in the complete circle of the 12 nine-step [tonalities]. I called it *Violoncelle bien tempéré* to underline the equality of flats and sharps which is characteristic of the nine-step scale.

3. Quite early in my life I had the urge to use pure rhythm liberated from any pitch. The first application of it was the reduction of the principal theme (motif) to its purely rhythmic value at the end of Message, Op. 39: the pianist has to beat it on the wood of the piano. A far more elaborate application of this urge for pure rhythm is in the second movement of the First Symphony (1927) which is for percussion alone. Here the thematic material of the first movement is reduced to its purely rhythmic value.

4. The "folklore" of birdcalls, of insects ("Katy did Katy didn't" etc.)—the sounds of nature, the rhythm of the spoken word—always had fascination for me. I started to use bird calls as musical material as early as 1924—the two themes of the last movement of my First Cello Sonata, Op. 29 (1924) are the calls of a "merle des roches" that I heard in Monte Carlo and "transposed" into the nine-step scale.

   The insects (fourth movement of the Duo) I heard during early autumn nights in Islip, Long Island, in the twenties.

   I have used the rhythm of the spoken word on many occasions. The third movement of the Sonatina for Timpani and Piano uses the prosody of the "Pater noster" recited in Russian.

5. At the end of the twenties I embraced the so-called "Eurasian" ideology, which is based on the idea that the Russian "Empire" inherited the empire founded by the Mongols, [with the result] that Mongols became assimilated with Russians (or vice versa). The opera *Hochzeit der Sobeide* and the Concertino, Op. 47, [reflected] this ideology. Then, after a visit to Egypt and Palestine where I looked for the familiar Orient came the Third Piano Concerto, [along with] the Duo that I baptized as No. 1 of *Cahiers Eurasiens*.

6. Eurasian ideology helped me [to escape from] the technicalities of my musical thinking which [had] culminate[d] in the Quintet, Op. 44 (1927). Yet [my approach] was still quite complex [in the period when] I was looking for simplification and renewal of my technical vocabulary.

7. Such simplification and renewal came via Folklore. I felt that, what the anatomy of the human body is for a painter—folklore is for a composer. The anatomy of the

human body gives the lines of "life survival." Every great painter has studied it—Michelangelo, Leonardo, Delacroix, Picasso—each one used it for his purposes (Picasso for abstract construction). [Similarly], Folklore gives us the lines of "musical survival." Operating with themes from Folklore, composers work with eternal material which they can use for any purpose.

8. My "cure" by Folklore started with the Russian Dances, Op. 50; then continued in China and Japan, where I became fascinated by the instrumental, theatrical, and vocal heritage of the Orient; then returned to Georgian Folklore: as there is a saying "proletarians of the world, unite!"—I would say that the Folklore of all countries and all races has the same eternal value.

   In my ballet *Trepak,* which I composed in 1937 on my return from China, I used musical themes from Russian Folklore that are pentatonic and treated them in a Chinese way.

9. There was a great decline in the quality of my production during the war years. To live through the occupation was not easy and I had to compose lots of trash—for dancers, for music halls, etc.—which had to be signed [with a *nom de plume*] because I was Russian. This helped *me* survive, but little of this war production of mine survived.

10. Immediately after the end of the occupation, even before the end of the war, my fertility returned. In one single summer (1945) I composed the cantata *Pan Kéou* in the Chinese idiom (which was produced at the Paris Opera for the celebration of the Chinese Double X), The Twelve, and the ballet *Déjeuner sur l'herbe;* then during the autumn and winter—*Jeu de la Nativité,* Showcase, and the ballet *Chota Rostaveli.*

11. The great change in my life occurred in 1949 when I came to live in the USA in Chicago; especially during the time between 1950–1958 during which I did not leave the USA. Numerous commissions gave birth to orchestral compositions. I orchestrated the Second Symphony, produced the Third using some older materials, then—Divertimento; Fourth Symphony.

12. The new musical language which I now used to express myself in larger orchestral forms synthesized all the technical devices of the past—which I outlined in [the previous pages]—and became combined with new research in form.

13. I see the profession of composer as a mission: a mission to serve the community to which he belongs, which stimulates him, in the first place, to give back to human beings what he receives from them, shaping it in the form of a work of art. When I say "serve" I do not mean to play down; on the contrary, to serve the community by art is to guide the community, just as a priest guides his congregation.

14. A work of art (a composition) as I see it must directly project the message it contains. Only if it communicates is it worth examining later on to [determine its principles of] "order," which are the technical means that the composer has used.

15. The technical devices employed by the composer can never be a goal in themselves, but only the means to express the message.

16. Above all is the imagination. Then comes personal taste that chooses among the products of imagination and after this the technical means that put in order the things imagined.

17. There are no "neutral" technical means. Each new idea needs new means, or extension of means.

18. So it is like building a house, extending it in all directions. Never reject what one had, but always add.

19. The greater the ideas—the larger the form.
    A large form cannot be filled up by extension of small ideas.

20. It is the Form and not the musical language that makes a composition long living. Every musical language becomes outdated sooner or later, but the message expressed by it in adequate form survives.

21. I do not believe in the so-called music of "tomorrow." The music that fully expresses "today"—which can be identified with the aims and with the cultural state of human beings in the community to which the composer belongs—is the music that may survive, by "fixing" a "memento" of the life of humanity.

22. Music is a construction in time: so many minutes of time put in order and "fixed" by the composer.

23. The reason why people like to listen to pieces of music heard before that projected [meaning to] them is a kind of "nostalgia" for the past.

24. Music is [a] uniting [of] people; [that] is its ultimate goal: its ultimate raison d'être is to make people feel united by contributing—[either] actively, in performing, or emotionally, in attending a performance of a work of art.

New York, January 10, 1962

Appendix 3
The Musical Heritage of Alexander Tcherepnin

Lists of Tcherepnin's works have been published in different years, in different countries, by different publishers, and for different reasons. What follows are two of these, a catalogue of works compiled by Lily Chou and a discography drawn from various sources by Benjamin Folkman, both included in the Tcherepnin compendium edited by Folkman. Titles are given in the language of the first publication. Not included in the catalogue are the numerous piano transcriptions, mostly of Russian composers' works, that Tcherepnin made for his performances, for pedagogical purposes, and on commission from publishers. Another exclusion is that of Tcherepnin's few incidental scores for film (1936; 1948), theater (1950–51), and television (1961–63).

The Music of Alexander Tcherepnin:
A Chronological Catalogue

compiled by Lily Chou

OPUS	TITLE	DATE COMPOSED	DURA-TION	PUBLICATION
Op. 1	**Toccata No. 1 for piano**	1921	6'	Belaieff 1922
	Revised ed. by the composer	1957		Belaieff 1957
Op. 2/1	**Nocturne No. 1 for piano**	1919	4'	Belaieff 1922
	Revised ed. by the composer	1957		Belaieff 1957
Op. 2/2	**Dance No. 1 for piano**	1919	4'	Belaieff 1922
	Revised ed. by the composer	1957		Belaieff 1957
Op. 3	**Scherzo for piano**	1917	3'	Durand 1927
Op. 4	***Sonatine romantique for piano***	1918	13'	Durand 1925
Op. 5	***Bagatelles* for Piano**	1912–18	12'	Heugel-Leduc 1923

OPUS	TITLE	DATE COMPOSED	DURATION	PUBLICATION
	Revised ed. by the composer	1958		Heugel-Leduc 1964
	Version for piano and orchestra	1958		Heugel-Leduc 1964
	Version for piano and string orchestra	1960		Heugel-Leduc 1965
Op. Posth.	**"Sunny Day" (forgotten Bagatelle) for piano**	1915	under 1′	Presser 1977
WoO	**"Old St. Petersburg" (Waltz) for piano**	c.1917	5′	MS
WoO	***Ballade* for piano**	1917	ca. 9′	MS
WoO	***Episodes* (*Priskaski*) (Fleas) 12 Simple Pieces for Piano**	1912–19 or 1920	10′	Heugel-Leduc 1923
WoO	**"A Contented Man" for bass and piano**	1918	2′	Chester 1938; Belaieff (in preparation)
Op. 6	***Petite suite* for piano**	1918–19	10′	Durand 1923
Op. 7	***Pièces sans titres* (Pieces Without Titles) for piano**	1915–17	9′	Durand 1925
Op. 8/1	**Nocturne No. 2 for piano**	1919	2′	Durand1925
Op. 8/2	***Dance* No. 2 for piano**	1919	3′	Durand 1925
Op. 9	**8 Preludes for piano**	1919–20	8′	Heugel-Leduc 1926
Op. 10	***Feuilles libres* (Loose Pages) for piano**	1920–24	9′	Durand 1924
Op. 11	**5 *Arabesques*** Andantino (piano) Allegro vivo (piano) Allegretto (piano) Presto (piano) Allegretto (violin and piano)	1920–21	5′	Heugel-Leduc 1925
Op. 12	**Concerto No. 1 for piano and orchestra**	1919–20	16′	Belaieff 1981
Op. 13	**9 Inventions for piano**	1920–21	8′	Eschig 1925 (Durand)
WoO	***Ode* for cello and piano**	1919	2′	Durand 1925
WoO	***Étude de concert* for piano**	1920	3′	Hamelle-Leduc 1924

OPUS	TITLE	DATE COMPOSED	DURA-TION	PUBLICATION
Op. 14	Sonata for violin and piano	1921–22	13′	Durand 1923
Op. 15	6 *Mélodies* for soprano or tenor and piano	1921	10′	Heugel-Leduc 1925
Op. 16	8 *Mélodies* for soprano or tenor and piano	1918–22	13′	Heugel-Leduc 1925
Op. 17	*Haltes* (Stops) for soprano or tenor and piano	1918–22	13′	Heugel-Leduc 1926
Op. 18	10 *Études* for piano	1915–19	25′	Heugel-Leduc 1925
Op. 19	2 *Novelettes* for piano	1921–22	10′30″	Heugel-Leduc 1923
Op. 20	Toccata No. 2 for piano	1922	7′	Simrock 1925
	Revised by the composer	1974		Simrock
WoO	*Romance* for violin and piano	1922	3′	Simrock 1925
	Version for violin and small orchestra	1922		Simrock 1925
Op. 21	6 *Études de travail* for piano	1922–23	12′	Heugel-Leduc 1923
Op. 22	Sonata No. 1 for piano	1918–19P	16′	Heugel-Leduc 1924
Op. 23	4 *Préludes nostalgiques* for piano	1922	7′	Heugel-Leduc 1924
Op. 24	4 Preludes for piano	1922–23	4′	Durand 1924
Op. 24/3 (posth.)	Prelude for 2 flutes, arr. by the composer	1971		Belaieff 1980
Op. 25	*Rhapsodie géorgienne* for cello and orchestra	1922	16′	Durand 1924
Op. 26	Concerto No. 2 for piano and orchestra (reorchestrated 1950) Original version for small orch.	1923	18′	Heugel-Leduc 1924
Op. 27	*Transcriptions slaves* (Slavic Transcriptions) for piano	1924	13′	Heugel-Leduc 1924
	1. *Les bateliers du Volga* (Song of the Volga Boatmen) 2. *Chanson pour la chérie* (Song for the Beloved)			

OPUS	TITLE	DATE COMPOSED	DURA-TION	PUBLICATION
	3. *Chanson granderussi-enne* (Song: The Great Russian People) 4. *Le long du Volga* (The Banks of the Volga) 5. *Chanson tchèque* (Czech Song)			
	2. Russian Song (new title) rev. ed. by the composer	1956		Heugel-Leduc 1956
	5. Czech Song rev. ed. by the composer	1956		Heugel-Leduc 1956
Op. 28	*Canzona* for piano	1924	5′	Simrock 1925
	rev. ed. by the composer	1974		Simrock 1974
Op. 29	**Sonata No. 1 for cello and piano**	1924	11′	Durand 1925
Op. posth.	**Canon for string trio**	1923–24	2′	Bardic 1987
	Canon (transcribed for piano by the composer)			Bardic 1987
Op. 30/1	**Sonata No. 2 for cello and piano** (second movement based on Canon for String Trio)	1924	10′	Universal 1925
Op. 30/2	**Sonata No. 3 for cello and piano**	1919–26	9′	Universal 1928
Op. 31	**4 *Romances* for piano**	1924	7′	Universal 1925
Op. 32	***Ajanta's Frescoes,* Ballet**	1923	30′	Universal 1933
Op. 33	***Concerto da Camera* for flute, violin, and chamber orchestra**	1924	13′	Schott 1925 Schott Prize, 1925
Op. 33a	**Intermezzo (2nd movement of *Concerto da Camera,* arr. for piano by the composer)**	1926	3′	Schott 1927 (The New Piano Book Coll/2, 1953)
Op. 34	**Trio for violin, cello, and piano**	1925	7′–8′	Durand 1925

OPUS		TITLE	DATE COMPOSED	DURA-TION	PUBLICATION
Op. 35		*Ol-Ol*, **Opera, first version in three scenes**	1924–25	58′	Universal 1926
		Final version in five scenes	1930	65′	Universal 1931
Op. 36		**String Quartet No. 1 (Love Offering by St. Thérèse of the Infant Jesus)**	1922	10′	Schott 1925
Op. 36a		***Musica Sacra* for string orchestra, arranged from String Quartet No. 1 by the composer and Kurt Redel**	1973	10′	Schott
Op. 37		**3 Pieces for chamber orchestra**	1921–25	28′	Universal 1927
	/1	Overture	1921	8′	Universal 1927
	/2	*Mystère* for cello and chamber orchestra	1925	11′	Universal 1927
		Version for cello and piano	1925		Universal 1927
	/3 /3b	*Pour un entraînement de Boxe* (For a Boxer's Training Bout) Prelude for chamber orch.	1922	10′	Universal 1927
		New version	1964		
		Training (unrealized ballet)	1922	10′	Universal 1927
Op. 38		**12 Preludes (The Well-tempered Violoncello) for cello and piano**	1925–26	25′	Durand 1927
		5 Preludes from 12 Preludes Op. 38, arr. by the composer: Nos. 2 and 4 for cello and percussion Nos. 3, 9, 10 for cello and strings	1925–26		Durand
Op. 39		**Message for piano**	1926	10′	Universal 1926
Op. 39b		***Voeux* (Wishes),** 6 Pieces for piano	1926	8′	Durand 1926

OPUS	TITLE	DATE COMPOSED	DURA-TION	PUBLICATION
WoO	*Pour la paix en Orient* (For Peace in the Orient) Originally one of the *Voeux*	1926	2 '	Durand 1926
Op. 40	**String Quartet No. 2**	1926	12 '	Durand 1927
Op. 41	*Magna Mater* for orchestra	1926–27	8 '–9 '	Universal 1931
Op. 42	**Symphony No. 1**	1927	24 '	Durand 1929
	Scherzo for percussion ensemble, from Symphony No. 1	(1927)	3 '	Presser 1974
Op. 43	*Elégie* for violin and piano	1927	6 '	Durand 1928
Op. 44	**Quintet for piano and strings**	1927	15 '	Universal 1930
Op. 44a	*Tanz* (Dance) for piano, arr. by the composer from 2nd movement of Quintet	1928	2 '	Bardic 1987
WoO	*Vocalise-Étude* for high voice and piano	1927	1 '	Leduc 1928 (No. 60 of Repertoire moderne de Vocalises-Études)
Op. posth.	**Study for high voice (or flute) and piano(** *Vocalise-Étude* **retitled)**			Belaieff 1980
Op. 45	*Die Hochzeit der Sobeide* (The Wedding of Sobeide), Opera in 3 scenes after Hugo von Hofmannsthal	1929–30	1 hr. 40 '	Universal 1931
Op. 45a	*Festmusik* (Celebration Music) for orchestra (Suite from *The Wedding of Sobeide*)	1930	10 '	Universal 1932
Op. 46	*Entretiens* (Conversations) for piano	1930	c. 13 '	Durand 1931
Op. 47	*Concertino* for violin, cello, piano, and string orchestra	1930–31	16 '	Universal 1931

OPUS	TITLE	DATE COMPOSED	DURA-TION	PUBLICATION
Op. 47	Original version for 4 violins, 2 violas, 2 violas da gamba, 2 cellos, bass, and piano	1930	16'	MS
	Version for clarinet, bassoon, piano, and strings	1944	16'	MS
WoO	**Triple Concertino for violin, cello, piano, and orchestra**	1965	16'	Universal 1973
	Version for violin, cello, and piano: Trio Concertante	1960		Universal 1974
Op. 48	**Concerto No. 3 for piano and orchestra**	1931–32	17'	Schott 1932
Op. 49	**Duo for violin and cello**	1932	12'	Benno Balan 1933
				Bote & Bock 1965
Op. 50	**Russian Dances for orchestra**	1933	10'	Benno Balan1935
				Universal
WoO	**Piano Method on the Pentatonic Scale**	1934–35		Shanghai Commercial Press 1935
Op. 51	***Étude du piano sur la gamme pentatonique*** **(Piano Study on the Pentatonic Scale)**	1934–35	19'	Heugel 1935
No. 1	1st Suite (7 pieces)	1934	3'	
No. 2	2nd Suite (7 pieces)	1934	4' 30"	
No. 3	*Bagatelles chinoises* (Chinese Bagatelles) (12 pieces)	1935	11' 30"	
Op. 52	**5 Concert Etudes**	1934–36	16'	Schott 1936
No. 1	Shadow Play			
No. 2	The Lute			
No. 3	Homage to China			
No. 4	Punch and Judy			
No. 5	Chant			

OPUS	TITLE	DATE COMPOSED	DURA-TION	PUBLICATION
Op. 53	**Technical Exercises for Piano on the 5-Note Scale**	1934–36		Peters 1936
WoO	*Die Heirat* **(The Marriage), Opera in 2 scenes by Mussorgsky– Tcherepnin**	1934–36	1 hr. 5′	Universal 1938
Op. 54	*Der Fahrend Schüler mit dem Teufelbannen* (The Wandering Scholar Who Exorcised The Devil), Ballet— piano version	1937	26′	Universal 1938
	New orchestral version (replacing lost original orchestration)	1964		
Op. 55	*Trepak*, Ballet	1937	40′	Universal 1938
WoO	*Autour des montagnes russes* **(Riding the Roller Coaster) for piano**	1937	4′	Eschig 1938 in the "Exposition 1937" Album
Op. 56	**7 Etudes for piano**	1938	9′ 30″	Belaieff 1938
Op. 57	*Suite géorgienne* **(Georgian Suite) for piano and string orchestra**	1938	20′	Eschig 1939
	Version for 1 piano, 4 hands by the composer	1938	20′	
	Version for 2 pianos by the composer	1952	20′	Eschig (Durand)
	Dialogue for piano solo (arr. by the composer from *Suite géorgienne*, 2nd movement)	1952	4′	Eschig
Op. 58	*Sonatine* **for timpani and piano**	1939	7′	Boosey & Hawkes 1940
	Revised edition for 2 or 3 timpani and piano	1951		Boosey & Hawkes 1951
	Version for timpani and orchestra			Boosey & Hawkes 1951
	Version for timpani and band	1966		Boosey & Hawkes 1966

OPUS	TITLE	DATE COMPOSED	DURA-TION	PUBLICATION
Op. posth.	**Sonata in One Movement for Bb clarinet and piano**	1939	6'	Schott 1980
Op. 59	**Trio for 3 flutes**	1939	6'	Belaieff 1950
Op. 60	**Quartet for 4 flutes**	1939	6'	Belaieff 1950
Op. 61	**Trio for 3 trumpets or 3 clarinets in Bb**	1939	6'	Marks 1952
Op. 62	**March for 3 trumpets or 3 clarinets in Bb**	1939	2'	Marks 1958
Op. 63	*Sonatine sportive* **for saxophone and piano**	1939	6'	Leduc 1943
	Original version for bassoon and piano	1939		Leduc 1975
	Version for piano	1939		MS
Op. 64	**Andante for tuba or bass trombone and piano**	1939	6'	Belaieff 1950
Op. 65	*Pour petits et grands: Douze pièces de moyenne difficulté* (For Young and Old: Twelve Pieces of Medium Difficulty) for piano	1940	25'	Durand 1940 (two volumes)
Op. 66	*Chant et refrain* **for piano**	1940	4' 30"	Durand 1940
WoO	*La légende de Razin* **(The Legend of Razin),** Ballet, Original Title: *Stenka Razine*	1940–41	50'	Belaieff
	Version for orchestra	1940–41		MS reduced
	Version for piano	1940–41		MS solo
WoO	*The Fair at Sorochinsk* Music by Mussorgsky, finished and orchestrated by Nicolai Tcherepnin, pub. Bessel 1941, Ballet version by Alexander Tcherepnin	1940	ca. 1 hr. 40'	MS
WoO	*Dionys,* **ballet mytho-logique**	1940	ca. 17'	MS

OPUS	TITLE	DATE COMPOSED	DURA-TION	PUBLICATION
WoO	*Suite populaire russe* (Popular Russian Suite) for small orchestra	1941	6′	Bessel 1949
WoO	*Badinage* for piano	1941	4′	Harold Lyche 1947
WoO	*Le retour du coche* (The Return of the Carriage) Original title: *Nevsky Prospect.* (original, longer version of Romantic Overture)	1942–43	13′30″	MS
Op. 67	Romantic Overture for orchestra	1942–51	9′	Schirmer 1955
WoO	*Vivre d'amour* (Hymn of Love), Cantata for soloists, chorus, organ, and orchestra	1942	ca. 6′	Belaieff
Op. 68	*Deux mélodies* (Two Songs) for soprano or tenor and piano	1943	5′	Durand 1946
WoO	*Atlantide*, Ballet with French text	1943		MS missing
WoO	*Valse orientale* for piano, flute, xylophone, and strings	ca. 1943	6′	MS
WoO	Polka for piano	1944	2′	Belaieff
	Version for orchestra	1955		MS available Belaieff rental
Op. 69	Evocation, *Enfance de St. Nino* (Childhood of St. Nino) for orchestra	1943–44	10′	MS available Belaieff rental
Op. 70	*Mouvement perpétuel* for violin and piano	1944	9′	Durand1946
Op. 71	7 Songs on Chinese Poems for soprano or tenor and piano (Chinese, Russian, English)	1945	12′	Belaieff 1956

OPUS	TITLE	DATE COMPOSED	DURA-TION	PUBLICATION
Op. 72	*The Nymph and the Farmer,* **Opera in 2 scenes (reorchestration of cantata Pan Kéou [Clam Shell], 1945)**	1952	40′	Boosey & Hawkes 1972
Op. 73	*Les douze* (**The Twelve**) **for narrator and small orchestra**	1945	16′	Belaieff 1946
	Version for narrator and piano			Belaieff
Op. 74	*Nativity Play,* **Cantata for 2 sopranos, tenor, bass, string quintet, and percussion**	1945	30′	Belaieff 1947
	Version for soloists, chorus, string orchestra, and percussion			1952
	Version for voice and piano			English translation 1962
Op. 75	*Le monde en vitrine* (**Showcase) for piano**	1946	15′	Boosey & Hawkes 1948
WoO	**2 Songs for high voice and piano**	1945	2′	Chester 1952
WoO	*Vendeur des Papillons* (**The Butterfly Salesman), Ballet**	ca. 1945		MS
WoO	*Chota Rostaveli,* **Ballet (2nd Act)**	1945–46	60′	MS
Op. Posth.	*Suite de ballet* (**Ballet Suite) arr. by the composer for 2 pianos and percussion, after the ballet Chota Rostaveli**	1946	ca. 20′	Belaieff 1982
WoO	*Rondo à la Russe* **for piano**	1946	3′	Gerig 1976
Op. 76	**Suite for solo cello**	1946	6′	Durand 1948
Op. 77	**Symphony No. 2**	1946–51	27′	AMP 1957
WoO	**"L'écolier paresseux" (The Lazy Scholar), folk song for voice and piano**	ca. 1947	2′	MS French and English

OPUS	TITLE	DATE COMPOSED	DURA-TION	PUBLICATION
WoO	"J'avais mal" (I Was Sick), French folk song for voice and piano	ca. 1947	2 '	MS
Op. 78	Concerto No. 4 (Fantasy) for piano and orchestra	1947	27 '	Hinrichsen 1949 Belaieff
Op. 79	*La Femme et son ombre* (The Woman and Her Shadow), Ballet	1948	30 '	AMP 1948
Op. 79a	Japanese Suite for orchestra, from the ballet *La Femme et son ombre*	1948	ca.15 '	MS available AMP rental
WoO	*La quatrième* (The Fourth Republic) for piano	1948–49	3 '	Heugel-Leduc 1954
Op. 80	Symphonic March for orchestra	1951	6 '	MCA 1956
	Version for band	1954		MS (available MCA rental)
Op. 81	*Expressions* for piano	1951	15 '	MCA 1951 Belaieff
Op. 82	*Songs without Words* for piano	1949–51	11 '	Peters 1953
Op. 83	Symphony No. 3, incorporating ballet materials from *Dionys* (1940), *Atlantide* (1943), and *Vendeur des Papillons* (1945?)	1951	28 '	Belaieff
Op. 84	*Songs and Dances* for cello and piano	1953	17 '	Belaieff 1950
Op. 85	12 Preludes for piano	1952–53	25 '	Marks 1956
	Rev. ed. by the composer	1972		Belaieff 1972
Op. 86	Concerto for harmonica and orchestra Arr. for harmonica and piano by the composer	1953	28 '	AMP 1956
Op. 87b	*Le gouffre* (The Abyss), Ballet	1949	30 '	Peters 1954
Op. 87a	Rondo for 2 pianos	1952	30 ' 30"	Peters 1957

OPUS	TITLE	DATE COMPOSED	DURA- TION	PUBLICATION
Op. 87	**Suite for orchestra (excerpts from Op. 87b, with Op. 87a [orchestral version])**	1953	18′	Peters 1954
WoO	*La colline des fantômes* (The Hill of Phantoms), Ballet	1953	26′	MS
Op. 88	**8 Pieces for piano**	1954–55	13′	Presser 1957
Op. 89	*The Lost Flute* **for narrator and orchestra**	1954	42′	Belaieff rental available
	Abridged versions for narrator, Piano, and percussion	1955	22′ and 18′	Belaieff 1956
	Abridged versions for narrator and orchestra	1955	22′ and 18′	Belaieff
WoO	**Pastoral for piano, arranged from** *The Lost Flute* (Introduction)	1955		Belaieff
WoO	**17 Piano Pieces for Beginners**	1954–57		Summy–Birchard 1955, 1957, included in "Contemporary Literature" selected and corrected by Frances Clark
Op. 90	*Divertimento* **for orchestra**	1955–57	25′	Boosey & Hawkes 1966
Op. 91	**Symphony No. 4**	1957	25′	Boosey & Hawkes 1959
WoO	*Exploring the Piano,* **12 duets for beginners and teacher-pianists**	1958	6′	Peters 1959
Op. 92	*Georgiana,* **Suite for orchestra (from** *Chota Rostaveli*)	1946/ 1958–59	18′	Eulenberg 1959
Op. 93	*Symphonic Prayer* **for orchestra**	1959	9′	Belaieff 1960
WoO	**Trio for flute, violin, and cello**	1960	10′	Amadeus 1977
WoO	**Fanfare for brass ensemble and percussion**	1961	6′	Boosey & Hawkes 1964
WoO	*Partita* **for accordion solo**	1961	6′	Pagani 1962

OPUS		TITLE	DATE COMPOSED	DURA-TION	PUBLICATION
Op. 94		Sonata No. 2 for piano	1961	12′	Boosey & Hawkes 1962
WoO		Processional and Re-cessional for organ	1962	9′	Peters 1965
Op. 95		Cycle of 7 Chinese Folk Songs for bass or soprano and piano	1962	15′	Belaieff
Op. 96		Concerto No. 5 for piano and orchestra; version for reduced orchestra	1963	21′	Belaieff 1964; Belaieff
Op. 97		*Serenade for Strings*	1964	16′	Kunzelmann 1966
Op. 98		*Vom spass und ernst* (Of Things Light and Earnest), Cantata for contralto or bass and string orchestra	1964	21′	Gerig-Breitkopf & Hartel
Op. 99		Concerto No. 6 for piano and orchestra	1965	24′	Belaieff 1967
Op. 100		Suite for harpsichord	1966	8′	Peters 1966
Op. 101		*Sonata da chiesa* for viola da gamba, and organ	1966	15′	Simrock 1969
		Version for viola da gamba, string quintet, flute, and cembalo	1967		Simrock1970
Op. 102		*Mass* (in English) for 3 voices (2 sopranos and alto) *a cappella*	1966	5′30″	C. F. Peters 1969
WoO		*Tzigane* for accordion solo	1966	2′30″	Pietro Oeiro 1968
Op. 103		6 Liturgical Chants for mixed chorus *a cap-pella*	1967		C. F. Peters 1969
	/1	"Cherubim Song"		4′20″	
	/2	"O My God, I cry to Thee"		4′15″	
	/3	"Light so Tender"		3′05″	
	/4	"Prayer to the Holy Spirit"		1′15″	
	/5	"Transfiguration"		2′45″	

OPUS		TITLE	DATE COMPOSED	DURA-TION	PUBLICATION
	/6	"Alleluia"		3′15″	
Op. 104		4 Russian Folk Songs for mixed chorus *a cappella*	1967		Peters 1969
	/1	"Hills"		3′20″	
	/2	"Shali-Vali"		1′30″	
	/3	"Complaint"		4′10″	
	/4	"Nonsense Song"		1′5″	
WoO		**"Ein kleines Lied" (A Little Song) for high voice and piano**	ca. 1967	1′	MS
WoO		**Invention for accordion solo**	1967	3′30″	Pagani 1969
WoO		***The Story of Ivan the Fool* (Music for a Radio Play) for narrator, chorus, solo voices, orchestra, and electronic sound**	1968	45′	MS
WoO		**Ascension for piano**	1969	1′	Choudens 1970 in album *Nouveaux Musiciens* Vol. 3
Op. 105		**Brass Quintet**	1970	10′30″	Peters 1972
Op. 106		**Russian Sketches for youth orchestra**	1971		MCA
		Version for band	1977		MCA
WoO		Baptism Cantata for soloists, children's choir, recorders, flutes, strings, organ, and congregation participation	1972	3′	MS
WoO		4 *Caprices diatoniques* for harp or Celtic harp	1973	4′	Belaieff
Op. 107 (posth.)		Woodwind Quintet	1976	15′	Peters 1984
WoO		**2 Pieces for Children** 1. "Indian Trail" 2. "Celebrations"	1976	1′	Willis 1977 in album Piano Compositions U.S.A.

OPUS	TITLE	DATE COMPOSED	DURA- TION	PUBLICATION
Op. 108 (posth.)	**Duo for 2 flutes**	1977	12′	Belaieff 1978
WoO (excerpts recorded as Op. 109)	*Opivochki* (Gradus ad Parnassum) About 40 short piano pieces	1975–77	ca. 35′	MS

Discography

CD Recordings

Orchestral Music

Symphony No. 1 in E, Op. 42; Symphony No. 2 in E♭ major, Op. 77   BIS CD-1017
  Singapore Symphony Orchestra; Lan Shui, conductor (1999)
  (w/ Piano Concerto No. 5)

Symphony No. 2 in E♭ major, Op. 77   First Edition FECD 0024
  Louisville Orchestra; Robert Whitney, conductor
  (w/ Piano Concerto No. 2; Suite Op. 87)

Symphony No. 3, Op. 83; Symphony No. 4 in E minor, Op. 91   BIS CD-1018
  Singapore Symphony Orchestra; Lan Shui, conductor (1999)
  (w/ Piano Concerto No. 6)

Symphony No. 3, Op. 83   THOROPHON Capella CTH 2021
  Staatsphilharmonie Rheinland-Pfalz; Peter Gülke, conductor (1988)
  (w/ Triple Concertino, Rhapsodie géorgienne)

Symphony No. 4, Op. 91, Suite for Orchestra, Op. 87   MARCO POLO 8.223380
Russian Dances, Op. 50
  Czecho-Slovak State Philharmonic Orchestra;
  Wing-Sie Yip, conductor (1991)

Divertimento, Op. 90   OLYMPIA OCD 640
  Musica Viva Orchestra; Alexander Rudin, conductor (1997)
  (w/ Nikolai Tcherepnin *Le Destin*; Ivan Tcherepnin Double Concerto)

Suite for Orchestra, Op. 87   First Edition FECD 0024
  Louisville Orchestra; Robert Whitney, conductor
  (w/ Piano Concerto No. 2; Suite Op. 87)

Magna mater, Op. 41	BIS CD-1247
Symphonic Prayer, Op. 93	
Singapore Symphony Orchestra; Lan Shui, conductor (2003)	
(w/ Piano Concertos Nos. 2, 4)	
Three Pieces for Chamber Orchestra, Op. 37	OLYMPIA OCD 584
Serenade for String Orchestra, Op. 97	
Musica Viva Chamber Orchestra; Alexander Rudin, conductor (1995)	
(w/ Chamber Concerto, *Rhapsodie géorgienne*)	

Concerted Music

Piano Concertos No. 1, Op. 12; No. 4 ("Fantaisie"), Op. 78; No. 5, Op. 96	OLYMPIA OCD 440
Murray McLachlan, piano	
Chetham's Symphony Orchestra;	Julian Clayton, conductor (1995)
Piano Concertos No. 2, Op. 26; No. 3, Op. 48; No. 6, Op. 99	OLYMPIA OCD 439
Murray McLachlan, piano	
Chetham's Symphony Orchestra; Julian Clayton, conductor (1994)	
Piano Concertos No. 2, Op. 26; No 4 "Fantaisie), Op. 78; No. 6, Op. 99	FORUM FRC 9110[a]
Murray McLachlan, piano	
Chetham's Symphony Orchestra; Julian Clayton, conductor (1994)	
Piano Concerto No. 2, Op. 26	First Edition FECD 0024
Alexander Tcherepnin, piano	
Louisville Orchestra; Robert Whitney, conductor	
(w/ Symphony No. 2; Suite Op. 87)	
Piano Concertos No. 2, Op. 26; No. 5, Op. 96	DG 453 157-2
Alexander Tcherepnin, piano	
Bavarian State Radio Orchestra;	Rafael Kubelik, conductor (1968)
Piano Concertos No. 2, Op. 26; No. 4, Op. 78	BIS CD-1247
Noriko Ogawa, piano	
Singapore Symphony Orchestra; Lan Shui, conductor (2003)	
(w/ Symphonic Prayer and Magna Mater)	
Piano Concerto No. 5, Op. 96	BIS CD-1017
Noriko Ogawa, piano	
Singapore Symphony Orchestra; Lan Shui, conductor (1999)	
(w/ Symphonies Nos. 1 and 2)	

[a] re-issue; [b] coupling; [c] coupling

Piano Concerto No. 6, Op. 99	BIS CD-1017
Noriko Ogawa, piano	
Singapore Symphony Orchestra; Lan Shui, conductor (1999)	
(w/ Symphonies Nos. 1 and 2)	
Ten Bagatelles for Piano and Orchestra, Op. 5	DG GALLERIA 463 085–2
Margit Weber, piano	
Berlin Radio Symphonie Orchestra; Ferenc Fricsay, conductor (1961)	
(w/ Falla *Nights,* Martin Concerto No. 5,	Weber *Konzertstück*)
Triple Concertino for Violin, Cello, Piano, and Orchestra, Op. 47	THOROPHON Capella CTH 2021
Göbel-Trio, Berlin	
Nürnberger Symphoniker; Uwe Mund, conductor (1978)	
Rhapsodie géorgienne for Cello and Orchestra, Op. 25	THOROPHON Capella CTH 2021
Reiner Hochmuth, cello	
Polnische Kammerphilharmonie;	Wojciech Rajki, conductor (1985)
(w/ Symphony No. 3, Triple Concertino)	
Rhapsodie géorgienne for Cello and Orchestra, Op. 25	OLYMPIA OCD 584
Concerto da Camera for Flute, Violin, and Chamber Orchestra, Op. 33	
Mystère for Cello and Chamber Orchestra, Op. 37b (in Three Pieces for Chamber Orchestra, Op. 37)	
Alexander Rudin, cello/conductor	
Nikolai Alexeyev, conductor (in Rhap. and Op. 37b)	
Olga Ivusheikova, flute; Nazar Kozhukar, violin	
Musica Viva Chamber Orchestra (1995)	
(w/ Serenade, Op. 97)	
Mystère for Cello and Chamber Orchestra, Op. 37b	AMATIUS CLASSICS ACCD 1002
Hai Zheng, cello	
Amatius Orchestra of New York; Paul Olefsky, conductor (1991)	
(w/ Tchaikovsky Rococo Vars., etc.)	
Concerto for Harmonica and Orchestra, Op. 86	URANIA US 5146 CD
John Sebastian, Harmonica	
Stuttgart Radio Orchestra; Hans Schwieger, conductor (1959)	
(w/ concertos by Villa Lobos and Ibert)	

Piano Music

Toccata No. 1, Op. 1	OLYMPIA OCD 681
Eight Preludes, Op. 9	
Sonata No. 1, Op. 23	

Canzona, Op. 28
Message, Op. 39
Seven Etudes, Op. 56
Le monde en vitrine (Showcase), Op. 75
  Murray McLachlan, piano (2000)

Toccata No. 2, Op. 20
Five (Chinese) Concert Etudes, Op. 52   OLYMPIA OCD 682
Twelve Preludes, Op. 85
Sonata No. 2, Op. 94
"Sunny Day" (Bagatelle oubliée), Op. Posth.
  Murray McLachlan, piano (2000)

Sonatine romantique, Op. 4   ETCETERA KTC 1033
Four Arabesques, Op. 11
Five (Chinese) Concert Etudes, Op. 52
Chant et refrain, Op. 66
Eight Pieces, Op. 88
Opivochki [Op. 109] (Nos. 3, 11, 9, 4, 17, 37)
  Bennett Lerner, piano (1985)

Bagatelles, Op. 5   CRI 896
Message, Op. 39
Voeux, Op. 39b (with ". . . pour la Paix en Orient")
Five (Chinese) Concert Etudes, Op. 52
Songs without Words, Op. 82
Sonata No. 2, Op. 94
  Martha Braden, piano (1991)

Autour des montagnes russes   NOBLESSE CD 87008
  Daniel Blumenthal, piano (1986)
  (w/ Auric, Honegger, Martinů, etc.: Souvenirs de
  l'exposition—Paris 1937)

Autour des montagnes russes   ETCETERA KTC 1061
  Bennett Lerner, piano (1988)
  (w/ Auric, Honegger, Martinů, etc.: Souvenirs de
  l'exposition—Paris 1937)

Five Concert Etudes, Op. 52   BIS 1110
  Jenny Lin, piano (2000)
  (w/ "Chinese" pieces by Arensky, Busoni, Adams,
  Chasins, Gould, Orenstein, Ketelby, Grainger, Scott,
  Rossini, Martinů, Waeber-Diaz)

Five Concert Etudes, Op. 52, Nos. 3, 4   THOROPHON CTH 2034
  Tsai Chai-Hsio, piano (1996)
  (w/ Buffalo Boy's Flute by He Luting, other Chinese pieces)

Petite suite, Op. 6: No. 3, *Berceuse*   GALL CD 564
  Christian Spring, piano
  (From Lullabies, w/ Schumann, Liszt, Chopin,
  Henselt, Grieg, Tchaikovsky, Brahms, Balakirev,

Rebikov, Busoni, Casella, Suk, Tansman, Vladigerov,
Villa-Lobos, Wendel, Ringger)

Chamber Music

Suite for Solo Cello, Op. 76 Yo-Yo Ma, cello (1999) (w/ Kodaly, Wilde, Sheng, O'Connor)	SONY SK64114
Complete Music for Cello and Piano Three Cello Sonatas (Op. 29; Op. 30, No. 1; Op. 30, No. 2) The Well-Tempered Cello, Op. 38 Songs and Dances, Op. 84 Ode for Cello and Piano (1919) Alexander Ivashkin, cello; Geoffrey Tozer, piano (1999)	CHANDOS CHAN 9770
Sonata No. 1 for Cello and Piano, Op. 29 Simca Heled, cello, Jonathan Zak, piano (1986) (w/ Rodrigo, Ries, Bazelaire, Breval, Mendelssohn, Weber, Rimsky-Korsakov)	CLASSICO 153 (formerly In- Sync C 4154)
Sonata No. 3 for Cello and Piano, Op. 30, No. 2 Yuri Semenov, cello, Ksenia Stegman, piano (2006) (w/ Rubinstein Sonata No. 1; Gretchaninov Sonata)	MELODIYA MELCD1000970
Ode for Cello and Piano (1919) Wolfgang Lehner, cello; Madeleine Stucki, piano (2001) (In *Russian Soul,* w/ Hovhanesian, Rebikov, Kar- jinsky, Tchaikovsky, Akimenko, Glière, Sokolow, Arensky, Cui, Rachmaninoff, Harsanyi)	GALL 1001
Ode for Cello and Piano (1919) Gaspar Cassado, cello; Michael Raucheisen, piano (w/ Cassado, Granados, Debussy, Handel, Mendels- sohn, Tchaikovsky, Liszt, Dvořák, Bruch, Glazunov, Saint-Saëns, Popper)	DANTE LYS 184
Duo for Violin and Cello, Op. 49 Eleonora Turovsky, violin; Yuli Turovsky, cello (1986) (w/ Stravinsky, Glière, Prokofiev)	CHANDOS CHAN 8652
Sonatine for Three Timpani and Piano, Op. 58 Duo Vivace: Albrecht Volz, Andreas Baumann (2000) (In *Pictures* for Piano and Percussion, w/ Tanner, B. Hummel, Desportes, Green)	AUDITE 95433
Andante for Tuba and Piano, Op. 64 Blair Bollinger, bass trombone; Hugh Sung, piano (1998)	D'NOTE DND 1033

(In *Fancy Free,* w/ Fetter, Spillman, Lassen, Vilette,
Ibert, Tomasi, Smith)

Piano Trio, Op. 34   PRO ARTE CDD 303
Odeon Trio (1986)
(w/ Taneyev Trio)

Trio for 3 Flutes, Op. 59   CLASSICO 258
Duo for 2 Flutes, Op 108
Prelude for 2 Flutes, Op. 24, No. 3
Etude (1927)
Bent Larsen, Henrik Svitzer, et al. (1999)
(In *The Russian Flute,* w/ Cui, Gretchaninov)

Trio for 3 Flutes, Op. 59   CLASSICO 199
Flutention Flute Trio (1997)
(w/ Boismortier, Mozart, Devienne)

Ten Bagatelles, Op. 5, arr. four guitars   ARS MUSICI AM13162
Take Four Guitar Quartet (2002)
(w/ Bach, Purcell, Britten, Pujol,
Vuong-Thatch, Mosca, Gershwin, Puccini)

String Quartet No. 2, Op. 40   VOXBOX2 CDX 5071
New World Quartet (1978)
(w/ Surinach, Hindemith, Bloch, Stravinsky,
Rosza, Korngold)

Quintet for Winds, Op. 107   CENTAUR CRC 2335
Cumberland Wind Quintet (1997)
(In *Shadows and Dreams,* w/ Baumann, Dollarhide,
Hoover, Jager)

Quintet for Winds, Op. 107   DYNAMIC 296
Prague National Theater Wind Quintet (2000)
(w/ quintets by Rubinstein, Ippolitov-Ivanov, Tansman)

LP Recordings

Orchestral Music

Symphony No. 2, Op. 77   Louisville-LS-645; RCA Gold
Louisville Orchestra; Robert Whitney, conductor   Seal, GL 25059[a]
(1964)

Symphony No. 4, Op. 91   Colosseum-SM551
Nürnberg Symphony; Rato Tschupp, conductor
(1974)

Symphonic Prayer, Op. 93   Colosseum-SM 543
Nürnberg Symphony; Günter Neidlinger, conduc-
tor (1972)

[a] re-issue; [b] coupling; [c] coupling

Suite for Orchestra, Op. 87
    Louisville Orchestra; Robert Whitney, conductor
    (1955)
	Louisville-545–2

Suite for Orchestra, Op. 87
    (identified as "from the ballet *The Abyss*")
    Nürnberg Symphony; Othmar M. F. Maga, con-
    ductor
	Colosseum-SM 560

Serenade for String Orchestra, Op. 97
 	
    Munich Chamber Orchestra, Hans Stadlmeir, con-
    ductor (1975)
	MHS 3752; Impromptu SM
	191506[a]

Georgiana Suite, Op. 92
    Frankenland State Orchestra; George Barati, con-
    ductor (1961)
	Lyricord 7103

Festmusik from *Die Hochzeit der Sobeide,* Op. 45a
    Bochum Symphony; Othmar M. F. Maga, conduc-
    tor (1977)
	Impromptu SM 191510

Russian Dances, Op. 50
    Nürnberg Symphony; Zsolt Deaky, conductor
    (1978)
	Colosseum-SM 578

Symphonic March, Op. 80
    Rhineland Philharmonic; Klaus Peter Seibel, con-
    ductor (1976)
	RBM 3052

Symphonic March, Op. 80
    (arranged for symphonic band)
    Gardiens de la Paix Band; Desiré Dondeyne, con-
    ductor (1977)
	Disques Serp MC 7040

Fanfare for Brass and Percussion Locke Brass Consort (1976)	Unicorn RHS 339

Concerted Music

Piano Concerto No. 2, Op. 26
    Composer, piano
    Louisville Orchestra; Robert Whitney, conductor
    (1961)
	LOUISVILLE-615

Piano Concertos No. 2, Op. 26, No. 5, Op. 96
 	
    Composer, piano
    Bavarian State Radio Orchestra; Rafaël Kubelik,
    conductor (1968)
	Deutsche Grammophon
	139379

Piano Concerto No. 5, Op. 96
    Weng Gi In, piano
    Rhineland Philharmonic; Pierre Stoll, conductor
    (1973)
	RBM 3016

[a] re-issue; [b] coupling; [c] coupling

Bagatelles for Piano and Orchestra, Op. 5	Deutsche Grammophon 138710; Heliodor 87938[a]
Margrit Weber, piano Berlin Radio Symphony Orchestra; Ferenc Fricsay, conductor (1961)	
Bagatelles for Piano and String Orchestra, Op. 5 Jürgen Meyer-Josten, piano Württemberg Chamber Orchestra; Jürg Färber, conductor (1973)	Turnabout TVS-S 34545
Bagatelles for Piano and String Orchestra, Op. 5 Michelle Roy, piano Nürnberg Symphony Orchestra; Michel Maynaud, conductor	Colosseum-SM 802
Triple Concertino for Violin, Cello, Piano and Orchestra, Op. 47 Gobel-Trio, Berlin Nürnberger Symphoniker; Uwe Mund, conductor (1978)	THOROPHON MTH 230
Concerto for Harmonica and Orchestra, Op. 86 John Sebastian, harmonica Stuttgart Radio Orchestra; Hans Schwieger, conductor (1959)	Heliodor HS 25064

Piano Music

Nocturne, Op. 2, No. 1 Composer (1954) (w/ Sonatine, Bagatelles, etc.)	Music Library MLR 7043
Sonatine romantique, Op. 4 Composer (1954) (w/ Bagatelles, Arabesques, etc.)	Music Library MLR 7043
Bennett Lerner (1985) (w/ Concert Etudes, *Opivochki*, etc.)	ETCETERA ETC 1033
Bagatelles, Op. 5 Composer (1954) (w/ *Sonatine, Arabesques,* etc.)	Music Library MLR 7043
Composer (1968) (w/ Sonata No. 1, Nostalgic Preludes, etc.)	EMI CVC 2124
Robert Howat (1979) (w/ Expressions, Preludes Op. 85, etc.)	Orion ORS 79329
Maria Kalamkarian (w/ Sonata No. 2)	German Columbia SMC 80 970
Helmut Roloff (1959)	Deutsche Grammophon 45 32 229 (45 rpm)

[a] re-issue; [b] coupling; [c] coupling

John Ranck (1959)

Zodiac LPZ 1001; International Piano Library IPA 2002[a]

Eight Preludes, Op. 9
   Monique Haas (1984)
      (w/ Sonata No. 2, *Voeux,* etc.)

Aulos Aul 53573

Four Arabesques, Op. 11
   Composer (1954)
      (w/ Bagatelles, *Sonatine,* etc.)

Music Library MLR 7043

   Bennett Lerner (1985)
      (w/ Etudes Op. 52, *Opivochki,* etc.)

ETCETERA ETC 1033

Sonata No. 1, Op. 22
   Composer (1968)
      (w/ Bagatelles, Nostalgic Preludes, etc.)

EMI CVC 2124

Four Nostalgic Preludes, Op. 24
   Composer (1968)
      (w/ Bagatelles, Sonata No. 1, etc.)

EMI CVC 2124

Voeux, Op. 39b
   Monique Haas (1984)
      (w/ Sonata No. 2, Eight Preludes, etc.)

Aulos Aul 53573

Five Chinese Concert Etudes, Op. 52
   Bennett Lerner (1985)
      (w/ Arabesques, *Opivochki,* etc.)

ETCETERA ETC 1033

Five Chinese Concert Etudes, Op. 52
   Jenny Lin (2000)

BIS 1110

Etude, Op. 56, No. 7
   Composer (1968)
      (w/ Bagatelles, Sonata No. 1, etc.)

EMI CVC 2124

Chant et refrain, Op. 66
   Bennett Lerner (1985)
      (w/ Etudes Op. 52, *Opivochki,* etc.)

ETCETERA ETC 1033

Showcase, Op. 75
   Robert Howat (1959)

Music Library MLR 7098

Expressions, Op. 81
   Robert Howat (1956)
      (w/ Preludes, Op. 85)

Music Library MLR 7072

   Robert Howat (1979)
      (w/ Bagatelles, Preludes, etc.)

Orion ORS 78329

   Composer (No. 9)
      (w/ Bagatelles, Sonata No. 1, etc.)

EMI CVC 2124

Five Songs without Words, Op. 82
   Robert Howat (4) (1979)
      (w/ Bagatelles, Preludes, etc.)

Orion ORS 78329

[a] re-issue; [b] coupling; [c] coupling

Twelve Preludes, Op. 85
  Robert Howat (1956) (w/ Expressions)   Music Library MLR 7072
  Robert Howat (4) (1979)
    (w/ Bagatelles, Preludes, etc.)   Orion ORS 78329

Eight Pieces, Op. 88
  Monique Haas (1984)
    (w/ Sonata No. 2, Eight Preludes, etc.)   Aulos Aul 53573
  Bennett Lerner (1985)
    (w/ Etudes, Op. 52, Sonatine, etc.)   ETCETERA ETC 1033
  Thérèse Dassault (1974)   Arion ARN 38263; Musical
                                                Heritage Society 3617[a]

  Composer (Nos. 4, 8) (1968)
    (w/ Bagatelles, Sonata No. 1, etc.)   EMI CVC 2124

Sonata No. 2, Op. 94
  Monique Haas (1984)
    (w/ Eight Preludes, Op. 9, *Voeux,* etc.)   Aulos Aul 53573
  Maria Kalamkarian
    (w/ Bagatelles)   German Columbia SMC 80
                                                970

Opivochki [Op. 109]
  Bennett Lerner (6) (1985)
    (w/ Etudes, Op. 52, *Sonatine,* etc.)   ETCETERA ETC 1033

For Other Solo Instruments

Suite for Harpsichord, Op. 100   Wergo S34 60028
  Antoinette Vischer (1967) (2 mvmts.)

Processional and Recessional for Organ (1962)   De Camera Magna SM 932 58
  Herbert Manfred Hoffmann

Suite for Solo Cello, Op. 76
  Paul Tortelier (1969)
    (w/ Piano Quintet, Duo, Trio, etc.)   HMV CSD 3226
  Ken Yasuda   Columbia (Japan) (UDI4)
                                                40x-9022–ND

Caprices diatoniques for Celtic Harp (1973)
  Denise Megevand (1974)   Arion 382 45
  Helga Stork (Nos. 3, 4) (1984)   Col 9002

Partita for Accordion (1961)
  Milan Blaha (1968)   Supraphon 0 11 0238
  Joseph Macerollo (1970)
    (w/ Tzigane for Accordion) (1966)   Kaibala

Chamber Music

Sonata for Violin and Piano, Op. 14
  Yehudi Menuhin, violin; Composer, piano (1972) BBC Records REGL 409
  Michael Appleman, violin; Diane Huling, piano   Vox Altéra (audio cassette)
  (1986)

[a] re-issue; [b] coupling; [c] coupling

Sonata No. 1 for Cello and Piano, Op. 29
S. Heled, cello; J. Zak, piano (1986)   Sync Labs C4154
Esther Nyffenegger, cello; Annette Weisbrod, piano
(1983)
(w/ Sonata No. 3, Preludes)   De Camera Magna SM 93718

Sonata No. 3 for Cello and Piano, Op. 30, No. 2 De Camera Magna SM 93718
Esther Nyffenegger, cello; Annette Weisbrod, piano
(1983)
(w/ Sonata No. 1, Preludes)

Sonatine sportive for Saxophone and Piano, Op. 63
Ed Bogaard, saxophone; Ton Hartsuiker, piano   Telefunken 6. 42841 AZ
(1982)
Daniel Deffayet, saxophone (1967)   Fidelio 3401
Marcel Mule, saxophone; Marthe Lenom, piano   London/Decca
(1955)

Sonatina for Three Timpani and Piano, Op. 58
Albrecht Volz, timpani; Andreas Baumann, piano   Audite 95433
(2000)

Twelve Preludes for Cello and Piano, Op. 38
Esther Nyffenegger, cello; Annette Weisbrod, piano
(1983)
(w/ Sonatas Nos. 1, 3)   De Camera Magna SM 93718
Seymour Barab, cello; William Masselos, piano
(Nos. 5, 7) (1950)   Paradox

Ode for Cello and Piano (1919)   Columbia (England) CX
                                                 1700

Janos Starker, cello

Andante for Tuba and Piano, Op. 64   RCA RL 303 21
Mel Culbertson, tuba; Michael Krist, piano
(w/ Brass Quintet, Op. 105)

Duo for Violin and Cello, Op. 49   HMV CSD 3226
Yan Pascal Tortelier, violin, Paul Tortelier, cello
(1969)
(w/ Piano Quintet, Suite, Trio, etc.)

Trio for Violin, Cello, and Piano, Op. 34
Composer, piano; Y. P. Tortelier, violin; P. Tortelier,
cello (1969)
(w/ Piano Quintet, Duo, Trio, etc.)   HMV CSD 3226
Gobel Trio   De Camera Magna SM 92112
Odeon Trio (1978)   RCA RL 303 24
Pro Musica Trio (1955)   Pro Musica PMT 201
Western Arts Trio (1979)   Laurel Records LR 109

Flute Trio, Op. 59   Corona, SM 30 001
Rehm, Daschler, Bold, flutes

Flute Quartet, Op. 60	Arion 30 A 071; Musical
Roger Bourdin Quartet (1970)	Heritage Society 3072[a]

String Quartet No. 2, Op. 40	
Y. & P. Tortelier, Groupe Instrumental de Paris (1969)	
(w/ Piano Quintet, Duo, Trio, etc.)	HMV CSD 3226
New World Quartet (1978)	Vox SVBX 5109
Quintet for Piano and Strings, Op. 44	HMV CSD 3226
Composer, Y. & P. Tortelier, Groupe Instrumental de Paris (1969)	
(w/ Quartet No. 2, Duo, Trio, etc.)	
Brass Quintet, Op. 105	
Annapolis Brass Quintet	Crystal S 207
John Taber, Rodney Miller, trumpets; Adrian van Woudenbert, horn; John Moore, trombone; Mel Culbertson, tuba (1978)	
(w/ Andante, Op. 64)	RCA RL 303 21

Vocal Music

Haltes, Op. 17	EMI Pathé Marconi 2C 065
Nicolai Gedda, tenor; Composer, piano (1973)	14028
(w/ Seven Songs, Op. 71)	
Seven Songs on Chinese Poems, Op. 71	EMI Pathé Marconi 2C 065
Nicolai Gedda, tenor; Composer, piano (1973)	14028
(w/ *Haltes,* Op. 17)	
Yi Kwe Sze, bass; Brooks Smith, piano (2) (1966)	Irmac 6517
Cantata, *Vom Spass und Ernst,* Op. 98	Pick70 119
Anton Diakov, bass; Annet Weisbrod, piano (3 excerpts)	

Tcherepnin's Recorded Performances

Commercial Releases

MUSIC BY TCHEREPNIN

Concertos

Piano Concerto No. 2, Op. 26	LOUISVILLE-615 (1961); RCA Gold Seal GL 25059[a]
Composer, piano	
Louisville Orchestra; Robert Whitney, conductor	

[a] re-issue; [b] coupling; [c] coupling

Piano Concerto No. 2, Op. 26	DEUTSCHE GRAMMO-
Piano Concerto No. 5, Op. 96	PHON 139379 (1968); CD
Composer, piano	435–157–2[a]
Bavarian Radio Orchestra; Rafaël Kubelik,	
conductor	

Solo Piano Music

Eight Bagatelles	ELECTROLA 78rpm
(from Ten Bagatelles, Op. 5, Nos. 1–3; 5–9)	G.DB 4440 (1935)
Ten Bagatelles, Op. 5 Music Library	MLR 7043 (1954)[b]
Ten Bagatelles, Op. 5	EMI CVC 2124 (1968)[c]
Chanson pour la chérie, Op. 27, No. 2	ELECTROLA 78rpm (1935)
Hommage à la Chine, Op. 52, No. 3	Japanese Victor VE 1003[a]
Sonatine romantique, Op. 4	MUSIC LIBRARY MLR 7043
Four Arabesques, Op. 11	(1954)[b]
Nocturne, Op. 2, No. 1	
Piano Sonata No. 1, Op. 22	EMI CVC 2124 (1968)[c]
Four Nostalgic Preludes, Op. 23	
Etude, Op. 56, No. 7	
Expression, Op. 81, No. 9	
Impromptu, Op. 88, No. 4	
Burlesque, Op. 88, No. 8	

Piano Rolls

from *Petite suite,* Op. 6 (three movements)	AMPICO (1926)

Chamber Music

Sonata for Violin and Piano, Op. 14	BBC RECORDS
Yehudi Menuhin, violin; Composer, piano	BEGL 409 (1972)
Quintet for Piano and Strings, Op. 44	EMI Pathé-Marconi C 063
	10912 (1969); HMV CSD
	3225[a]
Trio for Violin, Cello, and Piano, Op. 34	
Composer, piano; Y. P. Tortelier, violin; P. Tortel-	
ier, cello	
Groupe Instrumental de Paris	
(also String Quartet, No. 2, Duet for Violin and	
Cello, Suite for Solo Cello)	

Songs

Haltes, Op. 17	EMI Pathé-Marconi 2C 065
	14028 (1973)
Seven Songs on Chinese Poems, Op. 71	
Nicolai Gedda, tenor; Composer, piano	
(also songs by Nicolai Tcherepnin)	

[a] re-issue; [b] coupling; [c] coupling

Kiyose: Springtime in the Hills	JVC 78 rpm (1936)
Matsudaira: Prelude in D major	
Koh: Sketch, Op. 3A	
Ota: Traffic Sign	
Balakirev: Songs	EMI Pathé-Marconi 2C 063–10149 (1967); CZS 7 67496 2 (5 CDs)[a]

Boris Christoff, bass; Tcherepnin, piano
(also orchestral songs by Balakirev, conducted by
Georges Tzipine)

Borodin: Songs	EMI Pathé-Marconi 2C 063–10147 (1966); CZS 7 67496 2 (5 CDs)[a]

Boris Christoff, bass; Tcherepnin, piano
(also orchestral songs by Borodin, conducted by
Georges Tzipine)

Piano Rolls

Rubinstein: Nocturne in F	AMPICO (1926)
(transcribed by Tcherepnin)	

Unpublished Recordings for Broadcast

MUSIC BY TCHEREPNIN

As Pianist

Sonata No. 1, Op. 22	Columbia University (1965)
Sonata No. 2, Op. 92	
Préludes nostalgiques, Op. 23	
Prelude, Op. 85, No. 9	

As Conductor

Symphony No. 1, Op. 42 (1970)	BBC Symphony Orchestra
Symphony No. 2, Op. 77 (1968?)	Munich Philharmonic
Divertimento, Op. 90 (1968)	BBC Northern Symphony Orchestra
Symphony No. 4, Op. 91	BBC Symphony Orchestra

[a] re-issue; [b] coupling; [c] coupling

Notes

Preface

1. Diary entry dated September 15, 1976, PSF.

2. Guy Freedman, "Spanning the Generations (interview)," *Music Journal* 34, no. 7 (September 1976): 10–12; 46–47:12.

3. Ludmila Korabelnikova, "Exegi monumentum," *Muzykalnaya zhizn'*, no. 9 (1997).

4. Ludmila Korabelnikova, "Un premier aperçu sur les archives de Nicolas et Alexandre Tcherepnine (en parcourant les journaux intimes d'Alexandre Tcherepnine)," *Mitteilungen der Paul Sacher Stiftung* (Basel), no. 10 (1997).

5. In fact, the eldest son, Peter, learned to speak and read Russian as a child in Paris from his grandparents and tutors, not his father.

6. A. T. to Grigori Shneerson, March 7, 1968. SCMMC, coll. 375, no. 943.

7. Ibid., no. 944.

8. Willy Reich, *Alexander Tcherepnin* (Bonn: M. P. Belaieff, 1970).

9. Enrique Arias, *Alexander Tcherepnin: A Bio-Bibliography* (New York: Greenwood, 1989), p. 264.

10. Mark Aranovsky, ed., *Russkaia muzyka i dvatsatyi vek* (Moscow, 1998).

1. Introduction

1. Nikolai Slonimsky, "Alexander Tcherepnin Septuagenarian," *Tempo,* no. 87 (winter 1968–69): 16–23: 16–18. Elsewhere in his autobiographical notes, Tcherepnin claims an earlier acquaintance with musical notation.

2. A. Skidan, "Alexander Tcherepnin," *Novyi Zhurnal,* no. 132 (1978).

3. A. T. to his parents, July 16, 1927, PSF.

4. Freedman, "Spanning the Generations," p. 11. For the same story in similar words, see the "Short Autobiography" in appendix 1.

5. A. T. to Grigori Shneerson, April 2, 1972, SCMMC, coll. 375, no. 954.

6. Cf. A. Klimovitsky, "Lyudi dolzhny znat' chto ia khochu skazat': Schoenberg v Peterburge," *Muzykalnaia Akademia,* no. 4–5 (1995); no. 1 (1996).

7. Cited in *Vyacheslav Karatygin: Zhizn. Deiatelnost'. Statii i Materialy* (Leningrad, 1927), p. 232.

8. Arias, *Alexander Tcherepnin: A Bio-Bibliography,* p. 5.

9. A. T. to his parents, October 18, 1928, PSF (Tcherepnin's emphasis).

10. A. T. to Vasily Kiselev, May 2, 1968, RSALA, coll. 2985, register 1, no. 391, sheet 50. Regarding Beliaev, cf. also Ludmila Korabelnikova, "Dolgie Stranstviia Aleksandra Tcherepnina," *Muzykalnaia zhizn,* no. 9 (1997).

11. A branch of the International Society of Contemporary Music, the Association of Contemporary Music (ASM) existed until the early thirties, and included in its ranks Beliaev, Myaskovsky, Shaporin, Steinberg, Scherbachev, Shostakovich, and others.

12. Vyacheslav Karatygin, "Pamiati H. A. Sokolova," *Orphei: Sankt Peterburg* 1 (1922): 119.

13. A. T. to Vasily Kiselev, June 24, 1971, RSALA, coll. 2985, register 1, no. 392, sheet 11.

14. A. T. to Yuri Shaporin, September 21, 1960, RSALA, coll. 2642, register 1, no. 445, sheet 1.

15. A. T. to Vasily Kiselev, May 2, 1968, RSALA, coll. 2985, register 1, no. 392, sheet 53.

16. Alexander Gauk, *Memuary. Izbrannye statyi. Vospominania sovremennikov* (Moscow, 1975), p. 31.

17. Ibid., pp. 30, 111.

18. Sergei Prokofiev, *Avtobiographia* (Moscow, 1982), pp. 338, 412.

19. Ibid., pp. 409–410.

20. Vyacheslav Karatygin, "Noveishie techenia v zapadnoi musike," *Severnye zapiski,* December 1913.

21. M. Kozlova, ed., "'Chto vy dumaete o solntse?' an Autograph Album Collected by Prokofiev, 1916–1921," *Soviet Music,* no. 3 (1963): 49. Entry dated April 20, 1918, St. Petersburg.

22. BFM, pp. 253–254.

23. Ibid., pp. 255–256.

24. The "Mighty Five" refers to a circle of five Russian nationalist composers from St. Petersburg: Balakirev, Borodin, Cui, Mussorgsky, and Rimsky-Korsakov. After meeting regularly, they became known as the *Moguchaya kuchka* or "Mighty Handful," and the musical style associated with the group is sometimes referred to as *Kuchkism.* They were later called the "Five," as well as "Mighty Five" (*Moguchaya pyaterka*). This last term is best recognized by readers familiar with any of the common names for the group.

25. A. T. to Grigori Shneerson, April 7, 1962, SCMMC, coll. 375, no. 961.

26. S. Savenko "Muzyka Stravinskovo v stilisticheskom peizazhe epokhi," in *Isskustvo XX veka: ukhodiaschaya epokha?,* vol. 1 (Nizhni Novgorod, 1987), p. 179.

27. Nikolai Gumilev, "Nasledie symbolisma i akmeism," *Apollon,* no. 1 (1913); Sergei Gorodetsky "Nekotorye techenia v sovremennoi russkoi zhizhni," *Apollon,* no. 1 (1913).

28. BFM, p. 251.

29. Ibid., p. 259.

30. G. Sternin, foreword to Alexandre Benois, *Khudozhestvennye pisma, 1930–36, In Gazeta poslednye novosti* (Moscow, 1997), p. 5.

31. Mstislav Dobuzhinsky, *Vospominania* (Moscow, 1987), p. 209.

32. A. T. to Grigori Bernandt, January 21, 1970, SCMMC, coll. 449, no. 287.

33. Freedman, "Spanning the Generations (interview)," p. 11.

34. PSF, manuscripts, 1912–1915, undated.

35. PSF, manuscript, December 6, 1915.

36. All notations cited from manuscripts at PSF.

37. PSF, manuscript, November 14, 1917.

38. SCMMC, coll. 375, no. 920.

39. Freedman, "Spanning the Generations (interview)," pp. 11–12.

2. In the Hills of Georgia

1. See chapter 1, note 24.

2. A. T. to Grigori Bernandt, December, 13, 1969, SCMMC, coll. 449, no. 1150.

3. Tcherepnin's list of his Tiflis era works of musical criticism was published by Grigori Bernandt in volume 21 of the bibliographic dictionary *Kto pisal o muzyke: bio-bibliograficheskii slovar' muzykal'nykh kritikov i lits, pisavshikh o muzyke v dorevoliutsion-noi Rossii i SSSR*, ed. G. Bernandt, I. Iampol'skii, and T. Kiseleva (Moscow: Sov. Kompositor, 1971-89). Most of the clippings in the Paul Sacher Foundation archive are undated and from unknown sources; hence they are given in the text without source notations.

4. Clipping of article by A. T., PSF.

5. Alexander Tcherepnin, "First Quarterly Meeting of the Russian Musical Society," fall 1918, PSF.

6. Alexander Tcherepnin, "About Tchaikovsky," clipping of article, PSF.

7. Leo Gal, *Obnovlenie,* March, 10, 1919.

8. Author unknown, *Struggle,* December 12, 1920, PSF.

9. A. T. manuscript, PSF.

10. Clipping from *Struggle,* November 4, 1920. A friend of Tcherepnin, Iolanta Mirimanova, performed the violin solo. The renowned actor of St. Petersburg's Alexandrine Theater, N. Hodotov, performed Iokanan.

11. A. T. manuscript, PSF.

12. Tamara Tsulukidze, *Vsevo odna zhizn'* (Tbilisi, 1983), pp. 82-83.

13. A. T. to his parents, September 23, 1928, PSF.

14. Elizabeth Zhihareva to A. T., 1925, PSF.

15. Typescript copy of A. T. to Elizabeth Zhihareva, 1925, PSF.

16. Sergey Gorodetsky, "Zekh poetov," *Ars,* no. 1 (1919): 81.

17. Newspaper clipping from the Tiflis magazine *Ars,* November 1918, PSF.

18. Iakov Lvov, "Na lektzii Vladimira Kamenskovo," *Kavkazskoe slovo,* May 16, 1919.

19. Clipping, "V. Dolidze's Benefit Performance," January 11, 1920, PSF.

20. A. T. to Grigori Shneerson, 1962, SCMMC, coll. 375, no. 897.

21. A. T. manuscript, 1920, PSF.

22. A. T. to N. T., April 10, 1927, PSF.

23. *Poslednie novosti,* May 25, 1931.

24. Zakharia Paliashvili to N. T., December 13, 1925, Tiflis, PSF.

25. Iolanta Mirimanova to A. T., letters, 1925-1926, PSF.

26. Nikolay Vygodsky to A. T., February, 12 1923, PSF.

27. Nikolay Vygodsky to A. T., April 25, 1923, PSF.

28. Nikolay Vygodsky to A. T., December 9, 1924, PSF.

29. Nikolai Vygodsky, "Alexandre Tscherepnine. Bagatelles. 10 pieces pour Piano" (Paris, Heugel, [1923]); Alexandre Tscherepnine, "Nocturne et Danse pour Piano. Op. 2, No. 1, 2" (Leipzig: Belaieff, 1922); Alexander Tscherepnin, "Toccata d-moll. Op. 1" (Leipzig: Belaieff, 1922); *K novym beregam,* no. 3 (1923): pp. 54-55.

30. Nikolai Vygodsky to a friend, January 6, 1925.

31. Concert program, May 22, 1919, PSF.

32. Vladimir Ananov, "Concert by Alexander Tcherepnin, May 22, Conservatory Hall." Newspaper clipping inscribed "Kavkazskoe slovo," 1919, PSF.

33. Vladimir Ananov, "Concert by Alexander Tcherepnin, November 6, Conservatory Hall." Newspaper clipping inscribed "1920," PSF.

34. This excerpt is taken from editions in the Library of the Moscow Conservatory.

35. A. T. manuscript, inscribed to M. T., January 5, 1920, PSF.

36. A. T. manuscript, inscribed to M. T., November 21, 1921, PSF.

37. A. T. to Grigori Bernandt, August 20, 1964, SCMMC, coll. 449, No. 1133.

38. Newspaper clipping, signed "Es," PSF.

39. Thomas Hartmann, "Ob upotreblenie udarnyh instrumentov v orkestre," *Muzyka,* nos. 80, 82 (1912).

40. BFM, pp. 592–593.

3. Air and Bread of Emigration

1. Gleb Struve, *Russkaia literatura v izgnanii* (Paris: YMCA-Press, 1984), p. 22.

2. Wolfgang Kazak, *Lexicon russkoi literaturi 20 veka* (Moscow, 1996).

3. V. Shelohaev, ed., *Zolotaya kniga russkoi emigratzii. Pervaya tret 20 veka. Encyklopedicheskii slovar* (Moscow, 1997); L. Mnuhin, ed., *Russkoe zarubezhie: hronika nauchnoi, kulturnoi i obschestvennoi zhizni, 1920–1940. Frantziya,* 4 vols. (Paris, YMCA Press; Moscow: Eksmo, 1995–97).

4. Marc Raeff, *Russia Abroad: A Cultural History of the Russian Emigration, 1919–1939* (New York: Oxford University Press, 1990).

5. Karl Schlögel (Hrsg.), *Der grosse Exodus: Die russische Emigration und ihre Zentren. 1917 bis 1941* (München: C. H. Beck, 1994).

6. P. E. Kovalevsky, *Zarubezhnaia Rossia: istoria i prosvetitelskaya rabota zo pol-veka, 1920–1970,* 2 vols. (Paris: 1971, 1973); Roman Gul, *Ia uvez s soboi Rossiu: apologia emigratsii.* 2 vols. (New York, 1981, 1984).

7. BFM, pp. 192–193.

8. Newspaper clipping, "Teatr i muzyka: Chevstvovanie N. N. Cherepnina," inscribed "Presse du soir. Constantinople No. 155. Lundi 4.VII.1921," July 4, 1921, PSF.

9. Manuscript labeled "Na puti v Erevan," 1921, PSF.

10. Anna Markozova to M. T., 1922, PSF. Ilia Zlatin was a famous conductor and musical figure, a pupil of the St. Petersburg Conservatory, friend of Petr Tchaikovsky and performer of his works, head of the Kharkov department of the Imperial Russian Music Society. Feofan Pavlovsky was a baritone who sang in the opera theaters of Kiev and Tiflis, and in Moscow at Zimin's Theater and the Bolshoi. In 1926 he applied to Nicolas Tcherepnin for a position at the Russian Conservatory in Paris. S. Streicher was a Tiflis friend who by 1923 was already at the conservatory in Berlin, where Markozova later ended up as well.

11. Anna Markozova to M. T., April 16, 1922, PSF.

12. BFM, pp. 192–196.

13. Vladimir Scherbachev to his wife, *Statii. Materialy. Pisma,* (Leningrad, 1985), p. 161.

14. Vladimir Scherbachev to his wife, December 29, 1922, from Scherbachev, *Statii. Materialy, Pisma,* p. 111.

15. Scherbachev, *Statii. Materialy. Pisma, p. 131.*

16. Serge Prokofiev to Petr Suvchinsky, July 8, 1921. Music department of the French National Library, Paris. Suvchinsky Archive.

17. *Poslednie novosti,* June, 17, 1937, PSF.

18. Elena Balmont to the Tcherepnin family, August 20, 1923, PSF.

19. A. T. to his parents, April 17, 1927, PSF.

20. N. T. to A. T., September, 12, 1928, PSF.

21. A. T. to N. T., March 4, 1927, PSF.

22. A. T. to N. T., August 30, 1928, PSF.

23. N. T. to M. T., August 4, 1927, PSF.

24. M. T. to A. T., November 7, 1928, PSF.

25. Serge Prokofiev to M. T., February 27, 1924, PSF.

26. Linette Prokofiev to M. T., July 17, 1924, PSF.

27. Sergei Prokofiev to N. T., March 24, 1925, PSF.

28. Sergei Prokofiev to N. T., June 3, 1925, PSF.

29. Sergei Prokofiev to M. T., July 2, 1926, PSF.

30. Sergei Prokofiev to A. T., November 13, 1923, PSF.

31. Alexander Torletsky to M. T., November 12, 1922, PSF. Torletsky was the son-in-law of the renowned singer I. Ershov, who had performed the heroic tenor roles of Wagner's operas on the stage of the Mariinsky Theater.

32. Peter Saburov to N. T., PSF.

33. Feofan Pavlovsky to M. T., PSF.

34. Sergei Trailin to M. T., September 15, 1921, PSF.

35. *Poslednie novosti,* October 9, 1921.

36. Valentin Bulgakov to M. T., 1937, PSF.

37. *Kratki Putevoditel' po Byvshemy Spezkhranu Rossiiskovo Gosudarstvennovo Arkhiva Literatury i Iskusstva* (Moscow, 1994).

38. RSALA, coll. 2476, register 1, no. 46.

39. Paragraph 2 of the Parisian RMSA's charter.

40. RSALA, coll. 2476, register 1, no. 28.

41. Ibid., no. 1.

42. Ibid., no. 29.

43. Ibid., no. 11.

44. *Translator's note:* the term "barin," in Russian, means a wealthy landowner, lord of an estate.

45. N. T. to M. T., August 25, 1928, PSF.

46. N. T. to A. T., August 31, 1928, PSF.

47. Feodor Akimenko to M. T., regarding a concert to be held in the house of Comte Saint-Martin, PSF.

48. Viktor Walther, "Konzert Aleksandra Tcherepnina," *Poslednie novosti,* November 12, 1924.

49. Boris Shloezer, "Muzykalnye Zametki," *Poslednie novosti,* January 30, 1924, and February 16, 1925.

50. Emil Cooper, "Nezakonchennaia biographia muzykalnoi karriery," SCMMC, coll. 434, no. 1, sheet 178.

51. Vladimir Pohl, "Skazanie o grade Kitezhe," *Vozrozhdenie,* no. 1363 (1929).

52. *Vozrozhdenie,* December 9, 1934.

53. Mnuhin, *Russkoe zarubezhie: hronika nauchnoi, kulturnoi i obschestvennoi zhizni, 1920–1940.*

54. E. Shmurlo, "Chto takoe den' russkoi kultury," in *Arkhitekty russkoi kultury: collectsia statei* (Prague, 1926), pp. 9, 19.

55. *Poslednie novosti,* May 23 and 30, 1936.

56. Leri [V. Klopotovsky], "Nastanet den' (teper' on blizhe chem mozhno bilo ozhidat')," *Illustrirovanaia Rossia* 40 (125) (November 7, 1927): 4.

57. Leonid Sabaneyev, "Muzykalnoe tvorchestvo v emigrazii," *Sovremennye zapiski,* no. 64 (1937): 394–409.

58. Leonid Sabaneyev, "Tvorcheskii krisis v muzyke," *Sovremennye zapiski,* no. 67 (1938): 385–396.

59. Ibid., p. 386.

60. Ibid., p. 385.

61. Sabaneyev, "Muzykalnoe tvorchestvo v emigrazii," pp. 400–401.

62. The reasons for Prokofiev's departure were actively discussed. Some said that he had not been able to bear competition with "the Great Igor."

63. Ibid., pp. 397–398.

64. Ibid., p. 407.

65. Ibid., p. 409.

4. European Destiny

1. "Rasskazyvaet Aleksandr Tcherepnin," Sovetskaya muzyka, no. 8 (1967): 130–131. Tcherepnin was interviewed for this article by G. Haimovsky.

2. Janusz Cegiella, Dziecko szczęścia: Aleksander Tansman i jego czasy (Łódź, 1996), p. 89.

3. Ibid., pp. 163–165. Tansman's text was first published in Muzyka, no. 157 (1967): 22–25.

4. The original text wrongly lists "Nicolas Tcherepnin."

5. Cegiella, Dziecko szczęścia, p. 163.

6. Henri Prunieres, "Les tendances actuelles de la musique," La revue musicale, no. 166 (1936).

7. G. Erismann, "Bohuslav Martinů et la France," in Bohuslav Martinů: Anno 1981; Papers from an International Musicological Conference, 26–28 May 1981 (Prague, 1990), p. 65.

8. Larousse de la musique: Dictionnaire encyclopédique, 2 vols (Paris, 1957), 2:162.

9. Marcel Mihalovici, "Adieu à Alexandre Tcherepnine," Adam Magazine, 1978, pp. 18–19.

10. BFM, pp. 257–258.

11. A. T. to Vasily Kiselev, May 2, 1968, RSALA, coll. 2985, register 1, item 291, sheet 50 v.

12. Department of Music, French National Library, Paris.

13. I. Glebov [Boris Asafiev], Novaya franzuzskaya shkola: Shest': Milhaud, Honegger, Auric, Poulenc, Duret, Tailleferre (Leningrad, 1926).

14. Arthur Honegger, Ia—Kompositor (Leningrad, 1963), p. 116.

15. Glebov [Asafiev], Novaya franzuzskaya shkola, p. 46.

16. Ibid., p. 36.

17. Ibid., p. 45.

18. Ibid.

19. Ibid., pp. 34, 35.

20. A. T. to Grigori Shneerson, November 11, 1972, SCMMC, coll. 375, no. 955.

21. Schott Publishing House to A. T., March 21, 1925, PSF.

22. Allgemeine Musikzeitung, July 9, 1926.

23. Article in the Hannoverscher Kurier, written by Dr. Ch. Erpf [sic], date on photocopy provided by Schott Publications illegible, PSF.

24. Raymond Petit, "Concerto da camera (pour flute, violon et clavier), par Alexandre Tcherepnine (Récital Darrieux)," La revue musicale, no. 4 (1926): 160.

25. A. T. to Viktor Beliaev, SCMMC, coll. 340, no. 6488. Viktor Beliaev, "Sovremennaia muzyka i Alexander Tcherepnin," Sovremennaia muzyka, no. 11 (1925). Cf. the appendix to this chapter.

26. Neue Zeitung Hildesheim, signed "R," February 4, 1929, clipping in PSF.

27. Arthur Hoerée, *La revue musicale,* "Chroniques et notes," no. 5 (1925): 286.

28. Raymond Petit, *La revue musicale,* "Chroniques et notes, L'Edition musicale," no. 6 (1926): 82.

29. Raymond Petit, *La revue musicale,* "Chroniques et notes, Les Concerts," no. 5 (1924): 249–250.

30. Boris de Schloezer, *La revue musicale,* "Chroniques et notes, Réflexions sur la musique: Musique et littérature," no. 5 (1924): 258–259.

31. Boris de Schloezer, *La revue musicale,* "Chroniques et notes, Les Concerts," no. 6 (1926): 221.

32. *Editor's note:* This is, in fact, the Tiflis six-step scale, and does not represent Tcherepnin's mature principles. Tcherepnin moved beyond this when, early in his Paris period, he codified his nine-step scale, formed from the two superimposed six-step scales (ascending and descending). In his fully formed nine-step usage, the step-and-a-half intervals that early critics found overprominent become less frequent in his music.

33. A. T. to his parents, April 20, 1927, PSF. Hereafter, the dates of Tcherepnin's letters to his parents, all in PSF, are noted in the text.

34. The renowned violoncellist Paul Grummer was a constant partner and friend of the composer.

35. Slonimsky, "Alexander Tcherepnin Septuagenarian."

36. René Brancourt, "Concerts-Colonne," *Le ménestrel,* November 4, 1927.

37. Raymond Petit "Symphonie en mi, d'Alexandre Tcherepnine (Colonne)" *La revue musicale,* no. 3 (1928): 260–261.

38. A. T. to Grigori Shneerson, May 3, 1970, SCMMC, coll. 375, no. 963.

39. *Editor's note:* In these years Tcherepnin thought it would be doubly appropriate if the First Symphony were played by the New York Philharmonic, first, because it was now his hometown orchestra, and, second, because the score had been composed many years earlier in the city's metropolitan area. Leonard Bernstein expressed some interest to the composer, but to date [2007] the Symphony has not been performed by the Philharmonic.

40. Diary entry, August 10, 1967, PSF.

41. A. T. Typescript with editing, in Russian, PSF.

42. Ibid.

43. *Translator's note:* Here Tcherepnin alludes to an old myth of the earth being supported by three giant whales.

44. Note by Beliaev: "We can observe an 'aesthetic bent' in modern French primitivism reviving amid modern conditions the style of Rameau and Couperin. Italian primitivism, as expressed in the works of Casella, is considerably more full-blooded and saturated with sensual acuteness. German primitivism by virtue of particularly German characteristics, expresses itself in more serious forms than French and Italian primitivism. It is integrally tied to the problem of reforms in musical style, formulated as end goals. Today one can even speak of an American primitiveness, whose artistic offspring is the jazz band—born in the atmosphere of the particularly American bar (entirely not bourgeois) and promising to earn itself approximately the same position earlier conquered by the Viennese waltz. The jazz band bears the mark of such vital full-bloodedness as old Europe can no longer produce, while trying to 'utilize' this new art form for its 'hedonistic' (often in the most vulgar sense) needs."

45. *Editor's note:* Tcherepnin wrote only one violin sonata.

46. *Editor's note:* There are several inaccuracies in Beliaev's preceding sentence: Tcherepnin had written only one concerto for chamber orchestra and one violin sonata.

5. The Four Corners of the Globe

1. Alexander Tcherepnine, "Music in Modern China," *Musical Quarterly,* 21, no. 4 (October 1935): 391–400. All quotes that follow from this article are from this source.

2. A. T. to his parents, May 22, 1927, PSF. Hereafter, the dates of Tcherepnin's letters to his parents, all in PSF, are noted in the text.

3. A. T. to Grigori Shneerson, May 6, 1965, SCMMC, coll. 375, no. 975. *Etenraku* is a traditional composition of gagaku court music.

4. "Europe Takes an Interest in Chinese and Japanese Music," *Shanghai Dawn,* May 21, 1936. Interview with A.T., clipping, PSF.

5. Johann Goethe, *Sobrannye sochinenia,* 10 vols. (Moscow, 1980), 10:415.

6. Valentina Konen. "Znatchenie vneevopeiskikh kultur dlia muzyki XX veka," in *Etudy o zarubezhnoi muzyke* (Moscow, Muzyka), 1975.

7. E. Valina, "K probleme frantzuskovo muzykalnovo ekzotisma," in *O muzykalnom prosveschenii i obrazovania* (Maikop, 1995).

8. *Alexander Tcherepnin: 75 Jahre.* Zum 21. 1 (Frankfurt: V. P. Belaieff, 1974), p. 32.

9. Fr. G., "Ruska moderna opera in balet," *Slavenski narod,* October 20, 1933.

10. *New York City Sun,* February 3, 1934.

11. A. T. to Grigori Shneerson, SCMMC, coll. 375, no. 986.

12. Diary entry, PSF, September 24, 1975.

13. Ibid.

14. A. T. to Grigori Shneerson, August 9, 1968, SCMMC, coll. 375, no. 940.

15. Diary entry, November 19, 1949, PSF.

16. Philip Ramey, "Alexander Tcherepnin," *Ovation,* May 1984; idem, "Remembering Tcherepnin," *Chicago Magazine,* September 1979.

17. Enrique Arias, "The Symphonies of Alexander Tcherepnin," *Tempo,* no. 158 (1986); idem, "Alexander Tcherepnin's Thoughts on Music," *Perspectives of New Music,* no. 1–2 (1983).

18. Arias, *Alexander Tcherepnin: A Bio-Bibliography,* pp. 17–19.

19. A. T. to Grigori Shneerson, April 7, 1962, SCMMC, coll. 375, no. 939.

20. A. T. to Vasily Kiselev, August 1, 1969, RSALA, coll. 2985, register 1, no. 391, sheet 60.

21. A. T. to Grigori Shneerson, April 2, 1972, SCMMC, coll. 375, no. 954.

22. A. T. to Vasily Kiselev, RSALA, coll. 2985, register 1, no. 391, sheet 51.

23. *Editor's note:* Phillip Ramey reported a conversation in which pianist Rudolph Ganz described Alexander Tcherepnin's Paris performance of Schumann's Fantasy in C as the most compelling rendition he had ever heard.

24. A. T. to M.T., June 6, 1928, PSF.

6. In the Composer's Workshop

1. A. T. to Grigori Shneerson, February 2, 1965, SCMMC, coll. 375, no. 963.

2. Selections of Alexander Tcherepnin's thoughts, BFM, pp. 555–562.

3. A. T. autograph manuscript, PSF.

4. Ibid.

5. Boris de Schloezer, "Book Review of Igor Glebov's [Boris Asafiev] *I—Rimsky-Korsakov. II—Scriabin. III—Tchaikovsky.* Petrograd-Berlin: Svetozar, 1923; and Zveno, Paris, nos. 3, 4, 6 (1923).

6. Alexander Tcherepnin, "The World of Sound," *Music Journal* (March 1964); cited from BFM, pp. 635–636.

7. Alexander Tcherepnin. "La Percussion—est elle musicale?" *L'Age Nouveau,* no. 82 (1955). BFM, pp. 612–614.

8. A. T. to Grigori Shneerson, April 7, 1962, SCMMC, coll. 375, no. 961.

9. Ibid., June 11, 1966, SCMMC, coll. 375.

10. Alexander Tcherepnin "Let Underprivileged Instruments Play," *Music Journal* 20, no. 1 (1962); cited from BFM, pp. 615–616.

11. Undated piece by Alexander Tcherepnin that appears to be a lecture; cited in BFM, pp. 616–619.

12. A. T. to Grigori Shneerson, May 8, 1964, SCMMC, coll. 375, no. 889.

13. Ibid., February 7, 1967, SCMMC, coll. 375, no. 931.

14. Ibid., August 9, 1968, SCMMC, coll. 375, no. 940.

15. E. Denisov, "O Kompozitzionnom Prozesse," in *Sovremennaia muzyka i problemy kompositorskoi tekhniki* (Moscow, 1986.)

16. Diary entry, July 18, 1975, PSF.

17. Diary entry, August 17, 1975, PSF.

18. Diary entry, January 1, 1976, PSF.

19. A. T. musical manuscript, PSF.

20. Music notebook entry, October 20, 1928, PSF.

21. Diary entry, February 15, 1928, PSF.

22. A. T. to his parents, December 9, 1927. PSF. Hereafter, the dates of Tcherepnin's letters to his parents, all in PSF, are noted in the text.

23. Diary entry, July 12, 1970, PSF.

24. Hugo von Hofmannsthal, *Die Hochzeit der Sobeide* (Berlin: Fischer); *Svadba Sobeidy,* trans. O. N. Chumina, 2nd ed. (Moscow: V. Antik, 1899); no. 28 in the series *Universalnaia biblioteka.* This translation was the one used at the Vera Komissarjevskaya Theater.

25. This letter was written during the period of the First Symphony.

7. The Russian Composer

1. Reich, *Alexander Tcherepnin,* p. 105.

2. BFM, p. 127.

3. A. T. to Grigori Shneerson, February, 7 1962, SCMMC, coll. 375, no. 3.

4. A. T. to his parents, July 3, 1927, PSF. Hereafter only the dates are provided in the text for Tcherepnin's letters to his parents.

5. M. Borodin worked there as the main political adviser of the Central Electoral Committee of the Guomingdang from 1923 to 1927.

6. Unsigned, *Russkaya mysl,* August 31, 1958.

7. Feodor Aivaz to N. T., PSF.

8. *L'émigration russe en Europe: Catalogue collectif des périodiques russes. 1855–1940* (Paris, 1976), pp. 103–306.

9. RSALA, coll. 2481, register 1, no. 119.

10. *Poslednye novosti,* January 16, 1938.

11. Ibid., November 28, 1938.

12. Ibid., May 6, 1939.

13. Alexander Tcherepnin, *Russische Musik-Anthologie: 80 Beispiele vom Unsprung bis zum Beginn des 19 Jahrhunderts* (Bonn: M. P. Belaieff, 1966).

14. A. T. to Viktor Beliaev, April 7, 1966, SCMMC, coll. 340, no. 6482.

15. Yury Annenkov, *Dnevnik moih vstrech: Zikl tragedii,* 2 vols. (New York, 1966), p. 96.

16. Vladimir Belsky to N. T., April 10, 1925, PSF.

17. Ibid., August 6, 1925, PSF.

18. Ibid., September 1, 1926, PSF.

19. A. T. Autograph score, PSF.

20. A. T. Autograph score, PSF.

21. See n. 14, above.

22. Richard Taruskin, *Stravinsky and the Russian Traditions: A Biography of the Works through Mavra* (Berkeley: University of California Press, 1966).

23. T. [Tirscher, G.], "Alexander Tcherepnin," *Deutsche Musikzeitung,* no. 12 (September 1933): 101–103.

24. Lourié's diaries for the years 1946 to 1962 are kept in Paris in the private collection of the Ladua family.

25. *Translator's note:* The tsurn is a Middle Eastern reed instrument.

26. Published in a collection of the student songs of A. Aristov in 1904. A. Gluhovtsev alluded to the same song in his 1911 opera, *Days of Our Life,* which was staged at the Zimin Theater in Moscow in 1913. Tcherepnin could not have known this, however.

27. *Russian National Suite for Small Orchestra,* sketches and autograph clavier, PSF.

28. *Legend of Razin,* libretto, sketches, clavier, PSF.

29. *Trepak,* Libretto, sketches, and autograph manuscript of the finished score, PSF.

30. Similar work had been done a decade earlier in Moscow by Ippolitov-Ivanov, but the Tcherepnins likely knew nothing of this.

31. A. T. to Grigori Shneerson, January 10, 1970, SCMMC, coll. 375, no. 967.

32. The Dimitri Shostakovich archive in RSALA contains the letter from Alexander Tcherepnin.

33. SCMMC, coll. 375, no. 991.

34. A. T. to Vasily Kiselev, RSALA, coll. 2985, no. 391, sheet 18.

35. Ibid., January 27, 1968, RSALA, coll. 2985, no. 391, sheet 28.

36. Ibid., summer 1968, RSALA, coll. 2985, no. 391, sheet 46.

37. A. T. to Yuri Shaporin, September 21, 1960, RSALA, coll. 2642, register 1, no. 445, sheet 1.

38. A. T. to Grigori Shneerson, January 5, 1962, SCMMC, coll. 375, no. 894.

39. Ibid., May 8, 1964, SCMMC, coll. 375, no. 890.

40. Ibid., fall 1967, SCMMC, coll. 375, no. 903.

41. A. T. to Grigori Bernandt, fall 1967, SCMMC, coll. 449, no. 1133.

42. A. T. to Grigori Shneerson, October 8, 1975, SCMMC, coll. 375, No. 964.

43. Source unknown.

44. A. T. to Grigori Bernandt, after October 30, 1969, SCMMC, coll. 449, no. 1147.

45. Alexander Tcherepnin "A Trip to the Soviet Union" *The World of Musik: Quarterly Journal of the International Music Council,* no. 4 (1967).

46. A. T. to Grigori Shneerson, August, 4, 1966 SCMMC, coll. 375, No. 899.

47. Ibid.

48. The letters are in PSF. The work of Wyschnegradsky was practically unknown in Russia until the early 1990s. In 1991 the composer's son gave copies of important editions and recordings to this author.

49. Ivan Wyschnegradsky to A. T., October 1, 1968, PSF.

8. Finale

1. Slonimsky, "Alexander Tcherepnin Septuagenarian," pp. 19–23.

2. A. T. to Vasily Kiselev, RSALA, coll. 2985, register 1, no. 392, sheet 35 v.—sheet 36.

3. Ibid., March 9, 1974, RSALA, coll. 2985, register 1, no. 392, sheet 44.

a. *Editor's note:* Tcherepnin's *Divertimento* is a symphony in all but name, composed for Fritz Reiner who specified that he did not want a symphony.

4. A. T. to Grigori Schneerson, June 27, 1967, SCMMC, coll. 375, no. 936.

5. *Editor's note:* Ivan completed only the orchestration of the first movement from Alexander's "short" score, which consists of two unorchestrated movements. He had planned to orchestrate the second movement, then complete the symphony by composing a third movement which would be his own, and yet would incorporate some ideas based on conversations he had had with his father about the work. Ivan's further efforts were dashed by his untimely death in April 1998.

6. A. T. to Grigori Schneerson, June 27, 1967, SCMMC, coll. 375, no. 948. In 1994 the first thesis written in Russia about Tcherepnin was defended at the St. Petersburg Conservatory, but the author of the dissertation seems not to have published his thesis (S. Eisenstadt, "Fortepiannye Konzerty A. Tcherepnina: Cherty Stilya," Master's thesis, 1994.

7. A. T. to Grigori Shneerson, August 6, 1969, SCMMC, coll. 375, no. 951.

8. Ibid., 1970, SCMMC, coll. 375, no. 966.

9. Diary entry, August 7, 1976, PSF.

10. A. T. to Grigori Shneerson, SCMMC, coll. 375, no. 919.

11. Diary entry, July 18, 1975, PSF.

12. An Alsatian dish of pork and cabbage, a symbol of the Germanic.

13. Diary entry, January 24, 1976, PSF.

14. Diary entry, December 27, 1976, PSF.

15. Diary entry, January 1, 1971, PSF.

16. Diary entry, November 13, 1976, PSF.

17. Serge Tcherepnin, specifically for this book, photographed the tomb of the Tcherepnins near Paris. Maestro Gennady Rozhdestvensky photographed the memorial plaque on the house where Tcherepnin once lived.

18. SCMMC, coll. 449, no. 1138.

19. A. T. to Yuri Shaporin, September 21, 1960, RSALA, coll. 2642, register 1, no. 445, sheet 1.

20. Nikolai Struve, "Russkaia emigraziia: massovyi ishod v budutschee," *Strannik,* no. 1 (1997): 23–24.

Index of Works

General Index

Kalamkarian, Maria, 32, 233, 235
Kalugin, A., 61
Kamensky, Vassily, 22–24, 34, 162, 184
Kandinsky, Vasily, 39
Karatygin, Vyacheslav, 4, 6, 8, 241–242n
Karsavin, Lev, 154
Kashperova, Leocadia, 6, 184; *Children's Stories in Song,* 6
Kastalsky, Alexander, 32, 36
Kazak, Wolfgang, 41, 244n
Kedrov, Nikolai, 50, 52, 60
Khachaturian, Aram, 27, 30
Khlebnikov, Velimir, 156, 162
Khrennikov, Tikhon, 163, 166
Kibalchich, Viktor, 60
Kiladze, Grigol, 31
Kind, Anne, 3
Kind, Johann Friedrich, 1
Kirakosova, Maria, xv
Kiselev, Vasily, 70, 163, 171, 241–242n, 246n, 248n, 250–251n
Kiyose, Yasuji, 109–110, 239
Kobune, Kojiro, 109
Kochansky, Paul, 69
Kogoj, Marij, 112
Koh, Bunyah, 109, 239
Kolisch, Rudolf, 97
Komissarjevskaya, Vera, 140; Theater, 140
Komitas, Soghomon, 26–27; Society, 26–27
Kondrashin, Kiril, 163
Konen, Valentina, 111, 248n
Konoe, Hidemaro, 109
Konovalov, Alexander, 51
Korovin, Konstantin, 57
Korsh Theater, 21, 158
Kotshetz, Nina, 18, 20, 56
Koussevitzky, Serge, xi, 6, 47, 49, 52, 56–57, 136, 146, 167; Concerts, 4, 52, 56–57; Foundation, 164; Fund, xii, xvi, 136; Music Publishing, 6
Kovalev, Pavel, 42, 60
Kreisler, Fritz, 52
Kubelik, Raphael, xi, 114, 227, 232, 238
Kuchka (*see also* Mighty Five), 158–159, 242
Kuchkism, 19–20, 36, 144, 154
Kuprin, Aleksandr, 62
Kuzmin, Mikhail, 4, 150
Kuznetsova, Maria, 54, 58–59

Lamoureux Concerts. *See* Concerts: Lamoureux
Lao Chih-cheng, 109
Lapshin, Ivan, 53

Lee Hsien Ming, xiii, 104–105, 108, 113, 131, 166, 171, 176
Lehmann, Fritz, 74
Leibowitz, René, 128
Lermontov, Mikhail, 16
Les Six, 66, 70–1
Levy, Sylvain, 47
Li Yu, 164
Liadov, Anatoly, 4, 5, 50, 54, 149, 173, 183, 186
Liapunov, Sergei, 34
Lichké, André, xii, 92
Lifar, Serge, 60
Lineva, Evgenia, 157, 167
Liszt, Franz, 19, 115, 132, 175, 229–230
Literary and Art Circle of Youth, 50
Liturgical music, xiii, 44, 116, 144, 151, 162, 166–167, 173, 186, 206, 224
Litvinne, Felia, 50, 52, 58
Liu Xue-an, 109
Lomonosov, Mikhail, 150
Lourié, Arthur, 41, 56–57, 68, 77, 112, 146, 150, 156, 167, 250n; *Feast During the Plague,* 150; First Symphony, 57; *Japanese Suite,* 112, 222; *The Moor of Peter the Great,* 150; Toccata, 77
Lowtzky, Hermann, 146
Luboschits, Lea, 58
Lully, Jean-Baptiste, 67, 69

Mahler, Gustav, 114
Major-minor, 29, 36, 71–73, 94, 97, 101, 124, 138, 185–186, 193–194, 197, 207; hexachord, 94, 186–187, 198, 207; scale, 29, 36, 94, 97, 101, 124, 186, 193–194, 197, 207; sequence, 94; tonality, 71, 73, 101, 138; triad, 27, 94, 185–186
Malchevsky, Aleksei, 60
Malko, Nikolai, 5, 7, 56
Malyi Theater, 158
Mandelstam, Osip, 23
Maria Pavlovna, Princess, 60
Mariinsky Theater, 3, 5, 11, 49, 58, 245n
Markevitch, Igor, 42, 68, 148
Markozova, Anna, 43–44, 244n
Martin, Frank, 128
Martinů, Bohuslav, 66–70, 114, 229, 246n
Massenet, Jules, 17–18, 58; *Manon,* 17; *Werther,* 18
Matsudaira, Yoritsune, 109–110, 239
Mayakovsky, Vladimir, 8, 150
Medtner, Nikolai, 18, 20, 36, 41, 46, 52, 63, 100, 135, 146, 148

Scriabin, Aleksandr, 4, 6, 9, 55, 62, 76, 124, 162, 168, 170, 248n; *Divine Poem,* 9; *Poem of Ecstasy,* 9; *Prometheus,* 4, 9
Sdanovsky, Eugene, 58
Shanghai Conservatory, 108–110
Shaporin, Yuri, 7, 163–164, 181, 241–242n, 250–251n; *Decembrists,* 164; *Kulikov Fields,* 164
Shelley, Percy Bysshe, 19, 22
Shishkina, Anna, 59
Shneerson, Grigori, xiii, 9, 27, 72, 93, 114, 131, 134, 163, 165–166, 176, 241–243n, 246–251n
Shostakovich, Dmitri, xi, 5, 6, 25, 84, 163, 173, 241n, 250n; Eighth Symphony, 163; First Piano Sonata, 5; Second Symphony, 173; *The Nose,* 84
Shoukhaeff, Vassily, 47
Silver Age, 21, 40, 42, 111, 150, 156, 159, 162
Skidan, A., 3, 241n
Slavina, Maria, 58
Slonimsky, Nicholas, 1, 3, 84, 169, 241n, 247n, 251n; *Baker's Biographical Dictionary,* 1; *Music After 1900,* 1
Smetana, Bedrich, 114
Smirnov, Dmitri, 47, 58–59
Society of "Patriots of Russian Music," 43
Sokolov, Nikolai, 6, 12, 186; *The Foundations of Polyphony: Melodic Figurations,* 6
Sokolovski, Mikhail, 149; *The Miller-Magician, Swindler and Matchmaker,* 149
Sologub, Feodor, 48
Soros, George, xii
Souvchinsky, Pierre, xii
Spendiarov, Alexander, 6, 7
Spivakovsky, Tossy, 172
Steinberg, Maximilian, 4, 50, 241n
Stockhausen, Karlheinz, 134, 177–178
Stokowski, Leopold, 52, 57, 114
Strauss, Richard, 5, 7, 18, 22, 33, 52, 62, 101; *Elektra,* 5, 23
Stravinsky, Igor, xi, xii, 1, 4, 6, 9, 10, 16, 24, 36, 41, 54–56, 59, 62–63, 67–70, 73, 76–77, 99–102, 148, 153–155, 157–158, 168–169, 172–173, 181, 183, 230–231; *Apollo,* 10; *Baiser de la Fée,* 10; *Card Game,* 10; *Mavra,* 77, 250n; Movements for Piano and Orchestra, 10; *Octet,* 10; *Oedipus Rex,* 10; *Petrushka,* 1, 11, 158; *Pulcinella,* 10; *Story of a Soldier,* 10; *The Rite of Spring,* xii, 4, 70, 179; Three Japanese Lyrics, 112; *Threni,* 10
Streicher, S., 43, 44, 244n
Struve, Gleb, 41, 244n, 251n

Stuckenschmidt, Hans Heinz, 94
Sudeikin, Sergey, 23–24, 159, 162
Sudeikina-Stravinsky, Vera, 24
Sudermann, Hermann, 21
Suk, Josef, 114, 230
Suvchinsky, Pavel, 47, 154, 244n
Svetlov, Valerian, 146
Svoboda, Tomas, 114
Szymanowski, Karol, 69

Tailleferre, Germaine, 66, 246n
Taktakishvili, Vassily, 31
Taneyev, Sergei, 3, 6, 24, 39, 51, 62, 78, 135, 231, 252; Johann Damaskin, 78
Tansman, Alexander, 66–70, 74, 129, 230–231, 246n
Taruskin, Richard, 155, 250n
Tchaikovsky, Hippolytus, 2, 3
Tchaikovsky, Piotr, xii, 9–10, 17–20, 38, 52, 56–57, 59–60, 62, 80, 113, 127, 135, 147, 149, 161, 163–164, 179, 228–230, 243–244n, 252n; *Eugene Onegin,* 17, 161; *Iolanta,* 113; *Nutcracker,* 161; *Queen of Spades,* 17–18, 57; Sixth Symphony, 19, 147, 164; *Voyevoda,* 163–164
Tcherepnin, Nicolas, xv, xix, 1, 3–5, 7, 8, 16–17, 20–21, 27, 31, 33, 41, 46, 51, 53, 58–60, 63, 98, *103,* 112, 146, 148, 152, 244n, 246n; *Fairy-tale of the Fisherman and the Fish,* 20, 60, 151; *Joyzelle dans le Jardin,* 5; *Narcissus and Echo,* 21; *Pavillon d'Armide,* 1, 4, 13, 40, 50, 72, 151; *Svat,* 48; *Three Melodies,* 60; *Vanka Kluchnik,* 48, 98
Tcherepnin, Alexander: in Chicago, xii, xiv, 7, 114–116, 131, 189, 208, 248n; childhood years, xiii, 1–15, 19, 29, 31–32, 94, 165, 171, 183, 185; compositional process, xiii, 2, 12–14, 37–38, 55, 65, 80–81, 84–85, 88–89, 94, 119–126, 128, 137–139, 142, 188–190, 191–209; emigration, ix, xi, xii, xiv, xv, 3, 7, 11, 26, 40–43, 45–47, 49–53, 55–57, 59–63, 146–148, 180–181, 244n; music publishing (the Tcherepnin Collection), 6, 72, 109–110; in New York, xii, xiii, 1, 2, 15, 78, 79, 113–114, 116, 148, 151, 163, 165, 171–172, 180, 209; in Paris, xii, xiii, xv, 1, 2, 4, 5, 30–33, 41–43, 45–48, 50–58, 65–73, 77–78, 116, 150–151, 241n, 248n; in Petersburg, xii, xiii, 1–12, 14–17, 19, 21, 24, 34–36, 46, 50–51, 54–55, 71–73, 145, 166, 185–186, 243–244n; relations with his parents, xiii, xv, 6, 11–12, 27, 45, 47–49, 77–78, 93, 107, 113, 139, 179, 183–186, 241; nine-step scale, 25, 27, 36, 74, 84, 02. 94–

LUDMILA KORABELNIKOVA is currently Distinguished Musicologist and Lead Scientific Researcher in the music history department of the Russian State Institute for Art Research. She graduated from the Moscow Conservatory with degrees in theory and musicology and has served as director of research at the Tchaikovsky Archive in Klin. She was also a member of the research staff of the Glinka Museum. Her main area of interest is Russian music of the nineteenth and twentieth centuries. Her publications include several books on the life and music of S. I. Taneyev.

SUE-ELLEN HERSHMAN-TCHEREPNIN received her B.Mus. degree from Boston University and M.Mus. from State University of New York, Stony Brook. She has served as adjunct instructor at the Massachusetts Institute of Technology since 1991 and performs around the world as a professional flutist. From 1995 to 1999 she also served as president of the eighteen-hundred member American Federation of Musicians Local 9-535-Boston, and is currently a board member of the Tcherepnin Society.

ANNA WINESTEIN is a DPhil candidate in modern history at Oxford University and a former Fulbright Fellow. She has published writings on Russian art, theater, and dance history, including the book *The Magical Reality of Alexandre Benois,* which accompanied an exhibition she curated in 2005–2006 at the Boston Public Library.